Education of the trainable mentally retarded

CURRICULUM, METHODS, MATERIALS

RETARDED CHILD

Thomas S. Fee

Years past,
   retarded child,
      prejudice and ignorance
         of men's minds
            clouded his vision
            and you
               were hidden,
              shunned,
                 neglected,
                   and forgotten.

Slowly
   the light of knowledge
      began to penetrate the darkness
      to light the way
      and dissolve
         misconceptions,
           misunderstanding,
         and fear.

Years past,
   retarded child,
      your difficulty in handling
         the abstractions and demands
         of the academic world
           led you along the path
         of failure,
           frustration,
             and rejection.

Now—
   you find yourself
      in special classes
      designed to fit
         your abilities,
           needs,
           and interests—
              or you find yourself
                 in community training centers

Which help prepare you
   for a significant contribution
   to your fellow man.

You child,
   smiling up at me
      with affection and trust,
         have we done enough?

Reprinted with permission from The Pointer, Winter, 1969.

Education of the trainable mentally retarded

CURRICULUM, METHODS, MATERIALS

Freddie W. Litton, Ed.D.

Associate Professor of Special Education,
University of New Orleans,
New Orleans, Louisiana

with 122 illustrations

The C. V. Mosby Company

Saint Louis 1978

33040

The C. V. Mosby Company
11830 Westline Industrial Drive, St. Louis, Missouri 63141

Library of Congress Cataloging in Publication Data

Litton, Freddie W   1946-
    Education of the trainable mentally retarded.

    Bibliography: p.
    Includes index.
    1. Mentally handicapped children—Education.
I. Title.
LC4601.L57   371.9′28   77-10772
ISBN 0-8016-3023-1

CB/CB/B   9 8 7 6 5 4 3 2 1

To

Jeremy, Jennifer, and **Stephen**

PREFACE

Education of the Trainable Mentally Retarded: Curriculum, Methods, Materials is designed primarily for teachers in training who are enrolled in a university or in-service course on curriculum or methods and materials for teaching the trainable mentally retarded. The text can also be used as a resource book for those allied professionals (social workers, speech pathologists, rehabilitation specialists, counselors, physicians, etc.) who have contact with TMRs and their families and wish to expand their understanding and knowledge of the educator's delivery-of-service role.

Section one, Foundations, is intended to present basic information on the TMR and to establish a philosophy for the education of TMRs. This philosophy is a humanistic, reality based, pragmatic, behavioristic approach that allows implementation and optimal achievement of the desired skills of the curriculum section. Chapter 1 on the nature and cause of mental retardation provides current, basic information on educational philosophy, the multidisciplinary approach, definition, classification, and prevalence, characteristics, causes, and diagnosis. Chapter 2 on the educational, environmental, and instructional concerns covers curriculum goals, objectives, and content, instructional personnel (including the role of parents), organizational and administrative considerations, equipment, materials, and use of games, general principles of instruction, and individual education programs. Chapter 3 on behavior modification and the TMR discusses procedures to establish appropriate behaviors and eliminate inappropriate behaviors, and generalization.

Section two, Curriculum, contains seven chapters, each paralleling basic curriculum areas for the TMR. These chapters are concerned with developing self-care skills, basic communication skills, social skills, perceptual-motor and physical education skills, functional academic skills, recreation and leisure time skills, as well as economic usefulness and vocational skills. Each of these chapters discusses research findings relative to the TMR, general development of the curriculum area, assessment, behaviors or skills to develop, teaching considerations and procedures, activities, materials, and teacher resources.

Also included in the text are four practitioner-related appendixes: Appendix A lists publishers of tests, materials, and equipment for the TMR; Appendix B contains a directory of agencies, professional organizations, and publications contributing to the education and training of TMRs; Appendix C provides forms for teachers and administrators of programs for TMRs (emergency information card, parental consent or release forms, medical examination form, job analysis form, and checklist for program quality); and Appendix D is the *Litton-TMR Behavioral Assessment Checklist,* useful for a determination of behavioral functioning and growth in the seven basic curriculum areas.

After classroom teaching experience with the trainable mentally retarded, university teaching of undergraduate and graduate students in teacher training programs for the retarded, and conducting numerous workshops on teaching TMRs, I have recognized, as have many others, a critical need for a book that transposes scientific and theoretical aspects of teaching the retarded into a practical, consumable form. It is my sincere desire that *Education of the Trainable Mentally Retarded: Curriculum, Methods, Materials* offer a realistic, comprehensive approach to instruction yet not be restrictive nor stereotype TMR individuals. I have also attempted to incorporate and share current research and programmatic efforts taking place across the United States.

An undertaking of this nature must rely on assistance from a number of individuals. Acknowledgment and heartfelt appreciation are extended to those persons who contributed information and personal time to the text: Mollie Alarcon, Charlotte Ducote, Judy Stuart, Kathy Mix, Cliff Ouder, Jr., and many teachers and principals of schools for the TMR in the New Orleans area. Special thanks are due Dr. Jane Murdock for writing Chapter 3 on behavior modification and to Dr. Francis St. Peter and Betty James for securing photographs for the text. Appreciation is also extended to the typists of the manuscript, Jeannie Shapley and Deborah Casey, who were forced into impossible deadlines. I reserve the last thank you for my understanding and loving wife, Beverly, who endured along with me.

Freddie W. Litton

CONTENTS

SECTION ONE

FOUNDATIONS

The purposes of this section are threefold. It is intended to serve as a review of general but current and relevant information on retardation, with emphasis on philosophy, the multidisciplinary approach, definition, classification and prevalence, characteristics, causes, and diagnosis (intellectual and behavioral). It is also an in-depth description of educational environmental constructs for the trainable mentally retarded, including such aspects as curriculum goals, objectives and content, instructional personnel (including parents), organizational and administrative considerations, equipment and materials, and basic principles for instruction. Finally, it introduces the reader to a basic knowledge and understanding of the most viable approach to establishing appropriate and eliminating undesirable behaviors in the education and development of the trainable mentally retarded. This approach is applied behavior analysis or behavior modification.

CHAPTER 1

NATURE AND CAUSE OF MENTAL RETARDATION

The major purposes of this chapter will be to discuss the provision of services to the trainable mentally retarded (TMR) from a philosophical point of reference, to examine the disciplines that contribute to diagnosis, prevention, treatment, and management of retardation, and to present basic information on the definition, classification, prevalence, characteristics, and causes of mental retardation. Diagnosis, with specific emphasis on intelligence testing and assessment of adaptive behavior, will also be discussed.

PHILOSOPHY

Every business, agency, organization, or profession must have a basic philosophy on which to center its operations and functions. The United States of America and its system of education also have operating philosophies and beliefs. Our founding fathers declared in the Declaration of Independence on July 4, 1776, that "all Men are created equal, that they are endowed by their Creator with certain unalienable Rights, that among these are Life, Liberty, and the Pursuit of Happiness." These rights cannot be denied any residents of the United States. The rights of individuals with respect to education are also guaranteed. American education holds the belief that "all men are created equal" before the law and therefore have equal rights to an education, even though they do not have equal abilities to learn.

Forty-eight of the states value education to the extent that school attendance by youth is compulsory, and parents who fail to comply face criminal action. These laws reflect almost without question that education is essential to normal life in American society. The Supreme Court, in a 1954 ruling (Brown v. the Board of Education), stated: "In these days it is doubtful that any child may reasonably be expected to succeed in life if he is denied the opportunity of an education. Such an opportunity, where the state has undertaken to provide it, is a right which must be made available to all on equal terms."*

Although the first public school class for the mentally retarded was established in 1896, almost all school systems prior to the 1950s and most after 1950 chose to ignore this aspect of the population. These school systems and administrators held the belief that the TMR child, because of limited abilities and potential, would not return society's investment. In denying these

---

*From Brown v. the Board of Education, 347 U.S. 483, 74 S. Ct. 686 (1954).

individuals educational services, they denied the retarded citizen basic rights guaranteed by the Constitution. The two major cases that have clearly established the right of free access to public education for the TMR are Pennsylvania Association for Retarded Children v. the Commonwealth of Pennsylvania (1971) and Mills v. the Board of Education of the District of Columbia (1972). In the Pennsylvania case a federal district court entered a consent decree that Pennsylvania's public schools were to stop excluding children because of their mental retardation. Furthermore, if a school district wished to place a child in a special class or school, parents had to be notified prior to the change. In the Mills case a federal court ruled that the Constitution requires that every child, including the retarded, has a right to an educational program that will meet his individual needs and develop him to his fullest potential.

Presently it is the belief of most professionals in the field of mental retardation that the retarded should have the fundamental rights, freedoms, and privileges granted other citizens. This belief is reflected in the United States by the President's Committee on Mental Retardation (PCMR, 1971) and on an international scale by the United Nations' adoption of the Declaration of the Rights of Mentally Retarded Persons in 1971. The PCMR listed the general rights of the retarded to include training, medical treatment, psychiatric treatment, insurance, privacy, and marriage. Also included were the right not to be experimented on in institutions and the right not to be sterilized. The articles of the United Nations declaration follow:

United Nations Declaration of the Rights of Mentally Retarded Persons

Article I   The mentally retarded person has, to the maximum degree of feasibility, the same rights as other human beings.

Article II   The mentally retarded person has a right to proper medical care and physical therapy, and to such education, training, rehabilitation, and guidance as will enable him to develop his ability and maximum potential.

Article III   The mentally retarded person has a right to economic security and to a decent standard of living. He has a right to perform productive work or to engage in any other meaningful occupation to the fullest possible extent of his capabilities.

Article IV   Whenever possible, the mentally retarded person should live with his own family or with foster parents and participate in different forms of community life. The family with which he lives should receive assistance. If care in an institution becomes necessary, it should be provided in surroundings and other circumstances as close as possible to those of normal life.

Article V   The mentally retarded person has a right to a qualified guardian when this is required to protect his personal well-being and interests.

Article VI   The mentally retarded person has a right to protection from exploitation, abuse, and degrading treatment. If prosecuted for any offense, he shall have a right to due process of law with full recognition being given to his degree of mental responsibility.

Article VII Whenever mentally retarded persons are unable, because of the severity of their handicap, to exercise all their rights in a meaningful way, or it should become necessary to restrict or deny some or all of their rights, the procedure used for that restriction or denial of rights must contain proper legal safeguards against every form of abuse. This procedure must be based on an evaluation of the social capability of the mentally retarded person by qualified experts and must be subject to periodic review and to the right of appeal to higher authorities.

Inherent in the article's philosophy is found the principle of *normalization* (Nijre, 1969; Wolfensberger, 1972). This notion had its beginnings in the Scandinavian countries and has recently enjoyed widespread acceptance in the United States. Normalization consists of offering experiences to mentally retarded individuals that will enable them to live as much as possible like the rest of society. Included are vocational, recreational, social, and educational activities and opportunities. This book has as its philosophy the same principle, and with just cause. The problems and difficulties of mental retardation deserve our attention, not only for the more than 6 million retarded American citizens and their families but also for the good of all. The majority of retarded citizens can become useful, productive members of society, and, as PCMR (1974) states: "With appropriate training, retarded people are capable of continuing development in normal community settings."

DISCIPLINES CONTRIBUTING TO THE STUDY OF MENTAL RETARDATION

Although much has been written about the retarded individual for about thirty-six centuries, only in the last century have significant efforts been directed at educating, training, and treating TMRs, as well as preventing retardation. Historically, society has viewed the retarded with superstition, ridicule, persecution, and even divine reverence. From that status the retarded progressed to institutional care of a custodial nature. This idea was born in Europe and transferred to the United States in the middle 1800s. The present era has seen the establishment of public classes and schools for the TMR. Growth in this area has been phenomenal: from 2,500 classes in 1963 to about 25,000 in 1975 (Gearheart and Litton, 1975).

Care and concern through the centuries originated primarily from the disciplines of religion and medicine, the former because of religious interpretations of the condition and the latter because of the belief that retardation was an inherited disease. Today, however, we have a vastly changed society, with many professionals from diverse disciplines contributing to the identification, diagnosis, treatment, prevention, and management of the retarded. A Gallup poll (PCMR, 1975) indicated that 75% to 95%

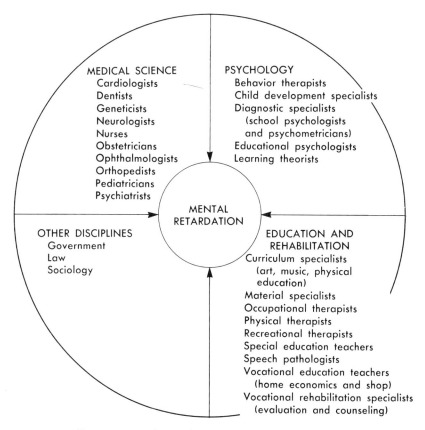

Fig. 1-1. Mental retardation: a multidisciplinary field.

of Americans surveyed expressed accepting attitudes toward retarded citizens as neighbors (up from 48% in 1970), and that 91% accepted the retarded as fellow employees (up from 30% in 1970).

The major disciplines contributing to the study of the retarded can be grouped into four categories: medical science, education and rehabilitation, psychology, and other disciplines. Each discipline or specialty, whether through a practitioner or researcher, with its area of expertise has made significant contributions to the field of mental retardation. More important than singular contributions is the recognition that with a concerted and collective effort, monumental achievements are possible. The direct beneficiaries are the retarded, and the ultimate beneficiary is mankind.

Medical science

Perhaps no other science has advanced as rapidly or made such substantial contributions as the field of medical research. Biomedical researchers have now made it possible to identify twenty-seven heritable metabolic disorders. Recent advances have also been made with regard to a more complete understanding of the functioning of genetic material called DNA (deoxyribonucleic acid) and chromosome analysis (karyotyping). Both these advances can help to reduce or prevent retardation effectively. Other significant advancements include the invention of new vaccines to control viral diseases, the development of a serum to combat the nervous system damage in the Rh-positive child of an Rh-negative mother, dietary modifications to prevent retardation caused by PKU (phenylketonuria) and galactosemia, and discoveries of substances that are toxic in certain persons, such as copper in Wilson's disease.

Practitioners in the field of medicine and related areas whose skills are frequently utilized in ameliorating or correcting physical disabilities and conditions often found in the TMR child include cardiologists, dentists, geneticists, neurologists, nurses, obstetricians, ophthalmologists, orthopedists, and pediatricians. Practitioners in the field of psychiatry also occasionally counsel and provide therapy to families of the retarded. The general functions of each medical science area follow:

cardiologists Provide medical treatment for congenital heart defects, diseases of the heart, as well as cardiorespiratory and cardiovascular dysfunctions.

dentists Provide care and treatment of teeth and gums that are defective due to abnormal development or disease.

geneticists Assist families who risk the transmission of serious hereditary disorders by determining the possibility of occurrence and explaining the alternative courses of action.

neurologists Render medical services involving the brain, spinal cord, and nervous system functions and disorders, (e.g., cerebral palsy, epilepsy).

nurses Aids the family in determining the problems of development in the young retarded child and devising strategies to cope with them.

obstetricians Provide medical care and service relating to pregnancy, labor, and puerperium (period of time after childbirth) and contribute greatly to preventing retardation.

ophthalmologists Diagnose and prescribe treatment for defects and diseases of the eye (e.g., fusion, accommodation, fixation, cataracts).

orthopedists Diagnose and treat diseases and abnormalities of musculoskeletal systems (e.g., clubfoot, congenital dislocation of the hip, Legg-Calvé-Perthes disease, cerebral palsy).

pediatricians Provide medical services relating to problems and diseases of young children and are usually the first professionals to detect abnormal or delayed development.

psychiatrists Assist families in coping effectively with problems generated because of the presence of a mentally retarded child.

Education and rehabilitation

The behaviorally oriented area of education and rehabilitation provides the bulk of the services to the TMR from childhood through adulthood. This group includes curriculum specialists (art, music, physical education), material specialists, occupational therapists, physical therapists, recreational therapists, special education teachers, speech pathologists, vocational education teachers (home economics and shop), and vocational rehabilitation specialists (evaluation and counseling). All groups work to develop the academic, social, personal, and vocational competencies necessary for success in community adjustment for the TMR. Specific role delineations follow:

curriculum specialists Contribute to the total curriculum for the TMR by adapting and modifying traditional objectives and developing skills in the content specialties of art, music, and physical education.

material specialists Major function to secure, develop, evaluate, and modify learning materials.

occupational therapists Contribute by teaching useful skills or hobbies to the TMR to promote their rehabilitation and recovery or to facilitate their ability to earn a living.

physical therapists Treat bodily ailments by various physical or nonmedical means and employ the use of heat, water, exercise, massage, and electrical current; their goal is to train the individual in performing essential activities.

recreational therapists Provide specially designed recreational and related activities to meet the needs of individuals who possess some significant degree of illness or disability.

special education teachers Design and implement curriculums for the preschool and school-age TMR; primary involvement is the day-to-day provision of learning experiences.

speech pathologists Evaluate, develop, and treat speech defects.

vocational education teachers Contribute in such areas as home economics (cooking, sewing, child care, domestic responsibilities) and shop to assist in the total educational program for the vocational and adult level TMR.

vocational rehabilitation specialists Provide evaluation, counseling, training, and job placement, with the goal of producing a wage earner.

Psychology

Important contributions to the field of mental retardation have been made by the discipline of psychology. Some branches concern themselves with the development, control, and eradication of particular human behavior, some with developmental processes, and others focus on observing, testing, evaluating, and characterizing behavior. The single most significant contribution of this science has been the development, refinement, and application of the principles and concepts of behavior modification to the education of the TMR. The groups that contribute to the total management of retardation include behavior ther-

apists, child development specialists, diagnostic specialists (school psychologists and psychometricians), educational psychologists, and learning theorists. Their contributions and roles follow:

behavior therapists Assist classroom teachers in designing and implementing effective programs for developing desired behaviors or eliminating and reducing bizarre and inappropriate behaviors found in many TMR children.

child development specialists Determine the developmental processes of the normal child, which becomes the basis for detection of an atypically developing child.

diagnostic specialists (psychometricians and school psychologists) Provide much of the academic, behavioral, and psychological testing in diagnosing mental retardation, as well as prescribing and transposing test data into educational and training programs.

educational psychologists Assist special educators in developing a better understanding of educational processes and focus on the learner, the process, and the situation.

learning theorists Contribute greatly to a better understanding of how and under what conditions students learn and individuals behave.

Other disciplines

Other disciplines whose roles often directly affect and contribute to the care of the retarded include government, law, and sociology. These are not all-inclusive but are only representative. Their primary functions are listed.

government Contributes politicians who create agencies at the federal, state, and local levels to regulate funds and programs.

law Provides litigation and legislation.

sociology Concerned with the function and relationship of the retardate in society; social workers also refer families to community resources, which provide services.

DEFINITION, CLASSIFICATION, AND PREVALENCE
Definition

The mentally retarded have been referred to in lay terminology as being dumb, stupid, dull, slow, and foolish and have been labeled feebleminded, idiots, imbeciles, morons, developmentally disabled, mentally defective, deficient, and handicapped. To label a condition or phenomenon is a simple and logical first step toward understanding, but to define it becomes an arduous task. A single accepted definition for mental retardation defies existence because of the condition's complexity, the multiplicity of causes, a wide range of levels, and diverse disciplines whose points of reference may differ.

Questions and disagreements have arisen in the past as to what should be included in the definition of mental retardation. Is it an intelligence quotient score, a capacity to learn, knowledge possessed, characteristics, thinking ability, social, personal, or vocational adjustment? The content of definitions has usually been indicative of current sociocultural standards, existing knowledge of the field, and the sophistication of assessment techniques. Table 1-1 is reflective of how definitions have changed in the last 65 years. It is interesting to note, how-

ever, that most of the quoted definitions mention the retardate's limited intelligence in relation to behavior. This may very well be the single characteristic common to all mentally retarded persons.

The most recognized and extensively accepted definition is the American Association on Mental Deficiency (AAMD) definition by Grossman (1973).

> Mental retardation refers to significantly subaverage general intellectual functioning existing concurrently with deficits in adaptive behavior, and manifested during the developmental period.*

The AAMD definition contains three important aspects worthy of amplification.

1. *Significantly subaverage general intellectual functioning.* This implies performance that is two or more standard devia-

---

*From Grossman, H., editor: Manual on terminology and classification in mental retardation, Baltimore, 1973, Garamond/Pridemark Press, p. 5.

Table 1-1. Historical development of definitions for mental retardation

Year	Primary focus	Originator	Definition
1910	Mental age	Doll	". . . intellectual retardation of two years at an age below nine or three years at an age above nine."
1937	Social incompetence	Tredgold	". . . a state of incomplete mental development of such a kind that the individual is incapable of adapting himself to the normal environment of his fellows . . ."
1941	Social incompetence	Doll	". . . a state of social incompetence obtaining at maturity, or likely to obtain at maturity, resulting from developed mental arrest of constitutional (hereditary or acquired) origin: the condition is essentially incurable through treatment and unremediable through training . . ."
1949	Characteristics	Wallin	". . . a condition of mental nondevelopment (agenesis), arrest, deficiency, or deterioration which is very grave and permanent, which dates from early life, and which always affects the intelligence, judgment, or understanding and the capacity for social and economic adjustment . . ."
1951	Education	Kirk and Johnson	". . . unable to profit sufficiently from the curriculum of the public schools but who can be educated to become socially adequate and occupationally competent . . ."
1954	Adult behavior	Benda	". . . incapable of managing himself and his affairs . . . and who requires supervision, control, and care for his own welfare and the welfare of the community."
1959	Physiology	Benoit	". . . a condition of diminished efficiency of the central nervous system . . ."
1961	Intelligence and/or adaptive behavior	AAMD (Heber)	". . . subaverage general intellectual functioning which originates in the developmental period and is associated with impairment in adaptive behavior."
1972	Developmental (Piaget)	Kolstoe	". . . a condition of intellectual arrest at some level below Piaget's level of formal thought."
1973	Intelligence and adaptive behavior	AAMD (Grossman)	"Significantly subaverage general intellectual functioning existing concurrently with deficits in adaptive behavior, and manifested during the developmental period."

tions below the mean of standardized individual intelligence tests developed for that purpose. For the *Stanford-Binet Intelligence Scale*, Third Edition, Form L-M, 1972 Norms Edition and *Catell Infant Intelligence Scale*, this represents intelligence quotient (IQ) scores below 68, and for the *Wechsler Intelligence Scale for Children—Revised* (WISC-R) (1974), scores below 70. (See Fig. 1-2.)

2. *Concurrent deficits in adaptive behavior*. Adaptive behavior is the degree to which an individual meets the social and personal standards expected of his age and culture. The three developmental levels and areas in which deficits might concurrently exist, according to the 1973 manual, are outlined below:

1. Infancy and early childhood
   a. Sensorimotor skills
   b. Communication skills
   c. Self-help skills
   d. Socialization (ability to interact with others)

2. Childhood and early adolescence
   a. Application of basic academic skills in daily life activities
   b. Application of appropriate reasoning and judgment in mastery of the environment
   c. Social skills (participation in group activities and interpersonal relationships)
3. Late adolescence and adulthood
   a. Vocational and social responsibilities and performances

3. *Developmental period*. The upper age limit at which significantly subaverage general intellectual functioning and adaptive behavior may exist is 18 years of age.

Classification

Equally confusing and perplexing as are efforts at defining retardation is the development of an acceptable classification system. A classification system, however, is necessary because it delineates more succinctly the functioning ability of the retarded, facilitates research efforts, allows for better communication between dis-

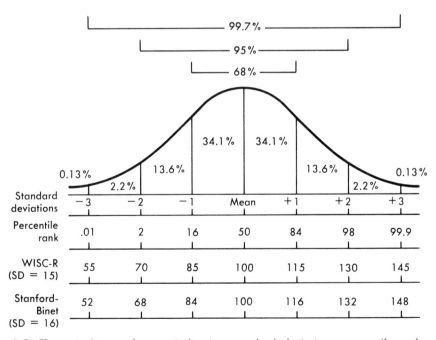

Fig. 1-2. Theoretical normal curve indicating standard deviations, percentile rank, and percentage of cases within each interval. The normal probability curve (Gaussian curve) is a symmetrical bell shape with many useful mathematical properties, including the division of test scores into standard deviation units. This allows for better test interpretation by indicating an individual's relative position in a group.

ciplines, and is more specific and descriptive of the levels of mental retardation. Also, a classification system with statistical data is of diagnostic value to physicians and researchers. Chinn, Drew, and Logan (1975), in a survey of the literature, found six parameters for classification: (1) severity of symptoms, (2) derivation of symptoms, (3) syndrome description, (4) adaptive behavior, (5) educability expectations, and (6) grouping on a manifested behavior basis. The major systems in contemporary use today, however, are classification by IQ scores, adaptive behavior, and origin of the condition.

IQ scores. Because standardized individual IQ tests have become one of the major diagnostic tools to indicate retarded functioning, the derived IQ scores are used for classification purposes. In a later part of this chapter intelligence testing will be examined further. (See Table 1-2.)

Adaptive behavior. Classification by adaptive behavior is another scale by which the diagnostician or educator may view those suspected of retardation. As previously mentioned, the AAMD recommends that to consider an individual retarded, deficits must exist in this area as well as in the cognitive or intellectual area. In many states these dual criteria are policy, and in at least one, California, they are law.

All behaviors of an individual (i.e., intellectual, social, physical, emotional) exist as a part of his total adaptation to the environment. Since IQ tests are samples of behaviors, IQ scores will often correlate positively with the ability to effectively adapt to the environment. Piaget identified intellectual development as a dynamic process whereby the individual continually assimilates (incorporates something from his environment into his mental structures) and accommodates (copes with environmental conditions by making necessary modifications) to the environment (Stephens, 1966).

As with intelligence, adaptive behavior is categorized in terms of levels. In 1970 the AAMD proposed six definitions of general adaptive behavior levels but recognized only four in 1973 (Grossman, 1973). These

Table 1-2. Classification by IQ scores

| IQ tests and scores | | Levels of retardation | |
WISC-R	Binet and Cattell	AAMD	Educational
55 to 69	52 to 68	Mild	Educable
40 to 54	36 to 51	Moderate ⎫	Trainable
25 to 39	20 to 35	Severe ⎬	
24 and below	19 and below	Profound ⎭	Severe

four levels of adaptive behavior, developmental stages, and corresponding characteristics are given. (See boxed material on p. 11.)

Origin. Etiological classification is yet another system and is used primarily by physicians. This AAMD (1973) medical classification system includes the ten categories of causes that follow. The more frequently occurring clinical types or possible specific causes are in parentheses.

1. Infections and intoxications (congenital syphilis, congenital rubella, congenital toxoplasmosis, Rh blood incompatibility, intoxicants)
2. Trauma or physical agents (maternal injury, birth injury, postnatal trauma)
3. Metabolism or nutrition (galactosemia, hypoglycemia, PKU, Wilson's disease)
4. Gross brain disease (neurofibromatosis, tuberous sclerosis)
5. Unknown prenatal influence (hydrocephalus, microcephaly, Cornelia de Lange syndrome)
6. Chromosomal abnormality (Down's syndrome, cri-du-chat, Klinefelter's and Turner's syndromes)
7. Gestational disorders (prematurity)
8. Following psychiatric disorder
9. Environmental influences
10. Other conditions

Reader guidelines. Since the primary reader of this text is the professional interested in educational aspects of care for one of the lower levels of mental retardation, the following term, definition, and IQ parameters for the TMR are suggested:

Trainable mentally retarded (TMR)—Individuals of this level are capable of learning in the

Preschool (0-5)	School age (6-20)	Adult (21+)
Level I (mild or EMR)		
Can develop social and communication skills; minimal retardation in sensorimotor areas; often not distinguished from normal until older.	Can learn academic skills up to approximately sixth grade level by late teens; can be guided toward social conformity.	Can usually achieve social and vocational skills adequate to minimum self-support but may need guidance and assistance when under unusual social or economic stress.
Level II (moderate or TMR)		
Can talk or learn to communicate; poor social awareness; fair motor development; profits from training in self-help; can be managed with moderate supervision.	Can profit from training in social and occupational skills; unlikely to progress beyond second grade level in academic subjects; may learn to travel alone in familiar places.	May achieve self-maintenance in unskilled or semiskilled work under sheltered conditions; needs supervision and guidance when under mild social or economic stress.
Level III (severe or SMR)		
Poor motor development; speech is minimal; generally unable to profit from training in self-help; little or no communication skills.	Can talk or learn to communicate; can be trained in elemental health habits; profits from systematic habit training.	May contribute partially to self-maintenance under complete supervision; can develop self-protection skills to a minimal useful level in controlled environment.
Level IV (profound or custodial)		
Gross retardation; minimal capacity for functioning in sensorimotor areas; needs nursing care.	Some motor development present; may respond to minimal or limited training in self-help.	Some motor and speech development; may achieve very limited self-care; needs nursing care.

From The problem of mental retardation, Department of Health, Education, and Welfare, Office of the Secretary, Washington, D.C., 1975, U.S. Government Printing Office, pp. 8-9.

areas of personal, social, and self-help skills and have limited achievement in academic areas. They will always be partially dependent and will need supervision for maintenance and help in adult daily living. Occupational performance will be primarily in noncompetitive conditions. The term TMR is approximately equivalent to the moderate and severe AAMD levels, levels II and III in adaptive behavior, and individual IQ scores of between 25 (± 5) and 50 (± 5).

As in any grade level or class, some students will possess abilities above and below those normally expected. There will be some TMR students capable of more than limited achievement in academics and some who possess little or no social or personal skills. These particular segments of the mentally retarded population, although grouped according to one or several common dimensions, should not be thought of as possessing the same skills or abilities. They are more heterogeneous than homogeneous in ability.

Prevalence

Current surveys on the prevalence and incidence of mental retardation are almost nonexistent, and earlier research is inconsistent, thus making precise answers relating to prevalence next to impossible. Twenty-eight prevalence surveys summarized by Heber (1970) found the range to be from 0.16% to 23%. Obviously, prevalence figures are dependent on many factors, for example, definition, IQ scores, tests administered (if the method of determining prevalence employed diagnosing the subjects), age, sources utilized, and geographical region.

Table 1-3. Incidence of retardation per 1,000 school-age children by educational classification and socioeconomic status*

SES	Educational classification		
	Educable	Trainable	Severe
High	10	4	1
Middle	25	4	1
Low	50	4	1

*Adapted from Chinn, P. C., Drew, C. J., and Logan, D. R.: Mental retardation: a life cycle approach, St. Louis, 1975, The C. V. Mosby Co., p. 6.

Table 1-4. Incidence of mental retardation by level*

Level	Total incidence (%)	Retarded (%)	Estimated number
EMR	2.6	76.7	5,460,000
TMR	0.3	20.0	630,000
SMR	0.1	3.3	210,000
Total	3.0	100.0	6,300,000

*Based on a population of 210 million.

The four frequently employed techniques for determining prevalence include geneological random test, birth register, period method, and census method (Farber, 1968). The census is the most widely used means whereby a survey is conducted by reviewing case files, analyzing data of various community agencies, and contacting persons in vocations where the probability of finding retarded persons is high. Surveys of the prevalence of mental retardation have generally indicated a higher incidence (1) during the school age years, (2) among males, (3) among ethnic and racial minority groups, and (4) among low socioeconomic groups (Kauffman and Payne, 1975). Table 1-3 indicates a significant number differential in the educable mentally retarded (EMR) incidence, depending on socioeconomic status (SES) and no difference in the TMR and severely mentally retarded (SMR) levels.

An IQ score of 70 has become the most widely accepted score for differentiating the retarded from the nonretarded. The normal probability curve for intelligence (Fig. 1-2) would suggest 2.33% of the population as being retarded, whereas the Stanford-Binet norms (1973) found 2.63% and the WISC-R (1974) found 2.2%. However, as Dunn (1973) points out, strong evidence exists to indicate that intelligence is not normally distributed but is positively skewed (to the lower end). This means an actual higher percentage exists than probability theory would indicate.

The Bureau of Education for the Handicapped (BEH, 1970), the United States Department of Health, Education, and Welfare (1975), and the President's Committee on Mental Retardation (1970), however, have chosen to recognize the estimated figure of 3%. In a population of 210 million, the number of retarded persons in the United States would therefore be 6,300,000, with the EMR level at 5,460,000, the TMR level at 630,000, and the SMR level at 210,000. (See Table 1-4.)

Prevalence figures for the mentally retarded are necessary for program planning, development of services, and allocation of funds. Of greater importance, however, is that these figures can be used to sample the impact and extent of efforts at combating retardation.

CHARACTERISTICS

Characteristics of any group serve only to assist others in obtaining a general idea of what the population is like. The task of listing characteristics of the TMR with any degree of accuracy is indeed complicated because as a group, variance is great in almost every dimension. Any single TMR individual cannot be expected to conform to all the characteristics of each dimension listed; instead, the various characteristics are intended to be representative and applicable to the majority of TMRs. The teacher or diagnostician should keep in mind the following characteristics in identifying or teaching the TMR. These are based on personal experiences and reports of Baumeister (1967), Heber and Stevens (1964), Huddle (1967), Kolstoe (1972), Liese and Lerch (1974), McLean, Yoder, and Schiefelbusch (1972), Nix (1969), Schiefelbusch, Copeland, and Smith (1967), Stein (1963), Waite (1972), and Wessel (1975).

Physical characteristics
1. Slightly below normal in height.
2. Tendency in many to be overweight.
3. More handicaps of vision and hearing.
4. Greater incidence of physical and multihandicapping conditions than found in the general population because the the vast majority have organic causes for the retardation.
5. Some individuals easily fatigued.
6. Posture often very poor.

Motor characteristics
1. Lag in motor performance abilities of about two to five years when compared to normal population.
2. Motor abilities organized similarly to those of normal children; attainment of these abilities follows similar developmental curves for both groups.
3. Significant relationship between IQ and physical fitness, although the relationship does not indicate cause.
4. Little or poor perceptual motor skills (i.e., body image, balance).
5. Physical abilities of institutionalized retarded at a lower level than those of children attending public school programs.
6. Disorders in daily motor activity—either hyperactive or hypoactive (lethargic).

Intellectual, learning, and academic characteristics
1. Poor performance; sometimes difficult to measure on standardized intelligence tests.
2. Can be expected to reach a mental age (MA) of 4 to 8 as young adults.
3. An intelligence quotient in the 25 to to 50 range on an individual test of intelligence.
4. Rate of mental development approximately one fourth to one half that of an average child.
5. Extreme slowness in development and attainment of specific intellectual functions needed for efficient learning—include the concepts of incidental learning, memory, discriminative learning, generalizing ability, and typical readiness skills.
6. MA of about 6 generally required to begin limited academic training; TMR cannot commence formal acquisition of these skills until chronological age (CA) of roughly 12 to 15.
7. Academic achievement generally commensurate with MA.
8. By adulthood and with adequate training, probable attainment at best only first or second grade achievement level.
9. Impairments and deficiencies in initial learning, transference, attending, and learning style.

Speech and language characteristics
1. Development of speech and language slow but sequential, following normal developmental patterns.
2. Language difficulties of varying degrees in over 90%.
3. Improper speech sounds common.
4. Poor expressive language.
5. Language development possible at all ages and levels.

The gains seem to be proportional to the degree of dedication, resourcefulness, and number of instructional personnel.

Personal, social, and emotional characteristics
1. Social maladaptation or inadequacy possible (violent, destructive, rebellious, untrustworthy behaviors).
2. Self-stimulating or self-abusive personal behaviors in many preschool and young school-age TMRs.
3. Limited imagination and creativity.
4. May be fearful, apathetic, disinterested, withdrawn.
5. May be overprotected or rejected by parents or other children.
6. Feelings of frustration and failure in many.

Occupational characteristics
1. At adulthood, most work in sheltered or closely supervised facilities.
2. Response to work better for money

incentives than competition or cooperation, although social approval very important.

3. Work best in individual and small group situations.

CAUSES

The factors and disorders responsible for mental retardation are numerous and may exist singularly or in various combinations. These factors also may be of prenatal (before birth), perinatal (during birth), or postnatal (after birth) origin.

Although the majority of retarded individuals are in the EMR range of intelligence with conditions that have unidentifiable environmental causes, the TMR category contains individuals who usually have known specific causes of clinical, pathological, or medical varieties. Only the more frequently occurring causes, types, and conditions associated with the TMR population will be described. A more detailed and comprehensive discussion of the causes, characteristics, and treatment of mental retardation can be found in the following medically oriented texts: *Atlas of Mental Retardation Syndromes* (Gellis and Feingold, 1968), *The Face in Genetic Disorders* (Goodman and Gorlin, 1970), *Congenital Mental Retardation* (Farrell, 1969), *The Genetic, Metabolic, and Developmental Aspects of Mental Retardation* (Murray and Rosser, 1972), *Handbook of Mental Retardation Syndromes* (Carter, 1970), *Mental Retardation: An Atlas of Diseases with Associated Physical Abnormalities* (Holmes, Moser, Hallodorsson, Mack, Pant, and Malyilevick, 1972), *Mental Retardation: Diagnosis and Treatment* (Poser, 1969), and *Prevention of Genetic Disease and Mental Retardation* (Milunsky, 1975).

Infections and intoxications

Maternal and childhood infectious diseases (particularly viral) and intoxications that destroy brain cells can be responsible for mental retardation. Discussed briefly will be congenital rubella, congenital syphilis, congenital toxoplasmosis, Rh blood incompatibility, and intoxicants (lead, carbon monoxide, drugs, etc.).

Congenital rubella. If the mother is infected during pregnancy with congenital rubella (German measles) and if occurrence is early in pregnancy, 50% to 60% of those children born may have one or several abnormalities. Such defects often include mental retardation, which might be accompanied by eye diseases (cataracts and glaucoma), cardiac anomalies, deafness, cerebral palsy, and microcephaly.

Congenital syphilis. Present at birth, congenital syphilis is a condition resulting from a transplacental bacterial infection of the fetus from syphilis present in the mother. There are two forms, early and late. The early form of syphilis damages the central nervous system, and manifestations with mental retardation usually include hydrocephalus and convulsions. The late stage, or delayed type, of congenital syphilis occurs from infancy to adolescence and may consist of progressive mental deterioration and retardation, severe antisocial behavior, hemiplegia, convulsions, nerve deafness, and sensory defects.

Congenital toxoplasmosis. Yet another possible cause of mental retardation is congenital toxoplasmosis. This maternal infection is caused by the protozoan *Toxoplasma gondii*, and, unlike fetuses affected by congenital rubella, the fetus is most susceptible to damage in the last half of pregnancy. In addition to retardation, there may also exist convulsions, microcephaly, hydrocephalus, deafness, and various physical and motor dysfunctions.

Rh factor. The Rh blood incompatibility factor is a hemolytic (breakdown of red corpuscles) disease, which, if left untreated, could cause mental retardation. This condition occurs in the newborn when the father is Rh positive (the blood contains the element known as the Rh factor) and the mother, Rh negative. The unborn child's blood becomes Rh positive because of genetic dominance of this blood factor. Antigens are formed by the mother to combat these factors (it usually takes two pregnancies for a dangerous level of antigens to form), which eventually destroy the red blood cells of the fetus and secrete bilirubin in the skin and brain. Various serums and blood transfusions have helped to reduce the incidences of this condition causing retardation.

Intoxicants. Intoxicants or poisons have just recently been recognized as producing profound and permanent damage to nerve tissue, thus causing retardation. The most common types include plumbism, or lead poisoning (primarily from lead-based paint on wood found in slum or old housing), carbon monoxide, and various drugs.

Metabolism and nutrition

Representative clinical types include the metabolic disorder of phenylketonuria (involving amino acids), galactosemia (involving carbohydrates), and hypothyroidism, or cretinism (an endocrine disorder).

Phenylketonuria. Phenylketonuria, or PKU, was one of the first recognized inherited metabolic defects and is a condition in which metabolism of the amino acid phenylalanine is deficient. This results in nerve and brain cell damage and ultimately mental retardation. Intelligence in the PKU child might range from severe to normal levels, depending on when intervention was initiated. About 90% have blond hair, blue eyes, and fair skin, and occurrence is twice as frequent in males. The effects of PKU can be minimized by excluding substances containing phenylalanine from the diet (milk is a primary source). Fortunately, this condition can be easily detected with

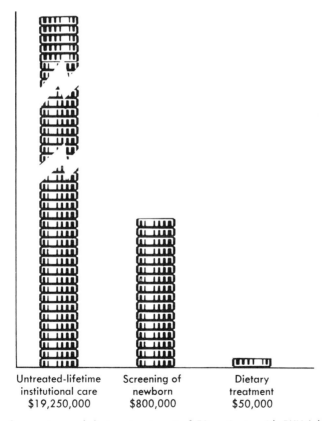

| Untreated-lifetime institutional care $19,250,000 | Screening of newborn $800,000 | Dietary treatment $50,000 |

Fig. 1-3. Cost of screening and dietary treatment of 50 patients with PKU (phenylketonuria) compared to untreated-lifetime institutional care. (From National Institute of Health, U.S. Department of Health, Education, and Welfare: What are the facts about genetic disease? Washington, D.C., 1975, Government Printing Office.)

screening tests, and if detection is early, retardation is prevented. Forty-eight states now require screening of newborns for PKU (National Institute of Health, 1975). Although it takes about $16,000 before one case of PKU is detected, the cost of detection and treatment is ten to twenty times less than the cost of a lifetime of institutional care. Aside from the humanitarian reason for screening and preventing this potentially serious condition, it is also economically sound. (See Fig. 1-3 for the cost of screening and dietary treatment for 50 patients versus a lifetime of institutional care.)

Galactosemia. The main carbohydrate disorder, galactosemia, exists when an individual is unable to metabolize galactose (sugar). A urine analysis is a common screening test, and if detection and dietary controls are instituted early, retardation and other conditions can be prevented or alleviated. One study (Komrower and Lee, 1970) indicated that children diagnosed and treated early had an average IQ of 84 and those diagnosed later, an average IQ of only 48.

Hypothyroidism. Sometimes called cretinism, hypothyroidism is the most common endocrine disorder and is caused by an absence or dysfunction of the thyroid gland. Cretinism is characterized by the clinical features of short thick hands and neck, large head, dry scaly skin, straight hair, protruding tongue, delayed bone development, short extremities, muscular hypertrophy (enlargement), and severe retardation. As a group, children affected with hypothyroidism are rather resistive and stubborn in their relationships with other children and adults (Hutt and Gibby, 1975). As in PKU and galactosemia, if this condition is diagnosed and treated early, the physical stigmas will be alleviated and the mental capacity increased.

Unknown prenatal influence

Conditions for which no definite cause can be determined but which existed at or prior to birth primarily include the cranial (head) anomalies of hydrocephalus and microcephaly.

Hydrocephalus. Hydrocephalus is a condition characterized by an unusually large head due to an excess of cerebrospinal fluid. In most cases there is a block in the circulatory system of the fluid because of tumors, infections, or injuries. Both the head size and the severity of mental retardation are dependent on the brain damage caused by the accumulation of fluid and resulting pressure. Surgery to drain away the fluid buildup (by means of a shunt) or correction of a valve defect are usually the accepted methods of treatment (Shulman, 1969).

Microcephaly. The opposite cranial defect of hydrocephalus is microcephaly. The chief feature is a small head circumference, usually less than 16 inches in adulthood or two standard deviations below the mean for age and sex. This is a developmental condition in which the brain does not grow or parts may even be missing, thus causing mental retardation. The two main types are primary (inherited) and secondary (acquired—by maternal infection, prolonged exposure to radiation, anoxia). Physical characteristics, in addition to the small head size, include a furrowed scalp, curved spine with stooping posture, and receding forehead. Microcephalic children have been observed to be alert, to have a sense of happiness, to shift interests quickly, to be echolalic (repeating the same sounds over and over), and to imitate the behavior of others (Hutt and Gibby, 1975).

Chromosomal abnormality

A brief explanation and understanding of basic human genetics is necessary before advancing into specific chromosomal abnormalities that cause retardation. Chromosomes, genes, and genetic counseling will be discussed.

A chromosome is made up of thousands of genes. Genes are composed of many hundreds of subunits called nucleotides, which are linked together in spiral form. These spiral forms (genes) constitute the

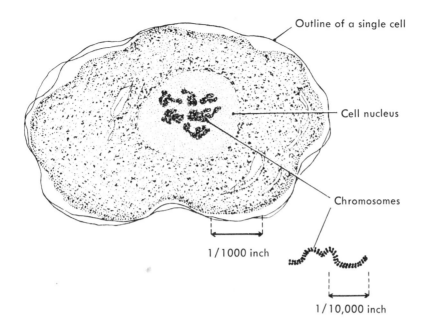

Outline of a single cell

Cell nucleus

Chromosomes

1/1000 inch

1/10,000 inch

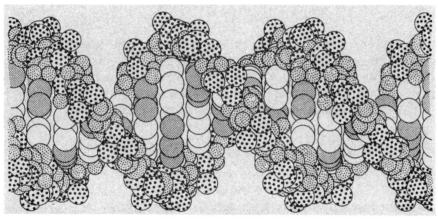

DNA = Genetic material

Fig. 1-4. Genes visualized as "beads" on a chromosome within a single cell. (From National Institute of Health, U.S. Department of Health, Education, and Welfare: What are the facts about genetic disease? Washington, D.C., 1975, Government Printing Office.)

genetic material called DNA, which is the main substance of the chromosomes. (See Fig. 1-4.)

Every individual has thousands and thousands of genes and carries between five and eight recessive genes for serious genetic defects. Genes, normal and faulty, are inherited by one of four ways—dominant, recessive, X- or sex-linked, and multifactorial inheritance.

Genetic makeup. Human cells normally have 22 pairs of chromosomes (autosomes), which govern the broad range of developmental aspects or abilities, and one pair of sex chromosomes, which govern sex characteristics. Females carry two X chromosomes and males carry one X chromosome and one Y chromosome. One chromosome of each of the 23 pairs is derived from the maternal egg cell and one from the paternal sperm cell—thus the normal constellation of 23 pairs. Any deviation or aberration in this chromosome makeup may produce serious mental and physical defects. The deviations may be numerical, structural, or multiple, a combination of number and structure (Grossman, 1973). Possible causes for the deviations are gene mutations, radiation, drugs, or viruses. The chromosomes are grouped (called karyotyping) into seven classifications. This systematic arrangement follows:

Group A—Chromosome pairs 1-3
Group B—Chromosome pairs 4-5
Group C—Chromosome pairs 6-12 plus X
Group D—Chromosome pairs 13-15
Group E—Chromosome pairs 16-18
Group F—Chromosome pairs 19-20
Group G—Chromosome pairs 20-21 plus Y

Genetic counseling. The science of genetics, because of numerous recent advances, has emerged as an important medical service for families with the risk of transmitting retardation. Genetic counseling, a specialized aspect of the genetics field, is a process whereby families are assisted in (1) comprehending the medical facts, including diagnosis and probable cause of the disorder, (2) determining the risk of recurrence, (3) understanding the alternatives for dealing with the risk of recurrence, (4) choosing the course of action based on family goals, as well as ethical and religious beliefs, and (5) making the best possible adjustment to the disorder in a family member.

Amniocentesis. A medical procedure for the assessment of the genetic status of a human fetus is called amniocentesis. This procedure (Fig. 1-5) is now considered relatively simple and safe. The process involves the withdrawal of amniotic fluid

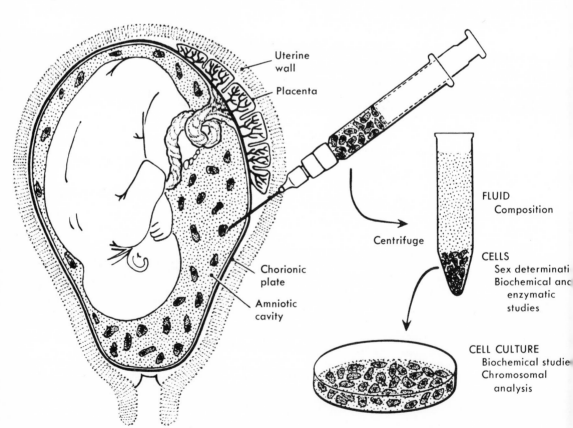

Uterine wall
Placenta
Chorionic plate
Amniotic cavity
Centrifuge
FLUID Composition
CELLS Sex determinati Biochemical anc enzymatic studies
CELL CULTURE Biochemical studie Chromosomal analysis

Fig. 1-5. Process of amniocentesis. (From National Institute of Health, U.S. Department of Health, Education, and Welfare: What are the facts about genetic disease? Washington, D.C., 1975, Government Printing Office.)

from an expectant mother's uterus in the sixteenth to twentieth week of pregnancy. The cells are then extracted from the fluid and cultured to determine if chromosomal defects exist. This procedure is useful in determining over sixty serious genetic disorders, twenty-seven of which can lead to mental retardation, among them Down's syndrome (National Institute of Health, 1975, and PCMR, 1971).

Down's syndrome. Chromosomal disorders causing retardation include Down's syndrome and cri-du-chat syndrome, both autosomal (first through twenty-second pair). Sex chromosomal disorders (twenty-third pair) include Klinefelter's syndrome and Turner's syndrome. Down's syndrome will be the only disorder discussed because of its relatively high frequency (about 20% to 25%) in members of classes for the TMR.

Dr. John Langdon Down, an English physician, first described this syndrome (a recognized pattern of altered development) in 1866, which later came to bear his name, Down's syndrome. Because of a resemblance in facial features to children of the Asian races and the evolutionary theories of that time, Dr. Down attached the word "mongol"—hence the terms mongolism and mongoloid. The more appropriate name for this disease is Down's syndrome (DS). The cause for this condition eluded detection until the development of a high-powered light microscope made karyotyping possible. Once this technique of chromosomal analysis and classification was perfected, Lejeune in 1959 precisely determined the factor common to all DS children—chromosomal abnormality. Prior to that time only theories as to the cause of DS existed, that of Benda (unfinished growth rate) in 1946 and Penrose (genetic factor) in 1950.

A child with DS typically has 47 chromosomes to a cell instead of the normal 46 (Fig. 1-6). The additional chromosome is found in the twenty-first chromosome pair; this is called trisomy 21 or nondisjunction. Trisomy 21 constitutes about 94% of DS cases; 5% are termed translocation (one of the twenty-first pair of chromosomes attaches to a chromosome of the D or G group). The remaining 1% is known as mosaicism because the cells contain a mixture of 45, 46, and 47 chromosomes.

Two possibilities exist for the trisomy 21

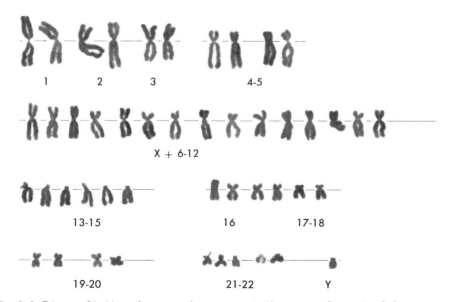

Fig. 1-6. Trisomy 21. Note the extra chromosome in the twenty-first pair of chromosomes. (From Reisman, L. E., and Matheny, A. P., Jr.: Genetics and counseling in medical practice, St. Louis, 1969, The C. V. Mosby Co.)

type of DS: (1) there can be a mistake in chromosome distribution from egg to sperm to form the first embryonic cell, or (2) the egg and sperm cells can be normal, but in the very first cell division the twenty-first chromosome pair does not divide correctly (Smith and Wilson, 1973).

The occurrence of DS is about one in 600 to 700 births, about 15,000 a year, and affects families regardless of socioeconomic level or race (PCMR, 1972). For young mothers the risk of having a DS child is low, but the chances increase progressively with maternal age. See Table 1-5 for a breakdown of this relationship.

Some of the more common clinical features of DS include hypotonic (flabby) muscles, small broad head, small flat nose, slanted eyes with epicanthic folds of the upper eyelids, Brushfield's spots (speckling of the iris), strabismus (cross-eye), small ears, small mouth with a tongue that often protrudes, small teeth, deep voice, skin folds across the back of a short neck, short stubby fingers with the little finger turned inward, a small gap between the first and second toes, dry skin, sparse, fine, and straight hair, short stature, mild to moderate obesity, and late and/or incomplete sexual development. Physical problems of a more serious nature include a high susceptibility to infection in the lungs and intestines, heart problems in about one third of DS children, leukemia (uncontrolled growth of white blood cells) in about 1%, and incomplete development of the intestine (Smith and Wilson, 1973).

Intellectually, the vast majority are in the TMR range, with an average IQ of 20 to 30 in institutionalized and 30 to 40 in noninstitutionalized DS individuals. Wunsch (1957) reported only about 4% are in the 50 to 70 IQ range. Also, there is a tendency for the IQ and social quotient to decrease with age (55 to 30 and 65 to 50, respectively) (Cromwell and Birth, 1969). The social development remains about two to three years above the level of mental functioning.

The DS child is typically happy, cheerful, and enjoyable. He experiences the same emotions as any other child but on a simpler level. Stubbornness and obstinance are the principal undesirable personality traits found in the DS child. Even in 1866 Down gave the following description:

> Another feature is their great obstinacy—they can only be guided by consummate tact. No amount of coercion will induce them to do that which they have made up their minds not to do.*

The mortality rate is about 20% to 30% within the first two years of life and rises to about 50% in the first five years of life (Holmes et al., 1972; Smith and Wilson, 1973). Defects in heart development account for two thirds of deaths, with the remaining causes of death due to intestinal blockage, infections, and pneumonia. The mortality rate today for those who survive the first few years is about the same as that for normal persons until around the age of 40, when the rate begins a sharp increase.

There is presently no known cure or treatment, and control seems to lie in prevention. The President's Committee on Mental Retardation (1972) believes DS can be eliminated as a cause of mental retardation through the technique of amniocentesis. Smith and Wilson (1973) offer this order of consideration for the performance of amniocentesis to decrease the occurrence of DS:

Table 1-5. Approximate frequency of Down's syndrome births according to maternal age*

Maternal age	Frequency of occurrence
< 30	1 in 1,500
30 to 34	1 in 750
35 to 39	1 in 280
40 to 44	1 in 130
> 45	1 in 65

*Data from Mikkelsen, M., and Stene, J.: Genetic counseling in Down's syndrome, Hum. Hered. **20:**457, 1970.

*From Down, J. L.: Observations on an ethnic classification of idiots, Clinical Lecture Reports of London Hospital 3:260, 1866.

1. The pregnant woman is a carrier of translocation type.
2. The father-to-be is a carrier of translocation type.
3. The couple has had more than one child with trisomy 21.
4. The prospective mother is in the older age group (over 40).
5. The woman has had one child with trisomy 21.

Of course, after amniocentesis helps to identify an abnormal fetus, the decision to have a therapeutic abortion is a personal concern dependent on the parents' moral and religious beliefs. The outlook for the child born with DS is much improved because of today's medical advances, behavioral knowledge, and comprehensive programming. Given a favorable home environment and early systematic training, the DS child's abilities can be greatly increased. Since parental involvement is so important in assisting the DS child in the development of his full potential, the booklet *Your Down's Syndrome Child: You Can Help Him Develop From Infancy to Adulthood* (Pitt, 1974), the article *A Home-Centered Program for Parents* (Eddington and Lee, 1975), and the news magazine *Sharing Our Caring* (for parents of DS children) are recommended reading for parents.

DIAGNOSIS

Total diagnosis or evaluation requires a multidisciplinary team of professionals (i.e., psychologist, educational specialists, physician, speech and hearing consultant, social worker). This segment of the chapter, however, will focus only on formal diagnosis of mental retardation with emphasis on intelligence testing and assessment of adaptive behavior, since these are the two criteria for mental retardation. This is not to diminish the value and contribution of the other disciplines; each is important. The other disciplines that assess and evaluate the abilities of the TMR as they relate to educational programming will be discussed in Section II, Chapters 4 through 10.

Intelligence tests

Intelligence tests are psychometric devices consisting of standarized questions and tasks for assessing an individual's potential for purposeful or useful behavior (Wechsler, 1974). Intelligence testing of the mentally retarded recognizes a number of basic assumptions and major generalities. These are listed to facilitate a better understanding of the values and limitations of intelligence tests.

Assumptions (Hutt and Gibby, 1975)
1. It is assumed that the examiner has had the background and experiences suitable to the test employed.
2. It is assumed that the test is given and scored by an examiner who has been adequately trained in its administration and interpretation.
3. It is assumed that the child performs on the test in a manner indicative of his true capacities.

Limitations (Gallagher and Moss, 1963)
1. It is agreed that intelligence test scores are not stable in all children and may fluctuate with age, especially the first ten years of life.
2. The same intelligence tests measure different cognitive functions at different ages.
3. Each test does not completely measure the phenomenon of intelligence.
4. Intelligence tests have three major functions, often forgotten: (a) to predict school achievement, (b) to determine abilities and limitations in a child, and (c) to provide information (with other tests) to clarify a child's problems.

Only standardized individual tests of intelligence should be employed with the mentally retarded. Individual tests allow for a better rapport between administrator and examinee and without question can provide the best possible estimate of a child's intelligence. Some concerns have been raised over the value of low IQ scores derived in formal testing with the TMR. Ross and Boroskin (1972) found that low IQ scores (below 30) are meaningful if the test is properly administered by a qualified examiner. They also found moderately high correlations between self-help scores and IQ scores for TMRs.

The two most widely employed and accepted individual tests of intelligence used in part to determine mental retardation are the *Stanford-Binet Intelligence Scale, Third Revision, Form L-M, 1972 Norms Edition* and the *Wechsler Intelligence Scale for Children—Revised*. These psychological tests have the necessary reliability, validity, and standardization to be considered effective measures for intellectual development. Other tests of value are listed in Table 1-6. The specific test selected, of course, depends on the child's age, suspected level of functioning, other handicapping conditions, tests to be given, and tests recently administered.

The *Stanford-Binet 1972 Norms Edition* (S-B) is the terminal product from the initial scales of Binet and Simon, first published in 1905 and revised in 1908 and 1911. The Stanford revision of the *Binet-Simon Intelligence Test* was first published in the United States in 1916 by Louis Terman of Stanford University, California. This test was revised in 1937 and again in 1960. In 1972, under the direction of Robert Thorndike, norm tables were developed to represent the performance of subjects in the 1970s.

The S-B undertakes to measure intelligence as general mental adaptability and makes use of age standards of performance. One of Binet's basic assumptions in the original scale was that an individual is thought of as normal if he can do the things persons of his age normally do, retarded if not, and advanced if his performance level exceeds that of persons his own age. The 1972 norm tables extend from the chronological ages of 2.0 to 18.0 and were based on approximately 100 subjects at each S-B age level, or 2,100 total subjects.

Administration of the S-B requires a professionally trained and certified examiner, is essentially verbal, and yields an IQ score. Test levels are spaced at six-month intervals from ages 2 to 5 and one year from ages 5 to 14; the remaining levels are Average Adult and Superior Adult Levels 1, 2, and 3. Each age level contains six tests, except the Average Adult Level, which contains eight tests.

The original edition of the test by Binet and Simon introduced the concept of men-

Table 1-6. Tests used in assessment of intellectual ability*

Test	Age range	Method of reporting	Publisher and date
Cattell Infant Intelligence Scale	3 to 30 mo.	MA and IQ	The Psychological Corp., 1940
Columbia Mental Maturity Scale—Revised (Third Edition)	3 yr. 6 mo. to 9 yr. 11 mo.	MA	Harcourt Brace Jovanovich, Inc., 1972
Leiter International Performance Scale	2 to 18 yr.	MA and IQ	C. H. Stoelting Co., 1948
McCarthy Scale of Children's Abilities	2½ to 8½ yr.	General Congnitive Index (possible conversion to MA)	The Psychological Corp., 1972
Peabody Picture Vocabulary Test	2½ to 18 yr.	MA, IQ, and percentile rank (deviation IQ)	American Guidance Service, Inc., 1965
Pictorial Test of Intelligence	3 to 8 yr.	MA and percentile rank (deviation IQ)	Houghton Mifflin Co., 1964
Stanford-Binet Intelligence Scale, Third Revision, 1972 Norms Edition	2 yr. to adulthood	MA and IQ	Houghton Mifflin Co., 1960
Wechsler Intelligence Scale for Children—Revised	5 to 15 yr.	Verbal IQ, performance IQ, full-scale IQ, and MA (test age)	The Psychological Corp., 1974
Wechsler Preschool and Primary Scale of Intelligence	4 to 6½ yr.	Verbal IQ, performance IQ, full-scale IQ, and MA (test age)	The Psychological Corp., 1967

*A list of publishers and their addresses appears in Appendix A.

tal age (MA). The average 12-year-old has a mental age of 12, the average 6-year-old has a mental age of 6, etc. Stern (1914) influenced Terman in the 1916 revision to use the concept of intelligence quotient (IQ) or ratio IQ because the MA alone was not a unitary measure of intelligence. It was thought that there should be consideration of the chronological age of the individual, hence the creation of the IQ formula. This is derived by dividing the MA by the CA and multiplying by 100 (to eliminate the decimal point):

$$\frac{MA}{CA} \times 100 = IQ$$

For example, a 10-year-old child with an MA of 4 years 3 months would have an IQ of 42 (the example below converts years into months):

$$\frac{48 + 3}{120} \times 100 = 42$$

The S-B shows substantial relationships with other tests of intelligence and is a good predictor of social maturity, learning, and some specific attributes of intelligence for the retardate (Himmelstein, 1968).

Wechsler (1944) introduced the deviation IQ to replace the MA concept, believing the MA an unjustified and unqualified indicator of mental level. The deviation IQ is a standard score on which the distribution of IQs is converted into a normal curve with an average of 100 and a standard deviation the same at every age level. IQs are obtained by comparing each subject's test performance not with a composite age group but exclusively with the scores earned by individuals in a single age group.

The *Wechsler Intelligence Scale for Children* was published in 1949 and contained two sections: a verbal, yielding a verbal IQ score, and a performance, yielding a performance IQ score. (A combination, or full-scale, IQ score is also computed). The *Wechsler Intelligence Scale for Children—Revised* (WISC-R) was published in 1974 and retains the IQ as an essential aspect. Wechsler believes that the IQ is still a

scientifically sound and useful measure but has been misinterpreted and misused (Wechsler, 1974). The WISC 1949 edition was revised because it had been standardized on a white middle class population and was considered unfair to children who differed from the sample. A stratified sampling plan was used in the recent revision to reflect selected variables as they existed according to the 1970 United States census. The variables used were age, sex, race (white and nonwhite), geographical region, occupation of head of household, and urban or rural residence.

The WISC-R consists of the same twelve tests (six verbal and six performance) that constituted the 1949 WISC, with only ten considered mandatory. The verbal and the performance sections each contain five areas of assessment plus one supplementary test. Both sections and their subtests are listed. The number following the test corresponds to the preferred order for administering the tests.

Verbal	Performance
Information (1)	Picture completion (2)
Similarities (3)	Picture arrangement (4)
Arithmetic (5)	Block design (6)
Vocabulary (7)	Object assembly (8)
Comprehension (9)	Coding (10)
Digit span (supplementary) (11)	Mazes (supplementary) (12)

Whereas the WISC age range was 5 to 15, the WISC-R is intended for use with children 6 to 16. The WISC-R also has numerous item changes and updating. The average correlation of the WISC-R full-scale IQ score and the S-B 1972 Norms Edition IQ is reported at 0.73, which is similar to the 1949 WISC (Wechsler, 1974).

Adaptive behavior

Although the intelligence tests and IQ remain some of the best indicators of mental functioning and fairly accurate predictors of potential for school success, they do not provide descriptive information on the way an individual maintains personal independence in daily living or how the social expectations of the environment are met. Both factors are crucial components in the education and training of the retarded.

Adaptive behavior ability or everyday behavioral functioning must be determined in the TMR because great variability in functioning of low IQ individuals exists; it also provides useful information in educational planning, home management, and training.

There presently exist numerous instruments for diagnosing adaptive behavior abilities and deficits (see Table 1-7 for a selected listing, areas of assessment, age range, publisher, date), but only three will be discussed: the *AAMD Adaptive Be-*

havior Scale, 1975 Revision (Fogelman, 1974), the corresponding *AAMD Adaptive Behavior Scale, Public School Version, 1975 Revision* (Lambert, Windmiller, Cole, and Figueroa, 1975), and the *T.M.R. Performance Profile for the Severely and Moderately Retarded, Third Edition* (DiNola, Kaminsky, and Sternfeld, 1968).

The current version of the *AAMD Adaptive Behavior Scales, 1975 Revision* (AAMD AB Scales) consists of two parts: developmental progress of skills essential to individual daily living (Part I) and measures of maladaptive behavior (Part II). The normative sample includes male and female

Table 1-7. Adaptive behavior instruments

Name of instrument	Age range (years)	Areas assessed	Publisher and date*
AAMD Adaptive Behavior Scale, 1975 Revision	All ages	Independence, physical, economic, language, numbers and time, domestic, vocational, self-direction, responsibility, socialization, and fourteen measures of personality and behavior disorders	AAMD, 1974
AAMD Adaptive Behavior Scale, Public School Version, 1974 Revision	7 to 13	Independence, physical, economic, language, numbers and time, vocations, self-direction, responsibility, socialization, and twelve measures of personality and behavior disorders	AAMD, 1975
Balthazar Scales of Adaptive Behavior for the Profoundly and Severely Mentally Retarded	5 to 57	Eating-drinking, dressing-undressing, and toileting	Research Press Co., 1971
Evaluation Form for Trainable Mentally Retarded Children	School age	Motor (gross and fine) conceptual, self-help, emotional, social, speech, and recommendations	Rocky Mountain Special Education Instructional Materials Center (no date given)
Five-point Rating Scale for the Young Trainable Child	Below 12	Self-care, social, language, economic, physical, arts and crafts, and music	Texas Education Agency, 1960
Louisiana Adaptive Behavior Scale	3 to 31	Practical knowledge, communication, self-help, motor, and social	Louisiana State Division of Mental Retardation, 1973
TARC Assessment System	3 to 16	Self-help, motor, communication, and social	H. & H. Enterprises, 1974
T.M.R. Performance Profile for the Severely and Moderately Retarded	School age	Self-care, body usage, practical skills, basic knowledge, communication, and social	Reporting Service for Exceptional Children, 1970
Y.E.M.R. Performance Profile for the Young Moderately and Mildly Retarded	Preschool	Social, self-help, safety, communications, motor manipulative, perceptual and intellectual, academics, imagination and creativity, and emotions	Reporting Service for Exceptional Children, 1967

*A list of publishers and their addresses appears in Appendix A.

children and adults (4,000 residents of sixty-eight United States residential facilities for the mentally retarded) at all levels of retardation. The administration of the scale may be conducted by first party assessment (an evaluator thoroughly familiar with the retarded person), third party assessment (an evaluator asking questions to an individual who is familiar with the retarded person), and interview method (obtaining the necessary information through interviewing parents or others who know the retarded person's abilities). Possible uses of the scale include (1) identifying areas of deficiency, (2) providing an objective basis for the comparison of ratings over time, (3) comparing ratings of the same individual under different situations (home, school, ward) to determine environmental effects, (4) providing a standardized reporting system for use between organizations, agencies, and schools, and (5) providing descriptions of the retarded to facilitate program planning and other administrative decisions (Fogelman, 1974). The mean reliabilities for this new version are reported as 0.86 for Part I and 0.57 for Part II.

Part I is organized along developmental lines of personal independence in daily living. It is designed to evaluate an individual's skills and habits in ten domains and twenty-one subdomains of behavior, which follow.

1. Independent functioning
   a. Eating
   b. Toilet use
   c. Cleanliness
   d. Appearance
   e. Care of clothing
   f. Dressing and undressing
   g. Travel
   h. General independent functioning
2. Physical development
   a. Sensory development
   b. Motor development
3. Economic activity
   a. Money handling and budgeting
   b. Shopping skills
4. Language development
   a. Expression
   b. Comprehension
   c. Social language development
5. Numbers and time
6. Domestic activity
   a. Cleaning
   b. Kitchen duties
   c. Other domestic activities
7. Vocational activity
8. Self-direction
   a. Initiative
   b. Perseverance
   c. Leisure time
9. Responsibility
10. Socialization

There are two types of items in Part I. The first requires the selection of only *one* of several possible responses. In scoring, the most difficult task the person can usually manage is circled and entered to. the right. For example, ability to drink under the subdomain Eating and the domain Independent Functioning is scored in the following manner[*]:

Drinking (circle only one)

Drinks without spilling, holding glass 3
in one hand.
Drinks from cup or glass unassisted— (2)
neatly.   **2**
Drinks from cup or glass unassisted— 1
considerable spilling.
Does not drink from cup or glass 0
unassisted.

The second type of item requires the administrator to check *all* statements that apply to the examinee. In scoring, the number checked is entered to the right. For example, the ability to ride public transportation under the subdomain Travel and the domain Independent Functioning is scored in the following way[*]:

Public transportation
(check all statements that apply)

Rides on train, long-distance bus,   ✓
plane independently.
Rides in taxi independently.   ✓
Rides subway or city bus for un-   **3**
familiar journeys independently.
Rides subway or city bus for familiar   ✓
journeys independently.
_____None of the above.

---

[*]From Fogelman, C. J., editor: AAMD adaptive behavior scale: manual, Washington, D.C., 1974, American Association on Mental Deficiency.

Part II of the scale surveys social expectations in fourteen domains and is designed to provide a measure of maladaptive behavior related to personality and behavior disorders. These domains of assessment follow:

1. Violent and destructive behavior
2. Antisocial behavior
3. Rebellious behavior
4. Untrustworthy behavior
5. Withdrawal
6. Stereotyped behavior and odd mannerisms
7. Inappropriate interpersonal manners
8. Unacceptable vocal habits
9. Unacceptable or eccentric habits
10. Self-abusive behavior
11. Hyperactive tendencies
12. Sexually aberrant behavior
13. Psychological disturbances
14. Use of medications

Part II contains only one type of test item, and the examiner selects those statements which are true about the examinee. In scoring, total each column and enter the sum of the totals to the right. An example is: Ignores Regulations or Regular Routines in the domain Rebellious Behavior and is scored as follows*:

	Occasionally	Frequently
Has negative attitude toward rules but usually conforms.	①	2
Has to be forced to go through waiting lines, e.g., lunch lines, ticket lines.	1	2
Violates rules or regulations, e.g., eats in restricted areas, disobeys traffic signals.	1	②
Refuses to participate in required activities, e.g., work, school.	1	②
Other (specify: _____)	1	2
_____ None of the above	—	—
Total	1	4

(5)

---

*From Fogelman, C. J., editor: AAMD adaptive behavior scale: manual, Washington, D.C., 1974, American Association on Mental Deficiency.

An individual Profile Summary Sheet (plotted in deciles according to age and percentiles) for Parts I and II (Figs. 1-7 and 1-8) can easily be constructed, making possible a graphical visual representation of an individual's functioning. This is critically important for identification of specific curriculum areas where the individual has needs. The profile can also be used to determine progress over a given period of time. On Part I of the profile, the higher the scores, the more acceptable the behavior for his age group; on Part II of the profile, the higher the score, the more behavior problems the individual exhibits in in that domain.

The *AAMD Adaptive Behavior Scale, Public School Version,* 1975 Revision, was standardized on 2,600 schoolchildren in California and is intended for use with public school TMRs, EMRs, and the educationally handicapped (emotionally disturbed and learning disabled). This revision also differs from the 1974 AAMD AB Scales in that items which do not pertain to school have been eliminated. The Domestic Activity domain in Part I and the Self-Abusive and Sexually Aberrant Behavior domains in Part II were deleted.

The administration and scoring is the same, and profile summaries can also be constructed. This standardization project represents a systematic, valid, and reliable means of evaluating the adaptive behaviors of noninstitutionalized TMR children ages 7 years 3 months to 13 years 2 months.

The *T.M.R. Performance Profile for the Severely and Moderately Retarded* is a scale for pupil performance based on teacher observation. The T.M.R. Profile is designed to identify the performance level of a pupil in a wide variety of daily living activities. The T.M.R. Profile was developed by classroom teachers and assesses six major curriculum areas, four subareas under each, and ten specific skill checks under each subarea. Each of the daily living skills consists of five descriptive levels of performance, ranging from a level of negative

Identification _MARY_

Age _16_

Sex _F_

Date of Administration _JANUARY 1, 1978_

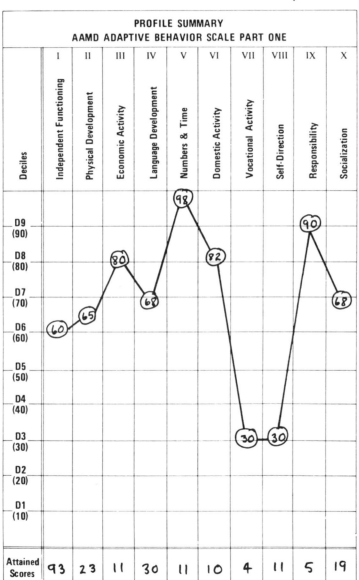

Fig. 1-7. Part one of sample profile summary sheet for a 16-year-old female.

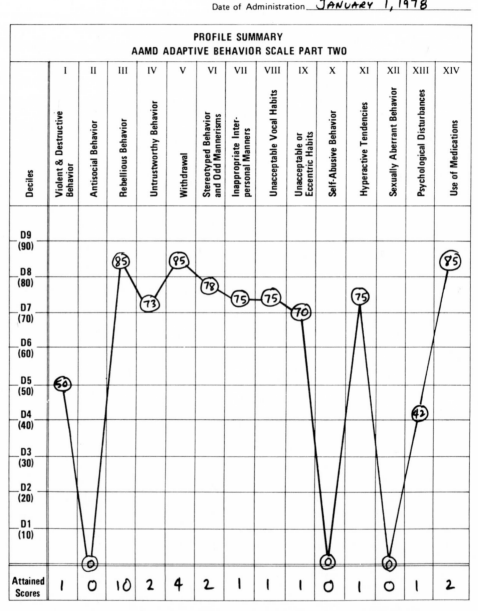

Fig. 1-8. Part two of sample profile summary sheet for a 16-year-old female.

or nonperformance to achievement. The six major areas and subareas follow.

1. Social behavior
   a. Self-control
   b. Personality
   c. Group participation
   d. Social amenities
2. Self-care
   a. Bathroom and grooming
   b. Dealing with food
   c. Clothing
   d. Safety
3. Communication
   a. Modes of communication
   b. Listening
   c. Language activities
   d. Language skills
4. Basic knowledge
   a. Information
   b. Numbers
   c. Awareness
   d. Social studies
5. Practical skills
   a. Tools
   b. Household items
   c. Family chores
   d. Vocational readiness
6. Body usage
   a. Coordination
   b. Health habits
   c. Fitness
   d. Eye-hand coordination

The T.M.R. Profile is designed to (1) record behavioral observations, (2) view these observations in graphic form, (3) identify areas of need and competence for an individual, (4) adapt curriculum materials and methods to meet the individual's needs, (5) review change and development, and (6) maintain a cumulative record specific to TMRs covering a ten year period (DiNola, Kaminsky, and Sternfeld, 1968).

The major area chart (Fig. 1-9) provides a Habilitation Level (HL) in each major curriculum area. The HL can be converted into a habile index, which is a numerical indication of the present performance level in daily living activities. This rating scale was not intended to give age norms, but merely to give indications of how a child is performing and progressing regardless of age, type, or sever-

ity of handicap. The manual recommends that the scores attained in the profile *not* be used for comparison between pupils.

Since adaptive behavior is not a unitary trait and any single score is nonproductive, there is no cutoff point at which the child is considered retarded in adaptive behavior. Instead, AB Scales assess numerous types of functioning and skills, and interpreting the results requires the application of professional judgment of the child's functioning in the context of school, home, and cultured environment.

SUMMARY

This chapter has intended to serve as an overview of mental retardation yet focus on those aspects which relate most to the trainable mentally retarded. The philosophy and rationale for the establishment of educational programs for the TMR were discussed with specific mention of the litigation that advanced this effort. Unquestionably, the TMR has rights, freedoms, and privileges granted other citizens under the Constitution.

Disciplines that contribute to the education, training, treatment, and prevention of mental retardation were discussed. These may be categorized into education and rehabilitation (curriculum specialists, materials specialists, occupational and physical therapists, special education teachers, speech pathologists, vocational education teachers, vocational rehabilitation specialists), psychology (behavior therapists, child development specialists, diagnostic specialists, educational psychologists, learning theorists), medical science (cardiologists, dentists, neurologists, nurses, obstetricians, ophthalmologists, orthopedists, pediatricians, psychiatrists), and other disciplines (government, law, sociology).

Subsequent discussion featured definitions, classifications, and prevalence of retardation. Numerous definitions were presented, with the AAMD (1973) definition analyzed and a specific definition for the TMR offered. The three principal methods

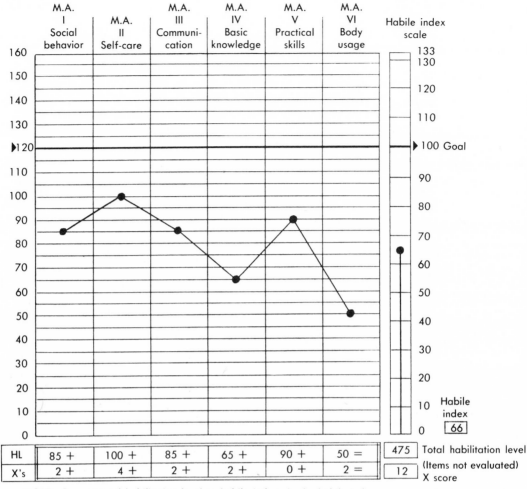

	M.A. I Social behavior	M.A. II Self-care	M.A. III Communi- cation	M.A. IV Basic knowledge	M.A. V Practical skills	M.A. VI Body usage	Total habilitation level
HL	85 +	100 +	85 +	65 +	90 +	50 =	475
X's	2 +	4 +	2 +	2 +	0 +	2 =	12

(Items not evaluated) X score

NOTE: Convert total habilitation level to habile index via the habile index conversion table. Place a dot to identify habile index on the habile index scale.

Fig. 1-9. Example of an individual's scores on the major area chart of the T.M.R. Performance Profile. (From Dinola, A. J., Kaminsky, B. P., and Sternfeld, A. E.: T.M.R. performance profile for the severely and moderately retarded, ed. 4, Ridgefield, N.J., 1970, Educational Performance Associates.)

used to classify retardation are IQ score, adaptive behavior, and physiological cause. Approximately 3% of the population is estimated to be retarded, which in raw numbers means over 6 million United States citizens.

Characteristics of the TMR population were also presented. Included were physical, motor, intellectual, learning, academic, speech and language, personal and social as well as occupational characteristics.

The major causes for the TMR level of retardation include infections and intoxications (rubella, syphilis, toxoplasmosis, Rh blood incompatibility, poisons), metabolism and nutritional disorders (phenylketonuria and hypothyroidism), unknown prenatal influences (hydrocephalus and microcephaly), and chromosomal abnormalities (Down's syndrome). The last segment of this chapter centered on diagnosing or identifying retardation using intelligence tests and adaptive behavior scales. The IQ tests described were the Wechsler Intelligence Scale for Children—Revised and the Stanford-Binet. The adaptive behavior scales described were the AAMD Adaptive Behavior Scale, 1975 Revision, the corresponding Public School Version of the scale, and the T.M.R. Performance Profile for the Severely and Moderately Retarded. These tests, used in conjunction with other measures, yield not only diagnostic information of the skills or disabilities of the child but also assistance in planning educational programs.

REFERENCES AND SUGGESTED READINGS

Baumeister, A. A.: Mental retardation: appraisal, education and rehabilitation, Chicago, 1967, Grune & Stratton, Inc.

Benda, C. F.: Psychopathology of childhood. In Carmichael, L., editor: Manual of child psychology, New York, 1954, John Wiley & Sons, Inc.

Benoit, E. P.: Toward a new definition of mental retardation, Am. J. Ment. Defic. 63:56, 1959.

Brown v. Board of Education, 347 U.S. 483, 74 S. Ct. 686 (1954).

Bureau of Education for the Handicapped: Better education for the handicapped, Annual Reports FY 1968 and FY 1969, Washington, D.C., 1970, U.S. Government Printing Office.

Carter, C. H.: Handbook of mental retardation syndromes, Springfield, Ill., 1970, Charles C Thomas, Publisher.

Chinn, P. C., Drew, C. J., and Logan, D. R.: Mental retardation: a life cycle approach, St. Louis, 1975, The C. V. Mosby Co.

Cronwell, A. C., and Birth, H. G.: Psychological and social development in home-reared children with Down's syndrome (mongolism), Am. J. Ment. Defic. 74:341-350, 1969.

Doll, E. A.: The essentials of an inclusive concept of mental deficiency, Am. J. Ment. Defic. 46: 214-219, 1941.

Down, J. L. H.: Observations on ethnic classification of idiots, Clinical Lecture Reports of London Hospital 3:259-261, 1866.

Dunn, L. M., editor: Exceptional children in the schools: special education in transition, ed. 2, New York, 1973, Holt, Rinehart & Winston.

Eddington, C., and Lee, T.: Sensory-motor stimulation for slow-to-develop children. A home-centered program for parents, Am. J. Nurs. 75: 59-62, 1975.

Ennis, B. J., and Friedman, P. R.: Legal rights of the mentally handicapped, vol. 1, Practicing Law Institute, 1973.

Farber, B.: Mental retardation: its social context and social consequences, Boston, 1968, Houghton Mifflin Co.

Farrell, G.: Congenital mental retardation, Austin, Texas, 1969, University of Texas Press.

Fogelman, C. J., editor: AAMD adaptive behavior scale: manual, Washington, D.C., 1974, American Association on Mental Deficiency.

Friedman, P.: Mental retardation and the law: a report on the status of current court cases (periodic issues), Washington, D.C., 1972, Office of Mental Retardation Coordination, Department of Health, Education, and Welfare.

Gallagher, J., and Moss, J.: New concepts of intelligence and their effect on exceptional children, Except. Child. 30:1-4, 1963.

Gearhart, B. R., and Litton, F. W.: The trainable retarded: a foundations approach, St. Louis, 1975, The C. V. Mosby Co.

Gellis, S. S., and Feingold, M.: Atlas of mental retardation syndromes, Washington, D.C., 1968, Department of Health, Education, and Welfare, U.S. Government Printing Office.

Goodman, R. M., and Gorlin, R. J.: The face in genetic disorders, St. Louis, 1970, The C. V. Mosby Co.

Grossman, H.: Manual on terminology and classification in mental retardation, Baltimore, 1973, American Association on Mental Deficiency, Garamond/Pridemark Press.

Heber, R. F.: Epidemiology of mental retardation, Springfield, Ill., 1970, Charles C Thomas, Publisher.

Heber, R. F.: A manual on terminology and classification in mental retardation, rev. ed., (monograph suppl.) Am. J. Ment. Defic. 65: 499-500, 1961.

Himmelstein, P.: Use of the Stanford-Binet form LM with retardates: a review of recent research, Am. J. Ment. Defic. 72:691-699, 1968.

Holmes, L. B., Moser, H. W., Hallodorsson, S., Mack, C., Pant, S. S., and Malyilevick, B.: Mental retardation: an atlas of diseases with associated physical abnormalities, New York, 1972, Macmillan Publishing Co.

Huddle, D. D.: Work performance of trainable adults as influenced by competition, cooperation and monetary reward, Am. J. Ment. Defic. 72: 198-211, 1967.

Hutt, M. L., and Gibby, R. G.: The mentally retarded child: development, education and treatment, ed. 3, Boston, 1976, Allyn & Bacon, Inc.

Kauffman, J. M., and Payne, J. S., editors: Mental retardation: introduction and personal perspectives, Columbus, Ohio, 1975, Charles E. Merrill Publishing Co.

Kirk, S. A., and Johnson, G. O.: Educating the retarded child, Boston, 1951, Houghton Mifflin Co.

Kolstoe, O. P.: Mental retardation: an educational

viewpoint, New York, 1972, Holt, Rinehart & Winston, Inc.

Komrower, G. M., and Lee, D. H.: Long-term follow-up of galactosemia, Arch. Dis. Child. **45:** 367-373, 1970.

Levitan, M., and Montagu, A.: Textbook of human genetics, New York, 1971, Oxford University Press.

Liese, J. E., and Lerch, H. A.: Physical fitness and intelligence, Ment. Retard. **12:**50-51, 1974.

McKusick, V. A.: Mendelian inheritance in man, ed. 3, Baltimore, 1971, The Johns Hopkins Press.

McLean, J. E., Yoder, D. E., and Schiefelbusch, R. L.: Language intervention with the retarded: developing strategies, Baltimore, 1972, University Park Press.

Mikkelsen, M., and Stene, J.: Genetic counseling in Down's syndrome, Hum. Hered. **20:**457, 1970.

Mills v. Board of Education, Civil Action No. 1939-71 (District of Columbia), August, 1972.

Milunsky, A., editor: Prevention of genetic disease and mental retardation, Philadelphia, 1975, W. B. Saunders Co.

Murray, R. F., and Rosser, P. L.: The genetic, metabolic and developmental aspects of mental retardation, Springfield, Ill., 1972, Charles C Thomas, Publisher.

National Institute of Health: What are the facts about genetic disease? Department of Health, Education, and Welfare, Washington, D.C., 1975, U.S. Government Printing Office.

Nihira, K., and Shellhass, M.: A study of adaptive behavior: its rationale, method and implications in rehabilitation programs, Ment. Retard. **8:**11-16, 1970.

Nijre, B.: The normalization principle and its human management implications. In Kugel, R., and Wolfensberger, W., editors: Changing patterns in residential services for the mentally retarded, Washington, D.C., 1969, President's Committee on Mental Retardation.

Nix, J. P.: Trainable mentally retarded: a guide to programming, Atlanta, 1969, Georgia Department of Education.

Pennsylvania Association for Retarded Children v. Commonwealth of Pennsylvania, Civil Action No. 71-42 (3 Judge Court, E. D. Pennsylvania), January, 1971.

Pitt, D.: Your Down's syndrome child: you can help him develop from infancy to adulthood, Arlington, Texas, 1974, National Association for Retarded Citizens.

Poser, C. M.: Mental retardation: diagnosis and treatment, New York, 1969, Harper & Row Publishers.

President's Committee on Mental Retardation: MR 70, The decisive decade, Washington, D.C., 1971, U.S. Government Printing Office.

President's Committee on Mental Retardation: MR 71, Entering the era of human ecology, Washington, D.C., 1972, U.S. Government Printing Office.

President's Committee on Mental Retardation: MR 73, The goal is freedom, Washington, D.C., 1974, U.S. Government Printing Office.

President's Committee on Mental Retardation: MR 74, A friend in Washington, Washington, D.C., 1975, U.S. Government Printing Office.

President's Committee on Mental Retardation: Silent minority, Washington, D.C., 1974, U.S. Government Printing Office.

President's Panel on Mental Retardation: A proposed program for national action to combat mental retardation, Washington, D.C., 1962, U.S. Government Printing Office.

Reisman, L. E., and Matheny, A. P.: Genetics and counseling in medical practice, St. Louis, 1969, The C. V. Mosby Co.

Rosen, M., Clark, G. R., and Kivitz, M. S.: The history of mental retardation, vols. I and II, Baltimore, 1976, University Park Press.

Ross, R. T., and Boroskin, A.: Are IQ's below 30 meaningful? Ment. Retard. **10:**24, 1972.

Schiefelbusch, R. L., Copeland, R. H., and Smith, J. O.: Language and mental retardation: empirical and conceptual considerations, New York, 1967, Holt, Rinehart & Winston, Inc.

Shulman, K.: Surgical treatment of mental retardation. In Poser, C. M., editor: Mental retardation: diagnosis and treatment, New York, 1969, Harper & Row Publishers.

Smith, D. W., and Wilson, A. A.: The child with Down's syndrome (mongolism): causes, characteristics and acceptance, Philadelphia, 1973, W. B. Saunders Co.

Stein, J. V.: Motor function and physical fitness of the mentally retarded: a critical review, Rehabil. Lit. **24:**230-242, 1963.

Stephens, W. B.: Piaget and Inhelder: application of theory and diagnostic techniques to the area of mental retardation, Educ. Train. Ment. Retard. **1:**75-86, 1966.

Stern, W.: The psychological methods of testing intelligence, Education and Psychological Monographs, no. 13, 1914.

Stevens, H. A., and Heber, R., editors: Mental retardation, Chicago, 1964, The University of Chicago Press.

Terman, L. M., and Merrill, M. A.: Stanford-Binet intelligence scale, rev. 3, Boston, 1973, Houghton Mifflin Co.

Tredgold, A. F.: A textbook of mental deficiency, Baltimore, 1937, William Wood & Co.

United States Department of Health, Education,

and Welfare, Office of the Secretary: The problem of mental retardation, Washington, D.C., 1975, U.S. Government Printing Office.

Waite, K.: The trainable mentally retarded child, Springfield, Ill., 1972, Charles C Thomas, Publisher.

Wallin, J. E.: Children with mental and physical handicaps, Englewood Cliffs, N.J., 1949, Prentice-Hall, Inc.

Wechsler, D.: The measurement of adult intelligence, ed. 3, Baltimore, 1944, Waverly Press.

Wechsler, D.: Wechsler intelligence scale for children—revised manual, New York, 1974, The Psychological Corporation.

Wessel, J. A.: Studies related to moderately (trainable) persons, Challenge 10:1-6, 1975.

Wolfensberger, W.: Normalization: the principle of normalization in human services, Toronto, Canada, 1972, National Institute on Mental Retardation.

Wunsch, W. L.: Some characteristics of mongoloids evaluated at a clinic for children with retarded mental development, Am. J. Ment. Defic. 62:122-130, 1957.

CHAPTER 2

EDUCATIONAL, ENVIRONMENTAL, AND INSTRUCTIONAL CONCERNS

The provision of services to the retarded has increased from 52% in 1969 (BEH, 1970) to 83% in 1974 (PCMR, 1975). Most of these services are directly or indirectly related to the recent establishment of classes and programs for the TMR. Now that a large quantity of services exists, the next and most vital component to be developed is quality. Even under optimal circumstances, the efficiency with which TMRs learn is limited, the progression of gains and achievements is slow, and the rate of mental development is significantly below normal. It becomes imperative then that special educators involve themselves with the various educational and instructional concerns that affect learning in the TMR.

As for a student in any educational program, the TMR should be considered first as an individual with the same basic needs and drives as other persons. The basic human needs, as identified by Maslow (1954), include physiological needs, safety needs, belongingness and love needs, esteem needs, and the need for a self-actualization. The utimate aim of programing should be to assist each TMR individual to satisfactorily realize his maximum potential and to fulfill basic needs and drives. This is more likely to be achieved by a comprehensive and systematic educational program involving the combined efforts of school, home, and community.

This chapter will center on curriculum goals, objectives, and content, instructional personnel (including parents), organizational and administrative considerations, materials, general principles of instruction for the TMR, and individual educational programs.

CURRICULUM GOALS, OBJECTIVES, AND CONTENT

Major prior criticisms relating to curriculum for the TMR, such as a lack of purpose, disagreement on educational objectives, and lack of a systematic instructional program (Daly, 1966), have little validity today and need not exist. Purposes and educational objectives have been determined (and with general consensus), and many states have recently developed systematic instructional programs for their TMR population (e.g., Florida, 1974; Illinois, 1972; Missouri, 1971; New Mexico, 1970; South Dakota, 1972). The problems today lie in dissemination of existing curriculum plans, development of materials specifically for the TMR, and training of teachers in those competencies which are of maximum benefit to the students and program.

Significant and vital components of any educational curriculum should include a stated operating justification or philosophy, general goals, specific objectives, and sequential content. The philosophical basis (that all children are entitled to the best program of instruction possible regardless of abilities) for this text on curriculum for TMRs was established in the beginning of Chapter 1; therefore only the goals and objectives need elaboration.

Adhering to the concept of normalization (Wolfensberger, 1972), even in curriculum, provides the basic purposes and goals of all education with applicability for the TMR. The three general purposes of education are to allow for development of knowledge, to provide a basis for vocations, and to allow opportunities for the development of self-realization. The TMR can acquire knowledge and facts, in most instances be trained for employment (sheltered or noncompetitive), and can certainly achieve personal fulfillment of self-actualization. Therefore the purposes of regular and special education are essentially the same; only the areas of emphasis, degree of attainment, and delivery service models differ.

The Educational Policies Commission of the National Education Association set up four main goals of education in 1946: (1) self-realization, (2) human relationships, (3) economic efficiency, and (4) civic responsibilities. These general goals were intended for all children regardless of physical, social, emotional, or mental limitations. These same educational goals may easily be adapted to fit the needs and abilities of TMR students.

1. Self-realization
   a. To develop a sense of security
   b. To realize worth as an individual
   c. To provide opportunities for successful achievement and development of capacities in all areas of curriculum
   d. To develop confidence and self-expression
   e. To enjoy and appreciate beauty in nature
   f. To develop leisure time activities
   g. To develop personal happiness and satisfaction
2. Human relationships
   a. To help the child work and play as a member of a group
   b. To develop common courtesy and good manners
   c. To practice good personal hygiene and health habits
   d. To develop respect for others and their property
   e. To encourage cooperation
   f. To teach right from wrong
   g. To teach acceptable social behavior
   h. To develop friendships
   i. To develop the concept of sharing
3. Economic efficiency
   a. To develop positive work habits and attitudes
   b. To develop a sense of responsibility
   c. To understand the relationship of money and work
4. Civic responsibilities
   a. To realize self as a citizen with rights and privileges
   b. To contribute to home, community, or work by being useful and productive
   c. To develop respect for home rules and community laws

Goals of education specific to the TMR must be developed from the needs, characteristics, abilities, and limitations of this particular group. Through the establishment of goals that are student oriented, curriculum can have a realistic base. The primary educational goals for the TMR include the following:

1. Ability to care for one's personal needs (self-care and personal health)
2. Effective communication or language usage
3. Appropriate social behavior and emotional stability
4. Development of perceptual-motor and physical skills
5. Some functional academic skills
6. Development of recreational and leisure time skills
7. Ability to be economically useful in the home or community and/or successful vocational adjustment

The content of the curriculum should

correspond to these general goals; only then will the day-to-day opportunities and experiences that allow the learner to achieve the desired goals be provided. In other words, these seven goals now serve as the seven domains around which to center curriculum for the TMR. Since these curriculum content areas or goals lack specificity, subareas of each domain must be delineated and then further refined by listing, in hierarchical form, specific skills to be developed.*

The curriculum areas, subareas, and specific skills to be developed can be more effectively taught by utilizing four instructional levels: primary, intermediate, prevocational, and vocational. The curriculum content for the TMR follows:

I. Self-care skills
  A. Feeding
    1. Eats soft and solid finger foods
    2. Drinks
      a. From a cup
      b. From a glass
      c. With a straw
      d. From a fountain
    3. Eats
      a. With a spoon
      b. With a fork
      c. With a knife
  B. Toileting
    1. Properly manipulates clothes before and after toileting
    2. Has bladder control
      a. Daytime
      b. Nighttime
    3. Has bowel control
      a. Daytime
      b. Nighttime
    4. Properly uses toilet tissue
    5. Flushes toilet after use
    6. Washes and dries hands
  C. Clothing
    1. Undressing and dressing
      a. Socks (off, on)
      b. Slip-on shoes or boots (off, on)
      c. T-shirt or pull-on shirt (off, on)
      d. Underwear (off, on)
      e. Pull-on pants (off, on)
      f. Slip-on dress (off, on)
      g. Coat (off, on)

---

*See respective chapters in Section II for specific skills, materials, and activities for each of the seven curriculum areas.

      h. Cap or hat (off, on)
      i. Mittens (off, on)
      j. Gloves (off, on)
      k. Slip (off, on)
      l. Scarf (off, on)
      m. Pajamas (off, on)
      n. Bra (off, on)
    2. Unfastening and fastening
      a. Unzips, zips
      b. Unsnaps, snaps
      c. Unbuttons, buttons
      d. Unbuckles, buckles
      e. Unlaces, laces
      f. Unhooks, hooks
      g. Unties, ties
    3. Appropriateness, care, and use of clothing
      a. Appropriateness
        (1) Identifies appropriate clothing for weather
        (2) Identifies appropriate clothing for different sexes
        (3) Identifies own clothing
        (4) Identifies dress clothing
        (5) Identifies work clothing
        (6) Identifies appropriate sizes
        (7) Identifies coordinated clothes
      b. Care and use
        (1) Selects clean clothing
        (2) Adjusts clothes on body for neatness
        (3) Uses a clothes brush
        (4) Folds clothes
        (5) Hangs clothes on hook, on hanger
        (6) Properly disposes of dirty clothes
        (7) Wipes shoes on mat when dirty
        (8) Polishes shoes
        (9) Uses umbrella
  D. Personal grooming and health skills
    1. Hands
      a. Washes hands when needed
      b. Dries hands after washing (cloth, paper, blower)
      c. Uses soap or soap dispenser (liquid, powder)
      d. Cleans nails
      e. Uses an emery board
      f. Uses fingernail clippers
      g. Applies and removes nail polish
    2. Nose
      a. Blows and wipes nose with handkerchief or tissue
    3. Teeth
      a. Brushes teeth
      b. Properly uses dental floss

4. Hair
   a. Combs hair
   b. Brushes hair
   c. Uses a hair dryer
   d. Puts hair in rollers
   e. Shampoos hair
5. Face
   a. Washes and dries face
   b. Applies makeup (e.g., powder, lipstick)
6. Skin
   a. Applies skin moisturizer
   b. Uses an electric shaver (face, legs, underarms)
7. Body
   a. Uses deodorant
   b. Bathes and showers independently
   c. Uses mouthwash
   d. Takes care of self during menstruation
E. Safety and first aid
   1. Home and sheltered employment
      a. Recognizes containers of poisonous substances
      b. Uses electrical devices safely
      c. Recognizes safety elements of fire or heat
      d. Identifies harmful or dangerous objects
      e. Uses bathtub or shower safely
      f. Properly disposes of plastic bags
      g. Recognizes stairways that are dangerous
      h. Uses tools safely
   2. School and recreation
      a. Enters, exits, and rides school bus in a safe manner
      b. Uses safe practices around playground equipment (e.g., slides, swings)
      c. Can cross a street or intersection safely
      d. Knows rules of safety with all recreational activities (e.g., swimming)
   3. Care of simple injuries
      a. Can apply antiseptic and creams
      b. Can apply adhesive or gauze bandages
      c. Can report or self-treat minor burns, animal and insect bites, small cuts, and nosebleed
II. Basic communication skills
A. Listening or receptive skills
   1. Motor imitation
   2. Development of auditory perceptual components of good listening behavior
      a. Auditory awareness

b. Auditory focusing
c. Auditory figure-ground
d. Auditory discrimination
e. Auditory memory
f. Auditory sequencing
g. Auditory blending
h. Auditory association
   3. Has a knowledge of environmental sounds
   4. Has a knowledge of sounds in isolation
   5. Can listen for information
   6. Can follow directions
   7. Can listen for enjoyment (e.g., music)
B. Speaking or expressive skills
   1. Development of physical prerequisites for speech
   2. Can gesture to communicate
   3. Motor and vocal sound
   4. Imitation
   5. Development of vowel sounds
   6. Development of consonant sounds
   7. Can repeat words (vocal word imitation)
   8. Can independently produce functional words
   9. Can identify pictures of commonly spoken words
   10. Can comprehend meaning of commonly spoken words
   11. Can repeat functional phrases and sentences
   12. Can independently produce functional phrases and sentences
III. Social skills
A. Self-control
   1. Is emotionally stable in most everyday situations
   2. Can control temper—not prone to verbal or physical outbursts
   3. Accepts changes in routine
   4. Can accept losing in game situations
   5. Can wait turn
   6. Responds positively to authority
   7. Respects criticism
   8. Feels secure
B. Social amenities
   1. Uses appropriate polite greeting and parting words (e.g., please, thank you, excuse me, hello, good morning, good-bye)
   2. Displays proper physical amenities (e.g., handshake, kiss, wave, clap)
   3. Can make simple introductions
   4. Displays proper eating and table manners
   5. Socially appropriate for specific en-

vironment (e.g., quiet at church services)

C. Group participation
   1. Participates appropriately in team games
   2. Interacts and enjoys group play
   3. Behaves appropriately while attending assemblies, plays, concerts, parties, movies, etc.
   4. Behaves appropriately on various modes of transportation (e.g., bus, train)
   5. Behaves appropriately on field trips
   6. Participates as a member of family, class, group home, residential unit, etc.
D. Personality
   1. Has a positive self-concept
   2. Is enthusiastic and has fun in most work and social activities
   3. Shows and accepts affection
   4. Participates and displays some leadership in play and work
   5. Takes care of and distinguishes between personal property and property of others
   6. Complies with rules and regulations of school and home
   7. Is truthful and honest
   8. Is dependable
E. Sex education
   1. Can recognize body parts and is aware of their function
   2. Able to recognize and understand physical changes during puberty and adolescence
   3. Is knowledgeable and exhibits some understanding of sexual self (e.g., menstruation, intercourse, masturbation, pregnancy)
   4. Can understand peer relationships (e.g., dating, masculine and feminine roles, family relationships)
   5. As a sexual being is responsible citizen of society (e.g., marriage, contraception, family responsibility, child care)

IV. Perceptual-motor and physical education skills
A. Basic movement skills
   1. Locomotor skills
      a. Crawls
      b. Creeps
      c. Dodges
      d. Gallops
      e. Hops
      f. Jumps
      g. Leaps
      h. Marches
      i. Rolls
      j. Runs
      k. Skips
      l. Slides
      m. Starts
   2. Nonlocomotor skills
      a. Bends
      b. Kneels
      c. Rotates
      d. Sits
      e. Squats
      f. Stands
      g. Stops
      h. Stretches
      i. Swings
      j. Turns
      k. Twists
   3. Manipulative skills
      a. Bounces
      b. Carries
      c. Catches
      d. Climbs
      e. Falls
      f. Hangs
      g. Hits
      h. Jumps
      i. Kicks
      j. Lands
      k. Lifts
      l. Pulls
      m. Throws
B. Perceptual-motor skills
   1. Body image
      a. Recognizes body parts
   2. Laterality
      a. Knows right
      b. Knows left
   3. Directionality
      a. Knows up/down
      b. Knows backward/forward
   4. Can coordinate eye-hand movements
   5. Can learn from touch and feel (tactile-kinesthetic ability)
   6. Has adequate balance
C. Physical fitness
   1. Organic performance
      a. Strength
      b. Flexibility
      c. Muscular endurance
      d. Power
   2. Motor performance
      a. Agility
      b. Speed
      c. Reaction time
      d. Overall general coordination
      e. Balance

V. Functional academic skills
A. Reading
   1. Basic visual perceptual skills

a. Can visually discriminate color, shape, and size
b. Can visually match color, shape, and size
c. Has visual sequential memory
2. Basic listening skills
   a. Auditory discrimination
   b. Auditory figure-ground
   c. Auditory association
   d. Auditory sequential memory
3. Produces left-right sequence patterns
4. Identifies and names letters of the alphabet
   a. Uppercase letters
   b. Lowercase letters
5. Identifies sight vocabulary words
   a. Safety words
   b. Public sign words
   c. Public building title words
   d. Months (and abbreviations) of the year
   e. Days (and abbreviations) of the week
   f. Family titles
   g. Public titles (with abbreviations)
   h. Basic color words
   i. Weather words
   j. Directional words
   k. Body part words
   l. Home and furniture words
   m. Clothing words
   n. Number words
   o. Fruit and vegetable words
   p. Action words
B. Writing
   1. Prewriting skills
      a. Holds pencil
      b. Can draw basic strokes
         (1) Down
         (2) Across
         (3) Slant right
         (4) Slant left
         (5) Circle
   2. Tracing skills
      a. Lines
         (1) Horizontal
         (2) Vertical
      b. Shapes
         (1) Cross
         (2) Square
         (3) Circle
         (4) Triangle
      c. Letters
         (1) Uppercase straight line letters
         (2) Lowercase straight line letters
         (3) Uppercase curved letters
         (4) Lowercase curved letters

(5) Uppercase circular letters
(6) Lowercase circular letters
d. Numbers
   (1) 0 to 10
e. Age
f. Telephone number
g. Name and address
3. Copying skills
   a. Lines
      (1) Horizontal
      (2) Vertical
   b. Shapes
      (1) Cross
      (2) Square
      (3) Circle
      (4) Triangle
   c. Letters
      (1) Uppercase straight line letters
      (2) Lowercase straight line letters
      (3) Uppercase curved letters
      (4) Lowercase curved letters
      (5) Uppercase circular letters
      (6) Lowercase circular letters
   d. Numbers
      (1) 0 to 10
   e. Age
   f. Telephone number
   g. Name and address
4. Writing independently
   a. Age
   b. Name
   c. Telephone number
   d. Address
   e. Important words
   f. Names
VI. Recreation and leisure time skills
    A. Participation in recreation
       1. Bicycling
       2. Bowling
       3. Camping
       4. Hiking
       5. Scouting
       6. Swimming
    B. Participation in leisure time activity
       1. Arts and crafts
       2. Music
          a. Rhythms
             (1) Free movement
             (2) Rhythm coordination
             (3) Basic locomotor rhythms
             (4) Nonlocomotor rhythms
             (5) Imitative or creative movements
             (6) Plays rhythm instruments
          b. Singing
          c. Dancing

3. Hobbies or other recreation–leisure time activities

VII. Economic usefulness and vocational skills
  A. Economic and domestic usefulness skills
    1. Uses common household items
      a. Can opener
      b. Dryer
      c. Iron
      d. Phonograph
      e. Radio-television
      f. Stove
      g. Toaster
      h. Washer
      i. Vacuum cleaner
    2. Contributions to family
      a. Cleans floors, rugs, sink, etc.
      b. Clears dishes from table
      c. Folds clothes
      d. Hangs up own clothes
      e. Makes own bed
      f. Prepares simple foods
      g. Serves food
      h. Sets table (dishes and utensils)
      i. Sews
      j. Takes out trash or garbage
      k. Washes and dries dishes (hand or machine)
      l. Washes car
      m. Washes clothes
    3. Gardening and yard work
      a. Picks up and carries away leaves
      b. Rakes leaves
      c. Trims shrubs or bushes
      d. Uses common garden or yard tools (e.g., rake, hoe)
      e. Waters lawn or garden
  B. Vocational skills
    1. Use of vocationally related tools
      a. Broom
      b. Hand saw
      c. Hammer
      d. Map
      e. Paintbrush
      f. Pencil sharpener
      g. Sandpaper
      h. Screwdriver
    2. Work habits and attitudes (work personality)
      a. Adjustment skills
        (1) Can work with adults
        (2) Can work with co-workers
        (3) Can adjust to new assignments
        (4) Can adjust to work environment
      b. Directional skills
        (1) Can and will follow verbally administered directions
        (2) Has self-directed work be-

havior (e.g., keeps working or reads work task)
        (3) Can accept correction
      c. Interpersonal skills
        (1) Acceptable personality
        (2) Acceptable social behavior
        (3) Socially responsible
        (4) Adequate self-concept
      d. Motivation
        (1) Desires to work
        (2) Has positive attitude toward work
        (3) Is willing to work routinely
      e. Personal appearance
        (1) Dresses appropriately for work
        (2) Has necessary personal hygiene habits
      f. Punctuality
        (1) Starts work on time
        (2) Attends work regularly
    3. Necessary or relevant functional academic skills
      a. Reading
        (1) Functional words (safety word signs, community words, etc.)
        (2) Specific job-related words
      b. Writing
        (1) Name, address, and telephone numbers
      c. Math
        (1) Recognizes and uses numbers
        (2) Recognizes and uses common measurements
        (3) Tells time
        (4) Has knowledge of money
    4. Specific vocational tasks
      a. Assembling (e.g., nuts, bolts, washers)
      b. Collating (e.g., pages for booklets)
      c. Folding letters
      d. Packaging
      e. Sorting (by color, texture, design, shape)
      f. Typing
      g. Weaving
      h. Wrapping
    5. Other necessary independent skills
      a. Uses time clock
      b. Uses public transportation
      c. Uses telephone (personal and public)

According to teachers of the TMR, the most important skill areas concern competence in the self-care and personal health as well as language (basic communication) areas (Geiger, Brownsmith, and Forgnone, 1976). To illustrate the change in curriculum area importance in the last several years, consider that Hudson in 1960 found teachers spending most of their instructional time on language and motor development. Personal health and self-care skills were listed sixth and ninth, respectively.

It is difficult to determine which curriculum areas are the most important, as all make contributions to developing the total self; certainly some curriculum areas demand more time, depending on the age of the students. The approximate percent of emphasis for each of the seven major curriculum areas per instructional level is depicted in Fig. 2-1.

INSTRUCTIONAL PERSONNEL

Teaching has been defined as "the creation or arrangement of an environment that produces specified changes in the behavioral repertoires of the students"* (Brown and York, 1974). Those who effect change in the education and develop-

---

*From Brown, L., and York, R.: Developing programs for severely handicapped students: teacher training and classroom instruction, Focus Except. Child. 6:4, April, 1974.

ment of the TMR or teach (some direct, some indirect) can therefore include administrators and supervisors, teachers, paraprofessionals (teacher assistants), aides, volunteers, and other school plant employees (e.g., janitors, bus drivers, secretaries, cafeteria workers), and, of course, parents. Each of these will be considered in the role of "teacher."

Administrators and supervisors

Administrators, including school principals of programs in special education and mental retardation, must first of all understand the total functioning of the school system in which they are employed. These individuals can be better understood and accepted by other school administrators if their philosophy of service is consistent with that of the system. The general duties of an administrator are (1) to continue effective programs and services, (2) to provide opportunities for improvement and expansion of these programs, (3) to provide leadership in the development of new services and programs, (4) to secure resources (financial and human) as needed, and (5) to keep lines of communication open (Gearheart, 1974; Selznick, 1966).

The term supervisor is used to describe the professional whose primary role is of a

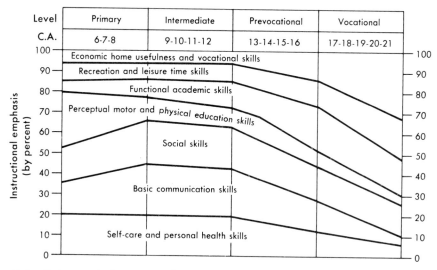

Fig. 2-1. Major curriculum areas by instructional level and approximate percent of emphasis.

more direct nature in the improvement of the educational environment.

Specific duties or tasks of the curriculum supervisor in mental retardation programs are assisting or encouraging each teacher or staff member to (1) gain a better understanding of her students, (2) develop individually and as a cooperating member of the school staff, (3) make more interesting and effective use of instructional materials, (4) improve her method of teaching, (5) develop evaluative techniques, (6) evaluate her own planning, work, and progress, (7) gain a sense of security in her work and in the community, and (8) participate in curriculum development and other in-service activities (Selznick, 1966).

Other duties might include making available ancillary personnel, working with parent and community groups, as well as informing students, other school administrators, and the community of goals and progress of the program.

Teachers

Because the retarded student has many unique learning problems, a teacher must have special training and possess certain personal traits. It is unclear as to which is more important, but certainly a combination of both maximizes the chances of an effective and competent teacher.

The reasons for a person becoming a teacher of the retarded are important. A prospective teacher should enter the field because of a genuine interest in developing the skills of the students and not merely to "help the less fortunate" or "fulfill some inner need." Satisfying one's own psychological needs by teaching the retarded is an undesirable situation and can be detrimental to the students (Blue, 1975).

The demands of teaching in this field of special education are numerous. Many teachers have to teach in less than desirable physical plants, try to teach with outdated and limited materials, and receive little support. The turnover rate for special education teachers has been found to be over 26% a year (Seater, 1972). The two leading factors associated with this teacher turnover are insufficient supportive services and inadequate administrative communication channels. This is unfortunate for students, the school system, and the profession as a whole because it generally takes three to four years of teaching (after student teaching) to produce any significant growth in teacher effectiveness (Millslagle, 1971).

In a 1972 survey (100% return) of state certification requirements for teachers of the mentally retarded, Simensen and Redding found that thirty-four states had statewide requirements, whereas the remaining sixteen allowed the preparing institutions to determine specific requirements for certification. Allowing the universities to dictate teacher certification standards seems to be a coming trend because no states allowed this in 1963 (Krause, 1963). All states required a course in methods and materials, and most required a practicum and introduction to exceptional children. Other courses listed covered characteristics, arts and crafts, language and speech, psychology, tests and measurements, vocational or parental counseling, and related electives.

The survey also revealed that only a few states differentiated between preparation for teaching educable and trainable retardates. More states today, however, are requiring certification in the TMR area of special education, and in addition to the above courses have added a characteristics and methods course for the TMR, a course in behavior modification, and a course in educational prescription and programming. Teachers of the TMR may also need courses in early childhood education because training in this area contributes to teacher effectiveness for the TMR (Blackwell, 1972). It is assumed and desired that competencies which constitute effective teachers for the TMR are obtained in certification programs. But what about personality traits? One study (Barns, 1966) simply asked teachers of the retarded to list the most desirable personality traits of effective teaching. Teachers listed patience, understanding, a sense of humor, love for children, emotional stability, kindness, acceptance of the retarded child, and firmness.

The following traits and characteristics (separate from instructional competencies or skills) are desirable in teachers of the TMR:

- Adaptability
- Calmness
- Cheerfulness
- Cooperative attitude
- Creativity
- Desire for knowledge
- Empathy
- Enthusiasm
- Health and vigor
- Maturity and stability
- Originality
- Resourcefulness
- Patience and tolerance

A novel system of explaining relevant characteristics needed by special education teachers was composed by Estelle Epstein (1968) and applies to the TMR.

ABC's for special education teachers*

A is for ACTION AND AFFECTION.
All children need movement; so do these;
Otherwise they'll be bored—not pleased.
Affection, too, is needed by all.
Does your program harken to that call?

B is for BALANCE AND BELONGING.
Do the children really have activities that change?
Quiet—active—in between—a range?
Do they feel that they belong,
And have a desire to "go along?"

C is for COHERENT, CLEAR, AND CONSISTENT.
Do the children know and understand
And realize you're ready to lend a hand?
Are the steps in the program in sequence . . . sequential,
To help each child develop to his potential?
Is the consistency tempered by needs, time, and place,
So that the children feel "they're on a safe base?"

D is for DYNAMIC AND DEMOCRATIC.
Is the program interesting, challenging, and forceful,
Making the children feel "a part of the circle?"
Are the rights of each individual child considered by you,
Leading to his self-respect and feeling of personal worth, too?

E is for ENJOYABLE AND EFFORT.
Do the children enjoy both the play and the work,
And get the feeling of success and therefore not shirk?
Are their efforts continuous and increasing with pride,
Instead of, "I can't do it" and letting it ride?

F is for FLEXIBILITY AND FIRMNESS.
Is the program flexible? Can it change to "fit the need?"
You may plan to study "wheels" and end up "planting a seed."
Are you firm—yet not too rigid?
We want children relaxed; not frigid.

G is for GROWTH AND GENEROSITY.
Does your program plan for growth—
For now? For the future? Yes, for both?
Are you generous with patience and time,
Helping the children feel secure and fine?

H is for HELPFUL AND HEALTHFUL.
Is the atmosphere healthful for each child?
Does he feel secure, calmer,—not wild?
Emotional and psychological health are important, too,
For the children, as well as for you.

I is for IMAGINATION.
Resourcefulness in finding new and better ways
Makes for happier, healthier, and more interesting days.
Invention, modification, as well as experimentation,
All should come within the range of your imagination.

J is for JOYFUL.
Joy of some success each day
Is the child's best reward or pay.
So include it and watch the child grow;
Even though the progress may be slow.

K is for KNOWLEDGEABLE AND KINDNESS.
Does the program include knowledge about retardation,
The help of doctors, counselors, clinics, and organization?

---

*From The Pointer 13(2):70-72, 1968.

Is kindness felt within the class
And imparted to each lad and lass?

L is for LIFELIKE AND LAUGHTER.
   Is the program planned on experiences that the children know,
   So that all can participate and have something to add or show?
   Is there a place of laughter to help the stress,
   To relieve anxiety and have children worry less?

M is for MEANINGFUL, MANAGEMENT, AND METHODS.
   Is the program complete? Is it real?
   For the children has it an appeal?
   Watch your methods, they mean ever so much;
   Use the five senses: sight, hearing, smell, taste, touch.

N is for NATURAL.
   The closer to home environment, the more comfortable the girl and boy;
   Then they can grow—step by step—even toy by toy.
   So use a natural setting whenever you can—
   By building upon the *known;* their knowledge you'll fan.

O is for ORDERLY AND OUTLETS.
   Sequence should be orderly, planned, not left to chance,
   So outlets into acceptable behavior it may enhance.
   These children need structured programs with order.
   This makes a happier son—or daughter.

P is for POPULAR AND PRAISE.
   Success grows with enjoyment and praise;
   Thus one's self-image he can easier raise.
   Have the program popular; give praise when due,
   Or it becomes as useless as an old shoe.

Q is for QUALITY AND QUIETNESS.
   Has the program quality—something to give,
   Enabling the participants a better life to live?
   Has it quietness, so needed for relief
   Of anxiety, excitement and inadequate belief?

R is for REPETITION AND ROUTINE.
   Repetition reinforces skill and ability;
   Familiar routine builds up security.
   Plan your program to include each,
   So that every child you will reach.

S is for SCIENTIFIC AND SECURITY.
   Does the program use ideas tested and scientific?
   If the child's on medication, find out what's in it.
   Build up a child's security—physical and emotional—to make him content.
   Is he being given all the help possible? That's what I meant.

T is for THOROUGH AND TOLERANT.
   Be tolerant—yet be thorough,
   Then the best results will show.
   Recognize each child's ability and weakness,
   And build upon his strengths for progress.

U is for UNDERSTANDING, USEFULNESS, AND UNIQUE.
   Understanding differences in each individual child,
   Remembering the interests and potentials all the while,
   Help the program to prove its usefulness to you.
   Also try hard to add uniqueness, too.

V is for VARIABLE AND VARIETY.
   A variety of presentations is needed by each,
   In that way every child you might be able to read.
   If an idea's good, don't wear it out;
   Change often—do a turnabout.

W is for WELL-FOUNDED AND WARMTH.
   Be able to explain aims and purposes of the program to others,
   To yourself, colleagues, children, fathers and mothers.
   Be ready to show affection and warmth the children need,
   Then they will progress much better—yes, indeed!

X is for X-RAY.
   X-ray your program with careful eyes,
   Help the children to really socialize.
   X marks the place to help—and how,
   Help the children when needed—then and now.

Y is for YIELDING AND YOU.
   Sometimes it is better to yield some,
   So to the teacher the child will come
   With confidence, trust, and a desire to learn,
   And be anxious to get the "wheels ready to turn."

Z is for ZEALOUS AND ZEST.
   Hard work pays a great dividend.
   Don't hesitate to give and bend.
   These children can learn with proper help from you,
   And develop zest for today and tomorrow, too.

Paraprofessionals (teaching assistants), aides, volunteers, and other school plant employees

Paraprofessionals, or teaching assistants, are paid employees of the school system. They should be qualified by education, experience, and character and be allowed to engage in instructional and noninstructional tasks. The use of paraprofessionals would allow the teacher more time for direct teaching, planning, testing, evaluating curriculum objectives, and parent contacts. Teaching assistants should undergo at least a month of orientation, training, and observation under master teachers. With proper training these paraprofessionals can assist in specific areas such as classroom management, selecting teaching material, and implementing prescribed programs. The training and employment of paraprofessionals in TMR programs has been used to alleviate teacher shortage problems (Luedtke, 1969).

Aides are also paid employees who assist the teacher or staff primarily in noninstructional time-consuming tasks. The general qualifications include acceptance of the TMR children, a pleasant disposition, emotional stability, ability to maintain confidentiality, and physical health (Gearheart and Litton, 1975). Specific duties include assisting the students in moving from room to room or building to building, supervising on the playground, assisting in snack or juice time, and general housekeeping (Hanson, 1969).

Volunteers are another important power source, and they perform a valuable service in programs for TMRs. Volunteers may be students, members of service clubs, senior citizens, and sometimes parents. Since it is difficult for many TMR students to make adjustments to different persons, regular attendance is necessary (Dillon, 1969). Volunteers are unpaid and, as a result, are often taken for granted. Their effectiveness can be increased by a procedure of training, supervision, and evaluation such as that which follows.

Training

1. Provide a general explanation of the overall program, including information on types of students, goals, content, facilities, and staff.
2. Explain how an aide's job fits into the program.
3. Detail specific aspects of each assignment, including administrative procedures, working hours, where to get help, and policies on supervision and evaluation.

Supervision

1. Carry out a general check to see that assigned jobs are completed.
2. Praise aides for jobs well done.
3. Provide constructive suggestions for job performance that needs improvement.
4. Provide additional training if needed.
5. Determine if each person's talents are utilized to the maximum.

Evaluation

1. Provide a checklist for evaluating aide performance.
2. Reward individuals for outstanding service by a certificate of appreciation.

School plant employees such as janitors, bus drivers, secretaries, and cafeteria workers can all, to a degree, assist in student development. Select students can receive vocational and social training by assisting these school workers. Also, since behavioral training requires continuity and consistency, the teachers may informally instruct these persons as to appropriate behavioral controls for disruptive or emotionally disturbed TMRs with whom they have contact.

Parents

Of particular significance in the last few years has been the diminution of the gap between parents and professionals. Today's parents are better informed and take a more active role in working for the best possible educational programs and services for their retarded children. Parents are serving as advisors, advocates, and teachers (Simches, 1975).

Parents can be utilized as "teachers" in the home or even in school, serving as volunteers. Since parents have the earliest and most prolonged contact with their

Fig. 2-2. Bus drivers, along with other ancillary school employees, should be a part of the instructional team. (Courtesy Bossier Parish, La., Public Schools.)

child, they can significantly assist in the development of self-help, motor and personal-social skills. If parents can develop these skills, they not only help the child to function more effectively, but their efforts may also prevent needless institutionalization. Early intervention training programs for parents have only recently been developed because professionals have become more sensitive to parent needs and have recognized that by training parents as behavior technicians, a valuable, economical, and effective existing force becomes utilized.

Some of the foremost needs of parents are understanding, counseling, and guidance. Parents need assistance in responding positively to the shock of having a trainable retarded child and in solving painful human problems thrust on them

without warning and for no comprehensible reason (Perske, 1973). These needs were reflected in a recent parent education program (Warfield, 1975) whereby parents ranked program topics in order of value and importance.

Rank	Topic
1	What is mental retardation
2	Understanding our own feelings
2	What is special education
3	How to manage family living problems
3	How to help children learn
4	The importance of social skills
5	Getting the most from professional help
6	Problems of adolescence
7	What testing tells us
7	Making plans for the future

Even for parents who understand and accept their TMR child, numerous behavior

Table 2-1. Problem behaviors of TMRs according to age*

Problem	Rank			
	Age 2 to 4	Age 4 to 6	Age 8 to 10	Age 12 to 17
Disobedience, stubbornness, noncompliance	1	1	1	4
Eating problems	1	2	4	3
Talking, communication problems	1	4	5	
Impulsivity, sensitivity, temperamental	1	3	4	4
Toilet problems	2	1	2	2
Problems with mobility, walking	3	6		5
Lack of social interaction skills	4		5	1
Aggressive behavior toward others		2	5	3
Temper tantrums, destructiveness		4	5	3
Problems with personal hygiene, dressing		4	6	5
Self-mutilating behavior		5	3	4
Rhythmic, stereotyped behavior		5	5	

*Adapted from Tavormina, J. B., Henggeler, S. W., and Gayton, W. F.: Age trends in parental assessments of the behavior problems of their retarded children, Ment. Retard. **14**(1):39, 1976.

problems are still posed by the child living at home. One investigation (Tavormina, Henggeler, and Gayton, 1976) identified four separate age groupings in which parents listed specific concerns (Table 2-1). The child between the ages of 2 and 4 has developmental problems, and professionals counseling or training these parents should focus on skill expectations and training. The child between the ages of 4 and 6 or 8 and 10 has problems in the personality development and self-care areas; counseling should center on parental understanding and teaching methods. The last age group, 12 to 17, exhibits social interaction problems, and counseling should deal with interpersonal skills, sexuality, and vocational training.

The involvement of parents with professionals is important, and Schaefer (1975) even suggests that parents influence the professionals' involvement with them and professionals influence the parents' involvement with the child. The model for parent, professional, and child interaction in Fig. 2-3 suggests that parents, teachers, and professionals from other disciplines influence both their direct involvement with the child and their interaction with one another. For more effective educational programming, teachers and therapists must be aware and know the significance of any

variables affecting student and parent behavior.

The training of parents of retarded children should be instituted as soon as the retardation is diagnosed. The education and training program should provide basic information on mental retardation, contain programs for skill development in various areas, and include a program for teaching parents basic behavior modification procedures. One excellent systematic program encompassing these criteria is called the Parent Trainer Technology System (Watson, 1975). This system is composed of nine programs: eliminating undesirable behavior, shaping self-help skills, language development, social-recreational development, motor coordination development, teaching academic skills, teaching behavior modification procedures, an evaluation program to assess effectiveness, and an administrative program designed to ensure effective operation of the system.

Specific suggestions for more efficient and effective parent training programs follow (Smith, 1976):

1. Utilization of regional parent training centers (several in a state) with strategically located satellite centers
2. Employment of a transdisciplinary training team consisting of a child

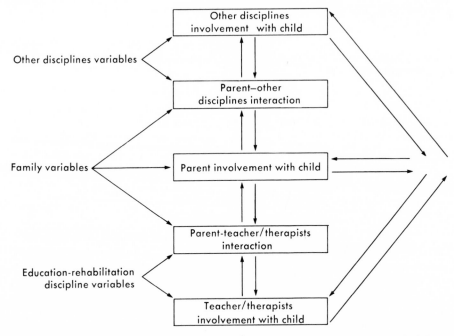

Fig. 2-3. Model of the interaction and involvement between the education-rehabilitation discipline, other disciplines, parents, and the retarded child. (Adapted from Schaefer, E. S.: Factors impeding socialization process. In Begab, M. J., and Richardson, S. A., editors: The mentally retarded and society: a social science perspective, Baltimore, 1975, University Park Press.)

development specialist and a social worker

3. Availability of training teams afternoons and evenings to be of service to both parents
4. Fifteen to twenty-five families assigned to each training team
5. Initial sessions in groups at the center and then informal and individual sessions in the home
6. Continuous assessment of the behavior of the retarded

Additionally, to be practical and of value, parent training programs should be comprehensive, focus on specific problems or needs, make other supportive services available to parents, and be economical.

When the child is in school, it becomes even more crucial to involve parents because of the extreme need for consistency between factors in the child's environments. A close relationship with parents is highly desirable and can be of significant benefit

to the child. Teachers can develop this relationship in the following ways:

1. Suggesting specific activities for developing and reinforcing skills
2. Discussing with parents effective behavioral and disciplinary measures
3. Being honest in the evaluation and assessment of the abilities of the child
4. Providing frequent communication regarding student progress
5. Serving as a referral agent for other services needed by parents
6. Involving parents in program planning
7. Remaining a consultant to parents and not a dominant authority

Another way to closely involve parents of a TMR child with the school and with their child is to have them serve as school volunteers. One successful program has been reported by Benson and Ross (1972). Program goals were (1) to provide students with more individualized instruction, (2) to promote parental interest and involvement in their child's educational growth so that they would be better able to work with their own child in the home, and (3) to encourage and develop community interest and support. All goals were achieved as students improved in self-care skills, academic skills, and fine-motor skills. Additionally, parents began working with their children at home, and parental and community support increased.

Books and programs written expressly for parents who desire to assist in the development of their preschool or school-aged TMR child include *The Mentally Retarded Child at Home: a Manual for Parents* (Dittman, 1959), *Home Care and Management of the Mentally Retarded Child* (Vulpe, 1969), *Management and Maintenance in the Home: a Guide for Teaching the Handicapped* (Walden, 1970), *Living With a Retarded Child: a Primer for Parents* (Buckler, 1971), *New Directions for Parents of Persons Who are Retarded* (Perske, 1973), *Isn't It Time He Outgrew This? or A Training Program for Parents of Retarded Children* (Baldwin, V. L., Fredericks, H. D., and Brodsky, G., 1973), *Families Play to Grow* (Kennedy Foundation, 1974), and *Every Child Can Learn . . . Something! For Parents and Teachers of Severely Retarded Children* (Thornley, 1973). Regular publications for parents include *The Exceptional Parent* (a magazine), *Mental Retardation News* (a newspaper), and *Sharing Our Caring* (a newsletter).*

Parents of the retarded now also have a national source of information in the National Information Center for the Handicapped, or Closer Look. This agency is funded by the United States Department of Health, Education, and Welfare, Office of Education, Bureau of Education for the Handicapped, and is under contract with the National Association of State Directors of Special Educators, Inc. Closer Look offers the following specific information products, free of charge (Dean, 1975):

1. A guide for parents in finding services for handicapped children
2. Parent information packets, including descriptions of parent organizations and reading lists
3. Explanation of state laws or public education programs for handicapped children
4. Periodic reports (The Closer Look Report) to help parents keep up with events in the world of the handicapped

Closer Look also provides information to professionals who work with other handicapped children, to students looking for career information, to parent groups seeking advice on organizing, and to the disabled adult.

Additional information on specific problems of home management or child development for the TMR is available by contacting the local, state, or national Association for Retarded Citizens.

ORGANIZATIONAL AND ADMINISTRATIVE CONSIDERATIONS

Additional aspects of the educational environment that primarily are organizational or administrative concerns include the service delivery model (i.e., special school), instructional levels and curriculum schedules, and student eligibility requirements.

Service delivery model

In the Cascade System of Special Education Services* (Deno, 1970; Reynolds, 1962), it is the special day school concept or model that is the most widely used and is also the most desirable for the TMR.

---

*Addresses are contained in Appendix B.

---

*Under this system the largest number of handicapped children and those with the least learning handicaps will be served in the regular programs, with and without modifications. These students are found in the upper levels of the system, which are less restrictive learning environments. At the lower levels of the system are found the special education students who possess more severe handicaps and are fewer in number. These lower levels are also more restrictive and self-contained.

(See Fig. 2-4 for the Cascade System of Special Education Services.) Providing services to TMR students utilizing this model allows for better community visibility, in-service training, better teacher morale and cooperation (the principal, staff, and all teachers have the same common interest), provision of supportive or ancillary services, an implementation of curriculum. Also, potential teachers (university students) who are engaged in field experiences can become exposed to many students with varying ages and functioning levels (Sontag, Burke, and York, 1973).

A TMR school should be near the campus of a regular elementary or middle school so that participation is possible in select school functions (e.g., pictures, concerts, assembly programs). Playground facilities and transportation services can also be utilized. A centralized program such as the special school model can save money for the school district, primarily in the area of specialized equipment and materials.

With adherence to the principle of normalization and emphasis on education in the least restrictive environment, the full-time special class model (in a regular school) and resource room model have been attempted recently. A study by Ziegler and Hambleton (1976) integrated young TMR children from a self-contained class into nonacademic (nonclassroom) regular school situations and found more positive interactions than negative between nonretarded and TMR students. Another project whereby TMR students were totally integrated with other exceptional (i.e., learning disabled, emotionally disturbed, educable mentally retarded) children and had some contact with regular class students was found to be beneficial academically but not socially (Truxillo, 1976).

Since the majority of TMRs exhibit a variety of difficult individual problems, specialized learning classrooms in the special school are needed. The basic and necessary physical components of the classroom include adequate lighting and ventilation, desks, chairs, carpet, cabinet and storage space, mirrors, sinks, chalkboards, bulletin boards, individual work areas, and easily accessible toilets.

Abeson and Ackerman (1965) formulated

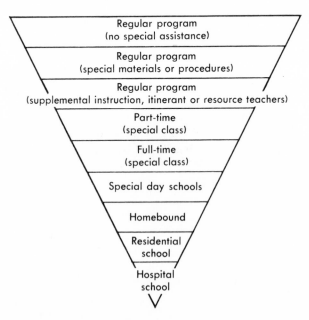

Fig. 2-4. Cascade System of Special Education Services. (Adapted from CEC: Teach children—not categories, Except. Child. **42**:234, 1976.)

several basic educational needs of the retarded student and made suggestions as to architectural solutions for each. Some of these follow.

1. *Many exceptional children will have a need to displace hyperkinetic energy.* This must be done without disturbing the other children, the teaching process, or the teacher. Small rooms or quiet areas adjacent to a central work area is an answer.

2. *Many children exhibit continuous negative verbal responses that require extinction.* There must be some control for excessive yelling and screaming. Carpeted rooms that mask or damp noise, the use of sound equipment and/or building withdrawal and isolation areas are possibilities.

3. *The teacher needs to be free from mechanical and nonteaching activities.* Teacher aides could be utilized in this area. Teaching freedom also requires easy access and manipulation of auditory and visual material, room space, and any mechanical adaptation of the environment or educational process.

4. *The four dimensions of architecture that may provide a sound base for manipulation of educational needs seem to be flexibility, mobility, multiplicity, safety.*

5. *Excessive and loud talking-out behavior must customarily be silenced to retain an adequate attention span of the entire group.* Individual masks, separate carrels, or sound-absorbent materials in space should be considered.

6. *The teacher has a need to withdraw from her class occasionally.* A teacher's office with adequate vision of the class should be provided.

7. *There should be an intimate relationship between the curriculum and the physical plant.* Since curriculum is generally meant to reflect the development of the child intellectually and physically, the child's environment must also reflect development. Consequently, individual rooms that grow with the child or group to form larger group rooms seem necessary. Physical arrangement of classes should reflect the growth from individual instruction through small groups to much larger public school classes.

8. *Allowances for teacher education must be made.* This is best accomplished by observation rooms adjacent to the classroom where a master teacher may effect radio communication with the practice teacher but not be visible to the class. The radio communication must be made through visually unobtrusive earphones.

9. *These exceptional children need individual instruction, particularly in the early or formative years.* All space must be convertible to individual space as necessary.

10. *Students need space in which to socialize and to interact with each other.* A classroom that includes flexible adaptation may encourage the socialization process.

11. *Adjunctive rooms are needed.* Major uses of these rooms are for observation, individual tutorial sessions, teacher's, nurse's or therapist's offices, offices for experimenters, and quiet rooms.

12. *Retarded children have a need to be routinized to the point of allocating certain spaces in rooms with certain functions.* It is thought that the same area can be used with multiple functions but can be changed with the use of lights, different shapes, movable walls, etc. All such rooms should work with the four variables of space, lighting, acoustics, and accessibility in determining the differential functions of its section and of its whole.

13. *Some young TMR children need a quieting period before the learning session begins.* Consequently, a reception room might be necessary. Such a room should be small and intimate, nonstimulating, geared for temporary or short-term occupancy, as well as a different space from that used for the learning process itself.

14. *Toilets and bathroom facilities must also meet the criteria of developmental progression.* Toilets should be adjustable in height and complexity of operation.

15. *Motivation incentives are needed.* Positive reward for work is possible by

allowing extension display space for exhibiting student productions.

Additional resources for administrators and school boards who plan to rennovate or design new educational facilities for TMR children include *Special Education Facilities: Schools and Playgrounds for Trainable Mentally Handicapped Children* (Ontario Department of Education, 1971) and *Florida's Educational Facilities for Exceptional Children, 1968-1973* (Florida State Department of Education, 1973). The first is a booklet that contains designs illustrating overall and specific room arrangements and playground areas for various sizes of schools and various age groups. Specific suggestions are also offered for the bathrooms, playroom, kitchen, craft room, principal's office, staff, and health room. The second source is a book containing a section on special schools for the TMR with specifics on several different buildings for students ranging in capacity from 64 to 200 and ages 6 to 21.

The model in Fig. 2-5 typifies the physical plant of a school specifically designed for TMRs. The school is Petree School in Pensacola, Florida. At present it serves 68 students, ages 6 to 18, and has eight class-

room teachers. The school was selected for illustration purposes because the educational program has four instructional levels (primary, intermediate, junior high, and senior high) and emphasizes self-care skills, language development, socialization skills, basic academic skills, and prevocational skills. The instructional levels and curriculum content coincide with this text's emphasis. Also, services of specialty areas (physical education, music, art, speech) are shared with another special school.

Instructional levels and curriculum schedules

The levels of instruction for the TMR, excluding preschool and postschool (see Chapter 11 for these levels), include the primary, intermediate, prevocational, and vocational levels. Small school districts often have only two or three instructional levels because of the small number of students. Suggested chronological ages (approximate), staff, and number of students in each class for each of the four levels follow:

Primary
    CA: 6.0 to 8.11
    Staff: 1 teacher, 1 aide, and volunteers
    Number of students in a class: 6 to 8

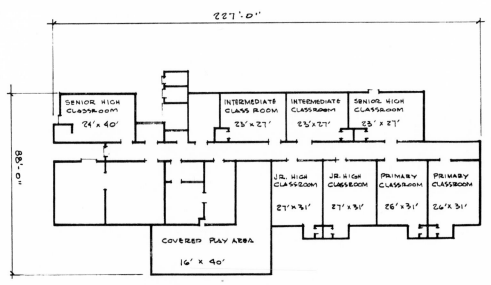

Fig. 2-5. Physical design for a TMR school. (From Florida's educational facilities for exceptional children, 1968-1973, Tallahassee, Fla., 1973, Florida State Department of Education.)

Intermediate
CA: 9.0 to 11.11
Staff: 1 teacher, 1 aide, and volunteers
Number of students in a class: 8 to 10
Prevocational
CA: 12.0 to 15.11
Staff: 1 teacher, 1 aide, and volunteers
Number of students in a class: 10 to 12
Vocational
CA: 16.0 to 21.0
Staff: 1 teacher, 1 aide, and volunteers
Number of students in a class: 10 to 12

Short periods of instruction, break and/or rest time in the morning and afternoon, and variety in activities are needed at all levels. Readiness skills for learning and the more demanding activities or tasks should be scheduled in the mornings and other activities in the afternoon. Typical daily schedules for each level follow:

Primary level schedule

9:00-9:15	Teacher preparation
9:15-9:30	Student arrival
9:30-10:00	Self-help skills
10:00-10:30	Social skills
10:30-10:45	Refreshment break
10:45-11:15	Listening and speaking skills
11:15-11:45	Sensory and perceptual-motor skills
11:45-12:30	Lunch
12:30-1:00	Rest period
1:00-1:30	Recreation and leisure time skills
1:30-2:00	Individual learning period; end of student day
2:00-3:00	Teacher planning and parent conference period

Intermediate level schedule

8:30-8:45	Teacher preparation
8:45-9:00	Student arrival
9:00-9:30	Self-help skills
9:30-10:15	Communication skills
10:15-10:30	Refreshment break
10:30-11:00	Academic readiness skills
11:00-11:30	Economic usefulness and leisure time skills
11:30-12:30	Lunch and free play
12:30-1:00	Rest or quiet period
1:00-1:30	Social skills
1:30-2:00	Perceptual-motor and physical education skills
2:00-3:00	Teacher planning and parent conference period

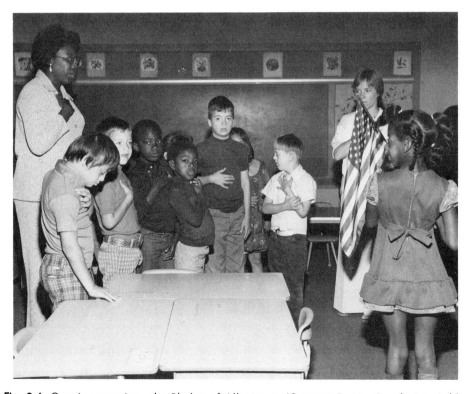

Fig. 2-6. Opening exercise—the Pledge of Allegiance. (Courtesy Bossier Parish, La., Public Schools.)

Prevocational level schedule

8:30-9:00	Teacher preparation
9:00-9:15	Student arrival
9:15-10:00	Functional academics
10:00-10:15	Refreshments or recess
10:15-11:00	Communication skills
11:00-11:30	Economic usefulness and vocational skills
11:30-12:30	Lunch and free play
12:30-1:00	Rest or quiet period
1:00-1:30	Social skills
1:30-2:00	Recreation and leisure time skills
2:00-2:30	Perceptual-motor and physical education skills
2:30-3:15	Teacher planning and parent conference period

Vocational level schedule

8:30-9:00	Teacher preparation
9:00-9:15	Student arrival
9:15-10:00	Functional academics
10:00-10:15	Refreshments or recess
10:15-11:00	Communication skills
11:00-11:30	Social skills
11:30-12:30	Lunch and free time
12:30-1:00	Recreation and leisure time skills
1:00-2:30	Economic usefulness and vocational skills
2:30-3:15	Teacher planning and parent conference period

Student eligibility requirements

The following criteria are representative of requirements in most states.*

1. A child not eligible for EMR placement
2. A child who meets legal school age (in many states a CA of 3.0; in others, 6.0)
3. A child whose physical condition, based on a medical examination, is such that:
   a. He has adequate physical health
   b. He is mobile (ambulatory or wheelchair)
   c. He is able to hear and see well enough to minimally relate to staff and activities
4. A child whose mental, emotional, and social development, based on individual diagnostic assessment, is such that:
   a. He possesses an IQ score of 25 to 50
   b. He possesses adaptive behavior skills in Level II or III

---

*The requirement of an individual being toilet trained before being admitted to TMR programs is still applicable in many states or school districts. Recent court cases, however, have ruled that it is no longer a prerequisite for admission because toilet training may now be considered a "reasonable educational objective" (Educational Facilities Laboratories, 1974).

c. He can communicate simple wants and needs and follow single directions
d. His behavior does not seriously endanger self or others

An admissions committee can best determine students who are eligible for classes. This committee should include the following professionals: teachers, school psychologists, social worker, supervisor of special education, building principal, and a physician (usually a pediatrician).

EQUIPMENT, MATERIALS, AND USE OF GAMES
Equipment

Of valuable assistance to any educational program are the amount and quality of equipment and materials. Audiovisual, outdoor, general, and housekeeping equipment and supplies necessary for functioning of a TMR special school program are offered here for the consideration of the school administrator or teacher. It is neither a maximum nor a minimum list but a composite of the suggestions of educators of the TMR. Materials for the seven major curriculum areas will be listed as each area of instruction is discussed in Chapters 4 through 11.

Audiovisual
  Language Masters
  Piano
  Projectors
    Filmstrip and individual filmstrip viewers
    Opaque
    Overhead
    16 mm sound
  Radio
  Record player and records
  Screens
  Tape recorder and headphones
  Television
Housekeeping and supplies
  Blankets
  Broom
  Buckets
  Cloth towels
  Detergent and cleanser
  Dustpan
  Iron and ironing board
  Mop
  Paper towels
  Pillows and pillowcases

Sheets
Vacuum cleaner
General
Aquarium
Balls
Beds or cots
Bookshelves
Bulletin boards
Cabinets
Camera
Chalkboards
Chart stand
Easels
File cabinets
First aid kit
Kitchen (fully equipped and supplied)
Mats
Mirror (full length)
Pencil sharpener
Rhythm band instruments
Student-sized desks and chairs
Tables (movable and stationary)
    Oblong
    Round
Teacher's and aide's desks and chairs
Toy shelves
Typewriter
Wastebaskets
Outdoor
Jungle gym
Ladders
Riding toys
Slides
Swings
Tires (old)
Trampoline (low)

When selecting classroom furniture, it is important to use the criteria of durability, maintenance, safety, and flexibility. Furniture should be of a heavy solid material (no upholstery) with a finish resistant to scratches, rough use, disinfectants, harsh detergents, and hot water. Do not purchase furniture with small or easily accessible bolts or screws or sharp corners, since these are potentially damaging to the students. Also, if possible, purchase furniture that is movable and can be easily stored or stacked when not in use (Bartholomew, 1976).

Materials

The educational materials aspect of the instructional program has become a distinct and important feature in special education in the last few years. The analyzing, appraising, and purchasing of materials by specialists or by the teacher becomes extremely important because each student must have the appropriate materials for his specific needs and maximum value for the dollar spent must be obtained. Following are additional reasons that attest to the importance of analyzing instructional materials (Brown, 1974):

1. With individual instruction becoming popular, a more precise selection of tasks and materials is required.

2. Mass production of materials is making it increasingly difficult for a teacher to become adequately familiar with all materials on a firsthand basis.

3. There is an increased emphasis on accountability in special education.

4. By analyzing materials, the application of basic principles of learning to the instructional process is facilitated.

5. Development of computer systems for storage and retrieval of materials is now possible.

A series of questions, categorized into teacher needs, student needs, and general needs, can serve as a general guideline for appraising instructional materials and programs. Some considerations and questions according to needs follow (Bleil, 1975):

Teacher needs
- What teacher skills are required?
- Is a presentation mode specified?
- Are the lessons sequences?
- Does it contain evaluation procedures?
- Are directions for teaching the skills and concepts clearly specified and understandable?
- Is the teaching strategy specified?
- How much time is required to use the material?
- Is the material intended for an individual or group?
- Can an aide or volunteer use the materials?
- Is there a teacher's guide or is it available separately?

Student needs
- Are individual behavioral objectives specified?
- Are the tasks in hierarchical form?
- What prerequisite skills are required?
- Is student response mode specified?

- Is criteria by which mastery is measured specified?
- Is there suggested follow-up or corollary material?
- Is the material an integral part of the curriculum objectives?
- Is the material attractive, motivating, or stimulating?

General needs

- What is the price?
- Is it consumable?
- If material is in "kit" form, can specific items be replaced?
- Is repair service available if the material is electronic?
- Is a scope and sequence chart provided?
- Is there a warranty?
- Are material parts dangerous, easily lost or stolen?
- Are materials durable?

A step-by-step guide to use before actually purchasing instructional materials is offered by a specialist in materials for the retarded (Boland, 1974). Her suggestions include the following eight steps:

1. Find out how much money has been allocated for instructional materials for your class.
2. Find out which equipment and materials are available on short-term or long-term loan from the school library, school district, or regional learning resource centers (LRCs).
3. Inventory all the instructional materials, textbooks, and workbooks that belong in your room.
4. Consider how you want to spend your budget (i.e., replacement, additional purchases of program parts, new materials).
5. Now take a very careful look at the needs of your children.
6. Consider any special needs you have as a teacher.
7. Look at materials from the LRC, instructional materials displays, advertisements in professional magazines, commercial catalogs, and talk to other teachers.
8. Now, purchase materials.

If these steps are undertaken, they can assist in spending your instructional materials dollar wisely.

The importance of materials for the handicapped has been recognized even at the federal level. In 1974 the Bureau of Education for the Handicapped restructured the Special Education Instructional Materials Center network of 1964. It is now entitled Learning Resource Centers (LRC) and administratively is under the Division of Media Services of the Bureau. To provide a more effective delivery of services to handicapped children, thirteen geographical regions, covering the United States and its territories, were established (Fig. 2-7). Each region has a Regional Resource Center (RRC) and an Area Learning Resource Center (ALRC). The RRCs provide services in four major areas: state program development, educational appraisal, educational programming, and sharing of resources. Each ALRC works with state education agencies within its region and facilitates the development, training, and implementation of effective delivery of media, materials, and educational technology (Howe, 1975). These agencies, especially the ALRC, are designed for the special education teacher and should be utilized. Teachers and other professionals engaged in work with TMRs are encouraged to contact the ALRC in their geographical region for information on available services. Resource centers, the states served, and their region number are provided in Table 2-2.

Use of games

Educational games are one of the techniques that can be used in helping retarded children learn with enjoyment. They are valuable in developing favorable attitudes toward schoolwork, facilitating the learning process, and aiding children to deal with their emotional and social problems in the classroom. The games, however, should be simple in organization, contain a minimum of rules, and have skills within the capabilities of the participants. Following are numerous occasions and specific reasons for utilizing games in school.

1. Motivation when the work has less intrinsic appeal than usual
2. "Hurdle help" when mastering a spe-

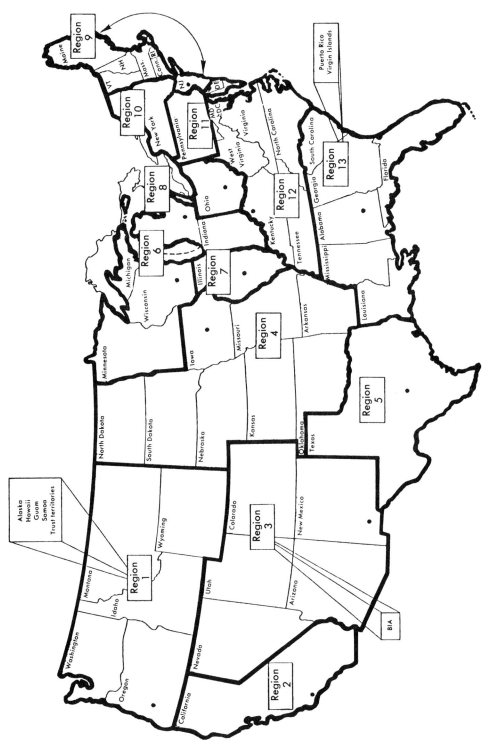

Fig. 2-7. Area learning resource centers.

Table 2-2. Area learning resource centers

Centers	States served	Region number
Northwest Area Learning Resource Center, University of Oregon, Clinical Services Building, Third floor, Eugene, Ore. 97403	Alaska, Hawaii, Trust Territory, Guam, Samoa, Washington, Oregon, Idaho, Montana	1
California Area Learning Resource Center, 600 S. Commonwealth Ave., Suite 1304, Los Angeles, Calif. 90005	California	2
Southwest Area Learning Resource Center, New Mexico State University, Box 3AW, Las Cruces, N.M. 88003	Nevada, Colorado, Utah, Arizona, New Mexico, BIA Schools	3
Midwest Area Learning Resource Center, Drake University, 1336 26th St., Des Moines, Iowa 50311	North Dakota, South Dakota, Nebraska, Iowa, Oklahoma, Kansas, Missouri, Arkansas	4
Texas Area Learning Resource Center, 2613 Whichita St., Austin, Texas 78701	Texas	5
Great Lakes Area Learning Resource, Michigan Department of Education, P.O. Box 420, Lansing, Mich. 48902	Minnesota, Indiana, Wisconsin, Michigan	6
Illinois Area Learning Resource Center, 1020 S. Spring St., Springfield, Ill. 62706	Illinois	7
Ohio Area Learning Resource Center, Ohio Division of Special Education, 933 High St., Worthington, Ohio 43085	Ohio	8
Northeast Area Learning Resource Center, 384 Stockton St., Hightstown, N.J. 08520	Maine, Vermont, New Hampshire, Rhode Island, Massachusetts, Connecticut, New Jersey	9
New York Area Learning Resource Center, New York State Education Department, Division for Handicapped Children, 55 Elk St., Room 117, Albany, N.Y. 12234	New York	10
Pennsylvania Area Learning Resource Center, 443 S. Gulph Rd., King of Prussia, Pa. 19406	Pennsylvania	11
Mideast Area Learning Resource Center, University of Kentucky, Porter Building, Room 123, Lexington, Ky. 40506	Delaware, Maryland, District of Columbia, West Virginia, Virginia, Kentucky, Tennessee, North Carolina	12
Southeast Area Learning Resource Center, Auburn University at Montgomery, 435 Bell St., Montgomery, Ala. 36109	Louisiana, Mississippi, Alabama, Georgia, South Carolina, Florida, Puerto Rico, Virgin Islands	13

cific skill, an understanding, or an important fact

3. Reinforcement of the learning of skills or material previously presented
4. Helping children review and organize information they have previously acquired
5. Providing relief from anxiety by emphasizing the fun aspect
6. Relaxation of tension caused by feelings of resentment or inadequacy
7. Channeling aggressive tendencies into constructive activities
8. Utilizing the values inherent in motor skills as an aid to learning—especially manipulative activities
9. Diversion tactics when a child, a group of children, or a teacher feels so angry or frustrated that it appears wise, for the good of the individual or the group, to postpone discussion, ventilation, or confrontation until some gratification (unrelated to the aggravating factor) has been enjoyed
10. Permitting the children to enjoy the "driver's seat" occasionally, acting in the position of authority figure, i.e., tester, asker of questions, evaluator of product, keeper of records (scores in the games)
11. Helping children learn quickly and thoroughly the value and importance of cooperation in group efforts (the

group wins or loses—rather than the *individual* in most of the games)

GENERAL PRINCIPLES OR TECHNIQUES OF INSTRUCTION FOR THE RETARDED

There are numerous general, fundamentally sound teaching principles or techniques for the retarded that, if used consistently, can better facilitate the learning process. Some of these instructional guidelines are amplified here.

1. *Recognize that the student must be ready to learn.* Maturity in responding in a consistent and accurate fashion is necessary. It will be unproductive to make demands or requests when the difficulty level of the task is beyond learner capabilities.

2. *Stimulate motivation and the desire to learn or participate.* Students cannot be motivated to learn but can be stimulated and rewarded, which can lead to their becoming eager to be involved in learning sessions. Teacher enthusiasm, activity variation, and positive rewards can foster a desire to learn or participate.

3. *Reinforce desired behavior.* When desired behavior occurs, positively reward the student for the behavior to increase the likelihood of its recurrence.

4. *Provide exercise and practice.* Exercise and practice are essential techniques in the learning process, since acquisition of skills is often difficult, slow, and easily forgotten.

5. *Keep learning sessions brief.* Because of the limited mental ability and short attention span in the retarded, periods of instruction should be brief. Once sessions become frustrating or tiring, the session should be ended or the activity changed.

6. *Encourage the student to be an active participant.* All learners, including the retarded, learn best by being active in the learning process. Little learning will take place if students are passive observers.

7. *Be sure the skill or concept being taught is mastered before proceeding to new or more difficult ones.* The concept of overlearning should be employed in teaching skills or concepts to the retarded. It is better to thoroughly learn and be able to effectively utilize only a few skills than to minimally (and probably inaccurately) learn a larger number of skills.

8. *Stress accuracy instead of speed in student work.* Correctness in student work is more important than how fast it is completed.

9. *Use small steps in learning a new skill.* The progression from one step to the next should be minimal to reduce the possibility of error and to make acquisition of new skills easier.

10. *Teach skills in hierarchical form.* Tasks should proceed from the simple to the complex.

11. *Make use of materials and teaching devices that are attractive and colorful.* The esthetic value of materials should not be overlooked, as it often adds incentive and motivation to learn.

12. *Provide immediate feedback.* If the students are not given immediate feedback, the wrong responses could be reinforced. The learner should know immediately if his responses are correct or incorrect.

13. *Use repetition.* Repeating activities in the same or a different way facilitates learning and overlearning.

14. *In initial learning sessions use only a one stimulus–one response set.* The initial learning session toward attainment of a skill should be uncomplicated. The student should not be bombarded with extraneous stimuli nor be expected to provide a complex response.

15. *Involve the various senses.* All senses should be developed and utilized to enhance efficiency in learning.

16. *Employ concrete materials.* Materials that can be manipulated, seen, etc. are more effective and desirable than those of a more abstract nature.

17. *Provide field experiences.* There are many areas of learning in which the community setting becomes a better classroom. Field trips provide real meaning in real settings but can also be used to reinforce

acquired skills (e.g., making a purchase, eating out).

18. *Establish routine*. Routine in scheduling activities and procedures lends order to the educational world of the retarded.

19. *Assess each individual's abilities*. It is imperative that the teacher and those who work with the retarded assess and have a knowledge of his functioning abilities in all curriculum areas.

20. *Evaluate the program*. The program of instruction must be periodically evaluated to determine the efficacy of the specific teaching approach, materials, and also to determine additional needs.

INDIVIDUAL EDUCATION PROGRAMS (IEPs)

One of the current mandates in teaching exceptional children is the development of individual educational programs (IEPs). This concept was developed out of federal legislation: Public Law 94-142, The Education for All Handicapped Children Act of 1975.

The primary purposes of this act are to guarantee that (1) all handicapped children have a free and appropriate education; (2) the rights of handicapped children and their families are protected; (3) a specific management process for the education of the handicapped at all levels of government is established; and (4) financial assistance is provided to state and local education agencies.

There are stipulations in P.L. 94-142 that must be adhered to for a program to be eligible for funding. Among these are the following:

1. Child identification procedures
2. Provision of full service to the handicapped child as a goal
3. Due process procedures
4. Regular parent or guardian consultation
5. In-service training
6. Provision of education in the least restrictive environment
7. Elements of nondiscriminatory testing and evaluation
8. Protection of confidentiality of data and information
9. Provision of a surrogate to act for a child if needed
10. *Inclusion of an individual education program (IEP)*

Benefits

The decision to include the IEP as a necessary part of programing for the handicapped child is a wise one because of its numerous benefits. An IEP will help to ensure consideration of the child as an individual during planning and provision of services. Other benefits include:

1. A common format for planning
2. Outline of a map for implementation
3. A means for communication
4. A standardization of quality of service
5. A basis for student evaluation and program accountability

Formulation

There are three general steps in formulating an IEP.

Identification for eligibility of the program. A child-find project can serve to locate children in the community who might be eligible for special education services. A screening program may also be of service in this initial step. Another procedure is to ask for referrals from physicians, social agencies, etc.

Developmental and physical evaluation. Once the decision has been made that the child is or may be eligible, an in-depth evaluation is needed. The physical diagnosis includes a medical evaluation of the child's health status, physical structure, sensory functioning, central nervous system functioning, etc. The developmental diagnosis should evolve into (1) a statement of the problem(s), (2) a profile of the child's capabilities as well as deficits, (3) statements of the child's needs, and (4) priorities of where to begin. This diagnostic effort must be shared among those responsible for implementing the educational program.

Development of the IEP. The plan is developed after the first two steps are implemented and must be periodically reviewed and revised. Included in development of the IEP should be (1) a representative of the child's school system (other than the teacher), (2) the child's teacher or teachers (special and regular), (3) one or both of the parents, and (4) where appropriate, the child.

Components

There are many versions of an IEP form, but to fulfill the mandates of the law the following components are suggested:
  1. The child's present levels of functioning (academic achievement, social adaptation, vocational skills, psychomotor development, and self-help skills)
  2. A description of the child's learning style, including strengths and weaknesses
  3. Specific educational services needed by the child, both special education and allied services (e.g., physical therapy)
  4. Short-term, measurable instructional objectives
  5. Necessary instructional media and materials
  6. A statement of annual goals
  7. The date services are to begin and the length of time needed for the services
  8. A statement or description justifying the specific special education environment utilized (Is it the least restrictive?)
  9. A list of persons responsible for implementing the IEP
  10. An evaluation component to determine the child's growth and development under IEP

For optimal achievement to take place in TMR individuals, assessment and teaching procedures must be, to a large degree, individual. The IEP concept then becomes a valuable approach for instruction. An IEP can be written for each student for the curriculum areas (if appropriate for age) of self-care, basic communication, social, perceptual-motor, and physical education skills, functional academics, recreation and leisure time skills, and economic usefulness

and vocational skills (Chapters 4 through 10, respectively). A general diagnostic tool to help identify specific behaviors that need development is the Litton-TMR Behavioral Assessment Checklist (see Appendix D). An extremely useful resource book on writing IEPs is *Resource for Workshops on Developing Individual Education Programs* (1977).*

SUMMARY

The major components of the educational environment and instructional concerns for the TMR were featured in this chapter. Included were curriculum goals, objectives, and content, instructional personnel, organizational and administrative considerations, equipment, materials, the use of games in teaching, and basic principles or techniques of instruction.

The four main goals of education (self-realization, human relationships, economic efficiency, civic responsibility) were presented as having applicability to TMR educational programs. Specific goals of education for the TMR were developed from the needs, characteristics, abilities, and limitations of this population. These include the ability to care and attend to one's personal needs (self-care and personal health skills), basic communication, appropriate social behavior and emotional stability, development of perceptual-motor and physical education skills, functional academic skills, development of recreational and leisure time skills, ability to be economically useful in the home or community and/or successful vocational adjustment (sheltered employment). Curriculum content then becomes these seven major goals. Each content area has several subareas, and each subarea contains numerous specific skills to be developed.

If teaching may be defined as creating or arranging the environment to produce change in the behavior of students, then "teachers" not only encompasses the special

---

*Available from National Association of State Directors of Special Education, 1201 Sixteenth St., N.W., Washington, D.C. 20036.

education classroom teacher, but administrators and supervisors, paraprofessionals, aides, volunteers, other school plant employees, and most certainly parents.

Those who desire to teach the TMR should do so only if they are genuinely interested in children and desire to produce positive change in the affective, cognitive, and motor domains of behavior. One should not teach the retarded merely to fill some inner or psychological need.

Many universities in a number of states now have teacher training programs for teachers of the TMR, and specific course work often includes introduction to the TMR, methods of teaching the TMR, behavior modification, prescriptive teaching, language development, parent counseling, and a practicum. In addition to instructional competencies developed in these courses, the following personality traits are also desirable: adaptability, calmness, cheerfulness, cooperative attitude, creativity, desire for knowledge, empathy, enthusiasm, health and vigor, maturity and stability, originality, resourcefulness, and patience and tolerance.

Since there is both need and value in training parents to accept and effectively manage their retarded child and his behavior, parent training programs are crucial and should be provided. A parent training program should have a team of professionals to work with, counsel, and inform parents on all aspects of raising a retarded child. These teams, to be of maximum value, should be available afternoon and evening hours and make home visitations. Parents should also be actively involved with the education programs of the school. Guidelines for successful parent involvement with the school were also given.

The third part of this chapter centered on organizational and administrative aspects of TMR educational programming. Discussed were the special school model (basic physical components and architectural solutions to the basic educational needs of the retarded), instructional levels (primary, intermediate, prevocational, vo-cational) with daily curriculum or activity schedules for each, and student eligibility requirements (medical, social, intellectual factors).

A list of school equipment (audiovisual, general, housekeeping, outdoor), specific information related to instructional materials (how to analyze, appraise, purchase) and the use of games with the retarded comprise the fourth part. Each is an important component in the education of TMRs.

The next segment of the chapter listed and described, relevant to the needs and characteristics of the TMR, twenty general principles of instruction necessary for the achievement of the seven basic curriculum goals.

The last section concerned individual education programs and their applicability to TMR educational programing.

REFERENCES AND SUGGESTED READINGS

Abeson, A., and Ackerman, P.: An architectural-educational investigation of education and training facilities for exceptional children, Washington, D.C., 1965, National Education Association.

Baldwin, V. L., Fredericks, H. D., and Brodsky, G.: Isn't it time he outgrew this? Or a training program for parents of retarded children, Springfield, Ill., 1973, Charles C Thomas, Publisher.

Barns, S.: Personality characteristics desired in teachers of children with mental retardation as compared to personality characteristics of teachers of regular classrooms, Pierre, S.D., 1966, Division of Pupil Personnel Services, State of South Dakota.

Bartholomew, R.: Furniture selection for MR institutions, Spec. Child. 2(2):18-20, 1976.

Benson, J., and Ross, L.: Teaching parents to teach their children, Teach. Except. Child, pp. 30-35, Fall, 1972.

Blackwell, R. B.: Study of effective and ineffective teachers of the TMR, Except. Child. 39:139-143, 1972.

Bleil, G.: Evaluating educational materials, J. Learn. Disabil. 8(1):19-26, 1975.

Blue, C. M.: An open letter to a prospective teacher of handicapped children, Focus Except. Child 7(4):8-10, 1975.

Boland, S. K.: Managing your instructional material dollar, Teach. Except. Child., pp. 134-139, Spring, 1974.

Brown, L. F.: The analysis of instructional materials, Ment. Retard. **12**(5):21-25, 1974.

Brown, L., and York, R.: Developing programs for severely handicapped students: teacher training and classroom instruction, Focus Except. Child. **6**(2):1-11, 1974.

Buckler, B.: Living with a retarded child: a primer for parents, New York, 1971, Hawthorn Books, Inc.

Bureau of Education for the Handicapped: Better education for the handicapped, Annual Reports FY 1968 and FY 1969, Washington, D.C., 1970, U.S. Government Printing Office.

Childs, R. E.: Fifteen basic components for an effective instructional program for the mentally retarded, Educ. Train. Ment. Retard. **10**:285-288, 1975.

Council for Exceptional Children: Teach children—not categories, Except. Child. **42**(4):234, 1976.

Daly, F. M.: The program for trainable mentally retarded pupils in the public schools of California, Educ. Train. Ment. Retard. **1**:109-118, 1966.

Dean, D.: Closer look: a parent information service, Except. Child. **41**:527-530, 1975.

Deno, E.: Special education as developmental capital, Except. Child. **37**:229-237, 1970.

Dillon, V. T.: Volunteer workers for the trainable, The Pointer **13**(3):61-62, 1969.

Dittman, L. L.: The mentally retarded child at home: a manual for parents, Washington, D.C., 1959, U.S. Department of Health, Education, and Welfare, Children's Bureau Publication, No. 374.

Educational Facilities Laboratories: One out of ten: school planning for the handicapped, New York, 1974.

Education Policies Commission: Policies for education in American democracy, Washington, D.C., 1946, National Education Association.

Epstein, E.: ABC's for the special education teacher, The Pointer **13**(2):70-72, 1968.

Florida State Department of Education: A catalogue of instructional objectives for TMR students, Tallahassee, Fla., 1974.

Florida State Department of Education: A curriculum guide for the intellectually disabled-trainable, Tallahassee, Fla., 1970.

Florida State Department of Education: Florida's educational facilities for exceptional children, 1968-1973, Tallahassee, Fla., 1973.

Gearheart, B. R.: Organization and administration of educational programs for exceptional children, Springfield, Ill., 1974, Charles C Thomas, Publisher.

Geiger, W. L., Brownsmith, K., and Forgnone, C.: Differential importance of skills of TMR students as perceived by teachers, unpublished manuscript, University of Alabama, 1976.

Gray, J. G.: The promise of wisdom: an introduction to philosophy of education, Philadelphia, 1968, J. B. Lippincott Co.

Hanson, F. M.: Aides for the trainable mentally retarded, C. T. A. Journal **65**:23-26, 1969.

Howe, N.: Coming soon—a learning resource center program, J. Develop. Disabil. **1**(3):43-45, 1975.

Hudson, M.: An exploration of classroom procedures for teaching trainable mentally retarded children, CEC Research Monograph, Series A, No. 2, Washington, D.C., 1960, Council for Exceptional Children.

Illinois State Department of Public Instruction: Systematic instruction for retarded children, Parts I, II, III, and IV, Urbana, Ill., 1972.

Joseph P. Kennedy, Jr. Foundation: Families play to grow, Washington, D.C., 1974.

Krause, J. B.: Requirements for teachers of mentally retarded children in the fifty states, Ment. Retard. **1**:38-40, 1963.

Luedtke, L. W.: Para-professional training program, The Pointer **14**(2):59-60, 1969.

Maslow, A. H.: Motivation and personality, New York, 1954, Harper & Brothers.

Millslagle, W. G.: Assessment of University of Northern Colorado special education student teaching evaluations and their relationship to future teacher success, unpublished doctoral dissertation, University of Northern Colorado, 1971.

Missouri State Department of Education: Curriculum guide for teachers of trainable mentally retarded children, Jefferson City, Mo., 1971.

New Mexico State Department of Education: A guide for the teacher of the trainable mentally handicapped, Sante Fe, N.M., 1970.

Perske, R.: New directions for parents of persons who are retarded, Nashville, Tenn., 1973, Abingdon Press.

President's Committee on Mental Retardation, MR 74, A friend in Washington, Washington, D.C., 1975, U.S. Government Printing Office.

Reynolds, M. C.: A framework for considering some issues in special education, Except. Child. **7**:367-370, 1962.

Schaefer, E. S.: Factors that impede the process of socialization. In Begab, M. J., and Richardson, S. A., editors: The mentally retarded and society: a social science perspective, Baltimore, 1975, University Park Press.

Seater, F. L.: An analysis of special education teacher turnover in Colorado, unpublished doctoral dissertation, University of Northern Colorado, 1972.

Selznick, H. M.: Administration and supervision considerations in programming for the mentally retarded, Educ. Train. Ment. Retard. **1**:119-123, 1966.

Simensen, R. J., and Redding, M. G.: State certification of teachers of the mentally retarded, Ment. Retard. 10:21-23, 1972.

Smith, R. W.: Parent training to prevent institutionalization, unpublished paper, University of New Orleans, 1976.

Sontag, E., Burke, P. J., and York, R.: Considerations for serving the severely handicapped in the public schools, Educ. Train. Ment. Retard. 8(2):20-26, 1973.

South Dakota Department of Public Instruction: South Dakota curriculum guide for trainable mentally retarded children, Pierre, S.D., 1972.

Special Education Facilities: Schools and playgrounds for trainable mentally handicapped children, Toronto, Canada, 1971, Ontario Department of Education.

Tavormina, J. B., Henggeler, S. W., and Gayton, W. F.: Age trends in parental assessments of the behavior problems of their retarded children, Ment. Retard. 14(1):38-39, 1976.

Thornley, M.: Every child can learn . . . something! For parents and teachers of severely retarded children, Seattle, Wash., 1973, Special Child Publications.

Truxillo, P.: The effects of resource room teaching on academic achievement of trainable mentally retarded students, unpublished manuscript, University of New Orleans, 1976.

Vulpe, S. G.: Home care and management of the mentally retarded child, Urbana, Ill., 1969, ERIC Clearinghouse on Early Childhood Education.

Walden, S. B.: Management and maintenance in the home: a guide for teaching the handicapped, Urbana, Ill., 1970, ERIC Clearinghouse on Early Childhood Education.

Warfield, G. J.: Mothers of retarded children review a parent education program, Except. Child. 4:559-562, 1975.

Watson, L. S.: Parent training technology: a potential service delivery system, presented at a Conference on Educating the 24-hour Retarded Child, March 31 to April 2, 1975, New Orleans, La.

Wolfsenberger, W.: Normalization: the principle of normalization in human services, Toronto, Canada, 1972, National Institute on Mental Retardation.

Ziegler, S., and Hambleton, D.: Integration of young TMR children into a regular elementary school, Except. Child. 42:459-461, 1976.

CHAPTER 3

BEHAVIOR MODIFICATION

Jane Y. Murdock, Ph.D.*

The purpose of this chapter is to provide teachers and others who work with the TMR with behavior modification procedures. There is an abundance of literature relating to behavior modification procedures appropriate to this level of retardation, ranging from establishing attending behaviors (Murdock and Hartmann, 1975) and developing the ability to imitate a model (Baer, Peterson, and Sherman, 1967) to programming generalized morphology (Guess, Sailor, Rutherford, and Baer, 1968) and generalized syntax (Garcia, Guess, and Byrnes, 1973; Wheeler and Sulzer, 1970). Such literature suggests the broad range of skills that can be taught to a TMR if appropriate procedures are used. It is possible that no single group has shown more dramatic improvement through the careful application of behavior modification principles than have TMRs.

According to Haring and Phillips (1972), educators are finding that the behavior modification methodology is quite effective with the moderately and severely handicapped. In some instances, programs for TMR student populations have expanded

*Department of Special Education, University of New Orleans, New Orleans, Louisiana.

their curriculum to include basic academic subjects: reading, writing, arithmetic, and language.

Educational programs for the trainable student have been developed that are true academic programs rather than programs which, in certain instances, simply provide parents or guardians with some relief from the care-taking responsibilities so long associated with the trainable child. It is the philosophy of some of these innovative educational programs that all children, regardless of initial diagnosis, can profit from learning basic academic skills as well as self-care and social-behavioral skills (Hoschauer, Hardman, and Smith, 1973). These programs embrace the philosophy that everyone is entitled to an opportunity to learn everything he* is capable of learning. This is considerably removed from the notion that particular individuals cannot learn certain things because they have been diagnosed as not having the ability to learn and are therefore untrainable. Consequent-

*Throughout this discussion, the student will be referred to in the masculine gender and the teacher in the feminine gender. This arrangement is purely for simplicity of exposition and does not imply that these roles cannot be reversed.

ly, they are denied an opportunity to try to learn those things which others have predetermined they are incapable of learning. This is not to take John B. Watson's (1924) environmentalist position to its extreme, but rather to attempt to maximize the possibility for each individual to use optimally whatever talents he may have. Brown (1973) suggested that, *"No amount of money will provide these students with the skills they are capable of acquiring.* The professional community simply does not have the instructional technology to teach them what they need to know and what they are capable of learning." The students that Brown is referring to are TMRs, and the instructional technology is behavior modification, or what he calls "behavioristic task analysis." Simply pouring money into TMR programs will not provide the students with the skills they are capable of acquiring. It is essential that teachers of TMR students be thoroughly trained in behavior modification procedures in addition to having adequate funding available.

BEHAVIOR MODIFICATION—WHAT IS IT?

Behavior modification involves interpreting and applying the empirical data derived from the experimental analysis of animal and human behavior. In layman's terms, it involves putting the results of scientific research to work in the real world with real people—in this case, with the TMR student. The following discussion includes definitions and examples of how reinforcement, punishment, time-out, response cost, and extinction procedures might be applied to TMR students, as well as contingency management.

Reinforcement

Reinforcement is the procedure of following a response with a reinforcing stimulus. For example, if a student makes an appropriate verbalization in response to the printed word "cat" and the question "What is this word?" and then is given a token

and praised by his teacher—*and* the frequency of reading "cat" correctly increases—then giving him the token and praising him is an example of positive reinforcement. By definition, reinforcement, positive or negative, must increase the rate of or otherwise strengthen the response it follows. If the frequency of reading the word "cat" had decreased, then giving that student a token and praising him would not have been an example of reinforcement. Another example of positive reinforcement would be if each time a student responds by looking at his teacher when the teacher says "Look at me," and he is given a taste of ice cream—and the rate of looking at the teacher increases—then the ice cream is an example of positive reinforcement.

Negative reinforcement also increases the rate of or otherwise strengthens the response it follows. However, this is somewhat different in that instead of delivering a positive stimulus—token, praise, or ice cream—some aversive stimulus is terminated. Following is an example of negative reinforcement. A teacher dismisses her class early for lunch because the students are yelling, running around, and generally misbehaving, and the frequency with which she dismisses her class early increases. Dismissing the class early results in the termination of aversive stimuli (students screaming, running around, misbehaving) for the teacher. However, examine the entire interaction closely. In all probability, being dismissed early would act as a positive reinforcer for the students, thus increasing or strengthening the screaming, running around, and misbehaving. Another example of a negative reinforcement procedure, which would not be used except when all other procedures fail, might be this: A child who soils his pants must wear them until he indicates to someone that he wants to go to the bathroom. The soiled pants are removed immediately contingent on an appropriate response relating to toileting behaviors, and such an appropriate response is strengthened. A procedure can be called negative reinforcement only if it increases or strengthens the response it follows.

Punishment

Punishment is the procedure of following a response with an aversive stimulus so that the response occurs less frequently or is otherwise weakened. For example, if a teacher claps her hands and says "No!" each time a student inappropriately gives an answer more than once (perseverates) and the rate of answering inappropriately more than once decreases, then clapping her hands and saying no is an example of punishment. By definition, punishment must weaken or decrease the rate of the response it follows.

Time-out

Time-out is a process of removing or withdrawing all reinforcers for a period of time following a response that you wish to weaken. Time-out is not typical punishment in the sense of administering an aversive stimulus, such as something painful and/or frightening.

For example, if a student is laughing and giggling during an academic session, the teacher closes her eyes and drops her head for a brief interval, during which she does not provide any positive reinforcement for the child. For this procedure to be effective, that is, reduce the rate of or otherwise weaken the response it follows, the teacher's attentive behaviors must have been reinforcing for the child—the time-out must be a *time-out* from reinforcement. Another example is a student spits, the teacher may quietly but firmly remove him from the classroom setting each time and place him in a time-out booth where there is no one for him to interact with and nothing to play with (but it is not dark or otherwise deliberately meant to be frightening). The child must remain there for a short period of time, perhaps 3 minutes, and the spitting behavior decreases. Once again, it cannot be considered time-out unless it

decreases the rate of or otherwise weakens the behavior it follows.

Response cost

Response cost is a form of punishment whereby a reinforcer is removed. If you have some form of tangible reinforcer (checks, tokens, stars, candy) you have something obvious and concrete to take away immediately following any response you wish to weaken. For example, if a student interrupts while it is another student's turn to respond, the teacher takes two of his tokens from him, and the interrupting behavior is weakened. Since this is a form of punishment, it must decrease the rate of or weaken the behavior it follows, or it is not response cost.

Extinction

Extinction is a procedure that involves the termination of a reinforcing stimulus that follows a response to weaken or decrease the rate of that response. An example of extinction is a teacher who does not attend to a student whenever the student is crying and the crying rate decreases or the intensity of the crying response is weakened. Another example is a teacher who does not call on students who raise their hands and the hand-raising decreases.

To some extent it is readily apparent when the use of each of these procedures is appropriate. Each procedure will be discussed in considerable detail later in the chapter. Establishment of appropriate behaviors and elimination of inappropriate behaviors will be included.

Contingency management

Contingency management involves clear specification of how and when a particular set of behaviors will occur. In other words, there is a clearly specified dependency between observable behaviors. The teacher of the TMR child must plan the contingencies ahead of time. What are the rules? What are the consequences? What behaviors will she reinforce? What behaviors will she punish? What behaviors will she place on time-out? What behaviors will she place on extinction? How is she going to accomplish each of these? The interaction between teacher and pupils constantly acts to strengthen or weaken behaviors. If the teacher does not understand and set up the contingencies so that she can manage them effectively, they will be mismanaged or occur haphazardly. To manage contingencies effectively, teachers must specify simply and clearly (1) what behaviors they wish to strengthen and what reinforcement procedures they will use and (2) what behaviors they wish to weaken and what punishment or extinction procedures they will use.

HOW TO ESTABLISH APPROPRIATE BEHAVIORS

Teaching essentially means establishing appropriate behaviors. It is the purpose of a teacher to teach that which society has determined appropriate for students to learn. Furthermore, many experts contend that it is also the teacher's responsibility to teach each student everything he is capable of learning within the prescribed curriculum. Consequently, the major emphasis should be placed on establishing appropriate academic and social behaviors rather than on eliminating inappropriate behaviors.

Logically, it is impossible for any person to exhibit behavior that equals more than 100% of his behavioral repertoire. If a TMR student comes into a classroom and 80% of his behavior is appropriate, then no more than 20% can be inappropriate. It is not uncommon for teachers to devote a disproportionate amount of time and effort toward eliminating the inappropriate behaviors before attempting to teach the appropriate social and academic behaviors that comprise the curriculum for the TMR student. This is usually not necessary, An alternative approach would be to teach the appropriate behaviors. As the rate of these behaviors increases, the rate of the inappropriate behaviors must necessarily decrease. Some behavior is going on constantly

with any living organism. As more of the organism's behavior becomes appropriate, less of it can be inappropriate. Consequently, the emphasis should be on teaching or establishing appropriate behaviors; reinforcers, by definition, must increase the rate of or strengthen the response they follow.

Kinds of reinforcers

There are two general kinds of reinforcers—unconditioned and conditioned. Unconditioned, or unlearned reinforcers are effective because of the biological make-up of the organism. Food and water are the prime examples of unconditioned reinforcers, as well as responses that terminate painful or aversive stimuli. However, most stimuli are originally neutral, that is, they have no reinforcing properties. These neutral stimuli can acquire reinforcing properties by being paired with or immediately followed by any stimuli that are reinforcing. When this occurs repeatedly, the previously neutral stimuli become conditioned, or learned reinforcers.

Most human behavior is learned and maintained by conditioned reinforcers. These may be social consequences such as smiles, praise, nearness, and attention, or they may be physical objects such as money, poker chips, points, or stars. Activity reinforcers are also conditioned, or learned, reinforcers. Premack (1965) conducted a number of studies which demonstrated that more preferred activities can be used to reinforce less preferred activities. The Premack principle, which is also known as "Grandma's rule," states that any higher-frequency behavior is likely to increase the rate of the lower-frequency behavior it follows. Grandma's rule is simply, "You do what I want you to do *before* you get to do what you want to do." Any activity a student likes can be used to reinforce performing tasks he likes less.

Reinforcer probing

Do not assume that what is reinforcing for you is necessarily reinforcing for others.

Also, do not assume that what reinforces one student will reinforce another. Even unconditioned reinforcers such as candy are not universally reinforcing. One teacher who was attempting to establish vocal verbalization in a relatively nonverbal child experienced considerable difficulty finding a reinforcer (Murdock, 1970). The teacher knew this because the child was not verbalizing more even though each vocal verbalization was followed by pieces of chocolate, sherbet, sugar-coated cereal, etc., which were also paired with smiles and praise. The teacher had made inquiries of parents, teachers, grandparents, and almost everyone immediately associated with the child in an attempt to discover something the child especially liked that would prove to be a reinforcer. The child's grandmother suggested pretzels. At the same time the teacher continued to vary the consequent stimuli used during the teaching sessions, that is, to probe for some consequent stimuli that would increase the rate of the vocal verbalizations and thus qualify as a reinforcer. During one session, the child placed the piece of pretzel, which she had received contingent on an appropriate vocal verbalization, into the teacher's mouth. That particular activity, feeding the teacher, proved reinforcing for the child in that the rate of vocal verbalization steadily increased during all remaining sessions (Fig. 3-1). Reinforcer probing is not usually this difficult, but it is almost always necessary to keep careful data to determine whether the consequent stimuli used with a student are, in fact, reinforcing.

Selecting reinforcers

Each teacher must determine the kind of reinforcers she will use based on their effectiveness and how little they interfere with ongoing academic behaviors. For example, some form of primary reinforcer is frequently used to establish vocal verbalization in TMR students. It is essential that the edible selected is not one requiring excessive chewing, such as caramels, since it is almost impossible to chew caramels and talk at the same time. It is also desira-

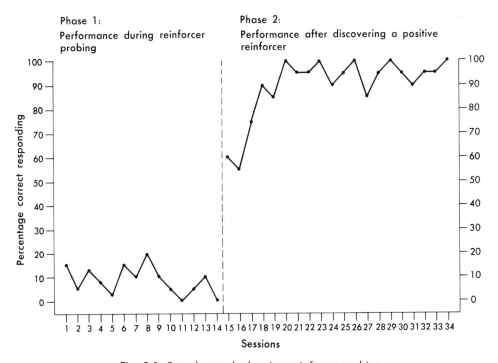

Fig. 3-1. Sample graph showing reinforcer probing.

ble to use a very small amount of sherbet because it is consumed very quickly.

The amount of reinforcer delivered is also important. It does not take great quantities, especially when delivering something edible, since satiation is also a factor. A student will satiate faster if he is given a tablespoonful of sherbet for each correct response than he will if he is given only a very small taste. It will also take him longer to swallow the tablespoonful; therefore, in the interest of maintaining the strength of your reinforcer by avoiding satiation and also not wasting valuable teaching time, it is better to deliver very small portions.

It is also useful to vary reinforcers and to present novel reinforcers to maintain reinforcer strength. Reinforcers can be varied in kind and degree. For example, if you are using edibles, you may have several kinds tucked away in the reinforcer pouch. As you reach into the pouch, pause appropriately to create an air of expectancy among your students. This entire interaction keeps the student's interest and attention, since they cannot predict exactly what kind of edible they will receive—it may be a piece of cereal, or a tiny piece of chocolate, or a piece of pretzel, etc. This also increases the probability that you have at least one powerful reinforcer for each student in the group.

Novel reinforcers are also effective for obtaining and holding the students' attention. An example of a novel edible reinforcer that meets all the requirements mentioned is punch or fruit juice, which can be squirted directly into the child's mouth, use plastic bottle with a nozzle on it that is normally used to apply hair tints. It is not necessary for the nozzle to ever touch the child's mouth, and, in any event, it can be washed. There is no limit to how the creative teacher can vary her reinforcers and discover novel reinforcers.

If your classroom is on a token system, variation of reinforcers is already provided, since every good token system has a wide variety of backups or payoffs that students can buy with their tokens. This is done to ensure that there is something reinforcing for every student in the program. However, it is possible to vary the *degree* of reinforcement by occasionally giving one or two more tokens than you normally would give for an especially good response. Do not do this on a predictable basis. The unpredictability is another attention-getting and attention-maintaining procedure.

Reinforcement schedules

When teaching new material, reinforce every correct response. This is called a continuous reinforcement (CRF) schedule. It is also a one-to-one fixed-ratio schedule (FR 1). Reinforcers should be delivered after every correct response (CRF or FR 1) until the student has mastered the new material at whatever criterion the teacher has established (normally at least 80% or better successful responding for two or more consecutive sessions). As soon as the student reaches the preestablished success criterion, thin the reinforcement schedule from a CRF schedule to a leaner fixed-ratio schedule (FR 2) in which every other correct response is reinforced.

When the student reaches the preestablished success criterion on this reinforcement schedule, change to a variable-ratio schedule (VR 3) in which approximately every third correct response is reinforced. For example, out of fifteen correct responses, the student would receive approximately five reinforcers, perhaps receiving one after four correct responses, then after two correct responses, after three correct responses, and so on. Each time the child reaches the preestablished success criterion on a particular reinforcement schedule, the schedule is thinned further on a variable-ratio schedule until it is possibly as thin as VR 10 (approximately every tenth correct response is reinforced).

It is essential to reinforce new material continuously for the material to be learned more efficiently, but it is also essential to reinforce mastered material on an intermittent unpredictable (VR) schedule. This results in greater resistance to extinction. If the student does not know exactly when a particular behavior will be reinforced, he will continue to emit that behavior over a longer period of time without receiving any reinforcement. Extinction occurs most rapidly under continuous reinforcement and least rapidly under unpredictable intermittent reinforcement. The positive effects of unpredictable intermittent reinforcement can readily be seen in the gambler who persists in playing the slot machine even after a long losing streak. Games of chance deliberately involve unpredictable intermittent reinforcement schedules.

When to reinforce

Reinforcement delivery must immediately follow the correct response. Any delay can result in reinforcing another response that has had a chance to occur in the interim period between the occurrence of the target response and the reinforcer delivery. Since reinforcers strengthen the behavior they follow, it is essential that they be applied immediately and discriminatively.

Data-recording procedures

When the teacher places emphasis on strengthening appropriate academic behaviors, it is relatively simple to keep data because graded samples of academic work are routinely available. When the target behavior you are keeping data on can be recorded, such as a written arithmetic answer, it is necessary only to examine the record and tabulate the responses. These are usually in the form of a percentage of correct responses. A teacher may assign ten arithmetic problems to be completed in a specified period of time. Consequently, the students receive 10% for each problem completed correctly. When the teacher reviews subsequent scores, it is easy to determine whether the student's performance in arithmetic is improving. If it is not, the student is not learning, or, put another way, he is not being taught. Once this is deter-

mined, it is necessary to discover the cause. The first assumption, particularly with TMR students, is that the material is too difficult. This may be true. However, an alternative assumption is that the student is not being reinforced, that is, whatever stimuli immediately follow his correct arithmetic responses are not reinforcing for that student. If they were reinforcing, the arithmetic performance would be improving. In the interest of expediency, it is advisable to operate under the second assumption and probe for a reinforcer before moving backward in the curriculum.

Most data recording is not as simple as counting the number of correct responses (either written or in some other relatively permanent form such as frequency data). When the target behaviors do no leave a record, there are three common data-recording methods used: tally, duration, and interval. These methods require data sheets of some kind and, of course, a human observer. The observer is usually the classroom teacher, an aide, or a volunteer. (See Fig. 3-2 for a sample data sheet.)

Tally method. For many behaviors, the easiest way to record data is to count, or tally, the number of times the target behavior occurs during a predetermined time interval. If the response is a gesture or a spoken response rather than a written response, some tally or record would have to be made as soon as the student makes the response. If you are attempting to determine a student's phonic reading responses, the response is either spoken by the child when the teacher points to the stimulus, or the child points to the printed symbol when the teacher verbalizes the letter sound or word. In neither instance does the child's response leave a written or otherwise permanent record. Consequently, it is necessary for some observer to record whether the child is correct or incorrect immediately following each response.

Duration method. The duration method is used when the length of the behavior rather than its frequency is the essential

Student _____   Type of data:

Instructor _____

Setting _____   Code: _____
                                           _____
                                           _____
                                           _____

Session number	Target behavior																								

Fig. 3-2. Sample data sheet.

feature. The length of the observation periods is determined in advance. For example, you may want to record the amount of time a child spends crying. As soon as the child begins to cry the watch is started. When he stops crying, the watch is stopped. Two watches are required. A stopwatch runs continuously while the child is crying, and another watch is used to time the duration of the observation period, perhaps 5 minutes. The duration method is the least used of the three common response measures. This may be because it is more efficient to estimate duration by using the interval method. However, Skiba, Pettigrew, and Alden (1971) used the duration method successfully to measure changes in thumb-sucking as a function of the contingent reinforcement of incompatible responses. O'Brien, Azrin, and Bugle (1972) used the duration method, as well as the tally method, to record changes in a child's locomotion from crawling to walking as a result of their training procedures.

Interval method. According to Gelfand and Hartman (1975), to use the interval method of recording, the observation periods must be broken into small equal intervals, and a record must be made of whether the behavior is observed to occur in each interval. The interval size usually varies from 5 to 60 seconds in duration, depending on the rate of the response and the average duration of a single response. The interval should be sufficiently small for high-rate behaviors so that two complete responses cannot occur in a single interval. However, the interval should be at least as long as the average duration of a single response. To use excessively long intervals results in underestimating the occurrence frequency of the target behavior and might result in underestimating the size of the reduction of an undersirable behavior as a result of a deceleration program. Using intervals that are too small would have the opposite effect.

Since interval recording provides a close approximation to either frequency or duration recording, it is applicable to a variety of behaviors. Barton, Guess, Garcia, and Baer (1970) used the interval method to record changes in mealtime behavior. It has also been used to record attending behaviors (Walker and Buckley, 1968), talking (Reynolds and Risley, 1968), disruptive behaviors (O'Leary, Becker, Evans, and Saudargas, 1969), and studying behaviors (Hall, Lund, and Jackson, 1968).

The teacher must adopt consistent rules as to when to record behavior regardless of the recording method she selects. The rule must be to record either (1) the portion of the interval during which the behavior took place (e.g., 50% or more of the interval), or (2) whether the behavior occurred at any time during the interval. This prevents the interference of unreliable data as a result of fluctuating standards. Determining whether the behavior occurred at any time during the interval requires less judgment on the part of the observer and is probably the easier procedure to employ. However, it may give an overestimate of absolute frequency or duration of the target behavior.

The particular form of data keeping the teacher selects depends on her particular situation and the target behaviors she is interested in. It is essential, however, for her to keep some formal record to ascertain whether her teaching procedures are working. In addition, these visual records, particularly in the form of graphs, can be a very powerful reinforcer for the teacher or parent. It is frequently difficult to determine accurately whether a student is making substantial progress. This is particularly true with many TMR students whose progress may be considerably slower than that of other students. A graph gives a teacher visual evidence of slow but consistent improvement. This not only lets her know that she has an effective teaching program, but it also reinforces her for her own appropriate teaching behaviors. Teachers need their reinforcers, too.

BASIC PROCEDURES TO ACQUIRE BEHAVIORS

It is possible that the particular social or academic behaviors the teacher wishes to strengthen are not presently a part of the student's behavioral repertoire. Consequently, the teacher may feel helpless. How can she reinforce (increase or strengthen) a behavior if that behavior never occurs? It is not necessary to simply wait for the behavior to occur, even in a very weak form. Instead, the teacher can model the correct response, prompt the correct response, or shape the correct response.

Modeling

Most human behavior is probably learned through imitating a model. Imitative learning is so important for the trainable mentally retarded student that it will be treated separately. (See discussion on imitating, pp. 78 and 79.) For now, it is sufficient for the teacher to know that if the desired behavior is not observed to be in the student's behavior repertoire, the teacher should first attempt to elicit that behavior by simply modeling it for the student to imitate. If the student cannot imitate, new behavior may be acquired through prompting.

Prompting

According to Becker, Engelmann, and Thomas (1971), a prompt is a previously taught task that the teacher can use to evoke a specified response when she is teaching a new task. For example, a student has been taught to say "mama" when he hears the word "mama;" he does not say "mama," however, when he sees the written letters *mama*. The teacher wants to teach the student to say "mama" when viewing the printed word *mama*. The teacher may prompt with the behavior the child has already mastered by pointing to the letters *mama* and saying, "This is 'mama.'" Remember that the student has already learned to respond correctly to such an auditory signal, and now the teacher is using that to prompt correct

responding to the visual signal *mama*. The prompt, or the auditory signal in this example, must be faded out gradually *but completely* to ascertain whether the child can respond correctly to the visual signal alone, that is, to know whether he has learned to read the word *mama*.

Prompting frequently involves using visual cues to prompt auditory learning and auditory cues to prompt visual learning. However, other senses may be used also, including the tactile and kinesthetic, and even the gustatory and alfactory. Such multisensory teaching is frequently useful when teaching TMR students.

Probably the strongest prompt involves physically moving the child completely through the desired behavior. Murdock and Hartmann (1975) designed teaching formats for students whose language abilities ranged from nonverbal to less than 4 years of age. Their teaching formats included prompts to be used as needed, ranging from the weakest to the strongest prompt. The weakest prompt required for the student to respond correctly was the appropriate prompt to be used. In the Murdock and Hartmann program, when a student responded correctly 80% of the time for two consecutive sessions, the prompt being used during those sessions was faded out and the next weaker prompt was used. This continued until all prompting was faded completely (Table 3-1).

If the teacher cannot motivate the student to respond appropriately by modeling the correct response or by using prompting procedures, then new behaviors can be acquired through shaping procedures.

Shaping

According to Sloane and MacAuley (1968), shaping involves the use of differential reinforcement and successive approximations to develop new behaviors. For example, with a TMR student certain responses that he currently produces resemble the desired terminal response more than others, however crude the closest

Table 3-1. Expressive language skills teaching format

Category I: Preverbal (preword) motor and vocal imitation

Move to next number in *each column* after child gives ten consecutive correct responses or responds correctly 80% or more for two consecutive sessions. For each task as the child reaches one of the defined criteria: (1) fade prompts, (2) thin reinforcement schedule, and (3) change verbal discriminative stimuli appropriate for the next task in this category.

Discriminative stimuli (instructor)			Response (child)	(2) Consequent stimuli (instructor)
(3) Verbal	Visual	(1) Prompts to be used if needed		
1. "Do this" followed by verbalization appropriate to action, e.g., "bye-bye" 2. Appropriate verbalization only, e.g., "bye-bye"	Instructor's action	1. *Completely physically* assist child with action 2. *Partially physically* assist child with action 3. *Touch* body part involved 4. *Tell* child what body part and movement to make	Correct imitation of instructor's action or gradual approximations of imitation	1. CRF social CRF tangible 2. CRF social FR 2 tangible 3. CRF social VR 5 tangible
			Incorrect response	No reinforcer

approximation to the terminal behavior may be. If the terminal behavior is saying the word "hi," only those variants of the student's speech that most closely resemble "hi" are reinforced and others are placed on extinction. Consequently, the range of speech sounds produced will shift in the direction of "hi." By providing *differential reinforcement* only for those response variants in the existing repertoire that more closely approximate the desired terminal behavior, new response variations are produced that were not previously emitted. The teacher gradually shifts the criteria for acceptable responding toward the terminal response as the student more closely approximates that response. The teacher accomplishes this by differentially reinforcing only those responses which match the desired production "hi" even more closely, thus again shifting the distribution of responses emitted. This gradual change, or shift, in reinforcement criteria (since the above procedure is repeated until the desired terminal form of the response is regularly produced) is described as the use of *successive approximations*.

Much new behavior does not involve learning totally new responses, but rather requires the student to relate existing responses to each other in particular ways or use existing responses to prompt new responses. As stated previously, much human behavior is learned through imitation rather than through direct shaping. Shaping is a very inefficient procedure to use compared with modeling or prompting. Consequently, shaping is used only when the child cannot imitate a model and when there are no prompts that can be used to initiate the new behavior.

Contingency management

Poor contingency management is probably the major cause of unsuccessful behavior modification programs. Contingency management involves clearly specifying how and when a particular set of behaviors will occur. There must be a clearly specified dependency between observable behaviors. To manage contingencies effectively when teaching appropriate behaviors, the teacher must (1) specify the behaviors she wishes to strengthen or increase, (2) ascertain what procedure she must use to get those behaviors started—modeling, prompting, shaping, (3) decide on a reinforcement procedure to use, having already made certain that she does, in fact, have a reinforcer, (4) choose a reinforcer delivery system to use that is simple, efficient, and does not interfere with ongoing academic behaviors, (5) determine what reinforcement schedule is appropriate to use, and (6) decide how she is going to keep data.

Consistency is essential for successful contingency management. Once a teacher determines these six criteria, she must follow her program consistently. There can be no relenting and giving a student a reinforcer when he has not earned it, for example, saying, "That's okay, Johnny, I know you meant to say 'It's a rabbit' not 'It's a cat,'" and giving Johnny the reinforcer *even though he responded incorrectly*. The teacher's intentions may be good, but she is reinforcing (teaching) incorrect responding.

Murdock (1969) investigated contingency management with TMR students in a public school setting. This was done in response to the teachers' complaints that behavior modification did not work with their students. Careful observations convinced Murdock that the teachers were delivering reinforcers noncontingently, that is, the students were receiving reinforcers for many behaviors that were not necessarily appropriate, and frequently they were receiving reinforcers for responses that were actually incompatible with correct responding. In addition, the students were not consistently reinforced for appropriate behaviors and correct responses. The teachers pointed out *how many* reinforcers (a combination of social reinforcers and tokens) the students were receiving without showing any significant improvement in their academic or social behaviors. A yoked-control design was used to demonstrate the importance of careful contingency management. This design required selecting two Down's syndrome students from each classroom being investigated. The two students were also close friends. They were alternately assigned to contingent and noncontingent teaching conditions. Whichever student was in the contingent condition was worked with first and received tokens paired with social reinforcers contingent on correct responding. The number of reinforcers delivered to the student in the contingent condition was carefully calculated before the student in the noncontingent condition was worked with. This was to ensure that each student received exactly the same number of reinforcers. However, for the student in the noncontingent condition, the reinforcers were delivered on an arbitrary time interval schedule ranging from 5 seconds to 3 minutes, independent of whether the preceding response was correct. The Down's syndrome students learned new material faster and responded correctly more consistently under the contingent reinforcement conditions.

Precise contingency management is essential to successful behavior modification programs. Behavior modification is much more than giving tokens to students and praising them. Praise, tokens, and all other reinforcers must be contingent on appropriate responding.

Stimulus control

So far the focus has been primarily on consequent stimuli, especially positive reinforcement. The *antecedent stimuli* must be considered also, since they become *discriminative stimuli* for particular responses. The consequent stimuli (reinforcers, punishers, etc. that follow a response) will vary, depending on the situation in which the response is emitted. When a response is reinforced in the presence of a particular stimulus and not reinforced in its absence, the stimulus is called a *discriminative stimulus* (S^D). In Table 3-1 examine the discriminative stimuli, which include verbal and visual stimuli as well as prompts to be used if needed. In a teaching situation the use of discriminative stimuli involves a sequence of events: (1) the stimulus is usually presented by the teacher, (2) the student responds to that stimulus, and (3) the teacher may or may not reinforce the response, depending on whether it is correct and also on the reinforcement schedule. Initially, however, each correct response to a particular stimulus or set of stimuli is reinforced by the teacher. With continued discrimination training, that is, continued exposure to the three-part relationship just described, the likehood of the response occurring becomes much greater in the presence of the discriminative stimulus that was the occasion for reinforcement than it is in its absence. Behavior is emitted that is appropriate to the different situations in which different consequences occur. After discrimination training, the likelihood of a particular response occurring will be greater in the presence of the S^D, and it will also be greater in the presence of other stimuli that are similar to the S^D than in the presence of other stimuli that are quite different. This is called *stimulus generalization*. How much stimulus generalization occurs depends on the number of factors and particularly on how similar the stimuli that were the occasion for nonreinforcement were to the S^D in the initial discrimination training.

People and setting can become discriminative stimuli. Teachers become S^D's for particular student behaviors, whether they realize it or not. Consider the situation in which Ms. Smith overhears Ms. Jones talking about Johnny Brown in the faculty lounge. Ms. Smith is describing Johnny as being cooperative, responsive to instruction, and generally a good student. Ms. Jones thinks there must be some mistake because the Johnny Brown in her classroom is uncooperative, unresponsive to instruction, and generally a poor student. Ms. Jones attends to (reinforces) Johnny when he is misbehaving and Ms. Smith attends to (reinforces) Johnny when he behaves appropriately. Mrs. Jones has become an S^D for inappropriate classroom behaviors, and Ms. Smith has become an S^D for appropriate classroom behaviors. It is also probable that Ms. Jones's *classroom* has become an S^D for inappropriate

academic behaviors just as Ms. Smith's classroom has become an S^D for appropriate academic behaviors.

Consider also the student who would not say one word for the new speech therapist, who had diagnosed the child as being nonverbal with a strong possibility of a moderate to severe hearing loss. However, when the child's teacher came into the speech therapist's room, the child responded to her by asking, "Can I go back to the room now and finish coloring my picture?" The teacher was an S^D for such vocal verbalization, but the new speech therapist was not.

Another example that is familiar to most teachers and others who frequent school settings is the classroom of students who are shouting, running around, knocking into desks and each other, throwing papers back and forth, when one student suddenly says, "Hey, here comes Ms. Smith." By the time Ms. Smith enters the classroom, all the students are seated at their desks and working quietly.

Attending

Attending is defined as listening to and looking at the person doing the instructing or looking at the educational materials involved in the instruction. In addition, there should be some observable evidence that the student is attempting to respond appropriately to the discriminative stimuli, that is, that he is not simply staring blankly at the teacher or materials.

To induce the student to attend, verbalize your instructions simply and clearly first. If the student does not attend in response to verbal instructions, model the desired behavior. If modeling fails, prompt the desired attending behaviors, even physically moving the child through the response if necessary. All prompts must be faded gradually but completely.

Initially, reinforce the child for attending on a CRF schedule. Pair the reinforcement with descriptive verbal praise, such as, "Thank you! I like the way you're watching me." Such descriptive praise takes time away from teaching, but it is time well spent if it establishes attending behaviors. As the attending behaviors are learned, thin the reinforcement schedule as described previously. Eventually, however, the teacher will be able to discontinue reinforcement completely for attending per se and will only reinforce correct responding at the end of a teaching chain. Observe the following teaching/learning situation:

1. Teacher: "Watch me and listen." This is usually accompanied by some gesture on the teacher's part, such as holding up her hand.
2. Student: Looks at the teacher.
3. Teacher: "Good watching me!" If she is using tangible rather than social reinforcers, she gives one to the student.
4. Teacher: "Now, do this." She models waving and says, "Bye-bye."
5. Student: Waves and says, "Bye-bye."
6. Teacher: "Very good!" She gives the student another reinforcer.

Such a typical teaching chain involves delivering two reinforcers to teach attending behaviors. As soon as attending behaviors are established, the reinforcer is delivered only at the end of the chain, and step 3 is omitted entirely. The same procedure applies to many school behaviors that become routine once conditioned (learned), such as coming in when the bell rings, going directly to seats, waiting for the teacher to begin the school day. Initially it may be necessary to reinforce each of these behaviors independently until the student have learned appropriate school behaviors. Once such behaviors become routine, they are not reinforced independently but only at the end of the behavioral chain they begin.

Imitating

The ability to imitate or "do as the model does" is essential to learn most of the social and academic behaviors outlined in a TMR curriculum, or any curriculum for that matter. Many of these behaviors can be taught through shaping procedures, but the time involved makes shaping an undesirable approach to have

to use for each behavior involved. Considerable research has been devoted to using behavior modification procedures to establish an imitative repertoire with moderately to severely retarded subjects. Some of these involved using shaping procedures to establish imitative behaviors. It is particularly important to note that once imitative responses were established, they generalized to include imitations that had never been specifically reinforced or trained. In other words, the retarded subjects had *learned to imitate.*

Baer, Peterson, and Sherman (1967) successfully trained over a hundred motor imitations in three severely retarded children. With two of their subjects it was necessary for them to place a vocal response at the end of a well-established motor chain to establish vocal imitation. For example, the subject may have reliably imitated getting up, walking across the room, and raising his hand. Consequently, raising his hand was followed by saying "hi." After reliable imitations were established, the motor chains were faded out. With a third subject, it was necessary to carefully shape imitative behavior, using differential reinforcement for successive approximations to the target behavior as described previously.

Sloane, Johnston, and Harris (1968) easily trained simple nonverbal motor imitation, then shaped simple imitation of the placement of the vocal musculature and associated structures, and finally evoked imitation of specific sounds and chains. Here, again, motor imitation was established before verbal imitation was attempted.

It may not always be necessary to establish motor imitation before attempting to establish the verbal imitation that is prerequisite to learning most academic skills. Garcia, Baer, and Firestone (1971) investigated the development of an imitative repertoire within preselected topographies of motor and vocal responses. They found that there was only generalization to the topographical type of imitation that was currently being trained or had been previously trained. This may indicate that the transition problem Garcia and associates experienced could have been anticipated when moving from one topography to another, that is, from motor imitation to verbal imitation, and that, in fact, there may be little, if any, relationship between the two. For further information related to modeling, see Bandura (1969).

GENERALIZATION*

Generalization requires that the student be able to respond correctly on all material mastered with the original teacher (1) in other physical settings, (2) for other people, (3) to different discriminative stimuli, and (4) to similar tasks. For example, assume a teacher is working with the child on an individual basis in an isolated area. The teacher points to a picture of the child's mother and asks, "Who is this?" The child responds correctly, "Mama." To have all four kinds of generalization, the child would also have to respond correctly (1) to the same picture and question when asked in other physical settings, such as classroom, home, (2) to the same picture and question when asked by someone other than the initial teacher, (3) to the actual mother rather than to a picture of his mother when asked the identical question or a variation of the question, and (4) by utilizing his mastery of the *m* phoneme to form other words (mom, me, my, etc.).

Generalization probing

Probing, that is, testing for generalization, should be done for each target behavior as soon as the child succeeds at some predetermined success criterion, for example, 80% or more for two consecutive sessions with the original teacher. To determine whether the child's behaviors are generalizing, the original teacher should

set up probes to test for each kind of generalization. Probes should not be reinforced.

1. For generalization to other physical settings, the original teacher simply encounters the child in any setting other than where the initial teaching occurred and presents him with the same visual and verbal stimuli.

2. For generalization to other people, the original teacher simply instructs another teacher, a volunteer, a peer, or one of the parents to present the same visual and verbal stimuli to the child and accurately report the response.

3. For generalization to different discriminative stimuli, simply vary the antecedent visual and/or verbal stimuli, still requiring the same response.

4. Generalization to similar tasks is more difficult to probe for. For example, when you are teaching vocal verbalization, generalization usually does not occur until the child has a fairly large verbal repertoire to work with, since new words that contain the same phonemes will probably have to be trained independently. However, the child should reach a criterion on such new words in considerably fewer and fewer trials.

Probes for similar task generalization are required as soon as the child has chaining responses, such as, "I want. . . ." For example, if the child has such a chain in his verbal repertoire, you can test his ability to generalize the use of this phrase by presenting him with a visual stimulus of any word in his repertoire and asking him, "What do you want? Say the whole thing."

Generalization training

If through the probing the teacher has determined that the child has failed to generalize, she should select a minimum of two other people who will give the child the same training she did in at least two different settings. The only difference between this training and the training given by the original teacher is the number of trials required and, consequently, the

---

°From Murdock, J. Y., and Hartmann, B.: A language development program: imitative gestures to basic syntactic structures. Salt Lake City, 1975, Word Making Productions.

Child _____

Date _____

Criteria for correct response:
(Example)
1. Audible sound for every syllable.
2. "gl" blend may be "gu" in "glass."
3. "Wawa" is acceptable for "water."
Desired response: "I want a glass of water."

Setting / Trainer	Probe (S^D) Visual: Point to glass of water. Verbal: "What do you want? Say the whole thing."	Trials (R) Correct (+) Incorrect (−) Prompted correct (p+) Prompted incorrect (p−) No response (0)				Reinforcement schedule (S^R) and tangible reinforcer to be used

1. When probing: Do not reinforce, model or prompt.
2. When training: Language instructor will fill in the reinforcement schedule
   to be used as well as the tangible reinforcer.

   Language instructor will provide prompt to be used under S^D
   in addition to the verbal and visual stimuli.

   The generalization trainer should model the correct response
   immediately following any incorrect (−) response the child
   makes. Then present S^D again and record as usual.
3. Return these cards to language instructor daily so that data can be analyzed and
   appropriate cards set up for your next session.

Fig. 3-3. Generalization training and probing card. (From Murdock, J. Y., and Hartmann, B.: A language development program: imitative gestures to basic syntactic structures, Salt Lake City, 1975, Word Making Productions.)

amount of time involved. Normally only three or four trials on each specified task should be required. These can be presented to the child during story time, math, or lunch, whenever it is agreeable for the person selected to do the generalization training. The original teacher must provide this person with materials that specify the discriminative stimuli, the criterion for a correct response, the reinforcement schedule, and space to record the data. Murdock and Hartman (1975) designed generalization training and probing cards for a language development program (Fig. 3-3). These cards are to be returned to the original teacher on a predetermined regular basis. When the child reaches criterion with both generalization trainers in both settings, probing identical to that just described must be done to determine whether the child has generalized his newly acquired behaviors to settings, people, and tasks *where no training has occurred.*

HOW TO ELIMINATE INAPPROPRIATE BEHAVIORS

When the emphasis is on establishing appropriate behaviors, there are considerably less inappropriate behaviors because they are not being reinforced (taught). There are very few academic settings so ideal, however, that inappropriate behaviors are *never* reinforced and therefore strengthened. Furthermore, there are no academic settings that do not have some students coming into them who have some or many inappropriate behaviors. Therefore teachers must be apprised of procedures that will weaken or eliminate behaviors as well as those which will strengthen behaviors. Differential reinforcement of other behaviors (DRO), extinction, and punishment are the general behavior-weakening procedures discussed here. Along with these, response cost and time-out, which are forms of punishment, and satiation and stimulus change will also be discussed.

Before going into each of these behavior-weakening procedures, it may be desirable to consider some of the reasons that teachers wish to weaken or eliminate behaviors and then to determine which behaviors most ethically should be weakened or eliminated. Once inappropriate behaviors present themselves, teachers feel a responsibility to do something about them, particularly when they interfere with learning. A student who spends a good portion of his time rocking back and forth, crying, or sleeping is not functioning in an optimal manner in a classroom. Neither is the student who does not attend or who does not follow instructions. These are behaviors that seriously interfere with the student learning. Screaming, crying loudly, fighting, grabbing materials from other students are behaviors that interfere with the learning of every student in the classroom.

The teacher has the responsibility of determining how inappropriate the behavior is. Does it warrant changing? Occasionally considerable time is spent modifying behaviors that are personally distressing to the teacher but may not actually interfere with learning. General appearance is one example of this. Does a student who wears a tie learn better than one who wears cutoffs? Does a student with neatly trimmed hair learn better than one whose hair grows past the middle of his back?

There are instances where it may be more appropriate to modify the teacher's attitudes than the child's behavior. Bernal, Williams, Miller, and Reagor (1972) investigated a situation in which a parent reported that her child was disobedient and hyperactive. The investigators found the child was acting quite normally, but his mother was imposing undue restrictions on him and was issuing commands at the rate of up to nearly 300 in an hour. The mother, not the child, was behaving deviantly.

After a careful analysis of the situation, the teacher has to determine to her own satisfaction which behaviors interfere the most with learning. Initially she has to identify the behavior she wants to weaken or eliminate. Then she has to determine whether she will use one of the behavior-weakening procedures or whether she will reinforce behaviors that are incompatible with the inappropriate behavior. The choices are differential reinforcement of other behaviors, extinction, or some punishment procedure.

Differential reinforcement of other behavior (DRO)

Differential reinforcement of other behavior is a procedure that involves reinforcing any behavior *except* the target behavior to be weakened or eliminated. The target behavior is placed on extinction, and behavioral alternatives are reinforced.

There are two forms of DRO. One is a method using reinforcement procedures to strengthen a behavior that is incompatible with the inappropriate behavior you wish to weaken. At the same time, the inappropriate behavior is placed on extinction and is *never* followed by a reinforcer. For example, if a student is reinforced for sitting at his desk and is ignored completely when he is not sitting at his desk, out-of-seat behavior is necessarily decreased or weakened. Since this is basically positive reinforcement, it is one of the most highly recommended behavior-weakening procedures for teachers. There is little, if anything, in this system that parents, principals, or others could object to. It also avoids the undesirable side effects of some of the other behavior-weakening procedures. Almost the entire segment of this chapter on establishing appropriate behaviors could also be incorporated in this part; remember that you are placing inappropriate behaviors on extinction (ignoring them completely) while reinforcing appropriate behaviors.

Examples of such differential reinforcement of other behaviors (DRO) that are incompatible with inappropriate behaviors are numerous. Teachers engage in many automatically without having to understand the principles behind them or the technical implications or explanations of what they are doing. For example, if a student pinches others at a very high rate instead of greeting them, teaching (reinforcing) the child to shake hands properly when meeting someone is an appropriate response that is incompatible with pinching. Using eating utensils properly at mealtime is incompatible with shoving food into the mouth with both hands. However, it is very unlikely that these same teachers would automatically place the inappropriate behaviors on extinction by completely ignoring them.

The second DRO procedure involves reinforcing *any* response other than the one specific response you wish to weaken. This method is particularly recommended in the absence of a well-defined incompatible response. Normally it is more desirable to use the first DRO procedure described because you are accomplishing two objectives at the same time, that is, weakening or eliminating an inappropriate behavior by placing it on extinction and strengthening an appropriate behavior that is incompatible with the inappropriate behavior, thus serving to weaken the inappropriate behavior even further. Research suggests that there is a greater suppression of inappropriate behavior when an alternative appropriate behavior is reinforced (Azrin and Holz, 1966; Herman and Azrin, 1964; Holz, Azrin, and Ayllon, 1963). This may be because the child is provided an alternative response that can earn reinforcers for him. However, when such an alternative appropriate behavior cannot be identified, reinforcing *any* other behavior is recommended because the child's net rate of reinforcement should not be reduced. In some instances he may even receive more reinforcers than he did before the procedure was implemented. Since the child is not being deprived of his usual reinforcers, he is less likely to protest against this procedure than he might be to other behavior weakening procedures, particularly punishment or extinction used alone.

Extinction

Extinction is a procedure that involves no longer presenting a reinforcing stimulus following a response that you wish to weaken, decrease the rate of, or eliminate. The child is not physically restrained or in any way prevented from emitting the behavior; but when he does emit the behavior, he does not receive a reinforcer.

Extinction is a procedure that has received a great deal of attention and enthusiasm from educators. On the surface it seems ideal because *nothing* happens, especially nothing aversive happens to the child as might occur in a punishment procedure. In practice, an extinction procedure is extremely difficult to implement. Not only the teacher, but *everyone* who encounters the child must place the target behavior on extinction. It is almost impossible to establish this necessary control over the child's entire environment. For example, as a teacher you have decided that you are going to place Johnny's crying on extinction. You are fortunate enough to have an aide, who is informed about the procedure and is agreeable and helpful in its implementation. The other students in the classroom are told not to pay any attention to Johnny when he cries, and they, too, are very cooperative. However, Susan's mother comes to pick Susan up for a dental appointment and, seeing Johnny crying, immediately goes over to him to console him and find out why nobody is attending to the poor child's needs.

Extinction alone is additionally difficult because reinforcement can be extremely subtle. Frequently just a glance, a moment's eye contact, physical nearness, etc. are strong enough reinforcers to strengthen or at least maintain some behaviors. It is almost impossible to eliminate such subtle reinforcers.

It is also very difficult to use extinction procedures when the behavior has been maintained on an unpredictable intermittent reinforcement schedule. As you will recall, unpredictable intermittent reinforcement is extremely resistant to extinction. It is the reinforcement schedule you want to use for those behaviors that you do not want to extinguish. When the response that you wish to weaken has been maintained

on a CRF schedule, the extinction procedure is most effective (Ferster and Skinner, 1957).

The teacher who determines (1) that she has adequate control of the environment and (2) that the behavior is one that will be responsive to extinction procedures because of its reinforcement history (CRF or nearly CRF) must also be alerted to one of the side effects of extinction. There is frequently an *increase* in the rate of the behavior or the behavior is *strengthened* at the beginning of extinction. This is called "extinction burst" and is only temporary if everyone in the child's environment persists in keeping the inappropriate behavior on extinction. However, remembering the effects of reinforcing a behavior on an unpredictable intermittent reinforcement schedule, it is obvious that one person (such as Susan's mother) reinforcing on what is now *a very lean unpredictable intermittent reinforcement schedule* makes the behavior even more resistant to extinction.

If you decide to implement an extinction procedure, do not discontinue it during the extinction burst because it does not seem to be working. This only strengthens the behavior. You must persist in the extinction procedure until you have succeeded in weakening the behavior to whatever level you have previously determined was an acceptable level or have eliminated the behavior completely.

Extinction should not be used to weaken or eliminate dangerous responses, such as hitting, biting, kicking, head banging, setting fires, climbing on the window ledge of the third floor. Such behaviors cannot be ignored but must be stopped immediately (Risley, 1968; Tate and Baroff, 1966).

Punishment

Punishment consists of delivering an aversive stimulus or removing a reinforcing stimulus contingent on a response that you wish to weaken, reduce the rate of, or eliminate. Removing a reinforcer is usually called response cost and is generally more desirable to use in a school setting than is an aversive stimulus.

Response cost. Response cost works on the same principle as fines do in the society at large. If you are caught speeding, the traffic court will impose a particular fine. If a student kicks someone sitting next to him, the teacher takes away so many tokens, points, etc. It is obvious that response cost could not be implemented if the reinforcers were consumed. Consequently, conditioned reinforcers such as tokens, points, or money are preferable to edible reinforcers, which are normally consumed immediately on delivery (Kazdin, 1972; Weiner, 1962).

Taking away privileges is also a form of response cost. Teachers routinely have deprived a student of recess or of leading the pledge of allegiance, etc. for being late for school or talking out of turn. Parents typically tell their children they cannot go to the movies or watch television because they told a lie or were involved in a fight. There is little research to indicate how effective this kind of response cost has been or the precise procedures that were used (Kazdin, 1972). If you decide to use this procedure, be especially careful to keep accurate data and manage the contingencies carefully. Usually, however, response cost has been maintained in token economy programs (Atthowe and Krasner, 1968; Phillips, Phillips, Fixsen, and Wolf, 1971).

Most studies relating to response cost reveal no undesirable side effects (Kazdin, 1972; Leitenberg, 1965). In studies that have suggested anecdotal undesirable side effects (Boren and Colman, 1970; Meichenbaum, Bowers, and Ross, 1968), the subjects were institutionalized delinquent soldiers and adolescent delinquent girls, respectively, who, in all probability, were considerably more sophisticated than TMR students in their ability to control others through threats or coercive techniques and to manipulate their environments in such a way that only positive reinforcement procedures could be implemented. According to Azrin and Holz (1966), as cited by

Gelfand and Hartmann (1975:189), effective response cost programs require the following:

1. Some level of positive reinforcement is administered to the child (so that you will have something to withdraw if necessary).
2. You have established the value of and are using conditioned reinforcers such as tokens, points, or money.

When you have met these two requirements, you must decide the exact cost to be attached to each instance and each type of inappropriate behavior. If such a decision is made on the spur of the moment when you are angry, there is a tendency to overcharge the student (Gelfand and Hartmann, 1975). Under these circumstances, the cost may become too high and the reinforcement rate too low, which causes the student to stop working.

The following word of caution from Gelfand and Hartmann (1975:190) summarizes the use of response cost:

Beware of relying too heavily on fines. It is often easier to think of how to fine a child than of how to shape a desired competing behavior. Be very sparing in the fines assessed or the whole learning situation will become aversive for the child and he will attempt to escape it. The police and courts make heavy use of fines—consider how popular they are.

Time-out. Time-out is another punishment procedure that can be used to weaken, reduce the rate of, or eliminate the behavior it is contingent on. Time-out is the process of removing or withdrawing all reinforcers for a period of time following a response you wish to weaken. Time-out makes positive reinforcement unavailable and is therefore associated with extinction. It differs from extinction in that no positive reinforcement is available for any behavior; in an extinction procedure, however, only the inappropriate behavior does not receive reinforcement.

Time-out is particularly effective when it is used simultaneously with the reinforcement of appropriate behaviors. This is similar to differential reinforcement of other behavior. However, instead of placing the inappropriate behavior on extinction, you remove the possibility of any positive reinforcement for a period of time. For example, if you place a student in a time-out area contingent on quarreling with other students, but he earns reinforcers for each pleasant interaction he has with his classmates, the quarrel-contingent time-out weakens his quarreling behavior and the pleasant-peer–interaction-contingent reinforcer strengthens that interaction behavior.

Time-out from positive reinforcement is particularly recommended when it is difficult to identify or isolate the reinforcer that is strengthening the inappropriate behavior. Under these circumstances, isolation or time-out effectively eliminates whatever reinforcer may be maintaining or strengthening the behavior because all reinforcers are eliminated, just as all behaviors are on time-out from reinforcement.

Again, teachers are cautioned to keep and observe their data carefully. There may be the rare child who responds to time-out as a reinforcer, that is, the behavior that it is contingent on is strengthened rather than weakened. Considering the temperaments of some exceptional students, it does not stretch the imagination far to understand that being alone for a period of time could serve as a reinforcer rather than as a form of punishment. Teachers must also use discretion in selecting a time-out or isolation area. A busy hallway, or anyplace where there are students or others who will in any way attend to the student placed in time-out, may provide him many positive reinforcers rather than eliminate all forms of positive reinforcement. It is also important to remove everything from the time-out area that can be broken or otherwise destroyed. In theory, time-out seems to be a very calm, matter-of-fact procedure. But, in fact, most children who are placed in time-out become extremely angry and will break or destroy anything they can get their hands or feet on.

It is just as important that the time-out area not be in any way frightening, stiffling, dark, etc. This is a punishment procedure that removes the child from positive reinforcement. It is not intended to present him with a frightening stimulus.

Time-out duration can be difficult to determine. Ideally, it should be left up to the child. He is told to come out when he thinks he can behave. Unfortunately, the students who are this cooperative are not usually the ones placed in time-out. As a rule, the time would range from 30 seconds to 10 or 15 minutes. At all times select the briefest time-out period possible. A word of caution also on when to remove a child from time-out. Removing a person from a situation which that person considers aversive will strengthen or increase the rate of the response it follows. Consequently, do not remove a child who is screaming, kicking, pounding on the door, etc. Removal should be contingent on an appropriate response from the child, such as being quiet for 3 to 60 seconds (Bostow and Bailey, 1969; Hawkins, Peterson, Schweid, and Bijou, 1966; Wolf, Risley, Johnston, Harris, and Allen, 1967).

As a teacher, you should be as calm and matter-of-fact as possible when taking a student to a time-out area. Under no circumstances should you scold, shove, or otherwise verbally or physically punish a student. Neither should you give the student lengthy explanations about why he is going to time-out nor should you argue with the student. Tell him simply and clearly what he did that resulted in your decision to take him to the time-out area, and then take him. Leave the area immediately. Hovering near the door of the time-out area tends to reinforce the student's protests. It is also advisable to invest in a kitchen timer if you use time-out procedures, since it is easy to become involved with the other students in the classroom and forget the child who is in time-out. When you remove the child, do not exhibit any negative behavior toward him. The time-out is over and now you will want to return to normal classroom activities and pleasant student-teacher interactions as quickly as possible.

Presenting an aversive stimulus. This procedure involves presenting either unconditioned or conditioned aversive stimuli contingent on a response that you wish to weaken or eliminate. An unconditioned aversive stimulus is one that is physically painful or frightening, such as a slap or a loud noise. A conditioned aversive stimulus is a previously neutral stimulus that immediately follows or has been paired with an aversive stimulus, until it takes on the qualities of the aversive stimulus. The best examples of conditioned aversive stimuli are the words, gestures, tone of voice, and facial expressions that usually accompany spankings, beatings, or other pain-producing stimuli. Punishment can range from saying, "No!" to beating a child severely. Under no circumstances should the latter occur in a school setting.

According to Becker, Engelmann, and Thomas (1971), there are two circumstances in which punishment may be required because reinforcement approaches are likely to fail: (1) whenever a certain type of behavior is so frequent that there is little or no incompatible behavior to reinforce and (2) whenever the inappropriate behavior is so intense that the child or others are physically endangered. Whenever a teacher plans a punishment procedure, she must keep the following rules in mind (Becker, Engelmann, and Thomas, 1971:171):

1. Punish immediately after the child emits the inappropriate behavior.
2. Use withdrawal or removal of reinforcers whenever possible.
3. Use a warning signal (usually words).
4. Carry out the punishment in a calm, matter-of-fact manner. (Do not use the occasion to vent your own frustration or anger.)
5. Reinforce behavior that is incompatible with the inappropriate behavior that is being punished.
6. Be consistent. The inappropriate behavior must never be reinforced.

Murdock and Hartmann (1975:5) described mild punishment procedures that could be used, if necessary, to eliminate nonattending behaviors:

1. If the child is not attending, verbalize instructions simply and clearly. Model the desired behavior. Physically place the child in the appropriate position and assist him in going through the desired behavior by guiding his arm toward his body or otherwise demonstrating precisely what it is that you want him to do. Caution should be used here to ensure that you are not reinforcing nonattending behaviors by talking to or physically handling the child. Keep accurate data to determine whether attending behavior is increasing with fewer prompts being required. If not, the following procedures should be used.
2. Withdraw your attention from the child. Do not attend to him until he has been attending appropriately for 3 seconds.
3. Take a reinforcer yourself, pairing it with the same social praise you would use with the child, e.g., "Very good sitting."
4. If the child exhibits hand-in-mouth, hands-over-eyes, grabbing behaviors, etc., establish arm-folding or hands-in-lap behaviors before proceeding with the program. This may be done by modeling the behavior and reinforcing the child's correct imitation. It may be necessary to physically move the child through the arm-folding or hands-in-lap behaviors, gradually fading out the physical prompting and reinforcing the child for each approximation to the desired behavior.
5. If the child emits a high rate of a specific inappropriate behavior, present an aversive stimulus immediately following that inappropriate behavior, e.g., loudly verbalize, "No!" This may be paired with a sharp rap on the table, desk, or chair or a loud handclap.

Note that only when all else fails is the most mildly aversive stimulus ("No!" possibly paired with a loud noise) presented to the student. Teachers should plan any punishment procedures sequentially so that the least punitive procedure that proves effective in weakening or eliminating the undesirable behavior is the one used.

There are undesirable side effects from punishment procedures that involve presenting aversive stimuli. They may produce disruptive emotional behaviors; they may have a general suppressing effect on all behaviors, not just the inappropriate behavior they were intended to suppress; they may result in escape or avoidance behaviors from the punishing agent and/or the punishment setting; or they may result in aggression toward the punishment agent (Azrin and Holz, 1966). Also, the person who administers the punishment sets a model for aggression (Bandura, 1962).

On the other hand, if anyone asks, "Does punishment work?" the unequivocal answer is "Yes." When the appropriate behavior poses a serious problem and all positive behavior modification procedures have failed, then some aversive procedure is warranted. Becker, Engelmann, and Thomas (1971) point out that, "When the long-term effects of using punishment are far more beneficial than the effects of not using it, the moral person will do what is best for the child and use punishment." It is also highly desirable that the punishment procedure eliminate the inappropriate behavior immediately so that the punishment can be discontinued as quickly as possible. See Azrin and Holz (1966) for further suggestions to follow should you determine it necessary to implement punishment procedure.

Satiation

Satiation is a method that involves presenting too much of a "good" thing, which results in weakening or eliminating inappropriate behaviors. Allyon (1963) presented a satiation procedure that he used with a psychotic woman who hoarded towels. He gave her so many towels that they lost their reinforcing properties. If you have a student who hoards crayons, pencils, paper, etc., you may provide these objects to such a degree that the student becomes totally sated. When this occurs, the stimuli that were once reinforcing (crayons, pencils, etc.) lose their reinforcing properties and become neutral or even aversive stimuli.

Satiation is also an effective technique when the particular reinforcer used by the child is not appropriate for his age, sex, etc. For example, for a 10-year-old child who sucks his thumb, the thumb-sucking is an inappropriate reinforcer because it subjects him to ridicule from his peers. If the child is required to suck his thumb for longer and longer periods of time, he will probably satiate on the thumb-sucking.

Gelfand and Hartmann (1975:192-193) give the following suggestions for implementing a satiation procedure based on the work of Ayllon (1963):

1. Remove any measures that may have been in effect to attempt to restrict the child's access to the reinforcer. If the stimulus has been hidden, you may place it out in full view; if you have been confiscating it, stop.

2. Offer the item frequently and repeatedly to the child. You may have to follow this procedure for a matter of days or weeks. Ayllon (1963) presented his towel hoarder with up to 60 towels a day for a period of three weeks.

3. Continue to supply the item to the child until he rejects it. It would be safest to continue until you encounter emphatic and repeated rejection of the former reinforcer. Good evidence of the time to stop is that the child avoids or attempts to escape from the stimulus.

Satiation does not weaken or eliminate behaviors as quickly as punishment. Consequently, if the inappropriate behavior is one that must be eliminated immediately, do not use satiation procedures. Satiation is also somewhat limited in that it is possible to recover from satiation, just as hunger returns shortly before time for the next meal.

Stimulus change

Sometimes it is possible to weaken or eliminate inappropriate behaviors simply by removing the discriminative stimuli (S^D's) associated with the response. This is a fairly common procedure used by teachers. If John and Jim spend most of their time talking to each other whenever they are together, simply rearrange the environment so that they are not sitting near each other when their talking would interfere with the ongoing academic activities. If watching television is an S^D for one of your overweight students to consume all the edibles in sight, reduce the amount of time that the child can watch television and place the edibles out of sight.

In these examples, changing the discriminative stimulus was quite simple. However, if the reinforcement contingency remains in effect after the stimulus change, the inappropriate response rate will probably recover (Azrin and Holz, 1966). As with other procedures that can be used to weaken or eliminate behaviors, this procedure is most effective when paired with reinforcing or strengthening a desirable alternative response.

SUMMARY

This chapter has presented an overview of behavior modification principles and their application to educating the trainable mentally retarded child. The primary purpose of teaching should be to teach students desirable social and academic behaviors rather than to focus on eliminating inappropriate behaviors. It is only reasonable that, as appropriate behaviors increase, inappropriate behaviors decrease. This is particularly true when the appropriate behaviors are incompatible with the inappropriate behaviors.

Reinforcement increases or strengthens any behavior it follows. There are two kinds of reinforcers: (1) unconditioned reinforcers such as food and water and (2) conditioned reinforcers. Most human behavior is controlled by conditioned reinforcers. Teachers should select reinforcers that are optimally effective; that is, the reinforcers should be varied and novel enough that the students learn efficiently without satiating readily, and the reinforcers should interfere as little as possible with the ongoing teaching.

If the response that you wish to reinforce (teach) is not presently in the student's behavioral repertoire, you should not simply wait for it to appear so that you can reinforce it. Modeling, prompting, and shaping are procedures teachers can use to help the student emit the desired response for the first time so that it can be reinforced and consequently strengthened. Modeling involves showing the student what it is that you want him to do so that he can imitate the behavior. You can also prompt him to emit a new behavior by using those responses which he has in his repertoire. It is recommended that you administer visual prompts to help train auditory skills and auditory prompts to help train visual skills. If modeling and/or prompting do not help the child produce the desired response, then it is necessary to shape the response by using differential reinforcement for successive approximations of the target behavior. Shaping is much slower and more laborious and should not be used unless other procedures have failed.

Poor contingency management is possibly the most common cause of failure in behavior modification programs. You must define precisely what behaviors you wish to strengthen or weaken, what procedures you are going to use, what your criteria for success are, and how you are going to record your data. Keeping accurate data is essential in any behavior modification program. It is necessary to determine whether the planned procedures are effective. When things go as planned, and they will if they are planned carefully, the data provide excellent reinforcement for the teacher.

When it is necessary to eliminate inappropriate behaviors, this can be accomplished through differential reinforcement of other behaviors (DRO), extinction, or punishment procedures. Differential reinforcement of other behaviors is the most desirable procedure to use because, basically, it involves reinforcing appropriate behaviors while ignoring inappropriate behaviors. The effort is still in the direction of teaching a student acceptable behaviors rather than punishing him for unacceptable behaviors.

Punishment can involve presenting an aversive stimulus or removing a reinforcer. Delivering an aversive stimulus is fraught with many dangers including, but not limited to, angry students, parents, and administrators, as well as the possibility of lawsuits as a consequence of their anger. Furthermore, people who are punished try to escape from or avoid the person who punishes and the setting where the punishment occurs. The person who punishes also presents a model for aggressive behaviors. If it is determined that the inappropriate behavior warrants a punishment procedure, it is preferable to remove a reinforcer, assuming that there are enough reinforcers in the student's academic environment that something can be taken away. This procedure is called response cost and is very similar to fines imposed in the world at large. Time-out is another punishment procedure that involves removing positive reinforcement. In this process, the possibility of any positive reinforcement whatsoever is removed.

Extinction is also a method that weakens behaviors, but it is much simpler in theory than in practice. It requires behavior that has been on a CRF or near CRF reinforcement schedule, an incredible amount of control over the student's environment, and behaviors that do not need to be weakened quickly. If these conditions are met, extinction can be used effectively to weaken or reduce the rate of inappropriate behaviors.

In some instances behavior can be weakened or even eliminated by simply presenting an overabundance of it, as Ayllon (1963) did with the psychotic and her towels. This procedure is called satiation. Sometimes behaviors can be diminished or removed by simply changing the environment so that the discriminative stimuli (S^D's) are no longer presented, just as appropriate behaviors can be evoked by presenting the S^D's.

There is no doubt that behavior modification principles can be successfully applied to the training of TMR students. Some of the finest success stories have come from experimental investigations with moderately to severely retarded individuals. Behavior modification is simple in theory but complex in practice. The teacher must be able to describe precisely what behaviors she wishes to modify, ascertain which behavior-strengthening or behavior-weakening procedures are the most appropriate, decide on the reinforcers and the reinforcer delivery sys-

tem, and determine the data recording procedures. She must also be committed to the program, at least as committed as any experimental investigator would be. A psychologist who is willing and able to assist the teacher on site should be involved in implementing any extensive behavior modification program. A psychologist should be available to monitor and follow up on such programs until the teacher has the competence to carry out the programs on her own, knowing at all times that she can consult with the psychologist whenever she feels the need to do so.

REFERENCES AND SUGGESTED READINGS

Atthowe, J. M., Jr., and Krasner, L.: Preliminary report on the application of contingent reinforcement procedures: token economy on a "chronic" psychiatric ward, J. Abnorm. Psychol. 73:37-43, 1968.

Ayllon, T.: Intensive treatment of psychotic behavior by stimulus satiation and food reinforcement, Behav. Res. Ther. 1:33-61, 1963.

Azrin, N. H., and Holz, W. C.: Punishment. In Honig, W., editor: Operant behavior: areas of research and application, New York, 1966, Appleton-Century-Crofts.

Baer, D. M., Peterson, R. F., and Sherman, J. A.: The development of imitation by reinforcing behavioral similarity to a model, J. Exp. Anal. Behav. 10:405-416, 1967.

Bandura, A.: Punishment revisited, J. Consult. Clin. Psychol. 26:298-301, 1962.

Bandura, A.: Principles of behavior modification, New York, 1969, Holt, Rinehart & Winston.

Barton, E. S., Guess, D. G., Garcia, E., and Baer, D. M.: Improvement of retardates' mealtime behaviors by time-out procedures using multiple baseline techniques, J. Appl. Behav. Anal. 3:77-84, 1970.

Becker, W. C., Engelmann, S., and Thomas, D. R.: Teaching: a course in applied psychology, Chicago, 1971, Science Research Associates, Inc.

Bernal, M. E., Williams, D. E., Miller, W. H., and Reagor, P. A.: The use of videotape feedback and operant learning principles in management of deviant children. In Rubin, R., et al., editors: Advances in behavior therapy, New York, 1972, Academic Press.

Bijou, S. W., Peterson, R. F., and Ault, M. H.: A method to integrate descriptive and experimental field studies at the level of data and empirical concepts, J. Appl. Behav. Anal. 1:175-191, 1968.

Boren, J. J., and Colman, A. D.: Some experiments on reinforcement principles within a psychiatric ward for delinquent soldiers, J. Appl. Behav. Anal. 3:29-37, 1970.

Bostow, D. E., and Bailey, J. B.: Modification of severe disruptive and aggressive behavior using brief time-out and reinforcement procedures, J. Exp. Anal. Behav. 2:31-37, 1969.

Brown, L.: Instructional programs for trainable-level retarded students. In Mann, L., and Sabatino, D. A., editors: The first review of special education, vol. 2, Philadelphia, 1973, JSE Press.

Ferster, C. B., and Skinner, B. F.: Schedule of reinforcement, New York, 1957, Appleton-Century-Crofts.

Garcia, E., Baer, D. M., and Firestone, I.: The development of generalized imitation within topographically determined boundaries, J. Appl. Behav. Anal. 4:101-112, 1971.

Garcia, E., Guess, E., and Byrnes, J.: Development of syntax in a retarded girl using procedures of imitation, reinforcement and modeling, J. Appl. Behav. Anal. 2:299-310, 1973.

Gelfand, D. M., and Hartmann, D. P.: Child behavior analysis and therapy, New York, 1975, Pergamon Press, Inc.

Guess, D., Sailor, W., Rutherford, G., and Baer, D. M.: An experimental analysis of linguistic development: the productive use of the plural morpheme, J. Appl. Behav. Anal. 1:297-306, 1968.

Hall, R. V., Lund, D., and Jackson, D.: Effects of teacher attention on study behavior, J. Appl. Behav. Anal. 1:1-12, 1968.

Haring, N. G., and Phillips, E. L.: Analysis and modification of classroom behavior, Englewood Cliffs, N.J., 1972, Prentice-Hall, Inc.

Hawkins, R. P., et al.: Behavior therapy in the home: amelioration of problem parent-child relations with the parent in a therapeutic role, J. Exp. Child Psychol. 4:99-107, 1966.

Herman, R. Z., and Azrin, N. H.: Punishment by noise in an alternative response situation, J. Exp. Anal. Behav. 7:185-188, 1964.

Holz, W. C., Azrin, N. H., and Ayllon, T.: Elimination of behavior of mental patients by response-produced extinction, J. Exp. Anal. Behav. 6:407-412, 1963.

Hoschouer, R. L., Hardman, M. L., and Smith, A. G.: Academic programs for the trainable mentally retarded, paper presented at the Southern Nevada Council for Exceptional Children, Las Vegas, Nev., March 30, 1974.

Kazdin, A. E.: Response cost: the removal of conditioned reinforcers for therapeutic change, Behav. Ther. 3:533-546, 1972.

Leitenberg, H.: Is time-out from positive reinforcement an aversive event? A review of the experimental evidence, Psychol. Bull. 64:428-444, 1965.

Meichenbaum, D. H., Bowers, K., and Ross, R.

R.: Modification of classroom behavior of institutionalized female adolescent offenders, Behav. Res. Ther. 6:343-353, 1968.

Murdock, J. Y.: Reinforcement therapy applied to the speech and language training of Down's syndrome subjects, unpublished master's thesis, University of Utah, 1969.

Murdock, J. Y.: Language program for nonverbal 4-year-old female: implications for reinforcer probing, unpublished manuscript, University of Utah, 1970.

Murdock, J. Y., and Hartmann, B.: A language development program: imitative gestures to basic syntactic structures, Salt Lake City, 1975, Word Making Productions.

O'Brien, F., Azrin, N. H., and Bugle, C.: Training profoundly retarded children to stop crawling, J. Appl. Behav. Anal. 5:131-137, 1972.

O'Leary, K. D., Becker, W. C., Evans, M. B., and Saudargas, R. A.: A token reinforcement program in a public school: a replication and systematic analysis, J. Appl. Behav. Anal. 2: 3-13, 1969.

Phillips, E. L., Phillips, E. A., Fixsen, D. L., and Wolf, M. N.: Achievement place: modification of the behaviors of pre-delinquent boys within a token economy, J. Appl. Behav. Anal. 4:45-59, 1971.

Premack, D.: Reinforcement theory. In Levine, D., editor: Nebraska symposium on motivation 1965, Lincoln, 1965, University of Nebraska Press.

Reynolds, N. J., and Risley, T. R.: The role of social and material reinforcers in increasing talking of a disadvantaged preschool child, J. Appl. Behav. Anal. 1:253-262, 1968.

Risley, T. R.: The effects and side effects of punishing the autistic behaviors of a deviant child, J. Appl. Behav. Anal. 1:21-34, 1968.

Skiba, E. A., Pettigrew, L. E., and Alden, S. E.: A behavioral approach to the control of thumb-sucking in the classroom, J. Appl. Behav. Anal. 4:121-125, 1971.

Sloane, H. N., Johnston, M. K., and Harris, F. R.: Remedial procedures for teaching verbal behavior to speech deficient or defective young children. In Sloane, H. N., and MacAulay, B. D., editors: Operant procedures in remedial speech and language training, Boston, 1968, Houghton Mifflin Co.

Sloane, H. N., and MacAulay, B. D.: Teaching and the environmental control of verbal behavior. In Sloane, H. N., and MacAulay, editors: Operant procedures in remedial speech and language training, Boston, 1968, Houghton Mifflin Co.

Tate, B. G., and Baroff, G. S.: Aversive control of self-injurious behavior in a psychotic boy, Behav. Res. Ther. 4:281-287, 1966.

Walker, H. M., and Buckley, N. K.: The use of

positive reinforcement in conditioning attending behavior, J. Appl. Behav. Anal. 1:245-250, 1968.

Weiner, H.: Some effects of response cost upon human operant behavior, J. Exper. Anal. Behav. 5:201-208, 1962.

Wheeler, A. J., and Sulzer, B.: Operant training and generalization of a verbal response form in a speech-deficient child, J. Appl. Behav. Anal. 3:139-147, 1970.

Wolf, M. M., Risley, R. T., Johnston, M., Harris, F., and Allen, E.: Applications of operant conditioning procedures to the behavior problems of an autistic child: a follow-up and extension, Behav. Res. Ther. 5:103-111, 1967.

SECTION TWO

CURRICULUM

This section is devoted to content and implementation of the seven major curriculum areas of instruction for the TMR. The curriculum areas include (1) self-care skills, (2) basic communication skills, (3) social skills, (4) perceptual-motor and physical education skills, (5) functional academic skills, (6) recreation and leisure time skills, and (7) economic usefulness and vocational skills.

For teaching TMRs the skills of the seven curriculum areas in Chapters 4 through 10, the following guidelines are offered as recommended procedure: (1) every student should be assessed in each curriculum area to determine where instruction should begin; (2) instruction should be structured, systematic and individualized as much as possible; (3) behavior modification principles and procedures described in Chapter 3 should be utilized; (4) student progress for each curriculum area should be carefully charted; and (5) a parent education and training program should be initiated in conjunction with the educational program.

Since this book is written primarily for teachers or teachers in training (those who must operate within the realities of curriculum implementation), the following considerations are offered.

There may sometimes be overlap in the skills to be taught in the seven basic curriculum areas because no area is so discrete in its skills that it excludes components of other curriculum areas. Development of language or social skills, for example, may be taught at certain scheduled time periods, but these same skills must also receive attention, reinforcement, and consideration in other curriculum areas.

General goals for the various curriculum areas are offered, but not by level. Instructional objectives for each curriculum area must remain specific to the individual and not his level of placement (e.g., primary, intermediate). It becomes inappropriate and unrealistic to relegate *specific* skills to a level of instruction, since what is taught by a teacher at a given level is dependent on the functioning level of the behaviors of each student she must teach.

CHAPTER 4

DEVELOPING SELF-CARE SKILLS

Many school districts are now assuming full responsibility for developing the self-care and personal health skills of TMR students, since state laws mandate education and training to begin at the age of 3 or 4 years. Most TMRs have not acquired these skills by this early age, and preschool programs as well as primary level programs should spend considerable time in developing these skills, about 35% and 20%, respectively. Also, with the trend for TMRs to remain in the home rather than in institutions, the school should assist in teaching any skill that would allow the retardate to attain the highest possible degree of normalcy and independence. By developing the self-care and personal health skills, the TMR and his parents can lead a happier and more satisfying home life.

The basic self-care skills include those related to feeding (eating and drinking), toileting, clothing (undressing and dressing, unfastening and fastening, and appropriateness, care, and use of clothing), personal health and grooming, as well as safety and first aid.

NORMAL DEVELOPMENT OF SELF-CARE SKILLS

Self-care skills are some of the earliest developed human skills, and in this area

parents may serve as teachers. Fostering development and teaching these skills to a normal child is usually achieved with a minimum of difficulty because of the child's rapid development and ease in learning. (See Table 4-1 for selected self-care skills and the ages at which they normally develop.) With the young TMR child's serious difficulties in learning, these self-care skills, which are often taken for granted, become a real challenge. A close working relationship with the parents is essential, since many of the skills will either be initiated in the home or be carried over into the home from the school. Parents of TMR children are usually eager to assist in the development of these skills but need help in knowing how and where to begin. One way to achieve this necessary harmonious relationship is by having regularly scheduled parent meetings and conferences. Meeting with parents individually allows topics to center on the individual needs of each couple, relative to training in the self-care area. Meeting with parents as a group allows them to interact and share ideas or successful techniques. Another less desirable, but sometimes necessary, means is sending periodic letters to the parents, describing the aims, goals, or skills being taught, explaining the prog-

Table 4-1. Developmental sequence of self-care skills related to feeding, clothing, toileting, and personal health

Age	Feeding	Clothing	Toileting	Personal Health
0 to 12 mo.	Finger feeds self Holds own bottle		Shows regular patterns in bladder and bowel elimination	
1 to 1½ yr.	Has discarded bottle Interested in helping to feed self Holds cup, will spill Grasps spoon and inserts into dish Poor filling and spilling is considerable	Cooperates in dressing by extending arm or leg	Indicates wet pants by pointing Cooperative toilet response for bowel movement	
1½ to 2 yr.	Fills spoon; difficulty inserting into mouth; some spilling	Can take off mittens, socks, cap Can unzip zippers Tries to unbutton Can remove shoes	Begins to indicate need for toileting (bowel and bladder) Requires assistance	Attempts to wash and dry hands
2 to 3 yr.	Holds small glass with one hand and drinks well Inserts spoon into mouth correctly Uses fork Gets drink unassisted	Helps pull up or push down pants Removes coat or dress Simple unbuttoning Tries to lace shoes; puts on shoes (often wrong foot) Will begin to choose clothes	Bowel control (some accidents) Bladder control during day Needs help with wiping	Washes and dries hands (neither very well) Attempts to brush teeth
3 to 4 yr.	Uses knife for spreading Likes to serve self Pours from pitcher	Undresses self Puts on major clothes (not always correct)	Goes to toilet by himself (occasional assistance)	Washes and dries hands fairly well Brushes teeth
4 to 5 yr.	Uses knife for cutting Social and talkative during meal	Able to dress and undress self without help Learns to lace shoes Can put away soiled clothes	Independence in toileting (flushing, wiping, clothing, washing) Full bladder and bowel control	Combs or brushes hair Can bathe self

ress of their child, and suggesting procedures or activities that can be utilized in the home to assist the school program.

Since rewards and reinforcement are such a major component of the teaching of self-care and personal health skills to TMRs, a simple diploma of achievement might be given when the student has successfully mastered a skill. The certificates serve as motivators and image builders. (See Fig. 4-1.)

Following are the major self-care skills to be developed in the TMR student:

A. Feeding
  1. Eating soft and solid finger foods
  2. Drinking
    a. From a cup
    b. From a glass
    c. With a straw
    d. From a fountain
  3. Eating
    a. With a spoon
    b. With a fork
    c. With a knife
B. Toileting
  1. Proper manipulation of clothes before and after toileting
  2. Bladder and bowel control (daytime)
  3. Bladder and bowel control (nighttime)
  4. Use of toilet tissue
  5. Flushing toilet
  6. Washing and drying hands
C. Clothing
  1. Undressing and dressing
    a. Socks (off, on)

Fig. 4-1. Certificate of achievement in the self-care area of curriculum.

b. Slip-on shoes or boots (off, on)
c. T-shirt or pull-on shirt (off, on)
d. Underwear (off, on)
e. Pull-on pants (off, on)
f. Slip-on dress (off, on)
g. Coat (off, on)
h. Cap or hat (off, on)
i. Mittens (off, on)
j. Gloves (off, on)
k. Slip (off, on)
l. Scarf (off, on)
m. Pajamas (off, on)
n. Bra (off, on)
2. Unfastening and fastening
   a. Unzips, zips
   b. Unsnaps, snaps
   c. Unbuttons, buttons
   d. Unbuckles, buckles
   e. Unlaces, laces
   f. Unhooks, hooks
   g. Unties, ties
3. Appropriateness, care, and use of clothing
   a. Appropriateness
      (1) Identifies appropriate clothing for weather
      (2) Identifies appropriate clothing for different sexes
      (3) Identifies own clothing
      (4) Identifies dress clothing
      (5) Identifies work clothing
      (6) Identifies appropriate sizes
      (7) Identifies coordinated clothing
   b. Care and use
      (1) Selects clean clothing
      (2) Adjusts clothing on body for neatness
      (3) Uses a clothes brush
      (4) Folds clothing
      (5) Hangs clothing on hook, hanger
      (6) Properly disposes of dirty clothes
      (7) Wipes shoes on mat when dirty
      (8) Polishes shoes
      (9) Uses umbrella

D. Personal health and grooming skills
   1. Hands
      a. Washes hands when needed
      b. Dries hands after washing (cloth, paper, blower)
      c. Uses soap or soap dispenser (liquid, powder)
      d. Cleans nails
      e. Uses emery board
      f. Uses fingernail clippers
      g. Applies and removes nail polish
   2. Nose
      a. Blows and wipes nose with handkerchief or tissue
   3. Teeth
      a. Brushes teeth
      b. Uses dental floss
   4. Hair
      a. Combs hair
      b. Brushes hair
      c. Uses hair dryer
      d. Puts hair in rollers
      e. Shampoos hair
   5. Face
      a. Washes and dries face
      b. Applies makeup (powder, lipstick)
   6. Skin
      a. Applies skin moisturizer
      b. Uses electric shaver (face, legs, underarms)
   7. Body
      a. Uses deodorant
      b. Bathes and showers independently
      c. Uses mouthwash
      d. Cares for self during menstruation
E. Safety and first aid
   1. Home and sheltered employment
      a. Recognizes containers that are poisonous
      b. Uses electrical devices safely
      c. Recognizes safety elements of fire or heat
      d. Identifies harmful or dangerous objects

e. Uses bathtub or shower safely
f. Properly disposes of plastic bags
g. Keeps stairways safe
h. Uses tools safely
2. School and recreation
a. Enters, exits, and rides school bus in safe manner
b. Uses safe practices around playground equipment (slides, swings)
c. Can cross street or intersection safely
d. Knows rules of safety for all recreational activities (e.g., swimming)
3. Care of simple injuries
a. Can apply antiseptic and creams
b. Can apply adhesive or gauze bandages
c. Can report or self-treat minor burns, animal and insect bites, small cuts, nosebleed

Some students can learn and master most skills in every area of self-care, whereas others will attain only a limited number at adulthood. The rate of attainment and ultimate level of achievement will depend on and be influenced by the degree of retardation, the presence of other handicaps (e.g., cerebral palsy), and the efforts of school and home.

In teaching new skills in the self-care area, one should make extensive use of the basic principles of behavior modification discussed in Chapter 3, especially the concepts of modeling, prompting, shaping, and fading. In teaching any of the skills, it is important to make the child understand exactly what you want him to do. Show him what you want, verbalize the task, assist him in doing it, and then immediately reward him for the attempt or task.

There has been some controversy over who makes the best teacher or trainer for self-care skills. Is it a college graduate, an aide, a volunteer, or the mother? Because an individual's position in life, education, or intelligence is unimportant in this area, the best instructor is one who possesses certain personality characteristics. According to Cassel and Colwell (1965), a successful instructor in the self-care area is one who:

1. Is able and willing to adjust to new situations
2. Is able to stay on schedule
3. Is consistent and even in temperament
4. Is able to get along with people
5. Speaks clearly and distinctly and can use gestures along with the spoken command
6. Is able to keep an objective attitude toward the child.

ASSESSMENT

A determination must be made of the skills or abilities the student possesses before actual instruction is initiated. The principal technique for assessment in this curriculum area include (1) rating scales or checklists (information obtained from observation or parent interviews), (2) selected sections of adaptive behavior scales, and (3) selected sections of formal instruments. Table 4-2 lists those scales, checklists, and instruments that may be utilized in assessing the TMR's self-care skills.

SKILLS RELATED TO FEEDING

Developing eating skills is an important part of the retarded child's early instructional program and is usually the first self-care skill to be mastered. The retarded child, as does the normal child, proceeds from total dependency to complete independence in dining skills and correlated behaviors. The objectives of the feeding program are to teach the basic physical coordination skills associated with finger feeding, drinking, and eating with utensils, as well as dining etiquette and appropriate behavior for various eating situations (e.g., cafeteria, picnic, party).

Good eating and drinking behavior may appear to be a simple self-care skill but when analyzed is actually a combination of many skills. The child who possesses good eating behavior must be able to enter the dining area, sit correctly, display only appropriate and relevant behavior during the meal, have the necessary physical skills, use correct utensils, and display appropriate manners for dining, such as placement of the noneating hand and use of a napkin.

Before you embark on teaching any developmental task related to feeding, the

Table 4-2. Examples of scales, checklists, and instruments for the assessment of self-care skills

Name of instrument	Sections of value	Publisher and date*
AAMD Adaptive Behavior Scale	Independent functioning (eating, toilet use, cleanliness, appearance, care of clothing, dressing and undressing)	AAMD, 1974
Balthazar Scale of Adaptive Behavior for the Profoundly and Severely Mentally Retarded	Eating-drinking, dressing-undressing, and toileting	Research Press Co., 1971
Cain-Levin Social Competency Scale	Personal care and mealtime skills	Consulting Psychologists Press, 1963
Louisiana Adaptive Behavior Scale	Self-help	Louisiana State Division of Mental Retardation, 1973
Skills Assessment for Trainable Mentally Retarded	Dressing, feeding, health	Georgia Division of Early Childhood and Special Education (no date)
TARC Assessment System	Self-help	Edmark Associates, 1974
T.M.R. Performance Profile for the Severely and Moderately Retarded	Self-care (bathroom and grooming dealing with food, clothing)	Reporting Service for Exceptional Children, 1970
Washington Guide to Promoting Development in the Young Child	Feeding skills, toilet training, dressing	University of Washington
Y.E.M.R. Performance Profile for the Young Moderately and Mildly Retarded	Self-help	Reporting Service for Exceptional Children, 1967

*A list of publishers and their addresses appears in Appendix A.

child must be ready to learn and the mother or teacher be willing and committed to the program. Readiness can best be determined by the pediatrician, nurse, and dentist. They will look at such factors as sucking and swallowing reflexes, physical skills (grasp, ability to hold the head up, upper extremity coordination), and mouth and teeth structures. If a child is not ready for any of these reasons, appropriate therapy should be undertaken by a physical therapist under the direction of a physician. Table 4-3 indicates methods of feeding, social and physical signs of readiness, form of food, and adaptations relating to feeding the retarded child. Also, activities to enhance feeding skills* follow:

1 to 3 months
1. Consider change in nipple or positioning if infant has difficulty in swallowing.
2. Pace feeding tempo to infant's needs.
3. Hold him in comfortable relaxed position while feeding.
4. Introduce solids, one kind at a time (use

*From The Washington Guide for Promoting Development in the Young Child, The University of Washington, Seattle.

small spoon, place food well back on infant's tongue).

4 to 8 months
1. Give finger foods to develop chewing, stimulate gums, and encourage hand-to-mouth motion (cubes of cheese, bananas, dry toast, bread crust, cookies).
2. Encourage upright supported position for feeding.
3. Promote bottle holding.
4. Introduce junior foods.

9 to 12 months
1. Bring child in high chair to table and include for part of or for entire meal with family.
2. Have child dry and in comfortable position, with trunk and feet supported.
3. Encourage self-help in feeding.
4. Offer a spoon when interest is indicated.
5. Introduce cup or glass with small amount of fluid.
6. Begin use of table foods.

13 to 18 months
1. Continue offering finger foods (wieners, sandwiches).
2. Use nontip dishes and cups. Dishes should have sides to make filling of spoon easy.
3. Give opportunity for self-feeding.
4. Provide fluids between meals rather than having child fill up on fluids at mealtime.

19 to 30 months
1. Encourage self-feeding with spoon.
2. Do not rush child.
3. Serve foods plainly but attractively.

Table 4-3. Development of feeding skills*

Method of feeding to be introduced	Social and physical signs of readiness	Form of food	Adaptations Social	Adaptations Positional	Equipment
Feeding by mouth					
Swallowing only	Child can swallow his saliva. Lip reflex may be present	Formula prescribed by doctor is offered by Breck feeder or by bottle with nipple with enlarged holes. Spoon feeding may be necessary	Feedings should be adapted to household routine as much as possible. More than one member of family should be taught to feed child. Child should be cuddled and talked to at intervals to promote his emotional developments	Child is held in a semireclining position; after feeding, he may be held upright to expel air from stomach. If child is too large to be held, he should be positioned in a semireclining position with body supported well	Breck feeder; bottle and nipple with enlarged holes; spoon
Sucking and swallowing	Child is able to suck his fingers or an object. He may be able to pull liquids from bottle by pressing action rather than true sucking. He can swallow saliva or water without difficulty	Prescribed formula is offered by bottle and nipple; holes of nipple may need to be enlarged. Feedings may gradually be thickened	Same as above		
Spoon feeding	Child is able to swallow formula easily; can swallow thickened formula from bottle. Opens mouth when spoon touches it; closes lips on spoon. Tongue may project as food is withdrawn. Manipulates food in mouth; smacks. Chokes at times	Strained food: fruits, vegatables, meats and custards	Child may join family for meals. May be put on schedule of three or four meals daily. Child's hand-to-mouth activity should be encouraged. Food should be placed where child can put fingers in it while being fed. His messiness should be accepted. Child should be told that he is eating	Child may be held on mother's lap with back to mother; mother has child grasp little finger of her hand, which holds spoon; mother conveys small portions of food to child's mouth; child thus learns hand-to-mouth activity that feeds him. When child can sit or be propped, mother sits at his right, slightly behind him and continues above technique until he can spoon-feed alone. Child's left or right hand may be restrained with mother's free hand; if child is right-handed, sit on left—if child is left-handed, sit on right	Large waterproof bib apron for mother and for child; newspapers on floor. Plate anchored with suction cup on bottom; 90-degree angle side-to-plate to facilitate child's effort to scoop. Chair to keep child in good anatomical position with feet braced. If child is clumsy or cerebral palsied, spoon may be adapted by bending

Cup feeding	Child can suck and can "nurse" rim of cup Can synchronize swallowing with sucking movements By 6-month developmental level child may put hands on cup Begins to put lips over cup but chokes often Child will anticipate cup with head-reaching and mouth-opening True drinking appears when child can take two swallows in succession and 2 ounces or more without stopping	Cup may be offered between feedings when parent has time to relax with child Child should be praised for his efforts He should be told that he is drinking	Cup may be offered by some technique Mother may place her hand over child's on cup Small amounts of fluid are offered at first	May use any type of cup or glass that seems to work; weighted cup with lid is often helpful
Self-feeding Finger foods	Munches rather than sucks Demands play objects at meals Shows eagerness or fusses if mother is slow in presenting food Pokes with index finger at nipple or food in dish Grasps objects with well-defined thumb and finger opposition Able to swallow small amounts of food	Let child munch on zwieback or cracker If child fingers food and immediately drops, put crust back into hand and guide to mouth Food should have taste, texture, and color appeal; for example: green beans, carrot and celery sticks, apple slices, green seedless grapes, banana, rice and meat balls,	Fixed routine—time and place of feeding Avoid distractions; child may do better in room alone with mother nearby Child should not be overtired or stimulated; observe for signs of lagging interest Finish meal by helping feed without comment Teach child to chew by moving jaws up and down	Comfortable and correct posture with head support if necessary If unable to sit, turn on stomach with pillow under chest Well-fitting table and chair Protective coverings for child and adjacent area

Continued.

*From U.S. Department of Health, Education, and Welfare: Feeding mentally retarded children, Washington, D.C., 1965, U.S. Government Printing Office.

Table 4-3. Development of feeding skills—cont'd

Method of feeding to be introduced	Social and physical signs of readiness	Form of food	Social	Adaptations Positional	Equipment
Self-feeding— cont'd Finger foods— cont'd	Moves food into chewing position; chews well and bites off food	tiny boiled potatoes, meat cubes, scrambled eggs, small nourishingly filled sandwiches, cereals, crisp bacon	Tell him what he is doing Watch that child does not stuff mouth without swallowing; be certain chewed food is swallowed Be sure new foods are introduced when child is hungry; offer new foods at evening meal		Plate with raised edge Straight-handled spoon with good-sized bowl Plate stabilized with suction cup
Spoon	Finger feeds small pieces of food from tray Rubs spoon back and forth on tray Demands feeding dish on tray Turns pages in book Builds tower of two blocks Hands over and releases objects	Select foods that adhere easily to spoon: squash, mashed potato, oatmeal, cream puddings	Minimal initial servings; allow child to serve seconds Liberal praise for accomplishments; no disapproval for mishaps Mirror may be helpful to stimulate interest and promote neatness, mirror not advised if any perceptual difficulty or while learning pattern of motion	Let child hold straight-handled spoon if possible Mother may stand or sit behind with child's back against her front or in front of child Mother assists only in filling and guiding spoon to mouth	
Cup and glass	Start with spoon Should swallow, not suck, liquids Possibly tilt head or place in semireclining position Drinks continuously, four or five swallows or more Grasps cup with both hands	Use liquids he especially likes	Try when child is thirsty or hungry Fill glass only quarter full Have child refill glass himself	Use semireclining position (seat is adjustable) until child learns to control flow into mouth Help raise and lower cup	Weighted cup or glass Try flexible plastic tumbler

4. Small servings will encourage eating.

31 to 48 months

1. Encourage self-help.
2. Give opportunity for pouring (give rice in pitcher to promote pouring skills).
3. Encourage child to help set table.
4. Have well-defined rules about table manners.

49 to 52 months

1. Socialize with child at mealtime.
2. Have child help with preparation, table setting, and serving.
3. Include child in conversations at mealtimes by planning special times for him to tell about events, situations, or what he did during the day.

A systematic approach in which the task is broken down into its component parts is axiomatic to teaching the retarded child to feed himself. For example, the child must perform a number of independent skills in feeding himself with a spoon:

1. Grasp the spoon
2. Lift the spoon to the bowl
3. Lower the spoon into the food
4. Scoop food onto the spoon
5. Lift the spoon to the mouth
6. Open the mouth
7. Insert the spoon into the mouth
8. Close the mouth
9. Remove the spoon
10. Chew the food
11. Swallow the food
12. Return the spoon to the bowl

The three behaviors directly related only to self-feeding include finger feeding, drinking, and eating with utensils. Since all children are natural finger feeders, this technique will not have to be taught but only refined. The students should be taught which foods can be eaten with the fingers, such as carrots, fruit, bread, potato chips.

In teaching drinking it is best to begin with a modified (covered) cup, as shown in Table 4-3. From there, use a small plastic glass, filling it only about one-fourth full. Physical assistance may be necessary when beginning instruction. It is important to use the child's preferred liquid (e.g., orange juice, grape juice, chocolate milk).

The two principal approaches to teaching eating are (1) a behavior shaping approach and (2) a fading technique approach. In shaping, each initial step is rewarded until the target or terminal behavior is attained. In fading, the trainer (teacher or parent) physically guides the student through the total behavior (Fig. 4-2). When the child begins to carry out the motion, the trainer loosens her grasp, or fades out of the task (Fig. 4-3).

The fading method is exemplified by the following steps*:

1. Get the child settled comfortably and securely at the table.
2. Determine your most comfortable working and teaching position.
3. Try to think of yourself as *this child*. ("I am his thoughts and hands for this feeding session.")
4. Introduce the spoon and get the child's attention on it by:
   a. Tapping it.
   b. Talking: "Look at the spoon."
   c. Turning the child's head in the direction of the spoon.
   d. Guiding the child's hand in touching it.
5. Give enthusiastic verbal praise every time the child makes an attempt to reach, touch, grasp, or move the spoon.
6. Do not allow the child to have the satisfaction of food unless he is holding the spoon (you may have to grasp his hand and guide him.) No finger feeding should be allowed.
7. Use active hand guidance to go through the feeding process. Do not guide him passively through any of the feeding stages when he is not looking at the spoon or bowl, since he will not learn if he does not see what he is doing.
8. Move the spoon to the bowl, scoop the food, deliver the spoon to his mouth.
9. Gradually decrease your grasp of the child's hand over a period of time. Increase your expectations for improved performance but remembers that repetition of the last step mastered is always the starting point for teaching the next step.
10. As you scoop food with your hand over his, exaggerate the scooping motion for emphasis.
11. Always be alert to changes in muscle tension in the child's hand as he exerts his own effort and begins to take over feeding himself.
12. The first independent effort will probably occur just before food enters his mouth. Loosen your grasp on his hand for this instant, but keep

*From Barnard, K. E., and Erickson, M. L.: Teaching children with developmental problems: a family care approach, ed. 2, St. Louis, 1976, The C. V. Mosby Co., pp. 130-132.

Fig. 4-2. Trainer physically guides the student through the motion of self-feeding. (From Barnard, K. E., and Erickson, M. L.: Teaching children with developmental problems: a family care approach, ed. 2, St. Louis, 1976, The C. V. Mosby Co.)

Fig. 4-3. Trainer decreases her involvement, or fades out of the skill. (From Barnard, K. E., and Erickson, M. L.: Teaching children with developmental problems: a family care approach, ed. 2, St. Louis, 1976, The C. V. Mosby Co.)

your hand positioned to exert full control as he moves the spoon from his mouth back toward the bowl. The distance covered by independent effort will increase gradually until the child can bring food from bowl to mouth without your guidance.

13. Reward the child for effort throughout the procedure.

    a. Be sure to give almost constant verbal approval for successes. Pleasant tone of voice, cheerful mood, and other rewarding touches are important.

    b. Be sure he gets some food to his mouth regularly—by your active guidance if necessary.

14. To avoid behavior that will interrupt the feeding sequence of hand to spoon, spoon to bowl, food to mouth, you may have to guide him very firmly. Remember that nonfeeding behavior has become established and has to be dislodged.

    a. Try to ignore interrupting behavior by keeping him busy scooping with the spoon, getting it to his mouth and back to the bowl for another scoop.

    b. After the child understands and demonstrates that he can follow, for the most part, the motion of self-feeding, it may be helpful to remove food immediately from his reach when he behaves unacceptably. Return the food only when acceptable behavior resumes —when he is sitting quietly, ready to eat again.

Often there are specific difficulties encountered when attempting to feed or teach self-feeding to the TMR. Some of the difficulties and inappropriate behaviors as well as suggestions on how to correct them are given in Table 4-4. Always remember, however, to reinforce appropriate or desired behavior in addition to the measures given.

SKILLS RELATED TO TOILETING

The general objective in toilet training is for the individual to appropriately use the toilet in an independent and consistent fashion. The child should also be able to successfully complete the associated toileting behaviors (e.g., manipulation of clothes before and after toileting, washing and drying the hands). The principal phases in developing an individual toilet training program include readiness, observation and recording, and implementation.

Generally, a child is considered physically

Table 4-4. Inappropriate eating behaviors and corresponding corrective measures

Behavior	Corrective measures
Dislikes food served	Provide 1 spoonful of desired food for each one of disliked food; gradually increase the schedule to a high ratio of low-preference food to a low ratio of high-preference food
Eats too slowly	Set a time for the main meal and a time for the dessert; remove food when reasonable time elapses (depends on individual)
Fills mouth too full by eating continuously	Replace eating hand in lap after each bite
Puts unused arm on table or uses unneeded hand to push food on spoon	Place unused or unneeded arm and hand in lap
Spills food	Reduce amount on spoon or fork or assist in motor movement
Has unsatisfactory posture	Remind and assist in correcting posture
Swallows food without proper chewing	Demonstrate procedure, verbalize "chew," and physically assist jaw to chew
Displays tantrum behavior	Ignore or remove student from table
Plays with utensils or throws food	Remove plate or objects immediately or slide student away from table
Eats someone else's food	Verbalize "no" and separate from others
Eats food from table	Verbalize "no"

ready for training if he can stand and walk alone, this ability indicating pertinent neurological development. The child should have a thorough physical examination prior to training to reveal any physical problems that prevent voluntary control of the bladder or bowels. These problems can then be corrected before initiating the training.

In the observation and recording phase, careful charting of the child's daily toileting habits are necessary to provide accurate information on which implementation is based. This record may also indicate readiness. If no reliable pattern is established after a period of three weeks, then the child is probably not ready to be trained. A daytime chart (Fig. 4-4) should be used

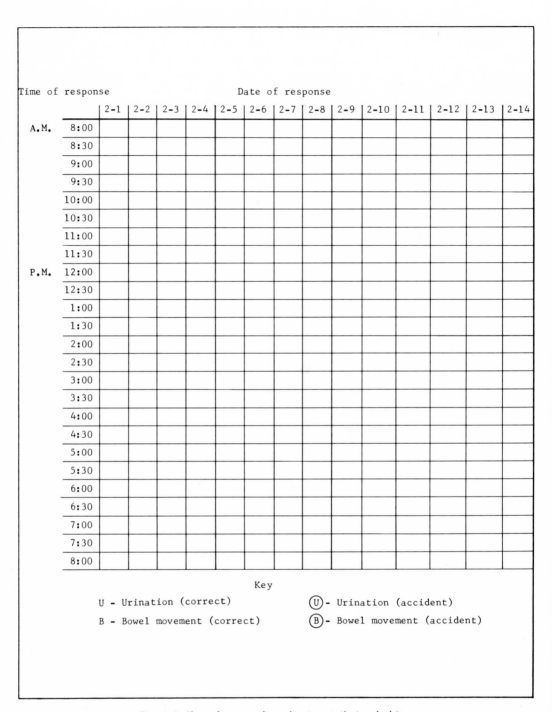

Fig. 4-4. Chart for recording daytime toileting habits.

to indicate times and dates for urination and bowel movements. This chart can also be used during and after training.

The implementation phase can begin after about a two-week baseline is established. You should begin teaching the most consistent response pattern first, be it for bowel or bladder control. In some cases the pattern is consistent for both, indicating the child is capable of simultaneous training in both areas.

The training consists of three phases: (1) eliminating (bladder and bowel) only when seated on the toilet, (2) self-initiated controlled toileting, and (3) training in the associated toileting behaviors. The procedures for the first two phases are essentially the same, although the degree of performance is different. The general components and considerations in training are explained:

1. *Scheduling.* Take the child to the bathroom a few minutes before the times indicated in the prerecording phase.

2. *Prompting.* This is a cue to the child that you want him to perform some behavior; the prompt may be verbal or gestural. A verbal prompt might be: "Mary, go to the toilet" or "Mary, go potty," and a gestural prompt might be pointing to the door, touching or physically directing her to the bathroom. Only the least amount of prompting necessary should be used. Also, use the prompt that the child successfully responded to in the previous training session.

3. *Fading.* First, fade the verbal prompts by reducing the number of words used or the sound of the words. Second, fade the gestural prompts by decreasing the amount or size of the gesture. Fading should be initiated when the child becomes more independent (i.e., no longer requires an outside force to initiate or assist in the behavior).

4. *Language.* The trainer should use language that is brief, clear, and consistent.

5. *Reinforcement.* Initially, reinforce continuously for the desired behavior or approximations of desired behavior and later change to an intermittent schedule. The reinforcers used depend on each child—it may be tangible (preferred food such as sugar-coated cereal, cookies, candy) or social (praise, smile, pat on the back) or both. Whatever the reward, it should be of high value to the child so that he will be motivated toward the activity again. Also, remember to always reward dryness (the incompatible behavior) throughout the day.

6. *Consistency.* It is critical that consistent procedures be used from day to day and from school to home.

7. *Accidents.* Accidents will occur during toilet training, and the response of the parent or trainer is important. Following are procedures for responding to accidents.°

    a. Let the child remain in his wet or soiled pants for a few minutes so that he may experience some discomfort. Make no comments.

    b. Change his pants, but show no facial expression, touch the child as little as possible, and say nothing to him. You are, in effect, virtually *ignoring* him when he has an accident.

    c. Reinforce him very frequently in the next few hours for being *dry*. For example, go to him fifteen minutes after the accident and, with smiles and hugs, praise him: Steve, good. You're dry!" The purpose is to give the child the clear message that it *pays to be dry*. When he is dry, he receives praise, physical contact, etc. When he is wet or soiled, he is ignored and uncomfortable.

    d. If accidents persist for a period of two months or more, perhaps still more undesirable consequences

°From Linford, M. D., Hipsher, L. W., and Silikovitz, R. G.: Systematic instruction for retarded children: the Illinois Program, Part III, Self-help instruction, experimental edition, Danville, Ill., 1972, The Interstate Printers and Publishers, p. 142.

could be applied following each accident. For example, the child might be left in his wet or soiled pants for longer periods of time, if this makes him uncomfortable. Again, it is critical to reinforce the child at a high rate when he is dry, particularly during the hours following the accident. Reinforcement for the child's being dry should be maintained throughout the program.

8. *Food and drink control.* It is an important part of a toileting program to maintain regular eating and drinking schedules. You might even give the child liquids an hour before his training time to enhance the possibility of the toileting behavior occurring.

The nighttime toilet training can be considered after the child develops a reasonable degree of independence in his daytime toileting behaviors. The training is essentially the same as first described. The following points will also assist parents in nighttime training: (1) do not give liquids after the evening meal; (2) make bedtime a routine procedure, (3) have the child go to the toilet immediately before bedtime and on awakening in the morning, and (4) reward the child for periods of dryness and give a special reward for all night dryness. Mechanical alerting or warning devices are also recommended and may be obtained from any major department store.

Specific aids or tips to remember in the toilet training program include (1) having the child dressed in easily manageable clothes (e.g., elastic waistbands), (2) having easily accessible toilets with easy-to-open doors, and (3) always having extra clothing nearby when training at school.

Following are additional suggestions and activities to develop independent toileting behaviors*:

---

*From the Washington Guide for Promoting Development in the Young Child, The University of Washington, Seattle.

9 to 12 months
1. Watch for clues that indicate that child is wet or soiled.
2. Be sure to change diapers when wet or soiled so that child begins to experience contrast between wetness and dryness.

13 to 18 months
1. Sit child on toilet or potty chair at regular intervals for short periods of time throughout day.
2. Praise child for success.
3. If potty chair is used, it should be located in bathroom.
4. Respond promptly to signals and clues of child by taking him to bathroom or changing his pants.
5. Use training pants once toilet training is begun.

19 to 30 months
1. Continue regular intervals of toileting.
2. Reward success.
3. Dress child in simple clothing that he can manage.
4. Remind him occasionally, particularly after mealtime, juice time, naptime, and playtime.
5. Take him to bathroom before bedtime.
6. Bathroom should be convenient to use, the door easy to open.
7. Plan to begin training when disruptions in regular routine are at a minimum, e.g., don't begin during vacation trip.

31 to 48 months
1. Child may still need reminding.
2. Dress him in simple clothing that he can manage.
3. Ignore accidents; refrain from shame or ridicule.

49 to 52 months
1. Praise child for his accomplishment.

SKILLS RELATED TO CLOTHING

The three primary behaviors to be developed by the TMR child related to clothing are (1) undressing and dressing, (2) unfastening and fastening, and (3) appropriateness, care, and use of clothing. The specific skills to be developed were listed earlier in this chapter.

Independent functioning related to the clothing area is the chief aim of instruction with the retarded child, but clothing also holds other values. It is important that the child be dressed similarly to other persons in the school and community because society is consciously aware and unconsciously accepting of others whose clothes are appropriate, clean, and attractive. An older retarded child's self-concept may also be affected by his type and style of clothing.

The prerequisite skills necessary for beginning instruction in the clothing area include mental and physical skills. The child should have associated mental abilities such as attending, watching, following physical cues or gestures, following verbal directions (sit down, push, pull, etc.), and matching clothing to appropriate parts of the body. Listed in Table 4-5 are gross and fine motor skills necessary to independently master dressing and undressing. If a child possesses most but not all of these skills, a teacher can either work on the difficult skills in a separate teaching session or in addition to the dressing session. Table 4-5 also provides suggestions to correct or develop the skill.

The training program for the TMR should begin with undressing. An undressing task (e.g., pulling socks off) is easier to perform and teach than its dressing counterpart (e.g., putting socks on). Undressing, whatever the article of clothing, does not involve handling the clothes in a particularly special way. Furthermore, each undressing and dressing skill should be broken down into a sequence of subskills and taught in a *backward* order. Following are examples of the steps in an undressing task (T-shirt) and a dressing task (pants) using this backward shaping technique.

Table 4-5. Prerequisite physical skills necessary for dressing*

Physical skill	Suggestions to correct or develop the skill
Stands alone	If child cannot stand alone, have him stand with support by use of pillow, or lean on bed or corner of room
Balances in chair or on floor without support	Support can be given for chair or floor
	Floor: sit in corner or with pillows
	Chair: strap armrests on chair
Leans freely from chair	Touch toes from sitting position
Raises each knee toward chest when sitting in chair	March while sitting down
	Assist leg by pulling on pants leg above knee
Places hand on opposite shoulder	Games: "Simon Says"; "Follow the Leader"
Places one or both hands on top of head	Song: "Put Your Finger in Your Hair"
	Game: "Simon Says"
Opposition with one or both hands (action of two hands pulling in opposite directions)	Game: "Tug of War"—pull on heavy rope
	Pull wagon
	Clasp hands and pull
Grasps and holds with right and left hands	Game: "Tug of War"—pull on heavy rope
	Swing on swing. Child must hang on to rope
	Hold and eat ice cream cone
	Shape child's hands around article of clothing and say "hold"
	Grasp drumstick or xylophone mallet
	Hang from crossbar
Picks up 1-inch button with thumb and forefinger	Place small pegs in board
	Put pennies in bank
	Any use of thumb/index finger
Pushes and pulls with one or both hands with full hand grasp, using all fingers and palm of hand	Pop beads—pull and push beads
	Songs: "Row, Row, Row Your Boat"; "See Saw, Margery Daw"
	"Tug of War" with nylon stockings tied together
	Pull wagon
	Elastic circle or rope
	Push doll buggy

*Adapted from Henderson, S., and McDonald, M.: Step-by-step dressing; a handbook for teaching the retarded to dress, Champaign, Ill., 1973, Suburban Publications.

Undressing—T shirt
1. Shirt covering only extended arms and hands
2. Shirt covering head, and arms extended
3. Shirt up around the chest
4. Shirt completely on

Dressing—pants
1. Pants at mid-hip level
2. Pants at knee level
3. Pants at feet level but on
4. One pants leg on, one off
5. Pants completely off

Any of the articles of clothing worn by children can be taught in this manner and include socks, shoes, shirt, underwear, pants, dress, coat, cap, mittens, gloves, slip, scarf, pajamas, and bra. It is important to remember that each step is demonstrated and reinforced when successfully completed.

The second clothing area concerns the child being able to unfasten and fasten the various parts of clothing. The skills to be developed include unzipping and zipping, unsnapping and snapping, unbuttoning and buttoning, unbuckling and buckling, unlacing and lacing, unhooking and hooking, and untying and tying.

The self-care area related to clothing cannot be completed by just teaching independence in taking off and putting on clothes. It should also include those behaviors related to appropriateness, as well as care and use of clothing. Such skills include identifying appropriate clothing for the weather and the sexes, the child's own clothing, dress clothing, work clothing, appropriate sizes, and coordinated clothes. Concerning care and use of clothing, the child should be able to adjust clothes, use a clothes brush, wipe shoes on a mat when dirty, hang up clothes (hook and coat hanger), use an umbrella, select his own clothing, fold clothes, dispose of dirty clothes, and polish shoes.

The following general suggestions relate to planning or designing clothing for the retarded individual.

> *Accessories:* avoid belts and cufflinks for younger children; knitted caps best (no ties); use clip-on neckties.
>
> *Blouse:* square cut along bottom, front opening, and large neck opening.
>
> *Colors:* use solid recognizable colors or large print because small print makes it more difficult to perceive arm and leg holes and front from back.
>
> *Construction:* sturdy with few seams double stitched at stress points.
>
> *Dress:* Large enough to pull on; no back openings.
>
> *Fabrics:* Durable material, washable, warm but lightweight, and wrinkle- and stain-resistant.
>
> *Fastenings:* front fastenings, few, but large, buttons; insert a ring on the tab of zippers.
>
> *Footwear:* slip-on shoes preferable, one-tone easier to care for than two-tone, no slippery or slick shoe soles; when laces are necessary (e.g., tennis shoes), buy shoes with a minimum of holes and use elastic laces.
>
> *Outerwear* (coats, jackets, and sweaters): avoid heavy and excessively bulky clothing; loose fitting best for coats, jackets, and sweaters.
>
> *Pants:* elastic tops desirable; avoid fly fronts for the young.
>
> *Shirts:* pullover shirts with large necks are best, but when regular shirts are necessary, select square cut at bottom or extra length for ease in tucking in.
>
> *Sleepwear:* One-piece pajamas best; few fasteners, loose fit.
>
> *Underwear:* half slips, nonslip elastic straps for bra and slip.

In teaching the skills of undressing and dressing to the retarded child, remember the following hints:

1. Establish routine for the instructional sessions (i.e., same trainer, same place, same time).

2. Teach for generalization to similar articles of clothing.

3. Provide oversize or loose clothes in beginning sessions for freedom of movement and ease in handling.

4. Color code front and back of clothing and left and right for shoes.

5. Have practice clothes at school.

6. Coordinate efforts with parents.

SKILLS RELATED TO PERSONAL HEALTH AND GROOMING

Another major area of self-care involves skills related to personal health and grooming. Instruction should concentrate on skills and habits related to the hands, nose, teeth, hair, face, skin, and body. Specific skills to be developed under each area are listed on p. 97. Skills taught depend in part on the child's sex. The students should be preassessed (parent interview) in these areas before instruction. A systematic progressive-step approach utilizing routine is important in the teaching of these skills. Also, parent cooperation is vital to the success and rate of accomplishment of grooming and personal health skills, since most of these skills are performed outside the school setting.

SKILLS RELATED TO SAFETY AND FIRST AID

The last major self-care area concerns an awareness and knowledge of safety concepts and self-administration of simple first aid. Safety is a difficult area to teach the TMR because the mastery of the con-

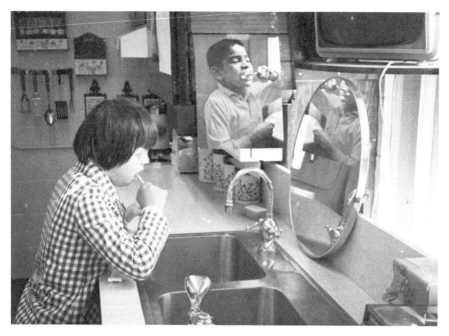

Fig. 4-5. Brushing the teeth is one grooming–personal health skill in which the TMR can achieve independence when given training. (Courtesy Greenwich, Conn., Public Schools.)

cepts of safety are only guides that must be applied to varied individual situations. It is, however, an extremely important aspect of curriculum for the TMR and must be taught in structured teaching situations as well as throughout the day. Care should also be taken to provide a safe environment for the TMR at home and at school.

The two major areas of safety instruction are (1) home and sheltered workshop and (2) school and recreational activities. The home and sheltered workshop segment should center on teaching safety related to poisons, electricity, fire, sharp objects, bathroom (bathtub and shower), plastic bags, tools, and stairways. School and recreational safety might center around the school bus (entering, exiting, riding), the playground, the street, and any recreational activity where safety should be taught (e.g., bicycling, playing ball, swimming).

The TMR can also be taught to take care of minor injuries and to self-administer needed and appropriate treatment (e.g.,

antiseptic, creams, bandages). Simple injuries might include minor burns, animal and insect bites, and small cuts. The procedure for controlling nosebleed for susceptible students might also be taught.

Vocabulary is an important aspect of safety, since so many regulatory signs for our safety are in existence. Following are some vocabulary words, according to instructional level, that the TMR should know.

Safety vocabulary*

Primary level

Bottle	Go
Cold	Glass
Cotton	Hot
Danger	In
Dial	Knife
Doctor	Mop
Do not	No
Down	Nurse
Exit	Out
Fire	Poison

*From Missouri State Department of Education: Curriculum guide for teachers of trainable mentally retarded children, Jefferson City, Mo., 1971, pp. 121-122.

Fig. 4-6. Recognition and understanding of danger and regulatory signs are important for the TMR. (Courtesy Bossier Parish, La., Public Schools.)

Primary level

Rags	Up
Scissors	Wait
Stop	Walk

Intermediate level

Bandage	Gas
Beware	Hospital
Bleach	Keep off
Broken glass	Keep out
Burn	Lye
Caution	Match
Cautious	Medicine
Clinic	Point
Danger	Police
Deep	Pull
Do not touch (handle)	Push
Entrance	Revolving door
Escalator	Slippery
Fire bell	Smoke
Fire escape	Street
Fire fighter	Telephone
First aid	

Prevocational and vocational level

Acid	Arrow
Ammonia	Beware of ice

Breakable	Move to rear
Bus stop	No admittance
Child's address	No hunting
Construction	No left turn
Crosswalk	No right turn
Disinfectant	No smoking
Do not enter	No trespassing
Elevator	Off limits
Emergency	Pedestrian crossing
Explosives	Pistol
Fallout shelter	Prohibited
Firecracker	Radiation
Fire extinguisher	Radiator
Firework	Rifle
Flammable	Sharp
Glue	Spray
Gun	Spray cans
Handle with care	Stairs
Harmful	This way out
High voltage	Turpentine
Inflammable	Use other door
Information	Use other exit
Insecticides	Warning
Low ceiling	Watch your step
Men working	Wet

In teaching safety and first aid skills, as in all self-care skills, instruction and training should be systematic and adhere to behavior modification principles.

MATERIALS AND SPECIALIZED PROGRAMS IN THE SELF-CARE AREA

There are numerous specific materials the classroom teacher should have in the room to effectively teach skills in the self-care area of curriculum. Following is a representative list of items a teacher might have or make. Also included are specialized programs and commercial aids that may be purchased (some rented). Prices are not included because of their frequent change, but the publisher or source is given. The addresses are listed in Appendix A.

CLASSROOM MATERIALS

Eating
Cups
Food
Powdered fruit drink
Napkins
Plates (plastic)
Salt and pepper shakers
Straws
Trays
Utensils (spoons, folks, knives)

Safety and first aid
Antiseptic
Bandages
First aid cream or spray
Gauze
Matches
Play equipment (bat, ball)
Plastic bags
Sharp objects (scissors, knife)
Tools (hammer, saw)
Traffic signs
Tricycle or bicycle

Toileting
Potty chairs
Reinforcers (candy, juice)
Toilet alerting devices (see commercial materials)

Clothing
Articles of clothing
Clothes brush
Dressing frames
Mirror (full length)
Play dolls with clothes
Shoe polish

Personal health
Comb
Cotton balls
Cotton swabs
Dental floss
Electric razor
Hairbrush
Hair dryer
Hair rollers
Hand lotion
Handkerchief
Makeup
Nail file
Nail polish
Nail polish remover
Preshave lotion
Soap
Shampoo
Tissue
Toothbrushes
Toothpaste
Towels (hand and bath)

Specialized programs

Project MORE (Mediated Operational Research for Education) Daily Living Skills Programs by James R. Lent, Project Director, Edmark Associates, 1976.

The Project MORE publications are the results of a federally funded program to teach normalization skills to institutionalized TMR populations. They can be easily adapted to meet the needs of a public school teacher of TMR students. Programs that can be used in the self-care and personal health areas include How to do MORE (an all-cartoon manual that provides the basics of behavior modification and data collection), Toothbrushing, Eating, Hand Washing, Use of Deodorant, Complexion Care, Hair Washing, Nose Blowing, Face Shaving, Leg and Underarm Shaving, Feminine Hygiene, Hair Rolling, Showering, Care of Simple Injuries, and Use of Public Restrooms.

Steps to Independence—a Skills Training Series for Children With Special Needs by Bruce Baker, Alan Brightman, Louis Heifetz, and Diane Murphy, Research Press, 1976.

A program for the handicapped, the purpose of which is to develop simple, vital skills needed for independent living. Its primary use is by parents, although teachers may also find it of value. This program consists of easy-to-read, illustrated manuals with the following content:

Early Self-help Skills—concentrates on prerequisite learning skills such as paying attention, following directions, eye-hand coordination, and gross motor abilities and covers beginning dressing, grooming, and mealtime skills.

Intermediate Self-help Skills—covers dressing, grooming, mealtime, and housekeeping skills.

Advanced Self-help Skills—covers advanced skills in dressing, grooming, eating, and housekeeping.

Behavior Problems—focuses on problem behaviors characteristic of TMR children, such as self-stimulation, self-abuse, and fearful behaviors.

Training Guide—designed for use by professionals working with parents and teachers, the training guide features a behavioral assessment guide for determining the appropriate training manual for each child.

Step-by-Step Dressing: a Handbook for Teaching the Retarded to Dress by Shirley Henderson and Mary McDonald, Suburban Publications, 1973.

This program provides the trainer (parent or teacher) with an in-depth comprehensive procedure to develop dressing skills. *Step-by-Step Dressing* also contains testing and progress charts for each dressing skill and a Mental and Physical Pre-Skills Evaluation.

A Program for Teaching the Independent Use of Zippers, Buttons, Shoes, and Socks by Alan Hofmeister, Project Director, Developmental Learning Material, 1977.

This field tested program requires no previous experience or training by the instructor and includes a precheck to determine learner readiness, sample instructions and learner's charts for recording progress, and a sheet of twenty-four colorful reward badges (sold separately). Sequential lessons and gamelike follow-up activities for teaching unbuttoning and buttoning a shirt, unzipping and zipping a jacket, taking off and putting on shoes and socks, and untying and tying shoelaces are included in this program.

A Program for Teaching Independent Dressing Skills by Alan Hofmeister, Project Director, Developmental Learning Materials, 1977.

This program contains step-by-step illustrated instructions for teaching the self-care skills of putting on and taking off three types of clothing: pants, tops that pull over the head, and tops that fasten down the front. The learner is given a demonstration of each task, accompanied by verbal directions and then assistance as necessary until independence is achieved. A precheck to determine readiness and learning charts for recording progress are also included.

Toilet Training the Retarded: a Rapid Program for Day and Nighttime Independent Toileting by Richard M. Foxx and Nathan H. Azrin, Research Press, 1973.

This program consists of a book and program forms pamphlet on how to provide step-by-step procedures to train self-initiated toileting. The program extensively employs behavior modification techniques to shape desired behaviors.

The Radea Program by Jean Walling, Melton Book Co., 1976.

Radea is a specific skills development program for the severely, profoundly, and multi-handicapped child (developmental ages 0 to 7). A task analysis, behaviorally managed approach, Radea is a comprehensive curriculum covering five areas: visual perception, auditory perception, perceptual-motor, oral language, functional living (self-feeding, tooth-brushing, dressing, etc.) and special problems (toilet training, swallowing, drooling, self-stimulation, echolalic speech). The program consists of a teaching manual, 564 task cards,

cassette tapes, picture cards, exercise material, task trial sheets, daily progress charts, and individual progress profiles. (A teacher training program is also available.)

Teaching Good Behavior and Personal Hygiene to the Retarded Adolescent, Harris County Center for the Retarded, Inc., 1968.

One guidebook for boys and one guidebook for girls.

Instructional aids

Stop and Go Signs and **Traffic Signals**, Community Playthings. Cards illustrating traffic signs and signals.

ETA Best Vests for Dressing Skills and Dressing Frames, Educational Teaching Aids.

Vests and frames to teach lacing, hooking, buttoning, zipping, snapping, tying, and buckling.

Dress Me Doll and **Bendi Baby**, Creative Playthings, Inc.

Cuddly Kitty and **Superboard Lacing Cards With Laces**, Developmental Learning Materials.

Cuddly Kitty is a put-together pet that teaches snapping, buckling, etc.

Educational Placemats, Educational Performance Associates. Paper place mats dealing with subjects such as colors, shapes, foods, numbers, clothing, seasons, days of the week, fruit, vegetables.

Raggedy Ann and **Raggedy Andy**, available at most larger department or toy stores.

Dolls to teach snapping, buttoning, etc.

Toilet Tutor, Bio-dyne Corporation.

A wet pants alarm for daytime training.

Reading for Safety: Common Signs of Community Service and Safety, I and II by Fern Tripp.

A series of two books showing, in color, 100 of the most common signs.

Wet Guard, Montgomery Ward, Inc.

A wet-bed alarm for nighttime training.

Lite-Alert Buzzer, Sears, Roebuck and Co.

A wet-bed alarm for nighttime training.

Star Tinkle Potty Chair, Peterson Co.

A potty chair for young retarded children that signals (plays music) when the child urinates.

Audiovisual aids

Washing Your Hands and Face, Brushing Your Teeth, Washing Your Hair, and **Trimming Your Nails**, Society for Visual Education, Inc. (Record/filmstrips.)

Care of Hair, Proper Clothing, Boys (Personal Talk), Girls (Personal Talk), Washing Face and Hands, Girls Bath, Boys Shaving, Boys and Girls Proper Clothing, Boys Shower, and

Menstruation, Harris County Center for the Retarded, Inc. (Filmstrips.)

Genesis, Hallmark Films and Recordings, Inc.
A film on how to train basic self-care skills dressing, eating, toileting) using behavior modification principles.

Safety and You, Teaching Good Manners and Behavior, Teaching Children Safety, and **Drugs, Poisons, and Little Children,** Educational Activities, Inc. (Records/filmstrips.)

Sing a Song of Safety (record) and **Safety First** (tapes), Learning Arts.

Sing a Song of Safety, Songs of Safety, Why Do I Have to Go to Sleep? Decca Records. (3 records.)

Safety First, Stop, Look, and Listen, Walt Disney, Publisher, (2 records.)

A Shoe Is to Tie, Department of Human Development, University of Kansas. A 16 mm color film demonstrating the steps and reinforcement used in teaching shoe tying.

SUMMARY

The self-care area of curriculum is one that serves many functional everyday human behaviors. Included are skills related to feeding, toileting, clothing, personal health and grooming, and safety and first aid. These skills can best be taught to the TMR by using established principles and practices of behavior modification, especially modeling, prompting, shaping, and fading. Once the behavior is developed, the student should be given ample opportunities for practice in day-to-day living.

Before attempting to teach any of the self-care skills, a determination of readiness and an assessment of the student's abilities must be made. Rating scales, selected sections of adaptive behavior scales, or selected sections of formal behavioral measures can be used for this purpose.

In developing eating skills for the TMR, the desired goal is total independence, including the associated behaviors relating to dining. The child, in addition to eating and drinking correctly, should sit properly, display the necessary table manners, and be adaptable to various eating situations.

Toilet training is a self-care skill that most TMRs learn at the preschool or primary instructional levels. The general goal is for the student to independently and consistently use the toilet, including associated behaviors (e.g., manipulation of clothes before and after toileting, washing and drying the hands). The toilet-training program should be individual and include the phases of readiness, observation and recording, and implementation.

Another self-care area, clothing, has as primary goals the skills of undressing and dressing, unfastening and fastening, appropriateness, care, and use of clothing. Liberal use of prompting and a backward shaping technique should be utilized in developing these skills.

Personal health and grooming is yet another important self-care area for the TMR. The specific skills taught include grooming and health habits relating to the hands, nose, teeth, hair, face, skin, and body.

Safety and first aid is the last curriculum self-care area of curriculum for the TMR. The two major environments where safety concepts and rules should be taught are the home-sheltered workshop (safety related to household and industrial poisons, electricity, fire, sharp objects, bathroom, plastic bags, use of tools, stairways) and school-recreational sites (school bus, playground, street and recreational safety). Important to safety is a recognition and understanding of related vocabulary words. Over 120 such words or phrases are necessary.

A list of classroom materials that can be used to develop skills in the self-care areas were provided along with a brief description of useful specialized programs and instructional aids.

REFERENCES AND SUGGESTED READINGS

Barnard, K. E., and Erickson, M. L.: Teaching children with developmental problems: a family care approach, ed. 2, St. Louis, 1976, The C. V. Mosby Co.

Baroff, G. S.: Mental retardation: nature, cause, and management. Washington, D.C., 1974, Hemisphere Publishing Corporation.

Cassel, R. H., and Colwell, C. N.: Teaching the

profoundly retarded self-help activities by behavior shaping techniques. In Bensberg, G. J., editor: Teaching the mentally retarded, Atlanta, 1965, Southern Regional Education Board.

Foxx, R. M., and Azrin, N. H.: Toilet training the retarded: a rapid program for day and night-time independent toileting, Champaign, Ill., 1973, Research Press.

Linford, M. D., Hipsher, L. W., and Silikovitz, R. G.: Systematic instruction for retarded children: the Illinois Program. Part III. Self-help instruction, experimental edition, Danville, Ill., 1972, The Interstate Printers & Publishers.

Louisiana State Department of Education, Division of Mental Retardation: One step at a time, Baton Rouge, La., 1974.

Perry, N.: Teaching the mentally retarded child, ed. 2, New York, 1974, Columbia University Press.

U.S. Department of Health, Education, and Welfare: Feeding mentally retarded children, Washington, D.C., 1965, U.S. Government Printing Office.

CHAPTER 5

DEVELOPING BASIC COMMUNICATION SKILLS

The ability to communicate is one of the major areas of behavior and plays a central role in almost every aspect of our daily lives. It allows for acceptance in society and is therefore most important. Our society demands that an individual be able to receive and interpret oral and/or written language and be capable of self-expression. In short, one must be an effective communicator. The achievement of these skills in education is translated into curriculum areas such as listening, speaking, reading, writing, and spelling.

The acquisition or remediation of communication or language skills is difficult and complex for the TMR because of the integrating or mediating system for language—the central nervous system (CNS). The CNS in many TMRs is defective, thus making effective communication more difficult. The focus of language training for the TMR should be on those aspects which can be most easily learned yet have the greatest utility. Most TMRs are so deficient in speech and language skills that nothing can be assumed regarding their abilities. Language gains are possible, but instruction must begin at lower levels than would normally be considered, and it must be systematic and rewarding to the student.

As Snyder, Lovitt, and Smith (1975) have indicated in a review of twenty-three language training studies, "it is definitely possible to improve the language skills of severely retarded children and adults through the application of systematic instructional techniques and reinforcement contingencies." This chapter will center on the earlier stages of speech and language development. The higher level communication skills (reading, writing, spelling) will be covered in Chapter 8 on functional academics.

NORMAL DEVELOPMENT OF COMMUNICATION SKILLS

Before normal developmental patterns in the communications area are presented, some of the terminology involved will be briefly defined and discussed. Terms included are communication, language, speech, and listening.

The term *communication* is used with the TMR because of its broad connotations. By simple definition it is the interaction that occurs between living organisms (Dickson and Jann, 1974). Fig. 5-1 illustrates this relationship between two individuals (*A*, the sender, and *B*, the receiver). According to the above definition, com-

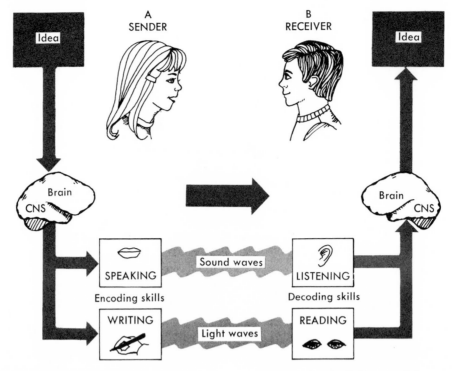

Fig. 5-1. Model of the communication process. (From Lerner, J. W.: Children with learning disabilities. Copyright © 1976 by Houghton Mifflin Co. Used by permission.)

munication includes more than listening, speaking, reading, and writing. It encompasses gesturing, signing, and other nonverbal communication skills sometimes used by young severely retarded or multihandicapped (e.g., deaf-retarded) children.

Language is the system used by humans to communicate and involves the expression of concepts. It is also defined as the symbolic formulation of ideas (Phillips, 1975). The process for acquiring language can be divided into the following three interrelated processes or systems:

1. Reception (input), which involves receipt of stimuli by the peripheral sense organs and some degree of understanding of these sensory experiences

2. Association, which involves integration, mediation, and internal manipulation of symbols of language between the processes of reception and expression

3. Expression (output), which involves the translation of ideas into oral (spoken) and graphic (written) language

It is important to remember that receptive skills (input) precede expressive skills (output) and that any interruption or discontinuity of this three-part system could adversely affect language functioning (McConnell, Love, and Clark, 1974).

Stages of language development can also be divided into three distinct levels (Myklebust, 1954):

1. Inner language, which refers to the experiences and meaning on which other language levels are based

2. Receptive language, which is understanding the spoken word

3. Expressive language, which is the last to occur and depends to a large extent on the development of the first two

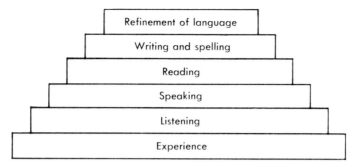

Fig. 5-2. Developmental hierarchy of traditional curriculum activities relating to language. (Adapted from Kellogg, R. E.: Listening. In Lamb, P., editor: Guiding children's language learning, Dubuque, Iowa, 1971, William C. Brown Co.)

Fig. 5-2 transposes the levels of language development into more traditional curriculum skills. These skills are also listed in typical order of attainment.

Speech, or speaking, is a unique characteristic of communication associated with humans. Cognitively it is a learned system of vocal symbols by which thought is conveyed; physiologically it is the motor act of uttering speech sounds. It is important to remember that speech and language do not develop in isolation from each other (Smith, 1974).

Listening is an auditory skill whereby the child has to internalize ideas; it involves some degree of evaluation. Listening is *not* synonymous with hearing. Hearing, or audition, is a physiological process. One can hear but not necessarily listen, a frequent characteristic of TMR students. There is a tendency for many educators to overlook the value of and take for granted the development of listening skills. Since listening is a major skill, the first receptive skill to develop, it provides a foundation for all language growth. If there are deficiencies or delays at this level, they will affect all other areas of communication to varying degrees—reception, or input, (listening) precedes expression, or output (speech).

The listening area contains a number of auditory-perceptual skills, which are listed and defined below. They appear in order of hypothesized development, but *no* two

skills can develop in isolation or be mutually exclusive.

auditory awareness Being aware of environmental sounds.

auditory focusing The ability to determine where a sound is originating.

auditory figure-ground The ability to attend to one aspect of the auditory field while perceiving it in relation to the remainder of the field.

auditory discrimination The ability to detect differences between sounds.

auditory memory The ability to store and recall what one has heard.

auditory sequencing The ability to remember and correctly repeat a sequence of items.

auditory blending The ability to blend single sounds into a complete word.

auditory association The ability to relate spoken words in a meaningful way.

Speech

TMR children have considerable difficulty developing adequate speech sounds and patterns. The reasons for this are directly related to the degree of possession or attainment of the requirements for effective speech. Following are some of the basic requirements:

1. Adequate physical structures—tongue, teeth, vocal cords, soft and hard palates, lips

2. Intelligence—primarily the physiological functioning and abilities of the speech-control area of the brain (cortex) as it relates to the articulation of speech sounds

3. Auditory discrimination—the ability

to contrast correct and incorrect sounds in isolation and in connected speech

4. Adequate feedback and monitoring system—the ability to continuously monitor and adjust our own speech behavior
5. Adequate models—since speech is a learned activity, a child's speech is in part influenced by those in his environment, primarily parents and siblings
6. Motivation—assists in the development of speech (Although teachers or parents cannot really motivate the child or student, they can stimulate, which will motivate him to develop speaking behaviors.)
7. Adequate emotional and social development—emotional or social problems can sometimes interfere with a child learning to speak (Desirable traits include a healthy self-image, good relationships with others, and a stable relationship with the physical environment.)

The TMR basically follows a normal sequence or pattern of speech development, although he proceeds at a much slower pace. Table 5-1 gives a basic outline of the normal speech development landmarks. It should be remembered that there is a range for rate of development, and not *all* children would follow exactly a normed reference guide.

The development of speech sounds in order of appearance is provided in Table 5-2. Most children acquire these sounds at an earlier age than is listed here. A child is considered to have defective speech (articulation) if the sound is not acquired by the specified age. The vowel sounds (a, e, i, o, u, and sometimes y) occur first and are usually mastered by the age of 3½. By the age of 8 a child should have mastered the blends and have errorless articulation (Phillips, 1975).

Table 5-1. Hierarchy of speech development behaviors*

Behavior	Age
Birth cry	Newborn
Undifferentiated crying	0 to 1 mo.
Differentiated crying	1 to 2 mo.
Babbling (vocal response to pleasant stimuli)	2 to 5 mo.
Lallation (listens and repeats sounds)	5 to 8 mo.
Echolalia (recognizes and imitates sounds)	8 to 12 mo.
First time words	12 mo.
Jargon (vocalization of a few words; must use inflection)	12 to 24 mo.
Practicing fluency	2 to 4 yr.
Completely intelligible speech	6 yr.
Mature articulation	8 yr.

*Adapted from Phillips, P. P.: Speech and hearing problems in the classroom, Lincoln, Neb., 1975, Cliffs Notes, Inc. p. 31.

Table 5-2. Normal attainment of individual sounds by age*

Age	Sound	Sound in words		
		Initial	Medial	Final
3½ yr.	b	boy	baby	tub
	p	pie	apple	cap
	m	man	hammer	gum
	w	wagon	away	
	h	hand	behind	
4½ yr.	k	key	turkey	book
	g	game	wagon	dog
	t	toy	butter	cat
	d	dog	daddy	bed
	n	no	penny	ran
	ng		singing	ring
	y	yes	barnyard	
5½ yr.	f	farm	coffee	puff
6½ yr.	v	visit	over	have
	sh	shoe	dishes	fish
	zh		treasure	garage
	th (voiced)	this	father	bathe
	l	look	milk	ball
7½ yr.	s	soup	bicycle	bus
	z	zipper	scissors	buzz
	r	rope	barn	car
	th (voiceless)	thumb	toothbrush	bath
	wh	what	somewhere	
	ch	chair	matches	watch
	j	jump	enjoy	page

*Adapted from Auditory Perception Activity Book, Jefferson Parish School Board, Gretna, La., 1974, p. 1.

ASSESSMENT

The assessment of the communication skills of the TMR has two basic purposes: (1) to determine the current level of functioning, compared with other children and with the child's own estimated potential and (2) to find out the child's strengths and weaknesses so an educational or therapeutic program can be planned. Most speech clinicians and language specialists strongly recommend that a diagnostic procedure precede the initiation of any program because the quality of the latter largely depends on the expended effort of the assessment. Although this part of the chapter will focus on informal and formal speech and language assessment, the assessor should always combine developmental information obtained with an estimation of a student's language environment so that a complete picture of current language needs may be examined.

Informal assessment

Many teachers of the TMR unfortunately do not have speech clinicians or language specialists available to them. Reasons for this condition might include a lack of trained personnel (common in rural areas) and a heavy case load of clients. Both reasons may restrict the availability of such professionals to TMR schools. Ideally these specialists would have TMR clients as a part of their assignment, but since the ideal does not always exist, the teacher may have to informally assess the speech and language abilities of her students.

Speech assessment. Since over 90% of speech disorders are articulation problems, only that area of assessment will be covered. A practical and informative procedure, if the child has some speech, is to systematically examine his verbal responses. A record should be kept of (1) misarticulations of vowels and/or consonants, (2) whether these errors are in the initial, medial, and/or final position in words, and (3) whether the errors consist of substitutions, omissions, or distortions. Once this has been determined, appropriate activities for that student can begin. Table 5-3 provides an informal speech (articulation) test for nonreaders.

Language assessment. Since the lowest level of language development, inner language, does not contain observable behavior, it is almost impossible to assess. The last two levels, however—receptive and expressive language—can be informally assessed, determining what language behaviors the child is able to perform using receptive and expressive language scales such as the following:

Table 5-3. Informal (speech) articulation test for nonreaders*

Sound	Suggested pictures or objects that illustrate the sound
[p]	pig, pie, pencil, apple, puppy, cap
[b]	bubble, bear, boat, boy, baby, tub
[t]	table, toes, kitty, bottle, hat
[d]	duck, dog, doll, candy, Indian, bread
[k]	ice cream cone, cup, kitten, chicken, cake
[g]	gun, girl, goat, wagon, tiger, egg
[f]	fish, finger, elephant, telephone, leaf
[v]	vacuum cleaner, valentine, stove, television
[θ] th	thumb, three, birthday cake, toothbrush, bath
[ð] th	feather, father, mother
[s]	Santa Claus, sleep, spoon, bicycle, horse
[z]	zebra, zoo, bees, nose, eyes
[ʃ] sh	shoe, sheep, shovel, washing, goldfish
[ʒ] zh	not necessary to test; if [ʃ] is defective, [ʒ] will in all likelihood be defective also
[tʃ] ch	chair, chicken, chin, pitcher, watch
[dʒ] j	jump, giant, soldier, engine, bridge
[m]	monkey, man, Christmas tree, hammer, comb
[n]	knife, nest, nose, running, banana, spoon
[ŋ] ng	swing, drink, monkey, finger
[l]	lion, lamp, balloon, yellow, ball
[r]	roller skate, rabbit, radio, tree, orange
[j] y	yarn, yellow, onion
[w]	window, wagon, watch, spider web, bow-wow
[h]	house, hat, horse, hand
[hw] wh	wheel, white, whistle, pinwheel

*Adapted from Anderson, V. A., and Newby, H. A.: Improving the child's speech, ed. 2, New York, 1973, Oxford University Press, pp. 47-48.

Language behavior	Language age equivalency
Receptive Language Scale	
Locates source of bell rung out of his sight.	6 mo.
Responds to name or "no-no" (activity ceases).	9 mo.

Waves "bye-bye" or "patty-cakes" on verbal request.   10 mo.

Comes when called; goes short distances to particular points when directed.   12 mo.

Gives toy on request accompanied by gesture. (Examiner holds out hand for toy child is holding.)   13 mo.

Recognizes a few objects by name.   14 mo.

Recognizes names of a dozen or more familiar objects when he hears them (and presumably sees them and can point to them).   16 mo.

Throws balls to examiner on request and carries out two of the following instructions: 24 mo.
"Put it on the chair."
"Put it on the table."
"Give it to Mother."
"Give it to me."

Identifies 5 or more pictures.   24 mo.

Recognizes objects by function.   2 yr. 3 mo.
"Show me what we drink out of."
"Show me what we buy candy with."
"Show me what goes on our feet."
"Show me what we can cut with."
"Show me what we ride in."
"Show me what we use to iron clothes."

Repeats 2 digits.   2 yr. 6 mo.
"Listen: say 2, now say _____."
a. 4-7
b. 6-3
c. 5-8

Identifies action in pictures.   2 yr. 9 mo.
"Show me the boy (girl) _____."
a. walking
b. running
c. jumping
d. sitting

Repeats one series of 3 digits.   3 yr.
"Say 4-2, now say _____."
a. 6-4-1
b. 3-5-2
c. 8-3-7

Follows preposition directions (must respond to at least 2).   3 yr.
"Put the ball _____."
a. on the chair
b. under the chair
c. in front of the chair
d. beside the chair
e. back of the chair

Interprets pictures.   3 yr. 3 mo.
"Look at these two pictures. See what they are doing here and here. Which one tells you (or makes you think) that it is nighttime."

Comprehends questions.   4 yr.
"What must you do when you are _____?"
a. sleepy
b. hungry
c. cold

Identifies object through function.   4 yr.
"Show me the one _____."
a. we cook on (stove)
b. we carry when it's raining (umbrella)
c. that gives us milk (cow)
d. that grows on a tree (apple)
e. that we read (book)
f. that a hen lays (egg)

Knows opposites.   4 yr.
a. Brother is a boy; sister is a _____.
b. In daytime it is light; at night it is _____.
c. Father is a man; Mother is a _____.
d. The snail is slow; the rabbit is _____.
e. The sun shines during the day; the moon at _____.

Repeats 4 digits.   4 yr. 6 mo.
"I am going to say some numbers and when I am through, I want you to say them just the way I do. Listen carefully and get them just right."
a. 4-7-2-9
b. 3-8-5-2
c. 7-2-6-1

Identifies object by hearing description of it.
"What is a _____ made of?"   4 yr. 6 mo.
a. chair
b. dress
c. shoe

Identifies (point to) coins on request.   5 yr.
a. penny
b. nickel
c. dime

Identifies 4 colors.   5 yr.

Carries out, in order, a command containing three parts. "Pick up the ball, put it on the table, and bring me the book."   5 yr.

Knows definitions.   5 yr.
"What is a ball?"
"What is a bat?"
"What is a stove?"

Expressive Language Scale

Vocalizes to toys; vocalizes for social contact.   6 mo.

Combines vowel sounds; says "m-m-mm" when he cries;   7 mo.

vocalizes recognition of familiar people.

Says "dada" or "mama" in babbling, but not with reference to parents; babbling acquires inflection.	8 mo.
Vocalizes "mama" and "dada" and has one other "word"; imitates sounds such as cough or tongue click.	10 mo.
Imitates a number of syllables as well as sounds; vocalizes 2 "words" other than "mama" and "dada."	12 mo.
Accompanies gestures by vocalization; spontaneously tries to imitate sounds such as adult exclamation.	14 mo.
Has a vocabulary of as many as 10 words; names ball when shown it; may name 1 picture (dog, shoe, cup).	18 mo.
Asks for wants by naming objects— milk, cookie, etc.	18 mo.
Has vocabulary of 20 words; combines 2 or 3 words that express 2 or more different ideas: "Daddy go bye-bye."	21 mo.
Expressive vocabulary of at least 25 words, mostly nouns, some verbs, adverbs, and adjectives; uses names of several familiar objects spontaneously and not merely when presented; talks in short sentences or phrases or subject-object combinations in a meaningful way.	24 mo.
Vocabulary may exceed 50 words; jargon is discarded in favor of understandable but simple 3-word sentences; uses pronouns I, me, and you, although not always correctly; soliloquizes, verbalizing his immediate experience, referring to himself by name. "Johnny fall down." Common expression— "mine."	2 yr.
Verbalizes for food, drink, and toilet. Asks for "another _____," wanting one for each hand.	2 yr.
Gives full name.	2 to 6 yr.
Gives use of some test objects: ball, shoe, penny, pencil; names test objects—shoe, ball, watch, telephone, flag.	2 to 6 yr.
Speech activities are repetitive.	2 to 6 yr.
Vocabulary has innumerable words; speaks in well-formed simple sentences.	3 yr.
Names pictures and on request tells the action: "Dog is running."	3 yr.
Names 8 pictures correctly: cup,	3 yr.

shoe, kitty, house, flag, clock, star, leaf, basket, book.	
Tells sex correctly in response to: "Are you a little girl or a little boy?"	3 yr.
Relates experiences; gives simple accounts of experiences or tells stories (unprompted) with sequential and coherent content and relevant detail.	3 yr. 6 mo.
Has vocabulary in excess of 1,500 words.	4 yr.
Counts 3 objects, pointing to each in turn.	4 yr.
Reads and tells a familiar story by way of pictures: *Three Bears.*	4 yr. 6 mo.
Gives a descriptive comment while naming objects in a composite picture.	5 yr.
Asks meaning of words: "What does _____ mean?"	5 yr.
Has vocabulary in excess of 2,500 words.	6 yr.
Can tell familiar story (*Three Bears*), including most details.	7 yr.

Formal assessment

The administration and interpretation of formal assessment instruments in speech and language should be performed by a trained, experienced, and certified pro-

Table 5-4. Formal articulation tests

Name of test	Age range	Publisher and date
Arizona Articulation Proficiency Scale	3 to 11 yr.	Western Psychological Services, 1970
A Deep Test of Articulation	Grade 2 and under; Grade 3 and over	Stanwix House, Inc., 1964
Fisher-Logemann Test of Articulation Competence		Houghton Mifflin Co., 1971
Goldman-Fristoe Test of Articulation	2 yr. and over	American Guidance Service, 1969
Photo Articulation Test	3 to 12 yr.	The Interstate Printers and Publishers, Inc., 1969
Riley Articulation and Language Test	Kindergarten to Grade 2	Western Psychological Services, 1966
Templin-Darley Tests of Articulation	3 to 8 yr.	University of Iowa, 1969

Table 5-5. Developmental language scales

Name of test	Age range	Author(s)	Publisher and date
The Bzoch-League Receptive-Expressive Emergent Language Scale	Birth to 36 mo.	Bzoch, K. R., and League, R.	The Tree of Life Press, 1972
Communication Evolution Chart from Infancy to Five Years	3 mo. to 5 yr.	Anderson, R., Miles, M., and Matheny, P.	Educators Publishing Service, 1963
Fokes' Developmental Scale of Language Acquisition	Birth to 7 yr.	Fokes, J.	Stephens, B.: Training the developmentally young, New York, 1971, John Day Co., pp. 104-129
Observational Rating Scale of Language	5½ to 14 yr.	Kolstoe, O. P.	Unpublished manuscript, 1963
Oral-Aural Language Schedule		Mecham, M. J.	Mental Retardation, **1**:359-369, 1963
Pattern of Normal Language Development	Birth to 6 yr.	Lillywhite, H.	Journal of American Medical Association, **167**:850-851, 1958
Preschool Language Scale	2 to 6 yr.	Zimmerman, I., Steiner, V., and Evatt, R.	Charles E. Merrill Publishing Co., 1969
Rating Scale for Evaluation of Expressive, Receptive, and Phonetic Language Development in the Young Child	4 wk. to 72 mo.	D'Asaro, M., and John, V.	Cerebral Palsy Review, **22**:3-4, 1961
Reynell Developmental Language Scales (experimental edition)	1 to 5 yr.	Reynell, J.	NFER Publishing Co., Ltd., 1969
The Verbal Language Development Scale	Birth to 15 yr.	Mecham, M. J.	American Guidance Service, 1959

Table 5-6. Formal language tests

Name of test	Age range	Dimensions assessed	Publisher and date
The Houston Test for Language Development	1½ to 6 yr.	Reception, conceptualization, and expression	Houston Test Co., 1963
Illinois Test of Psycholinguistic Abilities, Revised	2 to 10 yr.	Auditory reception, visual reception, auditory association, visual association, verbal expression, manual expression, grammatic closure, visual sequential memory, auditory sequential memory, visual closure, auditory closure (optional), and sound blending (optional)	University of Illinois Press, 1968
The Michigan Picture Language Inventory	4 to 6 yr.		University of Michigan Press, 1958
Peabody Picture Vocabulary Test	2 yr. 5 mo. to 18 yr.	Auditory word comprehension and association	American Guidance Service, 1970
Screening Tests for Identifying Children with Specific Language Disability, Revised	6 to 10 yr.	Visual copying (far and near point), visual perceptual memory, visual discrimination, visual perception, auditory recall, auditory perception of beginning and ending sounds, and auditory association	Educators Publishing Service, 1970
The Utah Test of Language Development, Revised	1½ to 14½ yr.	Comprehension and expression	Communication Research Associates, 1967

fessional. This might include speech clinicians, language specialists, educational diagnosticians, or psychometricians. Table 5-4 lists formal speech tests for diagnosing articulation difficulties, Table 5-5 lists language scales that can be employed to assess language age, and Table 5-6 lists formal language tests that can be used for diagnosing language difficulties.

SPEECH DEFECTS

The classroom teacher of the trainable child is, in effect, a speech teacher because of the extremely high incidence (90% to 95%) of speech problems among her students. Her speech-related functions include (1) the prevention of speech disorders, (2) general speech improvement for all children, (3) the refinement of speech skills, and (4) the correction of speech defects. Briefly discussed will be articulation disorders, stuttering, and voice disorders.

Articulation disorders

About 90% of all speech problems are articulatory by nature. When speech sounds are not produced in an accepted manner, articulation is defective. The main errors occur in the form of omissions, substitutions, and distortions.

Omission errors are the most severe and are characterized by the speaker omitting sounds that are present in normal pronunciation (e.g., "ni" for knife; "ate" for plate). Omissions are a common occurrence in the speech of the trainable mentally retarded.

Substitution errors occur when the speaker substitutes incorrect sounds for ones that are normally heard. Substitutions develop (1) when the correct sound has never been learned, (2) when the substitution has been learned (e.g., models at home), and (3) when only a few sounds are learned but used for all others (e.g., "tat" for cat; "momy" for money).

When the correct sound is approximated but not similar enough to be normally accepted, it is considered a *distortion*. Distortions are less noticeable than substitutions and are not nonstandard pronunciations involving incorrect vowels associated with dialectal speech patterns (e.g., "jist" for just; "git" for get).

Causes for articulation disorders include (1) physical abnormalities such as dental irregularities, tongue anomalies, tongue thrust (reverse swallowing), (2) organic conditions such as cleft palate, cerebral palsy, and partial or total deafness, (3) faulty learning from poor models, and (4) emotional maladjustment. The cause is important; often, if it is physical, it can be corrected.

As a speech correctionist for minor articulation problems, the teacher should begin by isolating and providing activities for the problem sounds. The help and advice from the speech therapists should be undertaken if a problem is suspected, but in the meantime the teacher can do the following:

1. Reassure the child about his importance as an individual.

2. Encourage the child to participate in activities in which he is successful.

3. Make the child's attempts at speech rewarding and pleasurable.

4. Use appropriate articulation.

5. Make every effort to understand the child's speech.

6. Build up the child's self-confidence with praise for work well done.

Stuttering

Although stuttering is a rare disability (less than 1% of the general population), it ranks second in incidence of speech disorders.. It is difficult to describe all behaviors associated with stuttering, but they have in common an interruption in the flow of speech, commonly described as a break in the rhythm and a disruption in fluency (Ainsworth, 1975). The two terms used to describe the severity of stuttering behavior are *primary stuttering* and *secondary stuttering* (Van Riper, 1972). A primary stutterer is in the beginning stages of stuttering and partly unaware of the

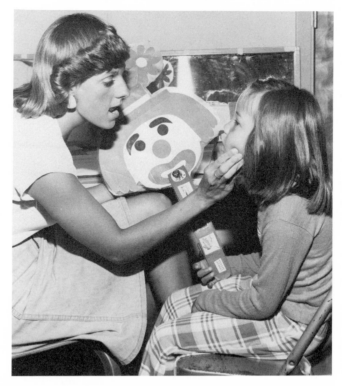

Fig. 5-3. Teacher or speech therapist must provide individual attention and make use of attractive innovative instructional devices in correcting articulation problems in the TMR. (Courtesy Bossier Parish, La., Public Schools.)

disfluencies; a secondary stutterer is well aware and has anxieties or fears. Associated characteristics of the secondary stutterer sometimes include tics or facial grimaces developed in reaction to the defect.

The teacher, in response to a stutterer, *should:*

- Create an atmosphere of ease and relaxation.
- React to stuttering in an unemotional and objective manner.
- Allow the child to complete his sentences.
- Listen in a relaxed but interested manner.
- Look at his eyes when he is speaking, not his mouth.
- Provide opportunities and tasks where success is easily obtainable.
- Ask questions that can be answered with short responses.
- Give sincere affection.

The teacher, in response to a stutterer, *should not:*

- Make an issue of speech.
- Tell him to "start over," "take your time," etc.
- Show impatience, embarrassment, or boredom.
- Stress perfection.

- Have an attitude of pity or sympathy.
- Accept wrong answers.
- Discuss his weaknesses or shortcomings in his presence.

Voice disorders

The three main voice disorders are faults in pitch (high or low), quality (harsh, nasal, guttural), and intensity (loudness) from either organic or functional causes. Voice disorders often go unrecognized and therefore untreated by the untrained speech correctionist. The most important point for the teacher is to always encourage pleasing voices. She may do this by helping the child hear himself or comparing voices with the use of a tape recorder. The area of voice therapy is a complex one and should only be handled by a speech clinician (Fox and Blechman, 1975).

MANUAL COMMUNICATION

For TMR children who are deaf, lack understandable vocal expressive skills, or

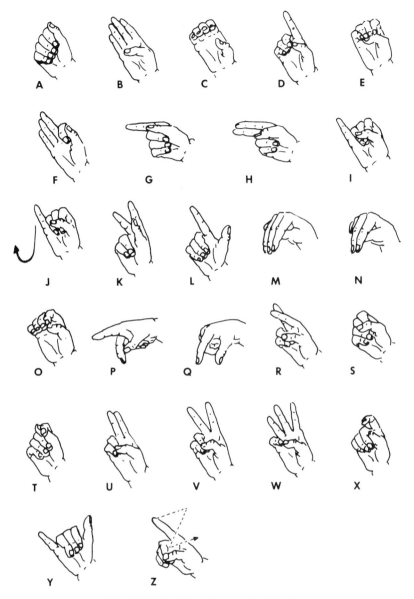

Fig. 5-4. Traditional manual alphabet.

have other serious language handicaps, communication can be achieved by using a system of total communication. This procedure employs simultaneous presentation of visual-manual language with spoken English. The trainer always speaks with clarity and firmness while signing, whether the child has normal or impaired hearing. Those with hearing will develop some spoken words, and those without hearing or with limited hearing can learn to speech read.

One recent experiment (Grinnell, Detamore, and Lippe, 1976) combined manual English and specific verbalization activities to teach language skills to severely and profoundly mentally retarded students 3 to 21 years of age. This multisensory approach used some of the traditional signs but added many new ones. Inflections were added, as well as endings, pronouns, articles, and other structural language elements.

The students of the program were either

nonverbal language-delayed (those who had not developed functional skills in receptive or expressive areas beyond rote learned direction following) or had limited verbal skills. The limited verbal group possessed so many inconsistent substitutions of sounds in words that their speech was unintelligible.

Results indicated that students not only learned and retained the correct manual English signs but also initiated signs and verbalized the corresponding word. This specialized technique increased the communication skills of most students. Signing classes were held for parents and other faculty to aid in reinforcing student use of appropriate signs. For some parents, signing was the first real communication exchange between them and their children.

The application of manual communication, even with the nonhearing-impaired child, will not harm the development of vocalizations but instead seems to facilitate receptive language skills (Bricker, 1972). The TMR child can be taught to understand and use signs to communicate simple words and concepts, simple commands, words for objects, body parts, etc.

A basic manual communication program must begin from the most elemental stages and proceed to more involved words for communication. Administration of such a program must also be structured, hierarchical, and sequential. One training program that meets these criteria was developed by Snell (1974) and consists of five phases. The words (signs) contained in these instructional phases follow:

A. Attending phase
1. Sit/chair
2. Still/quiet/be quiet
3. Now
4. Attend/watch
5. Look
6. Me
7. This/these
8. You

B. Motor imitation
1. Attend/watch
2. And
3. You

4. Do/activity

C. Vocal imitation
1. Say

D. Receptive phase
1. Show/demonstrate
2. Ears
3. Eyes
4. Face
5. Hair
6. Hands
7. Mouth
8. Nose
9. Teeth
10. Baby
11. Ball
12. Bell
13. Car
14. Comb
15. Hat
16. Key
17. Shoes
18. Go
19. Get
20. Box
21. Sit/chair
22. Door
23. Floor
24. Light
25. Table
26. Your/yours
27. Put/move
28. On
29. In
30. Under/below/beneath
31. Give

E. Expressive phase
1. What
2. Is
3. Are
4. That/those
5. Whose/who/whom
6. My/mine
7. Disappear/gone
8. Where

Once the child completes the phases, the possible combinations of communication (receptive and expressive) for learning purposes are endless. A manual or total communication language program holds great promise and merits serious consideration for many TMR students. Following are general techniques to use when teaching signing, as well as procedures for introducing new signs.

Techniques for teaching signing

1. Be thoroughly familiar with all signs before beginning and be able to sign at a consistent, smooth, and deliberate pace.

2. To avoid confusing the student, position all signs correctly.

3. Make signs close to the body, positioned below the shoulder and above the waist. The only exceptions would be those signs which should be made near the face.

4. Always directly face the person with whom you are manually communicating.

5. To allow generalization to other persons and situations, teach standard single signs. This will also eliminate the confusion associated with more than one sign for an object, person, or action.

Procedures for teaching new signs

1. Emphasize a new sign with slow, smooth, exaggerated rhythms.

2. Repeat new signs several times.

3. Maintain direct eye contact and use the appropriate facial and body expressions along with the new sign.

YOU (singular)
Point straight at the other
person with the right index
finger.

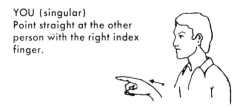

SAY
Hold the right index finger
parallel to the mouth; circle
it forward and down.

Fig. 5-5. Manual communication signs for *you* and *say*.

PROCEDURES FOR DEVELOPING SPEECH AND LANGUAGE SKILLS

As stated earlier, speech and language gains are possible in the mentally retarded, regardless of level of functioning. However, gains become dependent on a number of factors, including the skills and competencies of the teacher, the environment, and the approach employed.

The individual performing the language training should be skilled in the shaping procedures that are standard behavioral techniques. These procedures include positive reinforcement, modeling-imitation, shaping, prompting, fading, stimulus control, generalization, and extinction (Bricker and Bricker, 1970; Jens, Belmore, and Belmore, 1976).* Additional specific competencies that are necessary and relate directly to the instructional process include the ability to analyze language tasks and the ability to develop a sequential order of presenting tasks.

The environment for instruction in language should provide for control in presenting stimuli and delivering reinforcement. An optimal environment would contain separate rooms for individual instruction to supplement a student's group work. Group language instruction alone has not proved particularly effective for the TMR (Blue, 1970).

A number of approaches currently exist with regard to language instruction for

the TMR (Bricker and Bricker, 1970; Carrier and Peak, 1975; Chalfant, Kirk, and Jensen, 1968; Sailor, Guess, and Baer, 1973; Tawney and Hipsher, 1972). The principal characteristic of all approaches is that *instruction is systematic.* The severely retarded must have systematic exposure to a curriculum area as complex as language if gains are to be evidenced. One approach to an individual systematic language instruction program for the TMR is represented in Fig. 5-6. This approach consists of eight stages:

Stage 1: Assess individual language, formal and informal.

Stage 2: Analyze information and determine level of language functioning.

Stage 3: Identify skills to be developed and write sequential instructional objectives.

Stage 4: Begin instruction of objective 1 of skill 1 (checking also to see if prerequisite behaviors are necessary to begin objective 1).

Stage 5: Check for adequate progress (continue or make changes as necessary).

Stage 6: Continue plan while reducing prompts (using fading techniques).

Stage 7: Test for objective 1 for attainment of criteria.

Stage 8: Chart progress and proceed to next objective or step.

What language skills should I teach?

There are numerous basic communication skills to be developed in the TMR. The following guidelines developed by Jens, Belmore, and Belmore (1976) contribute to providing an answer to the question "What language skills should I teach?"

1. Teach the names of those objects the student comes in contact with most frequently during his daily activities.

---

*See Chapter 3 for a discussion of each technique.

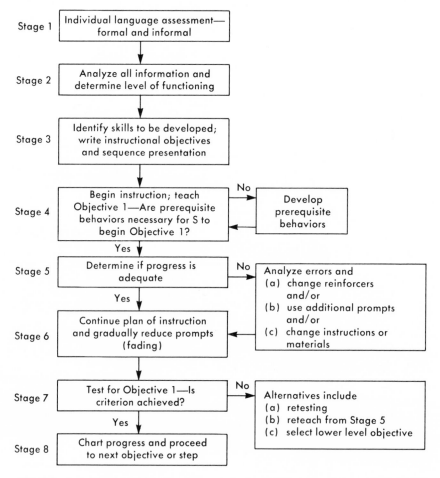

Fig. 5-6. Individual systematic approach to language instruction with the TMR.

2. Teach the names (or labels) of persons the student must frequently interact with.
3. Teach words or phrases the student hears most often in the instructional program.
4. Teach words and phrases commonly used in the student's home.
5. Teach those verbal responses the student is asked to make most often in his environment.
6. Teach those verbal responses the student will be asked to make in his future environment (sheltered workshop, etc.).

Another practical approach that has merit for the TMR is the expanding language environment concept (Chalfant,

Kirk, and Jensen, 1968). This concept, illustrated in Fig. 5-7, employs object words, action words, commands, statements, and questions found in the student's environment. It begins with the child and expands to the family, the home, the yard, the community, and the city and country.

Specific desirable communication skills to be developed in the TMR include the listening and speaking areas of language:

Listening or receptive skills
Motor imitation
Development of auditory perceptual components of good listening behavior
Auditory awareness
Auditory focusing
Auditory figure-ground
Auditory discrimination
Auditory memory

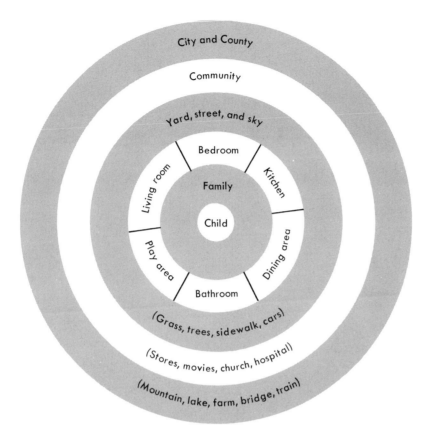

Fig. 5-7. Child's expanding language environment. (Reprinted from Teaching Exceptional Children by Chalfant, J., Kirk, G., and Jensen, K. by permission of The Council for Exceptional Children. Copyright © 1968 by The Council for Exceptional Children, Reston, Va.)

Auditory sequencing
Auditory blending
Auditory association
Knowledge of environmental sounds
Knowledge of sounds in isolation
Listening for information
Following directions
Listening for enjoyment (e.g., music)
Speaking or expressive skills
Development of physical prerequisites for speech
Gesturing to communicate
Motor and vocal sound
Imitation
Development of vowel sounds
Development of consonant sounds
Repetition of words (vocal word imitation)
Independent production of functional words
Identification of pictures of commonly spoken words
Comprehension of meaning of commonly spoken words
Repetition of functional phrases and sentences

Independent production of functional phrases and sentences

Techniques for promoting speech and language skills

1. *Parent as teacher.* Provide a good speech model for the child. Speak quietly and pronounce words clearly, distinctly, and with expressiveness.

2. *Talking is fun.* Create a warm relaxed atmosphere in the home that is conducive to communication. Be casual—do not pressure the child. Let him know that talking can be pleasant and enjoyable!

3. *Interaction.* Make a sincere effort to talk with the child as well as to really listen to what he says. Appropriate questions and comments regarding the content of what the child said or a statement such as, "How interesting . . . tell me some more

about that," might encourage the child to offer more conversation; this might also be useful if the adult does not understand what the child says and needs more information to do so.

4. *Word supply.* Provide the child with words, phrases, and sentences to describe or label objects, actions, feelings, and concepts (color, size, shape, time and space, etc.). This can be done throughout the day—in the house, outside in the yard or in the garage, while traveling in the car, when going on picnics, or while visiting the post office, doctor's office, stores, airport, zoo, or amusement park, and so on. When explaining the meaning of new words, use words that the child will understand.

  a. *Self-talk.* This procedure involves an adult talking out loud in the presence of the child about what he or she (the adult) is seeing, doing, or feeling at the moment. An example of this might be: "Mama's cooking . . . pot . . . put the pot on the stove . . . beans . . . put the green beans in the pot . . . turn on the stove . . . hot . . . the beans are cooking, they're getting hot . . . stir the beans."

  b. *Parallel-talk:* An adult talking out loud in the presence of the child about what the child is seeing, doing, or feeling at the moment is involved in this procedure. An example of this technique might be: "Look at Johnny . . . Johnny's playing with his blocks . . . he's building a tower. First, he puts a blue block, then a red one, and then another one . . . and some more blocks . . . look how tall Johnny's tower is getting!"

5. *Useful words.* Let the child experiment with new and old words, particularly ones that are important to him in his everyday life. Assist him in understanding the many uses of speech and language; help him learn that words can get him what he wants more quickly or that talk-

ing about problems can often lead to solutions. Gestures and grunts should generally not be accepted in the place of a speech attempt; for example, if the child points to the cookie jar while licking his lips, the parent might say, "Are you hungry? What would you like?" Verbal responses, which might range from "cookie" to "I'd like one of the homemade chocolate chip cookies that you baked this morning, please," should be encouraged.

6. *Expansion.* Add to or enlarge the child's utterances. For example, the child who says, "Kitty eat," may have this repeated to him by his parents as, "The kitty is eating," or "The white kitty is named Lulu. Lulu must be very hungry; she's so busy eating!"

7. *Read, read, read!* While reading a familiar story or rhyme to the child, ask him to point out pictures in the book or magazine. For example, you might say, "Show me the giraffe" or "Where's the mean old ogre?" Parents can let the child tell a story by way of the pictures, retell the story in their own words after the book has been read or put away, or, at the end of the reading, answer content questions such as "What was the little girl's name in the story?" or "Why did Joe want the car to go fast?" Bedtime might be a quiet and relaxing time to read to the child.

8. *Listening and learning.* Help the child increase his ability to "tune in" or pay attention and to remember or recall items.

  a. *Environmental sounds.* Listen for sounds in the house (voices, phones, doorbells, knocks, moving of chairs, running water, clocks, appliances), in the park or the woods (bird calls and other animal sounds, wind blowing, water fountains and streams, squeaking swings, and teeter-totters, footsteps), or while walking along a city street (cars, brakes screeching, train whistles, dogs barking, voices, shuffling of feet).

b. *Sound and word fun.* Reciting rhymes and singing songs will be fun for the youngster while benefiting the development of his skills in language and listening, inflectional patterns, fluency, and articulation.

c. *Games.* Play "Simon Says," "Follow the Leader," "Mother May I," and "Gossip" or "Telephone," a game in which a "secret" is whispered from one person to another in a circle; the last receiver has to compare his message with the original statement.

d. *Following directions.* Depending on the level of the child, require him to carry out one or more directions: (e.g., "Give me the ball"; "Pick up your shoes.") ("Go change your clothes, bring out the garbage, and then eat your snack"; "Turn around three times, hop on one foot, then put your left hand on your right knee.")

9. *Television guide.* Carefully choose the shows that the child will watch on television. Take time to talk to him about the things he has heard and seen relating to the selected programs.

Techniques for articulation development*

1. *Corrective feedback.* This approach will allow the child to hear the correct sound many times.

Johnny: Mom, whereth the thoap?
Mother: The *s*oap? Let me see. . . . Where's the *s*oap? Here is the *s*oap! We have green *s*oap. Do you hear the "s" sound? (Accept whatever response Johnny gives; patience is essential!) Here is the *s*oap? What is this?
Johnny: Soap (or *Th*oap).
Mother: Take the *s*oap now and wash your hands real good.

2. *Self-correction.* It is helpful for the adult to occasionally produce a speech

sound incorrectly in his own speech and then casually correct himself. For example, the parent might casually say, "My goodness! I see a *w*at . . . a dirty *w*at. No, not *w*at . . . *r*at. I see a big, dirty *r*at. Go away, *r*at!"

3. *Sound prolongation.* Subtle exaggeration of sounds will call attention to them. Every now and then, try something such as, "I *sss*py *sss*omething green. What is it?" Child guesses, "Is it the g*rath*?" Adult responds, "Yes (No), it is (isn't) the gra*sss* that I'm *sss*pying. Good gue*sss* (or gue*sss* again)!"

4. *Mirror work.* Occasionally use a mirror to observe the speech helpers (lips, tongue, teeth, etc.) in action while producing sounds. The child will be able to look and listen ("Our tongue peeks out between our teeth to say th - th - th" or "Put your lips together and hum; listen to the 'm' sound.").

5. *Sound scrapbooks.* Make sound scrapbooks with the child using pictures cut from old catalogs or magazines that contain a sound he is having difficulty with. Glue the pictures on cards or in a notebook.

6. *Look-listen-say.* Have the child name things he sees that contain a specific sound; or have him locate items in a certain category that contain "his" sound (foods, zoo or farm animals, toys, colors, etc.). Later, the child can draw or cut out pictures of some of these things.

7. *Hide and seek.* Hide pictures or objects that have a special sound in their names around the room. With the parent serving as a speech monitor, the child names the items that he found.

8. *Tongue twisters.* Make up sentences with the child that are loaded with a particular sound; for example, "Six swimming sailors saw seventy-six seahorses in the surging sea one September Sunday"; "Randy rabbit ran rapidly down the road."

9. *Songs.* Sing songs that have verses containing many words with particular speech sounds in them. There are endless possibilities, for example:

---

*These techniques were provided by Charlotte Ducote, Instructor of Special Education, University of New Orleans, New Orleans, La.

r: *"Row, Row, Row Your Boat"; "Rain, Rain Go Away"; "Ring Around the Rosy"*

l: *"London Bridge Is Falling Down"; "Looby Loo"; "Mary Had a Little Lamb"*

th: *"Three Blind Mice"; "Happy Birthday"; "This Old Man"*

s: *"Sing a Song of Sixpence"; "Eeensy Weensy Spider"*

A specific lesson plan to remediate and develop each needed speech sound should be devised. Examples of the "s" and "r" sounds are given below.

"S" sound

Materials

1. Seven similar objects (blocks, pencils, paper clips, etc.)
2. A crayon and piece of paper for each child
3. Pictures of "s" words to hide around the room (sun, sailor, six, socks, etc.)

Introduction

Listen to the "s" sound: s - s - s - s - s - s. "S" is the hissing snake sound. S - s - s - s - s - s. Let's try to make the "s" sound . . . place the sides of your tongue against the sides of your upper teeth (demonstrate). Blow air down the center and over the tip of your tongue and between nearly closed teeth (demonstrate). Hear the hissing sound? Let's say "s" again! (For students who persistently say "th" for "s" or touch the back of their upper front teeth with their tongue, suggest that the tongue must stay in its "house"—it can't "peek" out. A mirror might be used. For students who produce a slushy distortion or an "sh" for "s," try having them produce "s" while keeping a very narrow straw placed lengthwise and midway back down the center of the tongue. This should assist in keeping the sides of the tongue pressed against the sides of the upper teeth.)

Activities

"Now, let's do some things with the s sound."

1. Say, "On your piece of paper, draw some grass. Now, when I say the 's' sound, draw a snake in the grass." (Demonstrate: let the letter "s" represent a snake. The children will draw a "snake" for each time that the teacher says "s" in isolation.)

2. Have the children follow directions while playing "Simon Says" (sit up straight, stand up tall, sing a song, go to sleep, stir the soup, sweep the floor, swim, sip a soda, etc.).

3. Play "Hide and Seek" with "s" picture cards. Let the children search to see what they can find. When all cards have been found, teacher and children name the pictures. Emphasize the "s" sound.

4. Say, "The number seven has the 's' sound in it . . . Listen, s-s-seven. Let's count to seven . . . one, two, three, four, five, six, seven." Now say, "We use the number seven to count and to add.

Watch . . . I have two blocks in a pile and I'm going to add five blocks to the pile . . . How many blocks do I have? One, two, three, four, five, six, seven . . . Right, I have seven blocks." (Continue the activity with the children taking turns: 2 + 5, 6 + 1, 4 + 3.)

5. Sing the following with the children (hand movements can be used):

> A sailor went to sea, sea, sea
> To see what he could see, see, see
> And all that he could see, see, see
> Was the great big beautiful sea, sea, sea.

6. Tell the children to draw pictures on their "grass and snake picture" of objects they can see outside. Go to each child and ask him to name several of his pictures. Provide corrective feedback for "s" production.

7. Give each child a smiling "happy face" for work well done.

Other suggestions: sounds we hear; what we see at the zoo, on a farm, in the kitchen, etc.; "Sing a Song of Sixpence"; small and large; "I Spy"; days of the week, and so on.

"R" sound

Materials

1. A worksheet with a picture of a rooster on it for each child (Write six lowercase *r* letters in a row below the rooster.)
2. A small plastic rabbit (or one cut out of construction paper)
3. A small rug made out of construction paper or scrap material
4. A red crayon for each child
5. A worksheet of pictures of objects to be colored red: ball, shoe, sock, car, book, pencil, bird, star, chair, boat
6. A fishing pole made out of a yardstick, string, and a magnet: tie one end of the string to the yardstick; attach the magnet to the free end of the string.
7. Picture cards of "r" words (attach a paper clip to each card): rock, rooster, rabbit, rocket, rug, carrot, turtle, fork, tire, star, chair, car
8. Enough raisins or red apple pieces to use as reinforcements for the children.

Introduction

"Look and listen! Our special sound today is "r." (Show a picture of a rooster.) It is the rooster sound—er-er-er-er-errrrrrrrr! We can make the rooster sound by using our tongue. Lift your tongue to the top of your mouth and curl it back. Crow like a rooster—er-er-er-er-errrrrrrrrr." (If the children are having difficulty: (1) try having them say, "ah - r" or "ah - l - r," (2) emphasize tongue placement by holding out the palm of one hand and curling the finger tips backward to simulate "r" production, or (3) have them say the "y" sound as in "yes," before saying "r" if they need assistance placing the sides of their tongue against the sides of their upper teeth—y - r.)

Activities

"Remember the good 'r' sound. We'll be using it today!"

1. "The *rooster* wants to *run* in the *rain*. Everytime I say the *rooster* sound, 'r,' *draw* a *raindrop* on the *rooster* picture (demonstrate) . . . r - r - r - r - r - r - r . . ."

2. Tell the children, "I am going to sing a short song. My song has the word *rain* in it. *Rain* has the 'r' sound at the beginning—listen . . . *rrrain*. Everytime I sing the word *rain*, trace the letter *r* at the bottom of your *rooster* picture" (demonstrate using a red crayon). Sing the lines, "*Rain*, *rain*, go away, come again some other day," three times.

3. Play a fishing game with the fishing pole and "r" cards. Name all the "r" cards that are swimming in the pond. Let each child have a turn to go fishing and name his catch. Ask, "What did you catch?" Child responds, "A _____." Teacher says, "Right! You caught a _____." Say (point to child), "I caught a _____." (Encourage child to respond in a complete sentence.)

4. Say, "Let's put our fishing pole away and go *row* a boat. Watch . . . This is how we *row* a boat" (demonstrate). Sing, "*Row Row Row* Your Boat" several times with the children while *row*ing the boat.

5. Play "Ring Around the Rosy."

6. Teach prepositions while stressing correct "r" articulation. Put the *rabbit* on the *rug*, under the *rug*, or on the side of the *rug*. Ask, "Where is the *rabbit*?" (Wait for the child's response.) "The *rabbit* is _____ the *rug*."

7. Give each child the picture worksheet. Say, "Here are some pictures. Color them all *red*." When the children have finished coloring, point to a picture completed by each one and ask, "What is this?" Encourage the response, "It is a *red* _____."

8. Reward each child with a *raisin* or *red* apple piece for a job well done.

Additional procedures might involve activities geared around *relay races*, *ring toss*, left and right, get *ready*—get set—go, singing "*Rock-a-bye* Baby or "*Rudolph* the *Red*-nosed *Reindeer*," etc.

Physical exercises for speech production

Of vital importance to speech production are the physical organs and their capabilities. The child must be capable of inhaling, exhaling, sucking, swallowing, controlling the tongue, and chewing. Quite often the TMR child has physical organ defects, respiratory difficulties, or may be cerebral palsied and lack control of the necessary muscles. In these cases time may have to be spent developing physical skills. Following are exercises for inhaling, exhaling, sucking and swallowing, tongue control, chewing, and control of drooling.*

Inhaling exercises

1. Have the child inhale at any desirable rate any amount of air up to his maximum capacity. The use of a mirror for this activity may assist the child in observing his chest expansion, shape of lips, and depressed cheeks.

2. Encourage the child to be as noisy or as quiet as he wants while inhaling.

3. Have the child inhale, hold his breath, and then release the air.

4. Have the child inhale, hold his breath, puff his cheeks, and then exhale with his cheeks puffed.

5. Have the child inhale as much air as he can while you count up to three, four, five.

6. Hold a piece of paper touching the child's lips. Have the child inhale. The paper should stay on the child's lips as long as he inhales.

Exhaling exercises

1. Have the child blow candles, papers, cotton balls, and feathers.

2. Have the child stand or sit in front of a mirror. If he gets close enough to the mirror and blows, he will be able to see his breath marks on the mirror.

3. Have the child blow on a cold window during the winter so that he can see the frost marks left by his breath.

4. Have the child whistle: long and short, slow and fast.

5. Have the child blow on his own hand so that he may feel the force of his breath.

6. Have the child blow dandelion seeds.

7. Have the child exhale while you count to two, three, four.

*Information on pp. 135 to 137 from Gordon, M. L., Ryan, D. H., and Shilo, T.: Helping the trainable mentally retarded child develop speech and language: a guidebook for parents, teachers, and paraprofessionals, pp. 4-7, 1972. Courtesy Charles C Thomas, Publisher, Springfield, Ill.

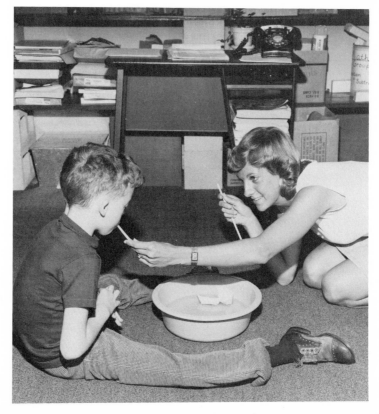

Fig. 5-8. Exhaling exercise to develop respiratory control—a necessary prerequisite skill for adequate speech. (Courtesy Bossier Parish, La., Public Schools.)

8. While the child exhales, have him feel and watch his abdominal (stomach) muscles.

9. Have a blowing contest with a few children. The child who can blow the object the farthest wins. Use bubbles, balloons, party horns, whistles.

10. When the child exhales, try to get him to produce a vowel sound: ah, oo, ee.

Sucking and swallowing exercises

1. For proper sucking and swallowing, have the child keep his head in an upright position.

2. To stimulate the child to suck, compress his cheeks.

3. Stroke the child's throat muscles while you are compressing his cheeks to stimulate him to swallow.

4. Spoon cold fluids to stimulate swallowing. Use nondairy unsweetened fluids such as unsweetened fruit drinks and water.

5. If the child can feed himself with a spoon, provide jams and jellies to help swallowing. As the child learns to swallow, introduce thicker foods.

6. Use lollypops for rewarding and reinforcing sucking and swallowing.

7. Have the child sip fluids through a straw. When he can do this with no trouble, pinch the straw.

8. Use ice cream as a reward but remember that it might inhibit swallowing, as it is a saliva-thickening food.

Note: Warm sweet fluids, citric acids, and milk products are hard to swallow. Salty and oily fluids are easier to swallow.

Tongue control

1. Apply pressure to the child's tongue with a tongue blade or a frozen ice pop stick. Start at the tip of the tongue and work toward the back with a *walking*

motion. The child's tongue will move back into his mouth automatically.

2. Play "Do What I Do" with the child. Have the child imitate your tongue movements. Some good tongue exercises are trying to touch the nose, trying to touch the chin, moving the tongue laterally, and extending the tongue as far as possible and retracting the tongue. As the child improves, he may be directed to increase the speed of these individual tongue exercises.

3. Have the child produce a la-la-la sound with alternating slow and fast rhythms.

Chewing exercises

1. Have the child bite down so that he will leave an impression of his teeth on substances such as soft candy and gum.

2. Have the child chew taffy as vigorously as possible.

3. Have the child chew on a wet cloth rag so that he will suck all the water out.

Drooling control exercises

1. Use humming, kissing, humming on a piece of paper, which gives a tickle sensation, and lip printing on a piece of paper (put lipstick on the child's lips) as exercises to encourage the child to close his lips. Lip printing shows the child the difference between open and closed lips.

2. When the child drools with his mouth open, tap under his chin to prompt him to close his mouth.

3. Have the child chew like a cow in front of a mirror.

4. Have the child exercise, protruding and retracting his lower jaw, to strengthen the muscles around his mouth and improve their coordination. These exercises should be done at a slower rate with a Down's syndrome child because of the larger size of the child's tongue.

5. Use biting exercises for jaw closure.

Listening, gesturing, and speaking activities

There exist a limitless number of successful individual and group activities that could be used in the basic communication area. The activities used often depend on the availability of resources or the inventiveness or ingenuity of the teacher. The child's in-school environment should not only be used for new learning experiences but also for generalizing what has been learned. Provide opportunities (by way of activities) to further develop and enhance those speech and language skills the child has acquired.

Following are some activities that can be used with TMRs in the areas of listening, gesturing, and speaking.

Listening activities

1. Identify community or home sounds (animals, bells, horn, telephone) from a tape recorder.

2. Have students put their heads on their desks and guess the classroom sounds that are made (knock on the door, door closing, paper rustling, whistle, writing on the board).

3. Have students imitate a series of sounds.

4. Recite nursery rhymes and ask questions about the rhymes that only require a yes or no ("Mary Had a Little Lamb," "Little Bo-Peep," "Little Miss Muffet," "Jack Be Nimble," "Pease Porridge Hot").

5. Recite simple but favorite children's stories and ask simple questions ("Three Little Pigs," "The Three Bears," "The Gingerbread Man").

6. Identify records.

7. Game: "Simon Says".

8. Game: "You Must"—a variation of "Simon Says" except that the teacher does not have to perform the act.

9. Game: "Bring Me"—play by having students in their desk. Then students perform the "bring me" request but only if it is sensible. If it is a silly request (e.g., bring me your house), students must sit still.

10. Listen and discriminate between loud and soft sounds (may be a clap, knock, word).

11. Listen and discriminate between sounds that are the same or different (the same for high and low pitch, fast and slow noises).

Gesturing activities

1. Have the child act out motions that accompany songs such as "Here We Go 'Round the Mulberry Bush," "Hokey-Pokey."

2. Act out concept words such as high-low, big-little, short-long, above-below, up-down, inside-outside.

3. Have the child "Show me what you can do with this," using various objects and tools (e.g., pen, hammer, saw, book).

4. Perform an action and have the child imitate your action and tell what you are doing (e.g., sleeping, waving, talking on the phone).

5. Have the child act out verbs (e.g., skipping, fishing, hitting a baseball).

6. Discuss the meaning of facial expressions (sad, happy) and various postures (e.g., tired, sitting).

Speaking activities

1. Use a telephone to practice speaking skills.

2. Have a "Talk and Tell Time."

3. Take field trips in or out of school and talk about them.

4. Talk about pets, hobbies, or weather.

5. Have a "surprise box"—student reaches in and withdraws an article and must then tell about it (color, shape, size, use, etc.).

6. Exchange greetings in the morning and afternoon.

7. Incorporate phrases from their language lesson into other activities (e.g., physical education) and have the child use them.

8. Perform an action and have the child name and describe the action.

9. Hide certain pictures or specific objects in the room and have the child find and then talk about them.

10. Play the game "I Am Thinking of Something Red—Do You Know What it Is?" Have the child or group guess the objects that are red in the room until he answers correctly.

11. Riddles: Ask any question using clues in the question and let the child or group guess the object. For example, "I am thinking of something you eat with, can you guess what it might be?"

12. Play store with the child using as many lifelike and labeled objects as possible. Have the child guess and talk about the items.

13. Game: "Spin the Bottle"—have the child spin the bottle; the child it stops on must tell about pictures the teacher has. The child can choose the picture.

14. Have the child think of as many words as he can to describe a particular object, for example, a ball (sound, hard, small, white).

15. Have the child tell what is missing in an incomplete picture.

16. Use action pictures for the child to describe.

17. Have a child describe scenes from a stereoscopic viewer (e.g., Viewmaster).

18. From pictures of objects on small cards, have the child draw one and think of the possible uses of that object.

MATERIALS AND RESOURCES IN THE BASIC COMMUNICATIONS AREA

With numerous published or commercial language materials and programs available today, reviewing and adopting the "right one" becomes perplexing to the teacher, therapists, or language specialists. It is wise to review as many programs as possible prior to selection. It is quite possible that several programs can be used, since the range of language deficiencies in TMR students is great. Another reason for adopting more than one for use is the variability of content in the different programs. Some are aimed only at lower levels of language development, and others are more comprehensive. Some school districts have adopted only certain facets of different packaged materials or modified the programs to suit their own needs. Whatever the case, several dimensions to assist in reviewing or adopting such programs are given.

Factors for adopting a speech or language program for TMRs

1. What are characteristics of the program's target population?
   a. CA, MA, IQ
   b. Institutionalized vs. noninstitutionalized
   c. Entering language level

Fig. 5-9. Use of language development kits such as the Peabody are effective in developing the receptive and expressive skills of the TMR. (Courtesy Greenwich, Conn., Public Schools.)

2. What language functions does the program cover?
   a. Listening (receptive) vs. speaking (expressive) skills
   b. Imitation
   c. Verbal vs. gestural, or both
3. What methods are employed in training sessions?
   a. Shaping, fading, extinction, or other behavioral training techniques
4. What specific materials are necessary and are they in the program package?
   a. Classroom materials
   b. Special apparatus
5. Who can best carry out the language sessions?
   a. Classroom teacher of the TMR
   b. Speech therapist
   c. Aide
   d. Other
6. Does the material provide for transfer and generalization?
7. What is the length of the program?
   a. Length of sessions
   b. Number of sessions each week
   c. Projected overall time
8. Are any modifications necessary?
   a. Planning time
   b. Other professional assistance

Specialized programs

Auditory Perception Activity Book by The Speech Therapy Department, Jefferson Parish School Board.

This activity book consists of a receptive and expressive language development scale plus activities to develop auditory reception, discrimination, association, sequential memory and sound blending. It was designed for use by speech therapists and teachers.

BKR Educational Projects by Louise Bradtke, William Kirkpatrick, and Katherine Rosenblatt, BKR Educational Projects, Inc.

This program consists of 15 basic language lessons relating to receptive, expressive, and nonverbal communication by sign. Also present are sections labeled cognition, visual skills, auditory (nonverbal) skills, fine motor skills, gross motor skills, social self, personal skills, and direction.

Distar Language I by Siegfried Engelmann and Jean Osborn, Science Research Associates, Inc.

A highly structured developmental program, *Distar* emphasizes receptive, expressive, and motor imitation language skills. It is designed for use by teachers and can be for individuals or groups.

Emerging Language by John Hatten, Tracy Goman, and Carole Lent, The Learning Business.

This book, with 144 language objectives, is designed for use by speech therapists or teachers concerned with language-disordered children.

For Speech Sake!: Activities for Classroom Teachers and Speech Therapists (revised edition) by Ruth E. Jones, Fearon Publishers.

Designed for the classroom teacher, this 66-page book contains four chapters: (1) speech correction and language development, (2) developing your classroom speech program, (3) working with speech sounds, and (4) more games and activities. This book is practical and offers classroom tested games, jingles, poetry, verse choir, story play, dramatization and other activities.

GOAL (Games Oriented Activities for Learning): Language Development by Merle B. Karnes, Milton Bradley & Co.

The GOAL kit contains 337 lesson plans on 8 × 9-inch cards plus other teaching aids and devices and is based on the clinical model of the Illinois Test of Psycholinguistic Abilities (ITPA). These game-oriented activities are designed to develop language processing skills.

Karnes Early Language Activities by Merle B. Karnes, GEM.

This program is designed for low-level language retarded children and consists of 200 model lessons with 1,000 activities. It is also based on the ITPA.

Language Acquisition Program for the Severely Retarded by Louise R. Kent, Research Press.

LAP is designed to develop language for the severely retarded individual and has three major sections: preverbal, verbal receptive, and verbal expressive. The program allows for development of an oral, manual, or combination language system and also contains a language inventory for determining a child's entry point.

Language Development Program: Imitative Gestures to Basic Syntactic Structures by Jane Murdock and Barbara Hartmann, Word Making Productions.

This behaviorally oriented program is designed for children whose language ability ranges from having no vocal verbalization to word order and form skills of a normal 4-year-old. Contents include informal receptive and expressive language placement tests, specific tasks, sequential list of environmentally useful words, and data recording sheets.

A Language Program for the Nonlanguage Child by Burl Gray and Bruce Ryon, Research Press.

This very structured language program in book form consists of 40 individualized language training units, with each unit having a screening test, pretests and posttests, and criterion tests.

Learning to Develop Language by Merle B. Karnes, Milton Bradley & Co.

This language program of 150 lessons is designed to train teachers to interact appropriately with children in developing language skills. It emphasizes receptive, expressive, motor-imitation, and nonverbal communication.

Manual Language Dictionaries: Functional Vocabulary for the Retarded by Mansfield Training School, Edmark Associates.

These three dictionaries comprise 60 basic signs and vocabulary necessary for everyday functioning.

Merkley Developmental Approach to Speech and Language by Francis A. Merkley, Project ADAPT.

Designed for the TMR (ages 2 to 8), this program emphasizes receptive, expressive, motor-imitation, and nonverbal communication.

Missouri State Department of Education Speech and Language Kit by John Heskett and Jess La Puma, State Schools for the Severely Handicapped.

In kit form, this program is designed to aid the teacher of TMR students in planning lessons involving speech and language development.

Motivation and Learning-Centered Training Programs for Language-Delayed Children by Merlin Mecham, Word Making Productions.

With the severely retarded student in mind, this program covers 15 units of language instruction under the general categories of gesture language, basic verbal languages, and transformations. The kit contains a manual, a picture packet, and a data recording book.

MWM Program for Developing Language Abilities by Esther Minskoff, Douglas Wisman, and J. Gerald Minskoff, Educational Performance Associates.

Although based on the ITPA model, this kit can be used without ITPA test scores. The primary purpose is for teaching disabled students with language problems, but its secondary purpose is for developmental teaching of language. The MWM kit contains an inventory of language abilities, 6 teaching manuals, workbooks, and various picture cards.

Non-Speech Language Initiation Program (Non-Slip) by Joseph Carrier and Tim Peak, H & H Enterprises, Inc.

Non-Slip is a set of procedures for teaching the nonverbal retarded to generate original seven-word sentences. The kit has 188 highly structured lessons with pretests, posttests, and probe tests, record sheets, and graphs.

Peabody Language Development Kit—Level P by Lloyd Dunn, J. O. Smith, and K. B. Horton, American Guidance Service.

Designed for students with a MA of 3 to 5 years, this highly structured kit contains 180 lessons, beginning with labeling language, and includes emphasis on syntactical and grammatical structures of language. Kit contents include cards, posters, records, puppets, fruit and vegetable models, and a variety of other materials.

Peabody Language Development Kit—Level 1 by Lloyd M. Dunn and J. O. Smith, American Guidance Service.

Level 1 has more auditory and visual stimuli and fewer tactual stimuli than Level P and is designed for oral language and intellectual stimulation. The format and kit contents are similar, but activities are designed for a MA of 4.5.

PEEK (Peabody Early Experiences Kit) by Lloyd M. Dunn, L. T. Chunn, D. C. Crowell, Liota Dunn, L. G. Slevy, and E. R. Yackel, American Guidance Service.

A highly structured program with 250 lessons, the PEEK kit has activities designed to focus on cognitive development (about 50%), affective development (about 25%), and oral language development (about 25%). The kit contains a teacher's guide, 2 manuals of 125 lessons each, puppets, cords, cassettes, posters, photographs, and assorted other objects and materials.

Portage Guide to Early Education (experimental edition) by David Shearer, James Billingsley, Alona Frohman, Jean Hilliard, Francis Johnson, and Marsha Sheaver, Cooperative Educational Service Agency No. 12.

This program is a sequential curriculum for the multiply handicapped in the areas of cognition, self-help, motor skills, socialization, and language. The language section is designed for all children with a MA of 0 to 5. Behavioral checklists are provided for assessment and development of each area.

Project MEMPHIS by Alton Quick, Thomas Little, and Ann Campbell, Fearon Publishers.

Another developmental comprehensive program containing 260 lesson plans designed for the mentally retarded and multiply handicapped, this program contains language and communication skills in one of the five curriculum areas. Instructional components of the kit include a developmental evaluation, individual educational program, and educational evaluation. The kit also contains numerous other materials, references, etc., and information for parents.

Speech Improvement for the Trainable Retarded: A Manual for the Classroom Teacher (revised edition) by Elizabeth Lynch and Jeanne Ross, Ohio State University Press.

This publication of activities, along with a comparison student worksheet, was developed for the classroom teachers of the TMR, especially those who do not have the services of a speech therapist. This program is developmental and contains 39 lessons.

Speech and Language Development for the Mentally Retarded by Michaela Nelson and Carolyn Saville, ESU No. 14.

Designed for TMRs with language problems, this kit contains 16 curriculum packets (eye contact, motor imitation, visual discrimination, auditory discrimination, etc.) of 12 lessons each and has a placement test to determine needed packets for each individual. Program contains a teacher's guide, graphs, and recording forms and packets.

A Speech Therapy Program for Mentally Handicapped Children by Linda Jensen, The Interstate Printers and Publishers.

Designed for teachers, parents, or therapists, the program contains two phases: the verbal behavior (basic articulation) and the higher level language process. Contents include a book, 8 duplicating masters, word lists, lessons, and procedures.

Suggestions for Teaching Language Skills to Use With Language Making Action Cards by Barbara Lippke, Word Making Productions.

This is not a program but a resource book describing the use of language materials and presenting activities that can be adapted to use with any language program for the TMR.

Visually Cued Language Cards by Rochana Foster, June Giddan, and Joel Stark, Consulting Psychologists Press.

This program consists of cards (pictorial representations) for use in teaching basic vocabulary and grammatical forms. Designed for TMRs with language problems, the program will eventually have 5 series of cards (only 3 at present).

SUMMARY

The basic communication skills area of curriculum is a vital one for the retarded because ability to communicate allows for acceptance into the mainstream of society. This chapter examined normal development of communication skills, assessment, speech defects, manual communication, procedures for developing speech and language skills, and materials and resources.

Language processes include reception, association, and expression. These language processes transposed into curriculum areas, in order of attainment, are experiences, listening, speaking, reading, writing and spelling, and refinement of language skills. The mentally retarded develop speech and language skills in the same developmental pattern as normal children but at a reduced pace.

Before language instruction is begun, an assessment of the child's current level of functioning and a determination of his strengths and weaknesses must be made. This may be accomplished by formal or informal measures, or both.

Besides general language instruction responsibilities, the teacher of the TMR has the tasks of preventing speech disorders, improving speech, refining speech skills, and assisting the speech clinician in correction of speech defects. Speech development and correction are important because of the high incidence of occurrence in the TMR. The most common problems include articulation errors (omissions, substitutions, and distortions), stuttering, and voice disorders (pitch, quality, and intensity).

Total communication (signing plus the spoken word) has been found to increase the communication skills of the TMR. It deserves strong consideration as a language approach for students who might be deaf (or hard of hearing), lack understandable vocal expressive skills, or have other serious language handicaps.

The most efficacious procedure for developing speech and language skills in the TMR must be individual and systematic. Such a procedure might include assessment, analysis, development of objectives, instructional activities, evaluation of instruction, continuance or reassessment, testing for criteria, and charting of progress. Basic fundamental skills that facilitate normalcy and independence should be taught first.

The teacher can contribute significantly to speech and language development with structural activities. The procedures section offered techniques for promoting general communication development, articulation development, and correction and physical exercises (inhaling, exhaling, sucking and swallowing, tongue control, chewing, and control of drooling). Practical listening, gesturing, and speaking activities were also listed.

Many sequential, structured, commercially prepared speech and language programs designed for the TMR exist. Twenty-seven such programs were described in this chapter's last section. Before selecting one, however, consider such factors as the ability level of your students, aims of the program, methods used, materials needed, length of the program, and cost.

REFERENCES AND SUGGESTED READINGS

Ainsworth, A.: Stuttering: what is it and what to do about it, Lincoln, Neb., 1975, Cliff's Notes, Inc.

Anderson, V. A., and Newby, H. A.: Improving the child's speech, ed. 2, New York, 1973, Oxford University Press.

Berry, P., editor: Language and communication in the mentally handicapped, Baltimore, 1976, University Park Press.

Blue, C. M.: The effectiveness of a group language program with trainable mentally retarded children, Educ. Train. Ment. Retard. 5(3): 109-111, 1970.

Bricker, D. D.: Imitative sign training as a facilitator of word-object association with low functioning children, Am. J. Ment. Defic. 76:509-516, 1972.

Bricker, W. A., and Bricker, D. D.: A program of language training for the severely language handicapped child, Except. Child. 37:101-111, 1970.

Chalfant, J., Kirk, G., and Jensen, K.: Systematic language instruction: an approach for teaching receptive language to young trainable children, Teach. Except. Child. 1(1):1-13, 1968.

Christopher, D. A.: Manual communication: a basic text and workbook with practical exercises, Baltimore, 1976, University Park Press.

Dickson, S., and Jann, G. R.: Diagnostic principles and procedures. In Dickson, S., editor: Communication disorders: remedial principles and practices, Glenview, Ill., 1974, Scott Foresman & Co.

Fant, L. J.: Ameslan: an introduction to American sign language, Silver Spring, Md., 1972, National Association for the Deaf.

Fox, D. R., and Blechman, M.: Clinical management of voice disorders, Lincoln, Neb., 1975, Cliff's Notes, Inc.

Fristoe, M.: Language intervention systems: programs published in kit form, J. Child. Comm. Dis. 8(1):49-77, 1976.

Gordon, M. L., Ryan, D. H., and Shilo, T.: Helping the trainable mentally retarded child develop speech and language: a guidebook for parents, teachers and paraprofessionals, Springfield, Ill., 1972, Charles C Thomas, Publisher.

Grinnell, M. F., Detamore, K. L., and Lippke, B. A.: Sign it successful—manual English encourages expressive communication, Teach. Except. Child. 8(3):123-124, 1976.

Hatten, J., Goman, T., and Lent, C.: Emerging language, Westlake Village, Calif.; 1973, The Learning Business.

Jefferson Parish School Board, Speech Therapy Department: Auditory perception activity book, Gretna, La., 1974.

Jens, K. G., Belmore, K., and Belmore, J.: Language programming for the severely handicapped, Focus Except. Child. 8(3):1-15, 1976.

Kellogg, R. E.: Listening. In Lamb, P.: Guiding children's language learning, Dubuque, Iowa, 1971, William C. Brown, Co.

Kent, L. R.: Language acquisition program for the severely retarded, Champaign, Ill., 1974, Research Press Co.

Lerner, J. W.: Children with learning disabilities, ed. 2, Boston, 1976, Houghton Mifflin Co.

Lynch, E., and Ross, J.: Speech improvement for the trainable retarded, Columbus, Ohio, 1975, Ohio State University Press.

McConnell, F., Love, R. J., and Clark, B. S.: Language remediation in children. In Dickson, S., editor: Communication disorders: remedial principles and practices, Glenview, Ill., 1974, Scott Foresman & Co.

Myklebust, H.: Auditory disorders in children, New York, 1954, Grune & Stratton, Inc.

Owens, M., and Harper, B.: Sign language: a teaching manual for cottage parents of nonverbal retardates, Pineville, La., 1971, Department of Speech and Hearing, Pinecrest State School.

Phillips, P. P.: Speech and hearing problems in the classroom, Lincoln, Neb., 1975, Cliff's Notes, Inc.

Riekehof, L. L.: Talk to the deaf, Springfield, Mo., 1963, Gospel Publishing House.

Sailor, W., Guess, D., and Baer, D. M.: Functional language for verbally deficient children: an experimental program, Ment. Retard. 11(3):27-35, 1973.

Smith, R. M.: Clinical teaching: methods of instruction for the retarded, ed. 2, New York, 1974, McGraw-Hill Book Co., Inc.

Snell, M.: Sign language and total communication. In Kent, L. R.: Language acquisition program for the severely retarded, Champaign, Ill., 1974, Research Press.

Snyder, L. K., Lovitt, T. C., and Smith, J. O.: Language training for the severely retarded: four years of behavior analysis research, Except. Child. 42:7-15, 1975.

Sperry, V. B.: A language approach to learning disabilities: a source book of activities for teachers, Palo Alto, Calif., 1972, Consulting Psychologists Press, Inc.

Tawney, J. W., and Hipsher, L. W.: Systematic instruction for retarded children: the Illinois program, part II, systematic language instruction (experimental edition), Danville, Ill., 1972, The Interstate Printers & Publishers, Inc.

Van Riper, C.: Speech correction: principles and methods, Englewood Cliffs, N.J., 1972, Prentice-Hall, Inc.

CHAPTER 6

DEVELOPING SOCIAL SKILLS

Social competence is a valued skill in American society. A requirement for social competence is the ability of an individual to understand and respond appropriately to social demands. This ability requires, among other things, a degree of intelligence. The attainment of social competence for the TMR then becomes a difficult task because of his limited intelligence. This chapter will discuss factors that affect development of social skills, assessment, skills to be developed, teaching considerations and procedures, and materials and resources for this area of curriculum.

FACTORS THAT AFFECT SOCIAL SKILLS

Being a socially acceptable individual in today's society is related to a multitude of dimensions and includes aspects of the personal self, emotional self, and self-concept. Among the many environmentally or genetically based personal factors that can affect the attainment of social skills, besides intelligence and mental age, are physical fitness, personal grooming, appropriate dress, and physical beauty or attractiveness. These factors, sometimes seemingly unimportant, can and should be given attention in their appropriate curriculum areas.

In a study of correlates of social competence among TMR children, Newman and Doby (1973) found that chronological age, environmental interaction, IQ, and teacher expectation explained 65% of the variance in social competence. Although teachers cannot control for biological-genetic variables such as CA and IQ, the other two primary variables, environmental interaction and teacher expectation, are amenable to change by educators.

Another dimension that could impede normal social development in the TMR is the emotional self. Disturbances of the emotions are often observed in TMR populations. The probability for increased disturbances in this group exists because of (1) their inflexible behavior, (2) their restricted background of experiences, (3) their difficulty in personal and social environmental perceptions, and (4) their greater number of negative or failure experiences. The effect of negative experience and failure to reach goals cannot be overemphasized. Fig. 6-1 indicates the types of behaviors that could result from a person not able to satisfy his perceived individual needs.

This thwarting of human goals can have serious effects on the development of the

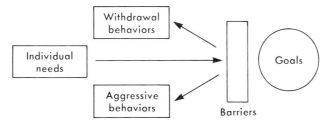

Fig. 6-1. Behaviors developed as a result of perceived needs not being met.

emotional self. Negative or unacceptable feelings are common by-products of frustration from an inability to achieve desired goals. According to Fagen, Long, and Stevens (1975), most, if not all, negative feelings and behaviors have their roots in the thwarting of goals. These relationships might also be applied to the retarded and are presented in Table 6-1.

The emotional needs of the TMR are fundamental and the same as for the intellectually normal:

1. The need to be loved and accepted unconditionally
2. The need for security—to be safe and relatively free of threat
3. The need to belong, to be a part of the group, and to feel identification and acceptance
4. The need to be recognized, to gain approval, to feel significant and accepted
5. The need to be independent, to take responsibility, and to make choices

It is important to recognize that when these needs are denied or unmet, the personal-social-emotional development of the child will be affected. Need deprivation must be recognized and action programs instituted to meet them. Teachers and parents must work jointly to meet these needs. Both can assist in child development by:

1. Assisting each individual in developing a positive, realistic view of self
2. Providing an environment of love and acceptance
3. Providing experiences and opportunities for the development of an individual's goals

Table 6-1. Relationship of feelings and thwarted desires*

Feeling	Thwarted desire
Resentment and feeling of neglect	Involvement with others
Withholding of effort and discouragement	Appreciation of effort
Rejection and coldness	Affection and warmth
Alienation and isolation	Friendship
Inferiority and despair	Mastery and competence
Helplessness and defeat	Autonomy and self-pride
Hostility	Love
Rebellion and defiance	Respect and inclusion

*Adapted from Fagen, S. A., Long, N. J., and Stevens, D. J.: Teaching children self-control, Columbus, Ohio, 1975, Charles E. Merrill Publishing Co., p. 63.

4. Developing capabilities for controlling the emotions

Basic to developing social skills is the development of a positive self-concept and self-identity. The self-concept appears to be the center around which human skills and personality revolve. A normal and healthy self-concept has also been found to correlate positively with higher achievements in retarded and nonretarded populations (Lawrence and Winschel, 1973; Purkey, 1970). Because the self-concept is critical to both social and academic skills, it merits further discussion.

Educational literature is replete with studies on the relationship of self-concept and other areas of behavior, but most of it relates to the intellectually normal and educable mentally retarded (IQ 50 to 70). Reviews of research on the self-concept of the mentally retarded indicate the TMR is being grossly neglected (Lawrence and Winschel, 1973; Schurr, Joiner, and Towne,

1970). Perhaps the neglect exists because self-concept in the TMR has been thought not to exist, not be important, or not be measurable. Whatever the alleged reasons, more definitive and descriptive data are needed by professionals and parents.

An array of scales do exist for measuring the self-concept of the mentally retarded. Five useful instruments with brief descriptions follow:

> *Laurelton Self-Attitudes Scale.* Developed by Guthrie, Butler, and Goulow (1961), the LSAS is a 150-item self-attitude questionnaire developed for use with retarded girls.
>
> *The Way I Feel About Myself.* Developed by Piers and Harris (1964), this instrument includes eighty statements easily answered by circling *yes* or *no*.
>
> *Tennessee Self-Concept Scale.* Developed by Fitts (1965), this scale provides separate assessments in self-criticism, identity, self-satisfaction, behavior, physical self, moral-ethical self, personal, family, and social self, and self-esteem.
>
> *Illinois Index of Self-Derogation.* Developed at the University of Illinois (Goldstein, 1964), each item contains a pair of statements, one describing a child with a socially undesirable ascription, the other a child with a neutral or socially desirable trait. The ITSD has a score sheet, utilizing pairs of stick figures, that permits the subject to record which of the two statements is representative of himself.
>
> *The Self Social Symbols Test.* Developed by Henderson, Long, and Ziller (1967), the SSST is a nonverbal test that requires the child only to point to the item he chooses. The test subareas are self-esteem, identification with others, preference for others, dependency or social interest, realism in size, and minority identification. A nonverbal instrument such as this may be more valid for measuring the self-concept because the TMR often does not understand verbal questioning during testing situations (Brengelman, 1964; Ringness, 1961).

A study to objectively measure the self-concept of the retarded and to test its clinical utility was performed by Zisfein and Rosen (1974). Results indicated that self-concept can be measured meaningfully in the retarded; more important, perhaps, is the finding that the measures have clinical utility. The four procedures used (self-evaluation scale, level of aspiration, risk-taking task, and self-comparison scale) were found to be clinically useful for detecting individual variations in personality functioning.

Another more recent study (Poudrier, Mercer, and Howard, 1976) found that even young TMRs possess measurable self-concepts and that a high correlation exists between scores of self-esteem and teacher-attendant predictions of the students' adult status.

Although there do exist some problems of measurement, use of less than appropriate instruments, and a general lack of data on self-concept development in TMRs, self-concept must be assumed to exist, to be important, and to be relevant to development of other areas of behavior.

ASSESSMENT

As in some other areas of human behavior, assessment of social skills can be performed using informal or formal (standardized) measures. Informal assessment by a teacher is possible by designing a behavior skills list or by using the list offered later in the chapter. Information can be obtained by child observation over a period of time or by the quicker method, the parent interview technique.

Formal assessment instruments that can be employed to determine a social skills levels for the TMR are contained in Table 6-2. Some of the instruments are adaptive behavior measures but contain an appropriate section or sections relating to socialization ability of the TMR. These useful subsections are identified in the table.

A social skills proficiency level determination for TMRs is important and has the following uses:

1. As a schedule of development
2. As a measure of specific individual differences or deviations
3. As a measure of improvement following a prescribed training program (Boruchow and Espenshade, 1976)
4. As a guideline for instruction in school or at home

Table 6-2. Tests and scales of social competence

Name of test	Sections of value	Age range	Publisher and date*
AAMD Adaptive Behavior Scale, Public School Version, 1974 Revision	Socialization and Part II, which consists of thirteen measures of maladaptive behavior related to personality and behavior disorders	7 to 13 yr.	AAMD, 1975
Cain-Levine Social Competency Scale	Social skills	5 to 13 yr.	Consulting Psychologists Press, 1963
Computerized Adaptive Behavior Assessments	Personal-social adjustment	5 yr. and over	Alla Associates, Inc., 1976
Children's Minimal Social Behavior Scale	All	All ages	Journal of Consulting Psychology, **21**:265-268, 1957
School Self-Control Behavior Inventory	All	All ages	Psychoeducational Resources, 1971
TARC Assessment System	Social	3 to 16 yr.	H & H Enterprises, 1974
Test of Social Inference	All	Low IQ—readers or nonreaders	Educational Activities, no date
T.M.R. Performance Profile for the Severely and Moderately Retarded	Social	School age	Reporting Service for Exceptional Children, 1970
T.M.R. School Competencey Scales	Personal-social	Form I—5 to 10; Form II—11 and up	Consulting Psychologists Press, 1976
Vineland Social Maturity Scale	Socialization	Birth to maturity	American Guidance Service, 1965
Y.E.M.R. Performance Profile for the Young Moderately and Mildly Retarded	Social and emotions	Preschool	Reporting Service for Exceptional Children, 1967

*A list of publishers and their addresses appear in Appendix A.

5. To assist in a determination of intergration potential into programs for the nonretarded

Finch and Ginn (1973) found one of the scales (CMSBS) to be useful in grouping for social activities to institutionalized TMR residents.

Two of the test instruments that are of long-standing use with the TMR and deserve special mention are the Vineland Social Maturity Scale (Doll, 1946) and The Cain-Levine Social Competency Scale (Cain, Levine, and Freeman, 1963). Each has withstood the test of time, has a number of uses, has significant correlations with mental age as well as with each other, and is fairly easy to administer (Congdon, 1969).

Vineland Social Maturity Scale. This scale is a developmental schedule that provides an outline of detailed performances with respect to the ability of an individual to assume responsibility and look after his personal needs. There are 117 items in this Binet-type scale in order of increasing difficulty. The Vineland is administered by the interview method, is untimed, and is individual. Information for scoring items should be secured from a person closely familiar with the individual, such as a parent, relative, or teacher. A child's total score can be converted into a social age and a social quotient. The scale is quite useful in determining general maturity in social competence and social independence.

Cain-Levine Social Competency Scale. The Cain-Levine is a forty-four–item behavioral rating scale for estimating social competence of TMR children. Goals are defined from a basis of social competency behaviors and assessed, like the Vineland, through the interview technique. The scale was developed to assess development of learned skills that will eventually permit the child to be self-reliant and a contributing member of society. The scale is useful in diagnosis, placement, planning, and evaluation of TMRs. Its greatest value lies in recognition and evaluation of the child's progress, rather than in comparing the child with others.

SKILLS TO BE DEVELOPED

General goals to be developed for the TMR in the social area include functioning as well as possible in social and interpersonal situations. The major skill areas include behaviors relating to (1) self-control, (2) social amenities, (3) group participation, (4) personality, and (5) sex education.

1. Self-control
   a. Is emotionally stable in most everyday situations.
   b. Can control temper—not prone to verbal or physical outbursts.
   c. Accepts changes in routine.
   d. Can accept losing in game situations.
   e. Can wait turn.
   f. Responds positively to authority.
   g. Respects criticism.
   h. Feels secure.
2. Social amenities
   a. Uses appropriate polite greeting and parting words (e.g., please, thank you, excuse me, hello, good morning, good-bye).
   b. Displays proper physical amenities (e.g., handshake, kiss, wave, clap).
   c. Can make simple introductions.
   d. Displays proper eating and table manners.
   e. Is socially appropriate for a specific environment (e.g., quiet at church services).
3. Group participation
   a. Participates appropriately in team games.
   b. Interacts and enjoys group play.
   c. Behaves appropriately while attending assemblies, plays, concerts, parties, movies, etc.
   d. Behaves appropriately on various modes of transportation (e.g., bus, train).
   e. Behaves appropriately on field trips.
   f. Participates as a member of the family, class, group home, residential unit, etc.
4. Personality
   a. Has a positive self-concept.
   b. Is enthusiastic and has fun in most work and social activities.
   c. Shows and accepts affection.
   d. Participates and displays some leadership in play and work.
   e. Takes care of and distinguishes between personal property and the property of others.
   f. Complies with rules and regulations of school and home.
   g. Is truthful and honest.
   h. Is dependable.
5. Sex education
   a. Can recognize body parts and is aware of their function.
   b. Is able to recognize and understand physical changes during puberty and adolescence.
   c. Is knowledgeable and exhibits some understanding of the sexual self (e.g., menstruation, intercourse, masturbation, pregnancy).
   d. Can understand peer relationships (e.g., dating, masculine and feminine roles, family relations).
   e. As a sexual being is a responsible citizen of society (e.g., marriage, contraception, family responsibility, child care).

All the social skill areas are, of course, related, but two deserve amplification: self-control and sex education. Self-control must become a primary social-educational objective if TMRs are to be adequately equipped to face the stresses of daily living. Sex education, an often neglected area of curriculum, warrants inclusion here because of the ever-increasing need. As the mentally retarded assume a more productive and integral role in society (according to the normalization principal) they must also assume more responsibility for their behaviors, including sexual behavior.

Self-control is defined as one's capacity to direct and regulate personal action (behavior) flexibly and realistically in a given situation. This definition (Fagen, Long, and Stevens, 1975) contains the following ingredients:

1. Self-control is viewed as "capacity."
2. Behavior must be willfully directed.
3. Behavior must be self-regulated.
4. The locus of action is the person himself.
5. Self-control implies flexibility in response.
6. Self-control involves realism.
7. Self-control should be considered in relation to a given situation.

Lack of self-control in the retarded is common, and development of self-control is difficult. Procedures for development of self-control in the retarded are discussed later in this chapter.

Sterilization and marriage are two problem areas of mental retardation. Both will be discussed, along with society's attempts to deal with sexuality in the retarded.

Historical efforts to cope with the sexual development of retarded persons have, in fact, been inhumane. Sterilization was the common practice in the early twentieth century and was performed for two reasons: (1) to keep retarded persons from having "defective" children and (2) to prevent a "nameless habit," which we now call masturbation (Perske, 1973). Further justification for sterilization then and now includes the following factors:

1. Benefits to society
   a. Reduction in the number of mentally retarded who are dependent on other members of society
   b. Reduction in cost to the state and tax-payers
2. Benefits to the retarded
   a. Removal of the threat of parenthood because they are unprepared or incapable
   b. No pressure on retarded parents to support their children adequately
3. Benefits to the unborn children
   a. Prevention of an uncertain rearing and future

Arguments advanced in opposition to mandatory sterilization for the mentally retarded follow:

1. Fear of an indiscriminate use of the legal power
2. A belief that the retarded are needed to fill society's menial jobs and for other societal reasons (e.g., surplus population, Farber, 1968)
3. Promiscuity encouraged
4. Possible harmful psychological effects from operation
5. Abridgment of individual human rights

With regard to state statutes, Krishef (1972) reported that two states prohibit sterilization of the retarded, twenty-two states have no sterilization laws, and twenty-four states permit sterilization.* Of the states where sterilization statutes exist, final authority either rests with the parent, guardian, or retardate (four states), courts,

*Two states did not reply.

agencies, or institutions (thirteen states, all but two with appeal procedures), or consent of both of the first two (four states). Additionally, three states have greater specificity of the final authority.

In general, a lack of mandatory sterilization procedures now exists in twenty-five states, indicating society's growing concern for the rights of individuals. However, about as many states (twenty-four) permit sterilization but with final authority given by parents, special boards, or both. This voluntary sterilization for retarded persons also seems to correlate with the attitudes of professionals and parents. Whitcraft and Jones (1974) found that over 85% of parents and professionals favored voluntary sterilization.

Most professionals once believed that marriage as a part of sex education programs for the retarded was an irrelevant concern because the obligations and responsibilities of parenthood were beyond their capacities. Caution, however, must always be exercised in stereotyping groups. Floor, Baxter, Rosen, and Zisfein (1975) found that there is no apparent reason to prevent once-institutionalized retardates from taking on the responsibilities of marriage and parenthood. However, it must be emphasized that a community preparation program was followed, and that the marriages investigated were of short duration. Gross generalizations of research can never be made, but certainly the accepted concept of retardates, especially from institutions, not marrying deserves additional attention.

The concern about retardates marrying is reflected in the state statutes. Seventeen states have no laws, twelve states prohibit marriages, and four states permit marriage (three of which are contingent on satisfaction of certain requirements). Fifteen states provided no information and two did not reply (Krishef, 1972). (See Fig. 6-2.)

The retardates' roles and attitudes toward sex in society have undergone dramatic change since the days of widespread sterilization. After sterilization came a stage of

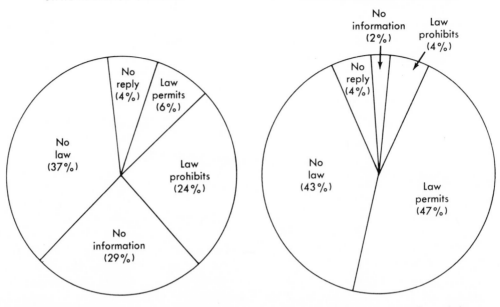

Fig. 6-2. State marriage and sterilization statutes for retarded persons. (Adapted from Krishef, C. H.: State laws on marriage and sterilization, Ment. Retard. **10**[3]:38, 1972.)

denial of the existence of sexuality; today, sexuality in all persons is considered normal and healthy within certain parameters. To teach sex education in the public schools today is far from standard accepted practice, yet the mentally retarded have unique needs relating to their sexual development. The sex drive is a known biological phenomenon existing in all human beings, retarded or not. The more intellectually capable individual can better cope with his or her sexual role in society. The mentally retarded are not capable of understanding the complex biological structure of the reproductive system nor can they anticipate the social consequences of inappropriate sexual behavior. The retarded are vulnerable, can be easily misled, and have the potential to fall prey to sexual seduction and exploitation.

Sex education is not simply the acquisition of facts about sexual body parts and their functions, but learning related to sexual feelings and emotions, normal heterosexual relations, and the responsibilities and consequences of sexuality. The necessity of teaching sex education to

TMRs is further reflected in needs expressed by parents (Fischer and Krajicek, 1974). Most parents interviewed were concerned about the management of their adolescent child's sexual development but did nothing until it was forced into the open by a crisis situation. A sex education program involving parents and school could prevent sexual crises. If normalization is to be maximized and if the mentally retarded can learn, then sex education must become a part of the socialization curriculum for the TMR.

TEACHING CONSIDERATIONS AND PROCEDURES

Education has only recently employed systematic methods and strategies for promoting social-emotional aspects of child development. These procedures are at last filtering down to programs for the mentally retarded. Evidence for the increased concern exists in the form of commercially prepared programs and research results indicating the impact of behavior modification procedures and techniques on the socialization process. This part of the chapter provides general procedures, considerations for teaching social development, a specialized techniques list, and, because of its uniqueness to curriculum, sex education program guidelines.

General procedures for effecting social skills*

1. Plan specific activities that allow for social interaction.
2. Establish classroom rules and boundaries.
3. Be consistent.
4. Be repetitious, since it assists the learning process.
5. Provide opportunity for self-control among students.
6. Avoid tension-producing situations.
7. Let the students understand that mistakes are a way of learning.
8. Accentuate the positive aspects of the child's behavior.
9. Maintain a pleasant, respectful teacher-student relationship.
10. Utilize all experiences as practical teaching opportunities.

Considerations for teaching social and self-concept development

Following are considerations of social and self-concept development that have implications in the formation and implementation of the social curriculum.

Social development

1. A child learns methods of appropriate social interactions in the family, with his peers, and from others important to him (e.g., teachers). The quantity and quality of these contacts could stimulate social development.
2. Children acquire social skills in line with their specific cultural expectations. The teacher must be aware of the cultural and subcultural expectations of each child to better understand the behavior of the child.
3. Acceptance and "forcing" are concepts

of achieving social independence important in the child's development. Parents and teachers must be willing to permit the child increased acceptance of responsibility yet not force those responsibilities on the child.
4. Many children may come to school as educationally disadvantaged TMRs. In educational planning we must recognize these differences and provide compensating experiences.
5. Democratic living has been found to enable the child to participate more effectively in the social area. An atmosphere that permits some choice and acceptance of the responsibility for one's choice should be provided.
6. The peer group is important to social development; thus peer relationship time must be provided.
7. Children vary in their readiness and need for social contacts. Adult respect for a child's attitudes promotes social development.
8. The skills necessary for forming adequate friendships are teachable and should be included early in a social curriculum.
9. Continual negative commands and focusing on the child's unacceptable behavior deters appropriate social development. Avoid rewarding this behavior by expressing undue concern, attention, and involvement.
10. Attitudes related to race and religion are learned early and generally reflect parental values and subculture. Attitude formation of acceptance and respect must be instituted early if change is needed (Dinkmeyer, 1965).

Self-concept development

1. Parents, teachers, and others of importance to the child must understand the significance of their role in formation of the child's self-concept.
2. The classroom atmosphere is important in producing feelings about self and therefore should be continually examined.
3. Positive self-concepts will develop if the child is given real responsibilities.
4. The teacher must understand the

---

*From Gearheart, B. R., and Litton, F. W.: The trainable retarded: a foundations approach, St. Louis, 1975, The C. V. Mosby Co., p. 115.

Fig. 6-3. TMR students can and should be encouraged to develop peer friendships in their neighborhood. (Courtesy Greenwich, Conn., Public Schools.)

child's self-concept and make use of available assessment techniques.

5. Methods of developing feelings of adequacy in the child should be utilized at all levels.

6. Parents and professionals should recognize that each child is unique and functions in terms of his self-concept (Dinkmeyer, 1965).

Specialized techniques

The lecture-discussion method of assisting children in understanding and developing satisfactory social behaviors holds limited value with TMRs. A number of other specialized strategies and techniques, however, are useful in assisting the development of social skills. These include behavior modification, play, sociodrama, videotaping, field trips, puppets, and games.

Behavior modification. Studies indicating the appropriateness and usefulness of the techniques and principles of behavior modification are endless. The concept of modeling as a technique should be employed because all students, especially the retarded, are influenced by teacher behavior. The social skills area is uniquely suited for modeling. Specific skills such as sharing, smiling, positive physical contacting, and verbal complimenting have been taught or increased using modeling (Cooke and Apolloni, 1976; Whitman, Mercurio, and Caponigri, 1970). Other techniques of behavior modification such as extinction, satiation, and time-out can be used to eliminate unwanted social behaviors (e.g., impulsivity, temper tantrums, exhibitionism). (See Chapter 3 for an in-depth discussion of techniques of behavior modification.)

Play. Play is the purposeful activity of childhood that facilitates the acquisition of neuromuscular, perceptual-motor, sensori-

Fig. 6-4. Group play provides opportunity for the TMR to develop personally and socially. (Courtesy Bossier Parish, La., Public Schools.)

motor, and interpersonal skill development (Moran and Kalakian, 1974). Through play, a child has the opportunity to develop socially and emotionally.

Social benefits are numerous, but, in particular, sharing and group participation behaviors are allowed to develop. Through playing in a group, a willingness and ability to follow directions, obey rules, and accept decisions and discipline are created. Play also provides socially acceptable channels for draining excessive energy.

Emotional benefits include the by-products of emotional insight, stability, and strength, all of which can result in a happier, more secure child. Because play is a natural medium for self-expression, retarded children can play out their inner frustrations, anxieties, tensions, insecurities, aggressions, fear, and confusion. By expression of the emotional self, the child puts his feelings out in the open, confronts them, and learns to control them.

Other benefits of play for the retarded include physical, communicative, and cognitive development. Play provides opportunities to learn basic motor patterns and skills, strength, develop cardiovascular and muscular endurance, and maintain general physical health. Also developed are eye-

hand coordination and other perceptual-motor skills.

Communicative and cognitive development are made possible through play because at group play the child learns to listen, follow directions, etc. He then begins to grasp relationships between words and concepts, which increases his understanding of language. He will also frequently verbalize his play experiences, since most are pleasurable and eventful. Conceptual skills develop as a result of the child using observation, memory, logic, and deduction in play activities.

Stages of play development are unoccupied behavior, solitary play, onlooker behavior, parallel play, associative play, and cooperative or organized play. The retarded generally follow this sequence of development.

Structured play activities have been found to increase the personal-social skills of the TMR. One study (Newcomer and Morrison, 1974) revealed that the development level of TMRs increased as a result of structured play activity. Members of the group that received unstructured play remained unchanged in their personal-social abilities, and it was suggested that unstructured play might contribute to environmental disorganization. Strain (1975) found that socialization ability activities (sharing, taking turns, building together, etc.) of TMR preschoolers can be increased by inserting into the curriculum socio-dramatic activities (i.e., acting out children's stories such as "The Three Bears"). Play is a technique that when used properly, can assist in the overall development of not only social skills but other areas of behavior as well.

Sociodrama. Sociodrama, or role playing, is a technique whereby it is possible to set up actual social situations and systematically reward desired responses. Role playing involves five steps: (1) identifying a specific problem, (2) describing the roles to be played, (3) selecting the participants, (4) dramatizing the problem or situation, and (5) reviewing the drama and considering other solutions (Smith, 1974). Role playing, as a social learning technique, is useful because (1) most students identify with their roles and act out real feelings, (2) it is an enjoyable experience, (3) it can illustrate an endless number of social situations, and (4) the teacher has a unique opportunity to observe the student in a sheltered social situation.

Videotaping. Of recent origin in developing or correcting social skills in the retarded is videotaping (Gajewski, 1974; Weisbord, 1976). Students can be videotaped at play, eating lunch, or while in class and then given feedback individually or in groups. This technique allows a student to "see himself in action" in a social situation. Videotaping holds promise for the TMR as a teaching tool in the social area because of the novelty of viewing oneself on "TV." It unfortunately is beyond the financial capabilities of many programs.

Field trips. Since socialization is a process involving the individual and his environment, one obvious technique to further provide this realistic interaction is the field trip. Riding the bus, eating out, and attending a cultural or sporting event are but a few ways in which the TMR would have opportunities to develop personally and socially. Group field trips, especially for the older students, should be an integral aspect of the total curriculum, since they hold numerous other values (Boruchow and Espenshade, 1976).

Puppets. Having TMR children act out social situations with puppets is a useful technique for developing social skills. Puppets have a high interest and appeal for all children, especially animal puppets or those of famous cartoon characters. Additionally, puppets have been found to make many students feel more secure and more expressive (Vittner, 1969).

Possible uses of puppets to enhance social and emotional development include (1) social or cultural awareness and human relations, (2) sociodrama and simulation of contemporary social issues, as well as acting out conflicts or other problem situations that occur in the classroom, school, or community, (3) as a tool to modify behavior, (4) for presentation of skits depicting historical events, special holidays, or current events, (5) to stimulate language communication skills, (6) as occupational, physical, vocational, and play therapy, (7) storytelling, (8) peer teaching and learning, (9) for cognitive skill development, (10) for diagnostic and prescriptive purposes, and (11) free play situations (D'Alonzo, 1974).

Puppets are inexpensive if homemade, and most types are easily constructed. Puppets can be created from cloth, socks, paper bags, boxes, mittens, cans, balls, papier-mâché, clay, and string.

Games. The use of games, commercial or teacher-made, develops group participation social skills. A detailed description of the application and value of games is available in Chapter 2.

Sex education

Sex education is an ongoing educational process and involves the home, the school, and the community. Following are steps for establishing a sex education program for TMRs that includes parents, profession-

Fig. 6-5. Planning and going on field trips can aid the socialization process of the TMR. (Courtesy Bossier Parish, La., Public Schools.)

als, and the community. Careful planning is essential for success.

1. *Selection of an advisory committee.* The composition of this committee should include parents, teachers, community leaders, and knowledgeable sex educators.

2. *Establishment of curriculum objectives.* The objectives should be developed in keeping with the level and ability of the students. They should also be easily understood by all persons involved in the program.

3. *Specification of curriculum content.* The instructional staff should outline the objectives sequentially.

4. *In-service education.* Because teaching sex education is new for the participating teachers, in-service education becomes essential. The attitudes, teaching skills, and resources should be the focus of this training.

5. *Relevance.* To achieve relevance and meaning in this area of curriculum, attempts should be made to integrate the teaching of sex-related information into the overall curriculum. A separate curriculum time may be required.

6. *Obtainment of administrative endorsement.* The support of the administration is essential to a sex education program.

7. *Experimentation with the program.* A pilot program with only one class is desirable for trying out the curriculum while select teachers gain experience. When the program becomes operational, these teachers can serve as consultants to the other teachers.

8. *Establishment of a parent program.* The parents should have input into the educational process; sex education discussion groups may be a part of this effort (AAHPER and SIECUS, 1971).

The parents' role is most important for a successful sex education program. Discussing sexuality with a retarded son or daughter is not an easy task, yet it must not be viewed as an impossible task. The child's general ability of accepting himself as a sexual being will derive from the parents' level of comfort about sex. Information about sex can be important to the child when he asks, but this should not be the only time. Some TMRs may never bring up the subject yet have need of sexual learning.

The discussion of sexual issues should be open, casual, and natural. Opportunities exist when observing a pregnant acquaintance, bathing, toileting, dressing. It should be emphasized, however, that sex, as a subject, should not be forced on the child. The accompanying parent questionnaire developed by Fischer, Krajicek, and Borthick (1973) can be used to determine student needs and curriculum objectives. Additionally, it may be used as a basis for parent group meetings.

Parent group meetings are recommended along with the educational program. Parents can benefit from mutual discussions of sexual issues. Comparing techniques for handling bodily changes or growing awareness of sexuality with other parents who have experienced it with their child is most helpful. Experienced parent discussion leaders state that, as a group, participants already have many answers, solutions, and alternatives to the posed problems. They find that their problem is not unique and that there are many ways to handle their

---

PARENT QUESTIONNAIRE ON SEX EDUCATION*

1. What particular issue of sexual development do you find most difficult to talk to your child about?
2. Do you feel you need some kind of help in discussing issues of sexual development with your child?
3. If so, what particular kind of help do you think would be most useful to you?
4. Is your child overly friendly to the point that it worries you?
5. Do you think your child will ever want to have dates with someone of the opposite sex? If so, will you allow this?
6. Do you think your child will ever want to get married?
7. If your child wanted to get married, do you think you could ever consider giving your permission?
8. Do you think your child would ever be capable of being a parent to a child?
9. Does your child know where babies come from? (Explanation)
10. Does your child know how babies begin to grow in the mother's body? (Explanation)
11. Does your child know how long babies grow in the mother's body?
12. Does your child know how a baby gets out of the mother's body? (Explanation)
13. Have you ever considered sterilization for your child to prevent (boys) his making a girl pregnant? (girls) her becoming pregnant?
14. Has masturbation been an issue in regard to your child?
15. How have you attempted to handle the issue of masturbation with your child?
16. How have you attempted to handle the issue of menstruation with your daughter? (where appropriate)
17. What would you consider the ideal situation for your (son) (daughter) when (he) (she) reaches the age of 20?
18. Do you think that you will be able to proceed with discussing sexuality with your child?

---

*From Fischer, H. L., Krajicek, M. J., and Bortnick, W. A.: Sex education for the developmentally disabled: a guide for parents, teachers, and professionals, p. 47. Copyright © 1973, University Park Press, Baltimore.

concerns. More importantly, however, is that, as the knowledge level and comfort increase, so does parent capability (Thurman, Bassin, and Ackerman, 1976).

It should be realized that not everyone working with the retarded will feel able and comfortable enough to discuss sexuality effectively. Teachers of sex education for the retarded, to be most effective, should (1) be knowledgeable and comfortable with their own sexuality and (2) have sensitivity in dealing openly with various expressions of human sexuality.

The teacher should also be attuned to the needs and feelings of each student if objectives are to be met. Not all students will respond to a lesson or objective, and many need not be exposed to all the objectives.

MATERIALS AND RESOURCES

Following are some of the excellent programs and resources that exist today for teaching social skills to the mentally retarded.

Developing Understanding of Self and Others by Don Dinkmeyer, American Guidance Service, Inc.

Kit D-1 consists of a manual (with day-to-day activities), 2 story books, 33 color posters, 21 records or 5 cassettes, 33 puppet- and role-playing cards, 6 hand puppets, 11 puppet props, and group discussion cards. It is designed to stimulate social and emotional development and is organized around the following eight unit themes:

1. Understanding and accepting self
2. Understanding feelings
3. Understanding others
4. Understanding independence
5. Understanding goals and purposeful behavior
6. Understanding mastery, competence, and resourcefulness
7. Understanding emotional maturity
8. Understanding choices and consequences

Kit D-2 contents are similar in nature to that of Kit D-1 but are designed for higher level students. The program is built around development of the student toward self-identity, friendship, responsible independence, self-reliance, resourcefulness and purposefulness, competence, emotional stability, and responsible choice making.

Training Fun With Activities of Daily Living by P. Kenner and J. Lantzer, Mafex Associates, Inc.

A program of 6 workbooks:
1. My home (family and personal hygiene)
2. My school (adjustment, eating in the cafeteria)
3. May I? (manners)
4. How to get along (social adjustment)
5. Where I live and play (community)
6. Common things around me (awareness)

When a Child Misbehaves by Alan Hofmeister (Project Director), Developmental Learning Materials.

This is a reference guide for teachers that provides specific examples for teaching desired behavior such as sharing, paying attention, picking up toys, and eliminating undesirable behavior such as arguing, hitting, and tantrums. The guide covers the use of praise (tangible and social), consistency, reasoning, ignoring, and discipline. Tally sheets, graphs to record learner progress, and reward badges are included.

Social Learning Curriculum by Herbert Goldstein, Charles E. Merrill Publishing Co.

This program consists of 10 phase books or manuals.

Each manual has a lesson objective, teacher information, materials needed, preparation necessary, and lesson strategies. Areas of the program include the following:

1. Perceiving individuality (self-awareness)
2. Recognizing the environment (in school)
3. Recognizing interdependence
4. Recognizing the body
5. Recognizing and reacting to emotions (in self and others)
6. Recognizing what the senses do
7. Communication with others
8. Getting along with others (acceptable behavior)
9. Identifying helpers (giving and getting help)
10. Maintaining body functions (how to take care of the body)

The kit also includes a set of stimulus pictures, supplementary books in academic areas, 10 spirit duplicating books with transparencies and evaluation checklists, and a scope and sequence chart. This approach is developmental and aimed at teaching basic social skills so that handicapped children can adjust to their environment. Liberal use is made of games and role-playing activities.

Social Perceptual Training Kit for Community Living by Barbara Edmonson, Ethel Leach, and Henry Leland, Educational Activities, Inc.

This kit consists of a book containing 50 lessons, slides, cassettes, drawings, and transparencies and is designed to develop social comprehension.

Focus on Self-Development by Judith Anderson, Carole Long, and Virginia Scott, Science Research Associates, Inc.

This program includes three major developmental areas:

1. Awareness
2. Responding
3. Involvement

All deal with the developing child's understanding of self, others, and the environment. All include sound filmstrips, activity books, records or cassettes, photo boards, and stories. Stage I is most suited for TMRs and contains 20 flexible units with topics such as self-concept development, socialization, and sharing.

Schools, Families, Neighborhoods by John Michaelis and Ruth Grossman, Field Educational Publications, Inc.

This audiovisual readiness program is aimed at developing self-understanding and appreciation of the roles and interaction of people in groups. This kit includes 95 study prints, photographic posters of people and their activities in schools, families and neighborhoods around the world, 3 sound filmstrips, 9 short stories, 4 wall charts, and a teachers' manual.

Teaching Social Behavior to Young Children by William Sheppard, Steven Shank, and Darla Wilson, Research Press.

This resource book is a training manual for teachers that focuses on the social environment of young children. It emphasizes principles and practices of behavioral supervision explained in lifelike situations.

Sex Education for the Developmentally Disabled: a Guide for Parents, Teachers, and Professionals by Henry Fischer, Marilyn Krajicek, and William Borthick, University Park Press.

This useful guidebook consists of three sections:

1. Structured client interview and picture series
2. Parent involvement
3. Teacher-professional workshops

Developed expressly for the mentally retarded, this manual presents a picture series covering sexual identification, sexual body parts, bodily functions, emotional functions, and pregnancy and birth.

A Resource Guide in Sex Education for the Mentally Retarded by SIECUS and AAHPER.

This practical curriculum guide covers four areas of sex education:

1. Awareness of self
2. Physical changes and understanding of self
3. Peer relationships
4. Responsibility to society

Each curriculum area is developmental but designed without mental and chronological ages to allow for flexibility. Each concept lists sample activities and resources.

On Being Sexual by Jeff Bassin and Teel Ackerman, Stanfield House.

This program contains a 22-minute color documentary film on sex education for the mentally retarded and is designed for parents and professionals. A *Workshop Training Package* accompanies the film and includes an orientation audio cassette tape for workshop leaders, a taped discussion for workshop participants, with emphasis on modeling the presentation of sex information to two retarded citizens, 2 tapes for workshop presentation on parent and child expectations, sex education for the retarded, dating, marriage and parenting, birth control, and the role of parents and teachers, as well as selected print materials.

Sexuality and the Mentally Handicapped by Winifred Kempton, Stanfield House.

This package of sex education materials is a series of 7 sets of slides (and teacher guides) and is intended to serve as a resource for teaching or counseling the retarded basic aspects of sexuality and related behavior. This slide series consists of the following sections:

1. Parts of the body—diagrams, drawings, and photographs of various parts of the male and female body emphasizing the uniqueness of each individual.
2. Male puberty—development of the male body through puberty. Presented are topics such as cleanliness, masturbation, and nocturnal emissions.
3. Female puberty—the changes, physical and emotional, that occur in the female body with an explanation of menstruation and body hygiene. A discussion of masturbation is included.
4. Social behavior—affection, love, sensuousness, homosexuality, and how to protect oneself from exploitation.
5. Human reproduction—a frank presentation of the process, including diagrams, drawings, and photographs of sexual intercourse, pregnancy, concluding with the birth of a baby.
6. Fertility regulation and venereal disease—explains birth control methods appropriate for the mentally retarded, including sterilization, abortion, and venereal disease.
7. Marriage and parenting—an examination of the marital partnership and the implications of having a family.

The following associations are important resources for additional information and materials on sex education for the mentally retarded.

Community Sex Information and Education Service
P.O. Box 2858
Grand Central Station
New York, N.Y. 10017

National Association for Retarded Children
2709 Avenue E, East
Arlington, Texas 76011

Planned Parenthood Association of Southeastern Pennsylvania
1402 Spruce St.
Philadelphia, Pa. 19102

SIECUS Publications
1855 Broadway
New York, N.Y. 10023

SUMMARY

Social competency is a difficult goal for TMRs yet not beyond attainment for most. The general socialization goal is for the individual to function as well as possible in social and interpersonal situations. Specific skills include behaviors relating to (1) self-control, (2) social amenities, (3) group participation, (4) personality, and (5) sex education.

Factors other than intelligence and chronological age that can affect the personal and social development of TMRs include physical fitness, personal grooming, appropriate dress, and physical attractiveness. Other major dimensions include emotionality, thwarting of goals, having one's needs unmet, and self-concept. All factors must be given consideration in total curriculum implementation of the social skills area.

Sex education as a part of the social curriculum is important and necessary for TMRs, since the retarded are assuming a more integral role in society. It is necessary to prevent exploitation, at the same time imparting a greater understanding of a normal human function. Sex education not only includes knowledge of sexual body parts and their function but feelings, emotions, and awareness of responsibilities and consequences relating to sexuality.

Among the techniques and specialized strategies available to the classroom teacher to develop the social skills in the TMR are behavior modification, play, sociodrama, videotaping, field trips, puppets, and games. Commercially prepared programs now exist in this curriculum area and can also be used in implementing a socialization program.

REFERENCES AND SUGGESTED READINGS

AAHPER-SIECUS: A resource guide in sex education for the mentally retarded, New York, 1971.

Bernhardt, M., and Mackler, B.: The use of play therapy with the mentally retarded, J. Spec. Educ. **9**:409-414, 1975.

Boruchow, A. W., and Espenshade, M. E.: A socialization program for mentally retarded young adults, Ment. Retard. **14**(1):40-42, 1976.

Brengelman, J. C.: Personality self-ratings in the mentally retarded, Train. Sch. Bull. **61**:120-128, 1964.

Cain, L. F., Levine, S., and Elzey, F. F.: Cain-Levine social competency scale, Palo Alto, Calif., 1963, Consulting Psychologists Press.

Carlson, B. W., and Gingland, D. R.: Play activities for the retarded child, Nashville, Tenn., 1961, Abingdon Press.

Congdon, D. M.: The Vineland and Cain-Levine: a correlational study and program evaluation, Am. J. Ment. Defic. **74**:231-234, 1969.

Cooke, T. P., and Apolloni, T.: Developing positive social-emotional behaviors: a study of training and generalization effects, J. Appl. Behav. Anal. **9**(1):65-78, 1976.

D'Alonzo, B. J.: Puppets fill the classroom with imagination, Teach. Except. Child. **6**(3):141-144, 1974.

Dinkmeyer, D. C.: Child development: the emerging self, Englewood Cliffs, N.J., 1969, Prentice-Hall, Inc.

Doll, E. A.: Vineland social maturity scale, Philadelphia, 1946, Educational Publishers.

Fagen, S. A., Long, N. J., and Stevens, D. J.: Teaching children self-control, Columbus, Ohio, 1975, Charles E. Merrill Publishing Co.

Farber, B.: Mental retardation: its social context and social consequences, Boston, 1968, Houghton Mifflin Co.

Finch, A. J., and Ginn, F. W.: Social behavior in institutionalized retarded adults, Am. J. Ment. Defic. **77**:468-469, 1973.

Fischer, H. L., and Krajicek, M. J.: Sexual development of the moderately retarded child: level of information and parental attitudes, Ment. Retard. **12**(3):28-30, 1974.

Fischer, H. L., Krajicek, M. J., and Borthick, W. A.: Sex education for the developmentally disabled, Baltimore, 1974, University Park Press.

Fitts, W. H.: Tennessee self-concept scale manual,

Nashville, Tenn., 1965, Counselor Recordings and Tests.

Floor, L., Baxter, D., Rosen, M., and Zisfein, L.: A survey of marriages among previously institutionalized retardates, Ment. Retard. **13**(2): 33-37, 1975.

Gajewski, F. J.: Using videotape as a hearing tool in special education prevocational programs, J. Spec. Educ. Ment. Retard. **11**(1):53, 1974.

Gearheart, B. R., and Litton, F. W.: The trainable retarded: a foundations approach, St. Louis, 1975, The C. V. Mosby Co.

Goldstein, H.: The development of the Illinois index of self derrogation, Project Report No. SAE 8204, Office of Health, Education, and Welfare, Washington, D.C., 1964.

Gunzburg, H. C.: Social competence and mental handicap: an introduction to social education, ed. 2, Baltimore, 1973, The Williams & Wilkins Co.

Guthrie, G. M., Butler, A., and Garlow, L.: Patterns of self attitudes of retardates, Am. J. Ment. Defic. **66**:222-229, 1961.

Henderson, E. L., Long, B. H., and Ziller, R. C.: Children's self-social constructs test: preschool form, unpublished test, 1967.

Kempton, W., Bass, M. S., and Gordon, S.: Love, sex, and birth control for mentally retarded: a guide for parents, Philadelphia, 1975, Planned Parenthood Association of Southeastern Pennsylvania.

Krishef, C. H.: State laws on marriage and sterilization, Ment. Retard. **10**(3):36-38, 1972.

Lawrence, E. A., and Winschel, J. F.: Self-concept and the retarded: research and issues, Except. Child. **39**:310-320, 1973.

Leland, H., and Smith, D. E.: Play therapy with mentally subnormal children, New York, 1965, Grune & Stratton.

Moran, J. M., and Kalakian, L. H.: Movement experiences for the mentally retarded or emotionally disturbed child, Minneapolis, Minn., 1974, Burgess Publishing Co.

Newcomer, B., and Morrison, T. L.: Play therapy with institutionalized mentally retarded children, Am. J. Ment. Defic. **78**:727-733, 1974.

Newman, H. G., and Doby, J. T.: Correlates of social competence among trainable mentally retarded children, Am. J. Ment. Defic. **77**:722-732, 1973.

Perske, R.: New directions for parents of persons who are retarded, Nashville, Tenn., 1973, Abingdon Press.

Piers, E. V., and Harris, D. B.: Age and other correlates of self-concept in children, J. Educ. Psychol. **55**:91-95, 1964.

Poudrier, B. R., Mercer, C. D., and Howard, D. P.: The use of a non-verbal instrument to assess the self-concept of young trainable mentally retarded children, unpublished manuscript, 1976.

Purkey, W. W.: Self-concept and school achievement, Englewood Cliffs, N.J., 1970, Prentice-Hall, Inc.

Ringness, T. A.: Self concept of children of low, average, and high intelligence, Am. J. Ment. Defic. **65**:453-461, 1961.

Schurr, L. T., Joiner, L. M., and Towne, R. C.: Self concept research on the mentally retarded: a review of empirical studies, Ment. Retard. **8**: 39-43, 1970.

Smith, R. M.: Clinical teaching: methods of instruction for the retarded, ed. 2, New York, 1974, McGraw-Hill Book Co.

Strain, P.: Increasing social play of severely retarded preschoolers with socio-dramatic activities, Ment. Retard. **13**(6):7-9, 1975.

Thurman, R. L., Bassin, J., and Ackermann, T.: Sexuality, sex education and the mentally retarded: one educational approach, Ment. Retard. **14**(1):19, 1976.

Vittner, D.: Structural puppet play therapy, Element. Sch. Guid. Counsel. **4**:68-70, 1969.

Weisbord, H. F.: Videotape feedback and behavioral change, Educ. Train. Ment. Retard. **11**(1):18-21, 1976.

Whitcraft, C. J., and Jones, J. P.: A survey of attitudes about sterilization of retardates, Ment. Retard. **12**(1):30-33, 1974.

Whitman, T. L., Mercurio, J. R., and Caponigri, V.: Development of social responses in two severely retarded children, J. Appl. Behav. Anal. **3**:128-133, 1970.

Zisfein, L., and Rosen, M.: Self-concept and mental retardation: theory, measurement, and clinical utility, Ment. Retard. **12**(4):15-19, 1974.

CHAPTER 7

DEVELOPING PERCEPTUAL-MOTOR AND PHYSICAL EDUCATION SKILLS

The physical domain of behavior is another vital area of curriculum for the TMR. Physical education and related activities have long been recognized as holding great value and providing many benefits for development of the total being. Yet offerings and opportunities for the mentally retarded have been minimal. Only in recent years have physical education programs surfaced as major concerns for the retarded. Reasons for past neglect include (1) a lack of structured curriculum and accompanying resources, (2) inadequate preparation of special education teachers to provide quality physical education programs, (3) few teacher training programs for adapted physical education, and (4) lack of information on the retarded's skills, abilities in, and benefits from physical education programing. Major advances have been made in these deficient areas, and now most educational programs for the TMR include a motor development or physical education class.

The importance of physical education to total development is significant and includes contributions to the physical, mental (cognitive), emotional, social, and academic aspects of self. Physical education can also serve as an end in itself. That

is, retarded and nonretarded children enjoy physical activities and games because they have *fun*. Although fun and enjoyment are not popularly espoused objectives for physical education scientists and theorists, they exist as reasons for students "liking" physical education class. Thus physical education functions as a unique medium for imparting other learning and behavior.

This chapter contains research findings about physical education for the retarded, assessment, skills to be developed (basic movement, perceptual-motor, physical fitness), teaching considerations and procedures, activities and games, the Special Olympics, and materials and resources.

PHYSICAL SKILLS AND MENTAL RETARDATION

For optimal programing to exist (as in other curriculum areas) a knowledge and understanding of the relationship between the skill area and mental retardation is essential. This body of information about physical education has been generated by researchers in the last ten to fifteen years, with impetus from professional organizations such as the American Association for Health, Physical Education, and Recreation, the Council for Exceptional Children, and the American Association on Mental Deficiency.

Reviews of research (Alarcon, 1974; Campbell, 1973; Ersing, 1974; Kral, 1972; Stein and Pangle, 1966; Wessel and Knowles, 1975) reveal the following factors concerning physical abilities and mental retardation.

1. The retarded are two to five years behind national norms on motor performance abilities.

2. The retardate's motor abilities are organized similarly to those of normal children; the attainment of these abilities is slow but follows similar development curves.

3. Poor physical fitness (e.g., strength, endurance) is characteristic of the retarded.

4. Improvement in physical fitness, motor skills, self-concept, social learning, and intelligence scores is possible as a function of physical education programs for the retarded.

5. The retarded in residential facilities score lower in motor ability and physical fitness than do those in public school programs.

6. Disorders of daily motor activity (e.g., hyperactivity, hypoactivity, clumsiness) are often found in the retarded.

7. Even the preschool-age TMR can derive benefits from a structured perceptual-motor, physical education program.

ASSESSMENT

The evidence of research efforts clearly indicates the retarded's need for physical exercise and involvement. To provide the necessary physical experiences an accurate and detailed assessment of individual physical abilities must be performed. The three major areas of total physical education assessment for the TMR include basic movement abilities, perceptual-motor skills, and physical fitness. Tables 7-1 to 7-3 list assessment instruments that can be used with the TMR in these three major physical education areas. A test representative of each area is provided.

Bruininks-Oseretsky Test of Motor Proficiency (BOTMP)

The BOTMP (1977) is a revision of the original *Oseretsky Test of Motor Proficiency*. Eight areas of motor performance are assessed in this individually administered test. The areas include running speed and agility, balance, bilateral co-

Table 7-1. Tests of basic movement skills

Name of test	Age range (yr)	Skills assessed	Publisher and date*
Bruininks-Oseretsky Test of Motor Proficiency	4½ to 14½	Running speed and agility, balance, bilateral coordination, strength, upper limb coordination, response speed, visual-motor control, upper limb speed and dexterity	American Guidance Service, 1977
The Teaching Research Motor Development Scale for Moderately and Severely Retarded Children	All	Standing balance, jumping, walking, imitation, timed fine motor abilities (placing, winding, tapping, drawing, and tracing), cutting, catching, bouncing a ball, hanging, pull-ups, sit-ups, push-ups, and running	Charles C Thomas, Publisher, 1972
University of Connecticut and Mansfield Training School Motor Skills Test	All	Crawling, rolling, walking up and down stairs, running, grasping, throwing, catching, balancing, jumping, stepping, bouncing, climbing, and kicking	In Fait, H. F.: Special physical education; adaptive, corrective and developmental, Philadelphia, 1972, W. B. Saunders Co.

*A list of publishers and their addresses appears in Appendix A.

Table 7-2. Instruments for perceptual-motor assessment

Name of test	Age range (yr)	Factors assessed	Publisher and date*
Adams County Checklist for Perceptual-Motor Deficiency	5 to 6	Gross motor skills, balance and motor control, eye-hand coordination and fine muscle control, visual and auditory skills	In The physical activities report no. 410, May, 1976
Developmental Test of Visual-Motor Integration	2 to 8 (short form), 2 to 15 (long form)	Global visual perception and motor coordination	Follett Publishing Co., 1967
Marian Frostig Developmental Test of Visual Perception	3 to 8	Eye-hand coordination, figure-ground discrimination, form constancy, position in space, spatial relations	Consulting Psychologists Press, 1964
Perceptual Forms Test	5 to 8	General visual-motor performance	Winter Haven Lions Research Foundation, 1969
Purdue Perceptual-Motor Survey	6 to 10	Balance and posture, body image and differentiation, perceptual-motor match, ocular control and form perception	Charles E. Merrill, 1966
Southern California Perceptual-Motor Tests	4 to 8	Balance, right-left discrimination, imitation of postures, crossing the midline and bilateral motor coordination	Western Psychological Services, 1969

*A list of publishers and their addresses appears in Appendix A.

Table 7-3. Tests of physical fitness

Name of test	Age range (yr)	Skills assessed	Publisher and date*
AAHPER/Kennedy Foundation Special Fitness Test	8 to 18	Flexed arm hang, sit-ups, shuttle run, standing broad jump, 50-yard dash, softball throw, 300-yard run/walk	AAHPER, 1968
Amateur Athletic Association Physical Fitness and Proficiency Test	School age	Abdominal endurance, arm-shoulder endurance, leg power, cardiorespiratory endurance	AAA, no date
Kraus-Weber Tests of Minimum Muscular Fitness	6 to 12	Muscle strength of abdomen, hip, upper and lower back, back-hamstring	In Kraus, H., and Hirschland, R.: Minimum muscular fitness test in school children, Res. Quart. **25**:179-188, 1955
Peabody Test of Physical Fitness	School age	Strength and speed, body build and growth, hand-eye coordination, cardiovascular endurance, muscular power	Institute of School Learning and Individual Differences, George Peabody College, no date
Physical Fitness for the Mentally Retarded	8 to 17	Muscular fitness of arms and shoulders, back flexibility, leg power, hamstring flexibility, cardiorespiratory endurance, physique	Metropolitan Toronto Association for Retired Citizens, 1964
Physical Fitness Test Battery for Mentally Retarded Children	School age	Speed, static muscular endurance of arms and shoulders, muscular endurance of leg and abdomen, static balance, agility, cardiorespiratory endurance	School of Physical Education, University of Connecticut, no date
Special Fitness Test Manual for the Mentally Retarded	8 to 18	Arm-shoulder and abdominal endurance, agility, leg power, speed, coordination, cardiorespiratory endurance	AAHPER, 1968

*A list of publishers and their addresses appears in Appendix A.

SUBTEST 1: Running Speed and Agility

1. Running Speed and AgilitySF

TRIAL 1: _____ seconds   TRIAL 2: _____ seconds

Raw Score >	Above 11.0	10.9-11.0	10.5-10.8	9.9-10.4	9.5-9.8	8.9-9.4	8.5-8.8	7.9-8.4	7.5-7.8	6.9-7.4	6.7-6.8	6.3-6.6	6.1-6.2	5.7-6.0	5.5-5.6	Below 5.5
Point Score >	⓪	①	②	③	④	⑤	⑥	⑦	⑧	⑨	⑩	⑪	⑫	⑬	⑭	⑮

○ POINT SCORE SUBTEST 1 (Max: 15)

□

SUBTEST 2: Balance

1. Standing on Preferred Leg on Floor *(10 seconds maximum per trial)*

TRIAL 1: _____ seconds   TRIAL 2: _____ seconds

Raw Score >	0	1-3	4-5	6-8	9-10
Point Score >	⓪	①	②	③	④

○

2. Standing on Preferred Leg on Balance BeamSF *(10 seconds maximum per trial)*

TRIAL 1: _____ seconds   TRIAL 2: _____ seconds

Raw Score >	0	1-2	3-4	5-6	7-8	9	10
Point Score >	⓪	①	②	③	④	⑤	⑥

○

□

3. Standing on Preferred Leg on Balance Beam—Eyes Closed *(10 seconds maximum per trial)*

TRIAL 1: _____ seconds   TRIAL 2: _____ seconds

Raw Score >	0	1-3	4-5	6	7	8	9	10
Point Score >	⓪	①	②	③	④	⑤	⑥	⑦

○

4. Walking Forward on Walking Line *(6 steps maximum per trial)*

TRIAL 1: _____ steps   TRIAL 2: _____ steps

Raw Score >	0	1-3	4-5	6
Point Score >	⓪	①	②	③

○

5. Walking Forward on Balance Beam *(6 steps maximum per trial)*

TRIAL 1: _____ steps   TRIAL 2: _____ steps

Raw Score >	0	1-3	4	5	6
Point Score >	⓪	①	②	③	④

○

6. Walking Forward Heel-to-Toe on Walking Line *(6 steps maximum per trial)*

TRIAL 1: ⬚⬚⬚⬚⬚⬚ = _____ steps   TRIAL 2: ⬚⬚⬚⬚⬚⬚ = _____ steps

Raw Score >	0	1-3	4-5	6
Point Score >	⓪	①	②	③

○

7. Walking Forward Heel-to-Toe on Balance BeamSF *(6 steps maximum per trial)*

TRIAL 1: ⬚⬚⬚⬚⬚⬚ = _____ steps   TRIAL 2: ⬚⬚⬚⬚⬚⬚ = _____ steps

Raw Score >	0	1-3	4	5	6
Point Score >	⓪	①	②	③	④

○

□

8. Stepping Over Response Speed Stick on Balance Beam

TRIAL 1: Fail   Pass   TRIAL 2: Fail   Pass

Raw Score >	Fail	Pass
Point Score >	⓪	①

○

○ POINT SCORE SUBTEST 2 (Max: 32)

Fig. 7-1. Scoring sheet for Subtests 1 and 2 of the Bruininks-Oseretsky Test of Motor Proficiency. (Reproduced with permission of American Guidance Service.)

ordination, strength, upper limb coordination, response speed, visual-motor control, and upper limb speed and dexterity.

The BOTMP age range is from 4½ to 14½ and requires 45 to 60 minutes for the complete battery, 15 to 20 minutes for the short form. A feature of the test is the scoring sheets, showing the student's pattern of strengths and weaknesses. (See Fig. 7-1.)

The BOTMP can be used for (1) a comprehensive assessment of motor development, (2) a brief general survey of motor proficiency, and (3) a specialized assessment of specific fine or gross motor skills. Test results are reported as age equivalents and as percentile ranks. These normative scores indicate the student's overall level of motor development. Age equivalents are reported for individual subtests, the fine and gross motor battery, the short form, and the total test. Percentile ranks are reported for all except the individual subtests.

Purdue Perceptual-Motor Survey (PPMS)

Developed by Roach and Kephart (1966), the PPMS is designed to pinpoint deficits in an individual's perceptual-motor development. The PPMS has five categories of performance, eleven subtests, and twenty-two test items. The child is assigned a score ranging from 1 (lowest level of performance) to 4 (highest level of performance) for each task.

The five performance areas are balance and posture, body image and differentiation, perceptual-motor match, ocular control, and form perception. See Table 7-4 for the eleven subtests.

The PPMS is administered individually and can be given by teachers, since the examiner's manual contains explicit scoring instructions for each subtest. The results can be used to prescribe remedial and developmental activities in the perceptual-motor area of behavior.

The teacher can also informally be on the lookout for visual and perceptual difficulties. An observation form developed

Table 7-4. Subtests and perceptual-motor skills evaluated by the Purdue Perceptual-Motor Survey

Name of subtest	Observed perceptual-motor skills
Walking board	Balance, postural flexibility, laterality
Jumping, skipping, and hopping	Symmetrical behavior and body control, laterality, body image, rhythm
Identifying body parts (auditory stimulus–motor response)	Body image, understanding significance of what is heard, proper translation of an auditory stimulus to a gestural response
Imitation of movements	Laterality, body control, directionality
Obstacle course	Body image in terms of its position in space, body control
Angels in the snow (visual stimulus-motor response with frequent auditory-vocal associations)	Body image, laterality, directionality, body control
Steppingstones (visual-motor)	Laterality, body control, eye-foot coordination, directionality
Chalkboard work	Laterality, directionality, motor movement, visual memory
Ocular pursuits (lateral, vertical, diagonal, rotary, monocular)	Ocular control, laterality
Visual achievement forms (copying various forms presented by teacher)	Form perception, figure-ground relationships
Kraus-Weber tests	Gross motor coordination, general postural adjustment, muscular fitness

by the American Optometric Association, 1975, for this purpose and specifically for the mentally retarded is the accompanying *Visual and Perceptual Checklist for the Retarded Child* (pp. 166 and 167).

American Alliance for Health, Physical Education, and Recreation/Kennedy Foundation Special Fitness Test (AAHPER Special Fitness Test)

The AAHPER Special Fitness Test, with accompanying awards program, is a modification of the AAHPER Youth Fitness Test and is designed for use with the mentally

Visual and Perceptual Checklist for the Retarded Child*

Child's name   Placement   Date of birth

                                                    Month   Day   Year

Please check or circle the appropriate answer.

VISUAL CONSIDERATIONS

1. Does the child have an eye that turns up, down, in, or out   ☐ Yes   ☐ No
   independently of the movement of his other eye?

2. Can the child follow with his eyes a moving target held   ☐ Yes   ☐ No
   approximately ten or twelve inches in front of him?

3. When following a moving target with his eyes, can he   ☐ Yes   ☐ No
   easily move his eyes past the body midline?

4. Does the child blink excessively?   ☐ Yes   ☐ No

5. Does he rub his eyes frequently?   ☐ Yes   ☐ No

6. Does the child turn or tilt his head to the side so as to use   ☐ Yes   ☐ No
   one eye only when looking at something?

7. Does he close or cover one eye frequently?   ☐ Yes   ☐ No

8. Does the child seem excessively sensitive and overly   ☐ Yes   ☐ No
   responsive to light?

9. Does the child have any unusual or different appearance   ☐ Yes   ☐ No
   in the structure and formation of the eyelids?

10. Are there involuntary tremor-like eye movements visible   ☐ Yes   ☐ No
    frequently?

11. Can the child converge his eyes almost to the bridge of   ☐ Yes   ☐ No
    his nose?

MOTOR CONSIDERATIONS

1. Can the child walk erectly?   ☐ Yes   ☐ No

2. If the child can crawl, can he fixate a target while crawling?   ☐ Yes   ☐ No

3. Is his gait smooth?   ☐ Yes   ☐ No

4. Does the child stand with one hip or one shoulder higher   ☐ Yes   ☐ No
   than the other?

5. Can the child move his eyes in coordination with his hands?   ☐ Yes   ☐ No

6. Can he catch a large ball?   ☐ Yes   ☐ No
   Can he catch a medium ball?   ☐ Yes   ☐ No
   Can he catch a small ball?   ☐ Yes   ☐ No

7. Can he catch a ball thrown from a short distance?   ☐ Yes   ☐ No
   Can he catch a ball thrown from a long distance?   ☐ Yes   ☐ No

8. Can he catch a bean bag?   ☐ Yes   ☐ No

9. Can he hop?   ☐ Yes   ☐ No

10. Can he skip?   ☐ Yes   ☐ No

11. Can he jump rope?   ☐ Yes   ☐ No

12. Can he button clothes?   ☐ Yes   ☐ No

*Reproduced with permission of the American Optometric Association.

13. Can he tie bows? ☐ Yes ☐ No

14. Can he zip zippers? ☐ Yes ☐ No

15. Does he have a problem tying his shoes? ☐ Yes ☐ No

Remarks: _____

_____

_____

_____

_____

_____

_____
Teacher or therapist's name

retarded (male and female), ages 8 to 18. The seven items of assessment follow:

1. Flexed arm hang
2. Sit-ups
3. Shuttle run
4. Standing broad jump
5. 50-yard dash
6. Softball throw for distance
7. 300-yard run/walk

Purposes of the testing program and award system are (1) to provide teachers, leaders, supervisors, parents, aides, attendants, and volunteers with a test battery to assess selected elements of physical fitness of the mentally retarded; (2) to serve as one way of diagnosing an individual retardate's specific strengths and weaknesses and of assessing his progress and development on selected elements of physical fitness; (3) to give the mentally retarded additional incentive to improve their levels of physical fitness, motor performance, and physical proficiency; and (4) to stimulate teachers of the retarded and schools that serve the retarded to upgrade their physical education and recreation programs.

An award system has been developed to recognize mentally retarded individuals who have demonstrated, by their test performance, attainment of certain levels of physical fitness. Standards, however, for the award levels are based on national norms obtained from results of testing public school EMRs. Awards are in the form of embroidered emblems designed to be worn on blazers, jackets, or sweaters. The award levels include the following:

AAHPER *Special Silver Award*—for those who attain the 50th percentile for their age and sex on *five of the seven items* on the Special Fitness Test.

AAHPER *Special Gold Award*—for those who attain the 75th percentile for their age and sex on *five of the seven items* on the Special Fitness Test.

Kennedy Foundation CHAMP Award—for those who attain the 85th percentile for their age and sex on *all seven items* of the Special Fitness Test. In addition, they must also engage in sports and recreational activities for at least 30 hours within a three-month period.

AAHPER *Progress Award*—certificates available to those who participate in the testing program and who show improved performance.

Since test items and norms were based on performances of EMRs, questions arise over the applicability and appropriateness of this program for TMRs. Although many TMRs can participate in these activities and achieve with the same criteria and standards as developed for EMRs, most cannot; therefore attainment of awards has been out of the question.

Major purposes of the test and award system are to motivate youngsters to participate actively in physical education and recreation activities and to give them feelings of accomplishment, success, and personal satisfaction. Important in attaining these goals is a personal challenge to achieve and to reach concrete goals that are meaningful to the participant. With these conditions and criteria as guidelines, some ways in which standards of the Special Fitness Test Award Program can be adapted and adjusted so that they are more appropriate and applicable for TMRs follow:

1. Using mental age rather than chronological age.
2. Reducing the number of test items that must be passed.
3. Using average percentile score rather than the listed standard on five of the seven items.
4. Changing (lowering or raising) percentile standards, according to the ability levels of individual participants.
5. Eliminating test items that are obviously unfair so that each participant has a fighting chance to succeed and achieve.
6. Grouping activities into two or three categories according to fitness characteristics—running events, endurance activities, power items; structuring these so that individuals have to attain a certain minimum standard in so many items from each category.
7. Substituting activities and items requiring the same basic skill, traits, and characteristics for those listed on the test battery.
8. Using improvement in raw score and/or percentile score as the basis for awards.
9. Using combinations of any of these suggestions.
10. Developing original, innovative, and creative approaches to challenge youngsters through these activities.

Physical fitness testing and evaluations of fitness need not be confined to formal or standardized tests. A teacher can use different activities that test the various components of fitness. The following activities can enable a teacher to observe students' capabilities in physical fitness:

Muscular endurance (abdominal): curls, leg lifts, sit-ups

Explosive power (arms and shoulders): throwing a medicine ball, softball, volleyball, or basketball for distance

Leg power: squat jumps, high jumps, long jumps

Strength: weight lifting, hand grips, isometrics

Speed: 25- or 50-yard dash, distance run in 5 seconds

General coordination: throwing and catching a ball, balance board activities, shuttle runs

Flexibility: back lifts, floor touching, leg raises

SKILLS TO BE DEVELOPED

Physical behavior skills for TMRs to develop are basic movement skills, perceptual-motor development, and physical fitness. Each will be discussed, and skills to be developed will be listed.

Basic movement skills

Basic movements are the foundation of a physical education program for the TMR, and they provide a starting point for all future movement experiences (e.g., games of low organization). Basic movement skills are also essential to performing many tasks of everyday living. The aim of movement education is to help the individual develop an awareness of himself, his body and its capabilities, and to encourage the use of movement as a means to learn about the environment.

The basic components, or elements, of movement are time, force, space, and flow (Conover, 1972). For movement to take place, all four elements must be present: time is consumed, force is expended, space is utilized, and movement is characterized by flow.

Movement exploration is a recent aspect of physical education for the retarded and provides many opportunities for the acquisition of important concepts. Such concepts include the following:

Directions: forward-backward, front-back, sideways, right-left, up-down, high-low, far-near, in-out, over-under
Intensity: hard-soft, loud-quiet, weak-strong, light-heavy, tight-loose
Speed: fast-slow, fastest-slowest
Size: large-small, tall-short, fat-trim, big-little
Space: wide-narrow, around-across-through, empty-full
Time: past-present-future, early-late, now-later, yesterday-today-tomorrow, last week–this week

Listed are basic movement skills for possible development in the TMR. The skills are classified as locomotor movements (through space), nonlocomotor movements (performed in place), or manipulative movements (giving and receiving of force).

Locomotor skills

Crawling	Marching
Creeping	Rolling
Dodging	Running
Galloping	Skipping
Hopping	Sliding
Jumping	Starting
Leaping	

Nonlocomotor skills

Bending	Stopping
Kneeling	Stretching
Rotating	Swinging
Sitting	Turning
Squatting	Twisting
Standing	

Manipulative skills

Bouncing	Jumping
Carrying	Kicking
Catching	Landing
Climbing	Lifting
Falling	Pulling
Hanging	Throwing
Hitting	

Perceptual-motor skills

The perceptual-motor area of development is global and encompasses a broad spectrum of interrelated perceptual attributes (visual, auditory, kinesthetic, tactual) with motor movements. Perceptual-motor theorists (Borsh, 1967; Cratty, 1969; Kephart, 1971) disagree on the components of this area but believe it to be critically important. Others (Mann, 1970) question the attributes of perceptual-motor training relative to academics. In spite of some confusion about this related physical education curriculum area, remember that (1) perceptual-motor skills do exist and are often deficient in the retarded and (2) the skills do have some importance, since they contribute to total human development. Perceptual-motor skills to be developed include the following:

1. *Body image or awareness*—concept of one's own body, its parts, and the role of the parts to each other and to the environment.
2. *Laterality*—ability to conceptualize one's self as having a left and a right side.
3. *Directionality*—ability to identify, in relation to one's self, left and right, up and down, backward and forward, etc.
4. *Auditory perception*—ability to aurally interpret or organize sensory data.
5. *Visual perception*—ability to visually identify, organize, and interpret sensory data.
6. *Haptic perception* (tactual and kinesthetic skills)—ability to learn from touch and the awareness of one's bodily position in space.
7. *Eye-hand coordination*—coordinated motor movements involving the hands and eyes.

Physical fitness skills

Physical fitness is the third aspect to consider in a physical education program for the TMR. Fitness is essential to overall development and is a state in which an individual possesses the necessary qualities to meet his everyday physical needs. TMRs generally possess poor physical fitness qualities but with proper training can be significantly improved (Campbell, 1973).

The two components of physical fitness are organic and motor performance. Organic performance refers to the body systems, namely circulation, respiration, and musculature. Motor performance pertains to the development of certain skills. The basic physical fitness skills and their definitions follow:

Organic performance

1. *Strength*—maximum muscular exertion of brief duration.
2. *Flexibility*—ability of body segments to move through normal ranges of motion.
3. *Muscular endurance*—less than maximum exertion over a long period of time.
4. *Cardiovascular endurance*—ability of the heart, lungs, and circulatory system to adapt

to the demands of prolonged total-body physical exertion.

5. *Power*—maximum release of force at a specific moment.

Motor performance

1. *Balance*—ability to maintain a proper relationship between the point of support and the center of gravity. Static balance is balance is balance without motion, and dynamic balance is balance while the body is in motion.
2. *Agility*—ability to rapidly and effectively change directions.
3. *Speed*—ability to move rapidly (usually refers to the skill of running).
4. *General coordination*—ability to integrate several different kinds of movement into a single effective pattern.
5. *Reaction time*—elapsed time between the nervous system's stimulus for movement and the individual's response to that stimulus.

Every child in an organized physical activity program should receive a thorough physical examination by a physician. Any physical limitations or activity restrictions for the child should be noted in the report. Care should always be taken not to overexert the child in an effort to develop fitness. Programs for the various skills must be considered on an individual basis.

Only when the retardate learns about his body and its abilities, has become comfortable and in control of his basic movements, and has the necessary physical fitness can he begin to enjoy higher organizational activities and games. Many older TMRs with training are capable of participation in the highest level of physical education activity—organized sports (individual, dual, team).

TEACHING CONSIDERATIONS AND PROCEDURES

In the physical education instructional program for TMRs the teacher or aide should be aware of considerations that allow for achievement of goals. Several considerations and procedures for teaching are provided:

1. Make the program motivational by the following:

a. Awarding ribbons for special events or activities
b. Displaying pictures in a physical education "Hall of Fame"
c. Displaying names for record performances or special accomplishments
d. Awarding certificates for program completion
e. Participating in the Special Olympics

2. Relate physical education to everyday skills of movement.
3. Make events, activities, and approaches challenging.
4. Instill the fun aspect of physical activity.
5. Provide daily physical experiences.
6. Provide opportunities for development of the other areas of curriculum such as language and social skills.
7. Concentrate on the process and activity; the finished product will soon be in evidence.
8. Allow for individual differences.
9. Modify games and activities as necessary.
10. Individualize for skill development.
11. Chart progress.
12. Provide a multitude of physical experiences.
13. Involve a maximum number of sense stimuli.
14. Always demonstrate and participate.
15. Stress safety as a chief concern for all activities.
16. Provide few and simple verbal directions.
17. Introduce only one new skill at a time.
18. Make use of music in teaching the basic movements.
19. Use task analysis for the individuals who cannot perform one of the basic movements and teach the steps of the sequence leading up to the task.
20. Watch for overfatigue.

ACTIVITIES AND GAMES

This part of the chapter contains a discussion of specific activities in the perceptual-motor area, an examination of task analysis as a way to teach basic movements, and a list of activities to make the retarded physically fit. Resources for other activities are described and listed later in the chapter. Also included are activity and game modification suggestions, how to use relays, and examples of specialized activities (parachute play, use of tires, beanbag, balance beam).

Perceptual-motor activities

Body image or awareness

1. The child can learn the names of the body parts, their location, their function, and their relation to each other.

Head	Waist
Hair	Hips
Eyes	Buttocks
Eyelashes	Arms
Eyebrows	Elbows
Ears	Wrists
Nose	Hands
Cheeks	Palms
Chin	Fingers
Mouth	Legs
Forehead	Knees
Neck	Ankles
Shoulders	Feet
Chest	Toes
Back	Soles
Abdomen	Heels

2. Have the students trace their body outline on a mirror with a grease pencil.

3. While the child is lying down, name and touch different body parts. Have the child identify them.

4. Have the child name and touch the body parts of the teacher or another student.

5. The child can lie down on a large piece of paper; then draw an outline around the child's body. This figure may be colored and/or cut into different body segments.

6. Using heavy cardboard, make a jigsaw puzzle of a man and have the child assemble the puzzle.

7. Using large magazine pictures of people, the child can cut out designated body parts.

Fig. 7-2. Knowledge of body parts is important in developing body awareness (image). (Courtesy Bossier Parish, La., Public Schools.)

8. The child touches one body part to one of a partner (e.g., knee to knee).

Laterality

1. Lying on his back with arms and legs together (with teacher assistance as necessary), the student can extend arms overhead, slide legs apart, move arms and legs simultaneously, move one arm, the other, one leg, the other, etc. Each time, the child returns to the starting position.

2. Standing erect, the student can swing arms and/or legs forward, backward, in unison, and in opposition.

3. On his back, the child can roll to the right, left, etc.

4. Have the child rock backward, frontward, right or left side, etc., while sitting on the floor. This can be accompanied by music, a drum, a metronome, or counting.

5. The student can pretend to or actually throw or kick a ball.

6. The student imitates a teacher's arm or leg movements.

7. See the balance activities later in the chapter.

Directionality

1. The student learns the terms basic to directionality activities.

Up-down	Over-under
Forward-backward	Top-bottom
Sideways-beside	Higher-lower
Behind–in front of	Between
Closer-away	In the middle–center
Near-far	Inside-outside
Above-below	

2. The child identifies the top, bottom, and sides of self, various objects, and the room.

3. Instruct the child to perform spatial commands (e.g., stand near the door, stand behind the desk).

4. Set up an obstacle course (inside or out) that requires the child to go over, under, around, etc., the obstacle.

5. Direct the child to move in specific patterns within a certain space (e.g., put your feet together, jump to the right).

6. Have the child jump over, in, on, to the right and left side of a tire.

7. See the balance activities later in the chapter.

Auditory perception

1. The child can:
   a. Listen for environmental sounds (e.g., cars, birds).
   b. Identify tape-recorded sounds.
   c. Listen and identify teacher-made sounds (e.g., writing on the chalkboard, using a stapler or pencil sharpener).
   d. Learn discrimination of near and far sounds, loud and soft sounds, and high and low sounds.

Visual perception

1. The child can:
   a. Reproduce colored pegboard designs.
   b. Reproduce colored parquetry blocks.
   c. Find and identify shapes in magazines.
   d. Reproduce bead designs.
   e. Work simple large-pieced puzzles.
   f. Use dominoes or playing cards for matching exercises.
   g. Perceive and discriminate letters and numbers.

Haptic perception

1. Have the child:
   a. Feel various textures (e.g., smooth, rough, wet, wood).
   b. Perform touch-board activities—materials attached to a board.
   c. Feel various geometric shapes.
   d. Use clay for tactile discrimination.
   e. Use sand to trace letters or numbers.
   f. Feel various temperatures.
   g. Feel weights.
   h. Smell various aromas.

2. Put various objects in a bag or hat and have students identify them by touch.

Eye-hand coordination

1. The child can develop coordination by:

Tracing
Cutting with scissors
Reproducing shapes with stencils or templates
Doing lacing activities

Hammering pegs into pegholes
Writing and drawing on chalkboard
Coloring
Doing dot-to-dot activities

Basic movements

Although nearly all the basic movements are easily learned by the average child, most must be painstakingly taught to the TMR child. Anyone of the basic movements at first glance appears to be a single large movement but is actually a series of discrete separate behaviors. When a child is unable to perform at a given movement, the task should be simplified to its basic components. Each be-

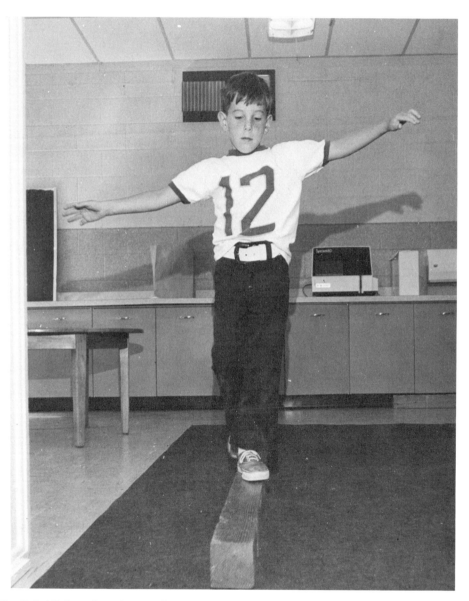

Fig. 7-3. Walking board, as well as the traditional balance beam, can be used to develop the perceptual-motor skills of the TMR. (From Gearheart, B. R.: Learning disabilities: educational strategies, St. Louis, 1973, The C. V. Mosby Co.)

havior can then be taught instead of the total movement. Following are examples of catching and kicking:

Catching
Stay in line with the oncoming ball or object.
Distribute weight evenly on both feet.
Relax the body.
Keep the eyes on the ball or object all the way to the hands.
Relax the fingers.
Cup the hands with the thumbs together.
Let the arms and body give with the impact of the ball.
Push the hands together to maintain control of the ball.

Kicking
Keep the eyes on the ball.
Step forward with the nonkicking leg.
Swing the kicking leg upward toward the ball.
Make contact with the ball.
Follow through with the body in the direction of the kick.

Physical fitness activities

The following activities contribute to more than one factor of physical fitness but are listed where they make the greatest contribution. They appear according to their degree of difficulty and appeal.

Strength, muscular endurance, and power
Race on tiptoes	Dual rocker
Seal walk	Chinese stand-up
Long jump	Walking chairs
Jumping jack	Wheelbarrow
Crab walk	Hand wrestle
High jump	Indian wrestle
Squat thrust	Indian leg wrestle
Modified push-up	Leg lifts
Leapfrog	Sit-ups

Cardiovascular endurance
Midnight	Cross tag
Drop the handkerchi	Chain tag
Bronco relay	Jumping rope
Circle relay	Swimming
Line relay	

Flexibility
Bird flying	Elephant walk
Dry-land swimming	Rocker
Twisting	Toe touches
Bending	Forward roll
Measuring worm	Backward roll

Activity and game modifications

Activities and games of the physical education program for the retarded are important. The retarded can participate in most of the same activities as can anyone else, but modifications of activities or games are often necessary to be more consistent with the child's needs and abilities. Adaptation consists of changing (1) distance and/or size of playing area, (2) rules, (3) equipment, (4) number of players, or (5) skills used or required. Modification of a popular low-organization game ("Red Light"), a team game (volleyball), and relays follows.

Red light
1. Starting and stopping signals may be given visually or with the body (back for green, front for red) instead of verbally.
2. "It" may count to 5 instead of 10.
3. "It" may sit instead of standing.
4. Opportunities to be "It" may be regulated by the teacher.
5. Movements to reach "It" may be other than running (e.g., crawling, hopping, or any of the other basic movement patterns).

Volleyball
1. Shorten the court dimensions.
2. Use a larger ball.
3. Move the serving area closer to the net.
4. Allow more than three hits to a side.
5. Allow more than six players to a side.
6. Allow students to throw and catch instead of volleying.

Relays. Relays are widely used and hold many values. General and specific motor activities, physical fitness, and socialization are some of the benefits from this one activity. To be most effective with this activity, the teacher should remember these points (AAHPER, 1966):
1. See that teams are as nearly even in ability as possible.
2. Demonstrate how the relay is to be conducted.
3. Have no more than five or six participants on a team.
4. Indicate clearly how and when each student is to begin and end.
5. Vary the relay activities from day to day.

Specialized activities

Parachute play. An increasingly popular item in physical education curriculum is the parachute. It can be used with children at all functioning levels and is especially good for developing flexibility, muscular strength, and cardiovascular endurance. The necessity for student cooperation in this activity aids social development.

Two parachute activity albums, "Rhythmic Parachute Play" and "Parachute Activities With Folk Dance Music," are available.*

Following are some suggested activities:
1. Shaking the chute up and down at waist level
2. Passing the chute
3. Pulling the chute toward oneself
4. Performing basic movements while the chute is held overhead

Tire activities. Discussed here because of the ease of obtainment and inexpensiveness are tire activities. They can be used in a variety of ways, and the activities are limited only by the imagination of the teacher. Listed are only a few activities:

*Educational Activities, Inc., Freeport, N.Y. 11520.

1. Jumping in and out of the tires
2. Walking and balancing on the edges
3. Rolling the tires
4. Following a training course
5. Following the teacher
6. Pulling the tire with a rope

The tires can also be used to anchor a pole for tetherball, used for swings, or used for target practice with balls or beanbags. The tires can be made attractive, appealing, and more functional by painting them (a good art activity for the class).

Beanbag activities. Beanbags can be used for developing a number of specific activities (throwing, catching, coordination, etc.). They are also inexpensive and can be used indoors or on the playground. Listed are individual tossing and catching activities:
1. Tossing upward underhand; catching with two hands; catching with one hand
2. Throwing for height
3. Throwing underhand and overhand for distance
4. Holding a beanbag in each hand; making large arm circles; releasing the beanbag so it flies upward, and catching it

Fig. 7-4. Parachute play serves many purposes in a physical education program. (Courtesy Bossier Parish, La., Public Schools.)

5. Tossing upward with one hand, catch with the other
6. Tossing two beanbags upward and trying to catch one in each hand
7. Tossing rapidly from one hand to the other—in front of the body, behind the body, closing the eyes
8. Passing the beanbag around the body from hand-to-hand—passing around the legs, between the legs, over the shoulders, behind the neck, etc.
9. While on back or knees, etc., tossing upward and catching
10. Holding the bag at arm's length in front of the body with palms up; withdrawing the hand rapidly from under the bag and catching it before it hits the floor
11. Tossing upward; making of a gesture or movement before catching (e.g., clapping hands, touching toes, turning around, beating chest)

Balance beam activities. This piece of equipment can be easily constructed and can be used for developing directionality, laterality, balance, postural orientation, and self-confidence. Following are possible activities:
1. Forward and backward activities
   a. Touching the heel first, then the toe on each step; feet are kept in a straight line; return, traveling backward touching the toe first, the then heel on each step
   b. Traveling forward and back walking on the heels
   c. Carrying a weight in one hand traveling forward and backward
2. Sideways activities
   a. Moving sideways using a step/close pattern, traveling the length of the beam and back
   b. Moving sideways the length of beam, crossing the left leg in front of the right; on the return trip, crossing the right leg in front of of the left
   c. Crossing one leg behind the other
3. Turning with the arms extended, folded, or behind the back, pivoting on the balls of the feet
4. Hopping across the beam on the left foot; returning on the right
5. Balancing on one foot, with the other leg extended to the rear, the knee straight, and the head up
6. Starting on all fours, moving forward and returning backward
7. Standing on both feet or one foot, picking up various objects from the floor
8. Starting at one end of the beam, stepping forward and across the beam using a crossover step
9. Sitting sideways on the beam, balancing on the seat
10. Lying across the balance beam on the stomach, extending the arms and legs, and holding the head up

SPECIAL OLYMPICS

The Special Olympics must be included when discussing physical education for the mentally retarded because of its national impact and current significance. Until the Special Olympics was organized, 45% of all mentally retarded children received no physical education, and only 25% received as much as an hour a week (Shriver, 1974). Today, the Special Olympics is one of the largest, most successful athletic programs in the world.

The Special Olympics was founded in the summer of 1968 when the Kennedy Foundation and the Chicago Park District instituted a 2-day olympic games experiment. Skeptics said "the retarded are too weak, they can't run, or jump, or anything else." Over the years, however, the doubters, and even the organizers, have come to realize that preconceived ideas about the retardate's limited ability to participate were invalid. For example, the high jump record for the Special Olympics is 5 feet 10 inches, the Silver Medal height for the regular Olympic Games of 1896.

The ultimate goal of the Special Olympics program is to create opportunities for sports training and athletic competition for all retarded children. It is the hope of those who participate in and sponsor the Special Olympics that the program will serve as a motivational framework within which physical education, recreation, and sports activities can take place. This is an area where the retarded can succeed and build a positive self-image, gaining confidence and self-mastery as well as physical development. As a child improves his performance in the gymnasium and on the playing field, he also improves his performance in the classroom, at home, and eventually on the job. Specific goals of the Special Olympics follow:

1. To provide motivation for the initiation of physical education and athletic programs where none exists.
2. To provide supplementary materials that will aid those currently conducting such programs.
3. To provide opportunities for athletic competition through local, state, regional, and international Special Olympics.
4. To give each retarded child a feeling of belonging by offering him membership in a national athletic club with membership certificates, periodic newsletters, etc.
5. To instill in the retarded child a sense of pride by giving him a chance to win an award, be honored at the school assembly, have his picture in a newspaper, or by giving him a chance to know success.

The Special Olympics is characterized by the "Special Olympics Oath," which follows:

LET ME WIN

BUT IF I CANNOT WIN

LET ME BE BRAVE IN THE ATTEMPT.

Special Olympics has competition in the following sports:

Fig. 7-5. Membership certificate for the Special Olympics.

1. *Track:* 50-yard dash, 300-yard dash, 220-yard dash, 440-yard dash, mile run, standing broad jump, high jump, softball throw, 440-yard relay, and pentathlon, which consists of five of the above events
2. *Swimming:* 25-yard freestyle, 50-yard freestyle, 25-yard backstroke, 50-yard backstroke, 25-yard butterfly, 25-yard breaststroke, and 100-yard freestyle relay
3. *Gymnastics:* scheduled series of movements
4. *Basketball:* free throw competition, pass, dribble, and shoot competition, as well as team competition
5. *Volleyball:* girls' and boys' mixed teams
6. *Floor hockey:* boys' and girls' teams
7. *Diving:* regular point competition
8. *Bowling:* regular bowling competition
9. *Ice skating:* regular point competition
10. *Football:* punt, pass, and kick competition

All these events are divided into *boys' and girls' competition* (with the exception of volleyball). After division by sex they are divided into *age groups:* 3 and under, 9 and 10, 11 and 12, 13 and 14, 15 and 16, 17 and 18, 19 to 25, 26 to 30, 31 and over. Then each sex and age group is divided into *levels of competence,* with the fastest runners, highest and longest jumpers, and longest throwers in the first division, middle achievers grouped in various divisions in the middle, and lowest achievers grouped in the lowest classes. Each category will have first-, second-, and third-place finishers. This process enables many children to achieve a level of success unavailable to them in any other area of participation.

Participation in the Special Olympics occurs at the school level (within the local school itself), the local level (several schools get together for competition), the area level (all schools in a geographical location have competition), the state level (all qualifiers within the state compete), the regional level (every two years, the states in a geographical area have competition), the international level (every four years, all states and some foreign countries get together for competition). At each successive level of competition there are less competitors from individual schools in at-

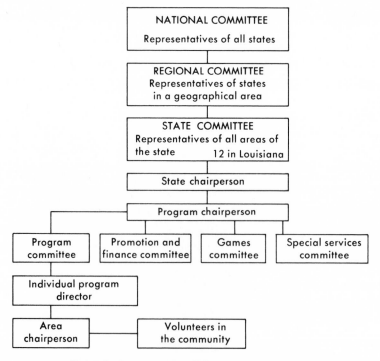

Fig. 7-6. Organization of the Special Olympics.

tendance because of the great number of individuals involved.

The same basic format is used throughout Special Olympic competition. The events begin with a runner carrying a torch to light the eternal flame, accompanied by a band if possible. There is an invocation, greetings to officials and dignitaries, the Special Olympics Pledge, a welcome to participants, sometimes a warm-up with the schools marching around the track, the competition itself, a closing speech, and the extinguishing of the Special Olympics flame. In the larger meets, state, regional, and international, where transportation and overnight lodging are necessary, many other activities are staged. Movies, dances, field trips, and clinics by local professional athletes and movie stars are held. At these larger meets the participants are treated to a happening that will be cherished forever.

The organization of the Special Olympics is illustrated in Fig. 7-6.

Special Olympics is a massive program that involves many individuals from all walks of life. It has grown from a thousand participants in 1968 to half a million in 1975. Its value to the participants is difficult to deny, yet one physical educator (Dunn, 1976) identified the following three problems or concerns of the Special Olympics:

1. Many children come to the meets unprepared (what to do, etc.).
2. In some educational programs the Special Olympics is being used as a replacement for well-rounded physical education programs.
3. Its value (social, intellectual, and physical growth) tends to be overstated.

The first two points, if true, can be easily corrected, the first by the additional involvement of specialists and more training and the second by administrators not allowing total replacement to occur. The validity of the third concern is questionable. Although the value of the Special

Olympics may not yet have been treated to rigid statistical analysis, very few participants and coaches will even question its worth.*

MATERIALS AND RESOURCES

Many of the materials necessary to provide a perceptual-motor and physical education program can be teacher-made or collected at little or no cost, although others must be purchased. Two invaluable items that can be constructed are the balance board and the balance beam. Diagrams and dimensions for teacher construction of a balance board and a balance beam are given in Figs. 7-7 and 7-8.

Specific materials necessary for a physical education program for TMRs might include items on the following list. Large equipment items, such as a jungle gym and swings, are listed in Chapter 2.

Balance beams
Balance boards
Balls (rubber and large, in addition to soccer balls, footballs, and basketballs)
Bats
Beads
Beanbags
Blocks (large and small wooden)
Clay
Form boards and templates
Horseshoes
Jump ropes
Ladders
Nets (volleyball and basketball)
Parachute
Pegboards and pegs
Puzzles
Quiet games (checkers, dominoes, etc.)
Ropes
Tires
Toys
Tumbling mats

Following are teacher resource materials and physical education programs for the mentally retarded.

*Further information is available through the Joseph P. Kennedy, Jr. Foundation, 1701 K St., N.W., Washington, D.C. 20006.

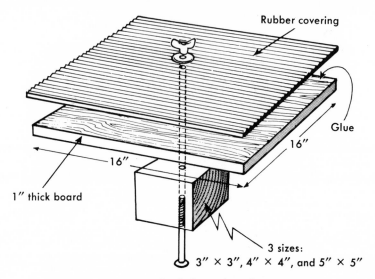

Fig. 7-7. Dimensions for balance board construction.

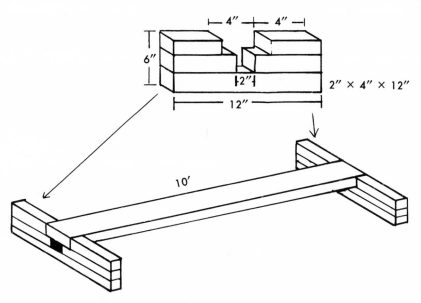

Fig. 7-8. Dimensions for balance beam construction.

I CAN (Physical Education Program) by Janet Wessel, Paul Vogel, Claudia Knowles, and Gina Green, Hubbard Scientific Co.

Developed at Michigan State University, I CAN is a complete physical education program for TMR children ages 5 to 14. Materials for each I CAN program are organized to implement an individualized teaching model (plan, assess, teach, reassess, record, and report) and include 2 notebooks of instructional activities, teaching guide, 2 sets of game activity cards, class per-

formance record sheets and individual achievement record sheets. Three of the four programs and skills are listed below; the fourth, Aquatics, is described in Chapter 9.

Fundamental skills
  Locomotor skills and rhythm
    Run
    Leap
    Horizontal jump
    Vertical jump

Hop
Gallop
Slide
Skip
Move to beat (even)
Move to beat (uneven)
Accent
Communication
Object control
Underhand roll
Underhand throw
Overhand throw
Kick
Continuous bounce
Catch
Underhand strike
Overhand strike
Forehand strike
Backhand strike
Sidearm strike
Body management
Body awareness
Body actions
Body parts
Body planes
Shapes and sizes
Spatial directions
Personal space
General space
Body control
Log roll
Shoulder roll
Front roll
Back roll
Static 2-point balance
Static 1-point balance
Dynamic balance
Balance on trampoline
Airborne on trampoline
Drop on trampoline
Health/fitness
Fitness and growth
Abdominal strength and endurance
Arm/shoulder/chest strength and endurance
Stamina and heart/lung strength and endurance
Trunk and leg flexibility relaxation
Posture
Standing
Sitting
Walking
Ascending
Descending
Pulling
Holding
Carrying
Lifting
Lowering

Physical Activities for the Mentally Retarded (Ideas for Instruction) by the American Association for Health, Physical Education, and Recreation.

This excellent book provides a list of physical activities for the retarded. It is designed for use by classroom teachers and contains four sequential levels of skills:

Level I—Basic movement patterns, fundamental motor skills, initial perceptual development, conceptual formation, development of self-awareness, body-concept, and self-image.

Level II—Activities of low organization in which patterns, movements, and skills developed at the first level are applied to more difficult situations.

Level III—Adapted and lead-up activities in which patterns, movements, and skills are used for the purpose of preparing the individual for participation in specific sports, games, and higher organized activities.

Level IV—Games, sports, and higher organized activities.

Families Play to Grow by the Joseph P. Kennedy, Jr. Foundation.

This unique physical education–recreation program was designed for the retarded child *and* his parents or family. This program teaches many favorite sports to the TMR with a step-by-step guide for each sport or activity. Included in the kit are the following family play guides:

1. Fun for the Very Young or Severely Retarded
2. Fun With Movement, Rhythm, and Dance
3. Fun With Soccer and Kickball
4. Fun With Basketball
5. Fun With Running
6. Fun in the Water
7. Fun With Hiking, Bicycling, and Nature Walking
8. Fun With Bowling
9. Fun With Volleyball
10. Fun With Baseball

Each guide contains techniques of teaching and suggested activities, all emphasizing family involvement. The kit also contains a Family Play manual, a Family Play calendar, and an "I'm a Winner" chart. The calendar is filled in every time a play-to-grow activity is finished, and when 30 hours are completed, it can be sent to the Kennedy Foundation for a Family Award of Achievement Certificate and Play to Grow 30 Hour Club Card for each family member who participated. The colorful "I'm a

Winner" chart is designed for the child to record each hour of play and can be put up in his room.

Movement Exploration and Games for the Mentally Retarded by Layne C. Hackett, Peek Publications.

Designed for the classroom teacher of the retarded, this book has activities in body image and space awareness, visual focusing and balance, strength and endurance, and eye-hand coordination.

Systematic Instruction for Retarded Children: The Illinois Program: Motor Performance and Recreation Instruction by Anthony Linford and Claudine Jeanvenaud, The Interstate Printers and Publishers, Inc.

This book presents specific lesson plans in the basic movement area of physical education. Plans and activities are included for walking, marching, kicking, throwing, pulling and pushing, rolling, jumping, crawling, hopping, climbing, swinging, squatting, catching, kneelin, hitting, running, hanging, and walking on a balance beam.

Project ACTIVE (All Children Totally Involved in Exercising) by Thomas Vodola and the Township of Ocean School District, Oakhurst, New Jersey.

Project ACTIVE is a series of manuals designed to help educators with assisting the mentally retarded and other handicapped children (K through 12) in physical development. These manuals, with activities and tasks, are listed:

Low Motor Ability: Developmental Physical Education—an individualized program for enhancing low-motor–perceptual-motor performance.

Developmental and Adapted Physical Education—a competency-based teacher training manual.

Developmental and Adapted Physical Education—Low Physical Vitality.

Developmental and Adapted Physical Education—Postural Abnormalities.

Developmental and Adapted Physical Education—Breathing Problems.

Frostig MGL (Move-Grow-Learn) by Marianne Frostig and Phyllis Maslow, Follett Publishing Co.

This is a movement education program to enhance the total development of children. The program consists of 181 exercise cards in the areas of body awareness, coordination, agility, strength, flexibility, balance, and creative movement. A move-grow-learn skills survey list (for evaluation purposes) can also be purchased to accompany this program.

Developmental Activities for the Primary Classroom by Vivien Richman and Lorraine Morgan, Instructional Media Inc.

This book contains 139 detailed suggestions for actual activities leading to development in 45 categories of gross motor skills, fine motor skills, and auditory and visual perception. All activities use teacher-constructed materials and can be used for individuals or groups.

Classroom Activities for Helping Perceptually Handicapped Children by Linda Anderson, The Center for Applied Research in Education, Inc.

A book of specific activities for developing visual perceptual skills, auditory perceptual skills, tactual and kinesthetic perception, fine motor coordination, laterality, directionality, and body image.

Teaching Through Sensory-Motor Experiences by John Arena, Fearon Publishers.

This book presents activities in eye-hand coordination, laterality and directionality, body image and awareness, tactile and kinesthetic perception, and visual perception and discrimination.

SUMMARY

Perceptual-motor development and physical education programs are important aspects of the curriculum for the TMR. Research indicates a significant motor performance lag, possession of few physical skills, and frequent motor disorders in this population. Yet, in past years, only minimal opportunities were offered for physical development. When appropriate structured programs are provided, however, improvement in mental, emotional, social, and academic areas is possible, in addition to motor skill gains.

The three principal areas of physical education include the basic movements, perceptual-motor skills, and physical fitness. The basic movements are locomotor, nonlocomotor, and manipulative behaviors: the perceptual-motor skills include body image, laterality, directionality, auditory, visual, and haptic perception, and eye-hand (fine motor) coordination; and the physical fitness domain includes organic performance (strength, flexibility, muscular and cardiovascular endurance, power), and motor performance (balance, agility, speed, general coordination, reaction time).

Each of the three main areas should be assessed by formal (standardized) or informal measures. A formal test battery for this curriculum area might include the Bruininks-Oseretsky Test of Motor Proficiency (movement skills), the Purdue Perceptual-Motor Survey (perceptual-motor skills), and the AAHPER/Kennedy Foundation Special Fitness Test (physical fitness).

In developing physical skills in the TMR it is important to remember that they can participate in most games and activities other students enjoy, but modification of the game or activity may be necessary. Adaptations might include changing the size of the playing area, amending the rules, reducing or increasing the number of players, or reducing the number of skills required. Although modification of some activities is necessary, there do exist specialized activities that are uniquely suited for TMRs. Of great benefit, and quiet and inexpensive fun, are parachute play activities, tire activities, beanbag activities, and balance beam or board activities.

Another specialized program of tremendous benefit for the TMR is the Special Olympics. Founded by the Joseph P. Kennedy, Jr. Foundation in 1968, the Special Olympics is now one of the largest, most successful athletic programs in the world. Competition is divided by sex, age, and level of competence. The sports areas include track, swimming, gymnastics, basketball, volleyball, floor hockey, diving, bowling, ice skating, and football.

REFERENCES AND SUGGESTED READINGS

AAHPER: Physical activities for the mentally retarded (ideas for instruction), Washington, D.C., 1968, American Association for Health, Physical Education, and Recreation.

AAHPER: Testing for impaired, disabled and handicapped individuals, Washington, D.C., 1975, American Association for Health, Physical Education, and Recreation.

Alarcon, M. M.: Movement expressions for the preschool trainable mentally retarded child: a descriptive study, Ed.S. thesis, University of Alabama, 1974.

American Optometric Association: Visual and perceptual checklist for the retarded child, St. Louis, 1975.

Anderson, L.: Classroom activities for helping perceptually handicapped children, West Nyack, N.Y., 1974, The Center for Applied Research in Education, Inc.

Arena, J. I.: Teaching through sensory-motor experiences, Belmont, Calif., 1969, Fearon Publishers/Lear Siegler, Inc.

Barsch, R. H.: Achieving perceptual-motor efficiency, Seattle, Wash., 1967, Special Child Publications.

Campbell, J.: Physical fitness and the mentally retarded: a review of research, Ment. Retard. 11(5):26-29, 1973.

Campbell, J.: Improving the physical fitness of retarded boys, Ment. Retard. 12(3):31-35, 1974.

Conover, D.: Physical education games and activities for the retarded, Focus Except. Child. 3(8):1-5, 1972.

Cratty, B. J.: Perceptual-motor behavior and educational processes, Springfield, Ill., 1969, Charles C Thomas, Publisher.

Curry, G. I.: Winter Haven's perceptual training and training handbook, Winter Haven, Fla., 1969, Winter Haven Lions Research Foundation, Inc.

Drawatzky, J. N.: Play education for the mentally retarded, Philadelphia, 1971, Lea & Febiger.

Dunn, J. M.: Special olympics—its strengths and problems, The Physical Activities Report, no. 409, April, 1976.

Ersing, W. F.: The nature of physical education programming for the mentally retarded and physically handicapped, J. Health, Phys. Ed. Rec. 45(2):8-9, 1974.

Fait, H. F.: Special physical education: adapted, corrective and developmental, ed. 3, Philadelphia, 1972, W. B. Saunders Co.

Hackett, L. C.: Movement exploration and games for the mentally retarded, Palo Alto, Calif., 1970, Peek Publications.

Hayden, F. J.: Physical fitness for the mentally retarded, Ontario, Canada, 1964, Metropolitan Toronto Association for Retarded Children.

Kephart, N. C.: The slow learner in the classroom, ed. 2, Columbus, Ohio, 1971, Charles E. Merrill Publishing Co.

Kral, P. A.: Motor characteristics and development of retarded children: success experience, Educ. Train. Ment. Retard. 7:14-21, 1972.

Liese, J.: Physical fitness and intelligence in TMR's, Ment. Retard. 12(5):50-51, 1974.

Mann, L.: Perceptual training: misdirections and redirections, Am. J. Orthopsychiat. 40(1):30-38, 1970.

Moran, J. M., and Kalakian, L. H.: Movement experiences for the mentally retarded or emotionally disturbed child, Minneapolis, Minn., 1974, Burgess Publishing Co.

Shriver, E. K.: A new kind of joy, Washington, D.C., 1974, Special Olympics, Inc.

Wessel, J. H., and Knowles, C. J.: Studies related to moderately (trainable) persons, Challenge 10(2):1-3, 1975.

Wheeler, R. H., and Hooley, A. M.: Physical education for the handicapped, ed. 2, Philadelphia, 1976, Lea & Febiger.

CHAPTER 8

DEVELOPING FUNCTIONAL ACADEMIC SKILLS

One of the controversies in curriculum design for the trainable mentally retarded is the inclusion or exclusion of "academics." Academic goals of TMR curriculum programs in past years were relegated to recognizing safety words (reading), counting to 10 or knowing one's age (arithmetic), and spelling and writing one's name (spelling and writing). Teachers of this particular population have long observed goals beyond these, although earlier research (Warren, 1963) demonstrated that even after instruction, poor academic performance prevailed. More recent research (Apffel et al., 1975; Ayllon et al., 1972; Bellamy and Buttars, 1975; Brown and Perlmutter, 1971; Fuller, 1974; Richardson et al., 1975), however, clearly negates the results of earlier efforts. Some of the reasons that may account for different findings between the early 1960s and the middle 1970s are (1) recently developed specialized instructional technology (behaviorist task analysis, programed instruction, backward chaining, etc.), (2) recently designed instructional materials for the population (Peabody, Rebus, etc.), (3) better quality teacher programs (competency based programs), (4) increased comprehensive educational programing (emphasis on pre-

school education), and (5) increased involvement in training parents as teachers.

The term "functional academics" is used in favor of "academics" because it appears to be more descriptive and realistic of attainable skills for TMRs. It should be emphasized that functional academics should only be a goal for those individuals which have demonstrated the necessary capabilities. Academic instruction for all TMRs without consideration of individual abiilties defies reason. Furthermore, academics is only one aspect of the curriculum, and primary emphasis, because of its inclusion in this text, is not intended. Other areas of curriculum (e.g., social or basic communication skills) hold greater overall importance for the TMR. At any rate, a program decision to include academics should be based on the child's demonstrated ability and learning rate and *not* on assumed potential implied by categorical labels.

This chapter on developing functional academic skills will examine the areas of reading, writing and spelling, and arithmetic. Each area will be discussed, focusing on development, assessment, skills to be developed, techniques, programs, materials, and activities.

READING

Learning beginning or basic reading skills is not, as was once thought, beyond TMRs' capabilities. Granted, reading is an exceedingly complex task, but only recently have specialized programs and strategies for teaching these skills been made available. As Apffel (1974) reported, past research indicating failure of TMRs to read may be due to the teaching methods and techniques used rather than their lack of requisite abilities. Correlated with these advances are teacher attitude and behavior changes. Ruvin (1970), for example, indicated that teachers of the TMR sometimes adversely affect their students' academic growth and success by overprotection, underexpectation, and tolerance of unacceptable classroom behavior. Fortunately, with increased quality teacher training programs and cumulative experiences in educational programing for the TMR, these teacher attitudes and behaviors are now rarely, if ever, observed.

To best relate the reading process to the needs of the TMR, it is necessary to understand the developmental reading process and factors that affect the attainment of reading skills. Each will be briefly discussed.

Developmental reading and factors affecting reading ability

Delchant (1970) lists the chief characteristics of reading as (1) a sensory process, (2) a perceptual process, (3) a response, (4) a learned process, (5) a development task, (6) an interest, (7) a learning process, and (8) communication. Beyond the characteristics of reading are two main skills: word attack and reading comprehension. These principal skills and their components are listed and defined here (Ekwall, 1976).

1. *Word attack skills (recognizing words)*—those techniques which are assumed to enable a child to "decode" an unknown word so that he can pronounce and understand it.
   a. *Phonetic analysis*—ability to identify the printed word symbols that represent words possessed in oral language.
   b. *Structural analysis*—involves the utilization of word parts, such as prefixes, suffixes, and compound words.
   c. *Context clues*—guessing at the meaning of an unknown word by looking at the position of the word in a sentence.
   d. *Configuration clues*—ability to identify words by their particular shapes.
   e. *Dictionary skills*—looking up the definition, the pronunciation, the usage, and the derivation of a word.
2. Reading comprehension—ability to understand and interpret what one reads (also includes critical reading).
   a. *Literal meaning*—a knowledge of the ideas and information exactly as stated.

Table 8-1. Typical grade level and mental age necessary for selected reading skills

Skill	Grade level	Mental age
Basic visual-perceptual skills (visual discrimination, visual matching, visual sequential memory)	Preschool	3 to 4
Basic listening skills (auditory discrimination, auditory figure-ground, auditory association, auditory sequential memory)	Preschool	3 to 4
Producing patterns in left-right sequence	Preschool	4 to 5
Recognizing rhyming words	Preschool	4 to 5
Recognizing consonant sounds	Preschool	4 to 5
Associating consonant sounds with letters	First	6
Knowing short vowel sounds	First	6
Knowing long vowel sounds	First	6
Blending consonant and vowel sounds	First	6
Recognizing root words	First	6
Forming plurals by adding s, es and ies	First	6
Recognizing consonant blends that represent two sounds (e.g., bl, st)	Second	7
Recognizing consonant blends that represent one sound (e.g., sh, th, wh)	Second	7
Recognizing vowel combinations (e.g., ee, ea)	Second	7
Recognizing compound words	Second	7
Adding common suffixes and prefixes to root words	Second	7
Recognizing contractions	Third	8
Recognizing possession	Third	8
Dividing words into syllables	Third	8
Using accents	Fourth	9

b. *Inference*—ability to use ideas and information as stated.

c. *Evaluation*—ability to judge and focus on qualities of correctness, appropriateness, and validity.

d. *Appreciation*—emotional and aesthetic sensitivity to the written work's psychological and artistic elements.

e. *Critical thinking*—ability to evaluate, judge fact from opinion, truth from fantasy, etc.

Table 8-1 provides basic reading skills, the typical grade level at which they are taught, and equivalent mental ages necessary for normal acquisition.

Certain factors are related to poor reading performance. Among them are low intelligence scores, physical factors (general health, visual and hearing disorders, neurological dysfunction), poor language skills, experiential factors (poor home conditions and low socioeconomic conditions, which influence interest and motivation and limit experiences), auditory, visual, and haptic perception, and emotional and social adjustment.

Assessment

Assessment of TMR reading abilities must concentrate on readiness skills and developmental levels. Reading assessment by diagnostic-remedial testing has little applicability with this population and therefore will not be discussed.

Readiness. No exhaustive list of reading readiness skills exists nor does there exist a readiness test that assesses all areas necessary for reading. Among the skills considered important, however, are visual and auditory discrimination, visual and auditory sequencing, listening for details, following directions, recognizing letters, using context cues, eye-hand coordination, seeing relationships, and interpreting pictures (Smith, 1974). Also, many reading specialists believe that a mental age of 6 is necessary for formal instruction. Following

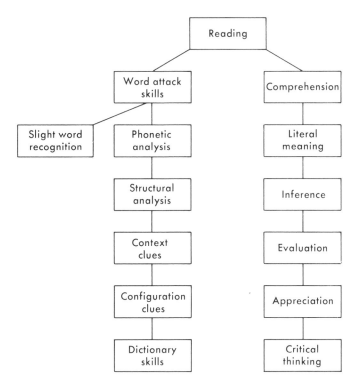

Fig. 8-1. Scope of the basic reading skills.

Fig. 8-2. Auditory skill training exercise to develop academic readiness. (Courtesy Bossier Parish, La., Public Schools.)

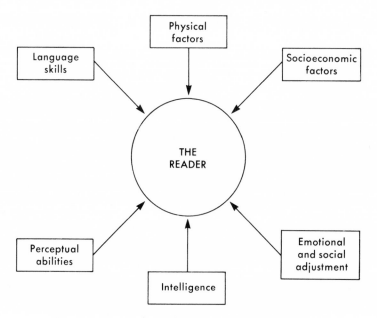

Fig. 8-3. Factors that influence reading capabilities.

Fig. 8-4. Visual matching is a basic visual perceptual skill for reading readiness. (Courtesy Bossier Parish, La., Public Schools.)

are probable chronological ages at which students with differing IQs would be ready to begin formal reading instruction:

	IQ	CA needed for reading
Average	100	6.0
	90	6.7
Slow learner	80	7.5
EMR	70	8.5
	60	10.0
	50	12.0
TMR	40	15.0
	30	20.0

A mental age of 6 was used as a requisite age for reading. Most TMRs would not be ready for formal reading until a chronological age of 11 or 12, and some lower IQ students would not be ready to read during a school career. Readiness skills and simple sight vocabulary words would comprise the "reading" program for most of these and other students.

Table 8-2 provides a description of several of the most popular standardized readiness tests in reading. All are designed for kindergarten or first-grade ability, so when you decide to select an instrument, make sure the child has a high enough ability to make the test valid and know what skill areas you want to evaluate.

Skills to be developed

A reading program for TMRs typically includes readiness skills, sight vocabulary, and functional reading skills. The sight vocabulary aspect of reading should be emphasized because of its benefits. Sight vocabulary skills for the TMR have been found to contribute to cognitive development, listening vocabulary, oral language, alphabet mastery, spelling, and memory skills (Feinberg, 1975). Some students may achieve more than the skills listed on pp. 191 and 192, but for the majority of students these skills will comprise a reading program.

Table 8-2. Selected standardized reading readiness tests

Name of test	Skills measured	Publisher and date
Gates-MacGinitie Reading Tests: Readiness Skills	Listening comprehension, auditory discrimination, visual discrimination, following directions, letter recognition, visual-motor coordination, auditory blending, word recognition	Teachers College Press, 1968
Harrison-Stroud Reading Readiness Profiles	Giving names of letters, auditory discrimination, visual discrimination, using auditory and context clues, using symbols, using context	Houghton Mifflin Co., 1950
Lee Clark Reading Readiness Test	Letter symbols, concepts, word symbols	McGraw-Hill, 1962
Maturity Level for School Entrance and Reading Readiness	Designed to determine whether children are mature enough to enter school and/or ready to read	American Guidance Service 1959
Metropolitan Readiness Tests (Level I)	Auditory memory, rhyming, letter recognition, visual matching, school language and listening, quantitative language	Harcourt Brace Jovanovich, Inc., 1976
Metropolitan Readiness Tests (Level II)	Beginning consonants, sound-letter correspondence, visual matching, finding patterns, school language, listening, quantitative concepts, quantitative operations	Harcourt Brace Jovanovich, Inc., 1976
Murphy-Durrell Diagnostic Reading Readiness Tests	Learning rate, letter names, phonemes test	Harcourt Brace Jovanovich, Inc., 1964
School Readiness Survey	Color naming, form discrimination, general information, listening vocabulary, number concepts, speaking vocabulary, symbol matching	Consulting Psychologists Press, 1969

Fig. 8-5. Visual form discrimination activity. (Courtesy Bossier Parish, La., Public Schools.)

1. Basic visual perceptual skills
   a. Can visually discriminate color, shape, and size
   b. Can visually match color, shape, and size
   c. Has visual sequential memory
2. Basic listening skills
   a. Auditory discrimination
   b. Auditory figure-ground
   c. Auditory association
   d. Auditory sequential memory
3. Produces left-right sequence patterns
4. Identifies and names letters of the alphabet
   a. Uppercase letters
   b. Lowercase letters
5. Identifies sight vocabulary words (suggested listing)

   a. Safety words

Walk	Poison
Stop	Caution
Fire exit	Keep out
Railroad crossing	Glass
Danger	Do not enter
Flammable	Explosives
Beware of dog	Restricted area
	Warning

   b. Public signs

Telephone	
Men	No eating
Women	No smoking
No trespassing	Keep off the grass
Wet paint	Private
Entrance	Posted
Don't walk	School zone
This way out	Keep out
Exit	Self-service
Restroom	Out of order
	One way

   c. Public building titles

Fire Department	Train depot
Post office	Police station
Bus station	Airport
Hospital	Bus stop
Library	Subway

   d. Months(and abbreviations) of the year

January (Jan.)	July
February (Feb.)	August (Aug.)
March (Mar.)	September (Sept
April (Apr.)	October (Oct.)
May	November (Nov.
June	December (Dec.

   e. Days (and abbreviations) of the week

Monday (Mon.)	Thursday (Thur.
Tuesday (Tue.)	Friday (Fri.)
Wednesday	Saturday (Sat.)
(Wed.)	Sunday (Sun.)

   f. Family titles

Mother	Niece
Father	Grandfather
Grandmother	Brother

Sister	Cousin
Aunt	Nephew
Uncle	

   g. Public titles (with abbreviations)

Doctor (Dr.)	Mrs.
Principal	Miss
Mr.	Ms.

   h. Basic colors

Black	Brown
Blue	White
Green	Purple
Orange	Red
Pink	Yellow

   i. Weather words

Hot	Warm
Cold	Foggy
Cloudy	Humid
Windy	Snow
Rainy	Sleet
Sunny	Hail
Cool	

   j. Directional words

Open	Back
Close	Front
Up	Left
Down	Right
Off	Above
On	Below
Over	Ahead
Under	Behind
Push	In
Pull	Out
Stop	Between
Go	

   k. Body parts

Hand	Elbow
Toe	Mouth
Lips	Teeth
Hair	Shoulder
Nose	Chin
Head	Eyelash
Foot	Nails
Knee	Heel
Leg	Ankle
Eye	Thigh
Nose	Waist
Tongue	Chest
Ear	Ribs
Arm	Wrist
Stomach	Fingers
Thumb	Neck

   l. Home and furniture words

Chair	Kitchen
Table	Bedroom
Window	Door
Bathroom	Stove
Television	Refrigerator
Ceiling	Sink

Living room | Wall
Den | Curtains (drapes)
Dining room | Bed
Basement | Garage (carport)
Attic

m. Clothing words

Shoes | Underwear
Socks | Tie
Dress | Sandals
Coat | Belt
Pants | Jacket
Hat (cap) | Gloves (mittens)
Shirt | Suit
Slip | Tennis shoes
Bra

n. Numbers

One | Six
Two | Seven
Three | Eight
Four | Nine
Five | Ten

o. Fruits and vegetables

Orange | Coconut
Apple | Lettuce
Banana | Squash
Peach | Corn
Potato | Peas
Tomato | Pumpkin
Carrot | Celery
Onion | Watermelon
Raisins | Cantaloupe

p. Action words

Sitting | Walking
Standing | Jumping
Running | Eating
Laughing | Drinking
Climbing | Throwing
Creeping | Catching

Programs and materials

There are many programs and associated materials for developing reading and reading readiness skills, all using a particular approach. Popular approaches include basal readers, phonics, individualized reading, language experience, linguistics, and programed instruction. Very few programs of any approach have been developed with the TMR as one of the target consumers. The *Peabody Rebus Reading Program, DISTAR*, and *Edmark Reading Program* will be examined as possible approaches because they (1) are structured, (2) are personalized, (3) are interesting and motivational, (4) provide immediate feedback,

(5) contain an evaluation component, and (6) have been successfully used with the TMR (Apffel et al., 1975).

Peabody Rebus Reading Program (REBUS). Developed by Woodcock, Clark, and Davies (1969), this is a programed approach to introductory reading using rebuses (picture words). Also included is a combination of rebuses and traditional spelled words.

The rebus level includes two full-color programed workbooks, each containing 384 frames. At completion of these two readiness books, the student will be able to use a rebus vocabulary of sixty-eight words in complex reading tasks. The transitional level is a continuation of Books 1 and 2 and contains one programed workbook. This book is correlated with two rebus readers. On completion of the readiness and transitional programs, a student will have a reading vocabulary of 120 spelled words, including the names of numbers and colors as well as the words most common to the major basal reading program.

A supplementary lessons list is also available for the readiness level and includes seventeen lessons designed to facilitate group instruction and to extend the introduction to the program. A word card deck representing the rebuses and words is also available. A unique aspect of REBUS is the marking system: the student marks his response with a moistened pencil eraser, and a special ink reveals whether the selection is correct. This is often motivational to some students.

DISTAR. The DISTAR (Direct Instruction Systems for Teaching Arithmetic and Reading) program was developed by Englemann and Bruner (1969) and contains Reading I, II, and III, Language I, II, and III, and Arithmetic I, II, and III. Of concern for TMRs is Reading I and, in some cases, Reading II.

The DISTAR reading program is designed to teach children the skills they need to read. Englemann (1967) has stated that "virtually all children with mental ages of 5 or over can learn to read." This of course

a	a		can		have		run
	airplane		car		here		see
	and		cat		house		sit
	are		chair	I	I		table
	at		coat		in		the
	ball		come		is		they
	banana		dog		it	3	three

Fig. 8-6. Sample of vocabulary from *Introducing Reading: Book Two* of the Peabody Rebus Program. (American Guidance Service, Circle Pines, Minn., 1969.)

refutes traditional belief that a mental age of 6 to 6½ is necessary to learn to read. This idea also supports some teachers of TMRs who have students "reading" with MAs of less than 6. Although mental age is a fairly good predictor of school success and academic achievement, it may not always be absolute.

Reading I concentrates on basic decoding skills necessary to look at a word, sound it, and say it. Features include learning the sounds for forty letters, blending these sounds together, modification of look-alike confusing letters (b and d), special aids (markers, left-to-right directional arrows, etc.), and rhyming exercises. The letter symbols in DISTAR are taught as sounds rather than as names of letters, with the purpose of helping students to blend more effectively and accurately. Following are examples for teaching pronunciation of two letters (m and s).

m

mmm, as in him (continuous, voiced)
To pronounce, take a deep breath and hold the first sound in *me* for several seconds: mmmēēē. Say *am* slowly: aaammm.
Wrong pronunciations
  muh—There should be no *uh*.
  em—This is the letter name. Drop the *e*.

m, m, m—Do not repeat the sound. Say it once and hold it.

s

sss, as in kiss (continuous, unvoiced)
To pronounce, take a deep breath and say the last sound in *miss* for several seconds: mmmiiisss. Say *so* slowly: sssōōō.
To help the child, make sure he has his teeth showing, his lips spread, and his tongue not touching his teeth. Say: "Smile and bite. Now say sss."
Wrong pronunciations
  suh—There should be no *uh*.
  es—This is the letter name. Drop the *e*.
  sih—There should be no *ih*.

Reading I contains teacher presentation notebooks and take-home materials. Teacher materials are a teaching guide, the related skills book (*Sounds and Reading Sounds*—books A, B, and C), and records of sounds presented. Student materials include take-home blending sheets, take-home sound-symbol sheets, stories, writing sheets, and workbooks of worksheets.

Reading II is a continuation of the skills book (books D, E, and F), a recycling book, plus other related materials. This level is intended for a two-year program and emphasizes comprehension.

A unique teaching technique in this phonics approach is its presentation. In

DISTAR the lessons are conducted with small groups of children of similar ability (determined by pretests) who sit around the teacher. Each lesson is about 20 to 30 minutes in length. A DISTAR Library Series (Englemann and Bruner, 1971) and DISTAR games are also available to reinforce the skills contained in DISTAR I and II.

Edmark Reading Program. Developed by Bijou (1972), this developmental reading program utilizes aspects of programed instruction and operant learning principles. Programed instruction components include lessons that contain small, discrete, sequential steps, reinforcement (social or token), progression by a student at his own rate, and a small teaching machine to frame the lessons. Cuing, shaping, fading, and stimulus response chaining are some of the operant learning principles of Edmark.

The Edmark Program was designed to teach reading to the retarded and non-readers and uses a 150-word vocabulary. There are 227 lessons of four types: (1) word recognition lessons (teaches one or two words with increasing distractor difficulty), (2) direction books (teaches following printed directions), (3) picture-phrase matching lessons, and (4) storybook lessons (sixteen stories to read orally). Each lesson indicates the activity to be taught and the criteria for each.

Other features of Edmark include pretests and review tests, procedures for chart-

Fig. 8-7. Programed instruction reading program (System 80) for the TMR. (Courtesy Greenwich, Conn., Public Schools.)

ing student progress (a student record book), and a prereading unit for determining if the student has the necessary skills to benefit from the program. Added in 1976 was a 950-word illustrated twelve-

Table 8-3. Reading materials and publishers

Program or material	Publisher
Auditory Perception Training	Developmental Learning Materials
Beginning to Read, Write, and Listen	J. B. Lippincott Co.
Developing Learning Readiness	Webster Publishing Co.
A First Course in Phonic Reading	Educators Publishing Service
First Experiences (letters and sounds)	McGraw-Hill Book Co.
First Phonics Series	Educators Publishing Service
Fitzhugh Plus Program	Allied Educational Council
Intersensory Reading Method	Book-Lab, Inc.
Learning About Sounds and Letters	Ginn and Co.
Learning the Letters	Educators Publishing Service
The Look, Listen, and Learn Series	Millikin Publishing Co.
Michigan Tracking Program	Mafex Associates, Inc.
Perceptual Skills	Teaching Resources, Inc.
Phonovisual Series	Phonovisual Products, Inc.
Primary Phonics Series	Educators Publishing Service
Reading Achievement Program for the Moderately and Severely Retarded	The Interstate Printers and Publishers
Sanders Touch Type Reading System	SLM, Inc.
Sounds, Letters and Words; More Sounds, Letters and Words; and Skill With Sounds	J. B. Lippincott Co.
Structural Reading Series	Random House, Inc.
System 80	Borg-Warner Educational Systems
Target Red: Auditory-Visual Discrimination Kit	Field Educational Publications, Inc.
Training for Independence (recognition of functional words, understanding of functional words and phrases, and retention of important oral phrases and numbers)	Developmental Learning Materials
Vowel Sounds	Milton Bradley Co.
Vowel Sounds and Consonant Sounds	Milton Bradley Co.
Words in Color	Xerox Education Division

page book using every word taught in the program. This book is designed to be used as a take-home reward when a student completes the program. Advantages of this program are that it is sequential, based on learning principles, moderately priced, and requires little specialized training for the teacher (Gillespie and Johnson, 1974).

Other possible reading programs and teaching materials include those in Table 8-3. The teacher interested in any of them should consult the publisher's brochure or catalogue.*

WRITING AND SPELLING

Writing is a highly complex process requiring the integration of perceptual, motoric, and conceptual abilities (Hammill, 1975). It is one of the highest forms of communication and therefore one of the last to be mastered. There is always some skepticism about teaching the retarded person to write, but any informal survey of teachers or formal research (Sharp, 1973; Stasio, 1976) will demonstrate that many TMRs can learn to write.

Teaching the TMR to write is included because (1) writing is a purposeful and meaningful activity, (2) writing itself can improve eye-hand coordination, although some eye-hand coordination is necessary to learn to write, (3) writing reinforces the ability to recognize safety and sight vocabulary words and useful numbers, and (4) writing is within the capabilities of many TMRs.

Assessment

Assessment will once again only focus on determination of readiness skills. Whereas traditional writing curriculum is also concerned with penmanship (legibility and speed of writing) and conceptual writing (grammatical correctness and meaningfulness of the product), these have limited concern for TMRs.

The primary readiness skills are ade-

---

*Addresses of publishers are contained in Appendix A.

quate language and experiences, both providing something meaningful to say through written communication. The secondary readiness skills are those which pertain to the perceptual-motor proficiency necessary to execute graphical symbols.

A list of possible readiness skills (secondary), as well as formal and/or informal techniques for their evaluation follows:

1. Visual-motor integration
   a. Eye-hand coordination (Eye-Hand Coordination subtest of the Frostig Developmental Test of Visual Perception)
   b. Copying (Copying subtest from the Metropolitan Readiness Test)
   c. Ocular control (Ocular Control subtest of the Purdue Perceptual-Motor Survey)
   d. Left-right progression (Does he begin to read on the left side of the page? Does he connect dots from left to right?)
   e. Small muscle coordination (Observe the child stringing beads, using a pegboard, or holding a pencil.)
2. Laterality
   a. Handedness (Observe the child in various activities, e.g., eating, brushing his teeth, throwing a ball, cutting, coloring.)
   b. Eyedness (Have the child observe with both eyes a small object through a small circle in the middle of a sheet of paper. The paper should be about 20 inches from his face. Have the child close his right eye. If he can still see the object, he is left-eyed, if he cannot, he is right-eyed. The eye used to sight the object is the dominant eye.)

As the TMR learns to write, many errors in penmanship will occur. Their writing may be illegible, too slow, or otherwise unsatisfactory. This is normal and to be expected for a period of time. Writing, like other skills, is slow to develop. However, if the errors still persist after a period of time, the child may not be ready for writing, and a reevaluation of his prewriting skills should be made.

Skills to be developed

The basic prewriting and writing skills to be developed in the TMR, besides basic readiness skills are listed:

Prewriting skills: Holds pencil; can draw the basic strokes (down, across, slant right and left, circle).

Tracing skills: Can trace lines (horizontal and vertical), shapes (cross, square, circle, triangle), letters (uppercase and lowercase straight line letters, then uppercase and lowercase curved and circular letters), numbers (0 to 10), age, telephone number, and name and address.

Copying skills: Has same skills as listed for tracing.

Writing independently: Can write age, name, telephone number, address, important words, and names.

Refinement: Shows improvement in quantity, quality, and size of words.

Procedures, techniques, and materials

The normal procedure for teaching handwriting consists of four basic stages: (1) teaching introductory movements using the chalkboard, (2) seat work activities using learned movements, (3) teaching cursive writing movements using the chalkboard, (4) seat work using learned movements, and (5) seat work on cursive letters. This sequence can also be adapted for the TMR, but keep in mind that the rate of progression will be slow.

There are two basic issues relating to procedures for teaching writing: cursive writing vs. printing and uppercase vs. lowercase letters. Proponents of teaching cursive writing first collectively state that (1) it establishes a sense of direction; (2) it eliminates errors of reversals; (3) the need to transfer from one form of writing to another is eliminated; (4) it is easier because there exists a rhythmic continuity and wholeness missing from printing; and (5) it provides greater academic success. Those who favor printing first state that (1) it is easier to learn because it consists of only circles and straight lines; (2) the letter form is like that found in published material; and (3) the child does not have to transfer because printing is legal and just as legible (Hildreth, 1963; Lerner, 1976; Stuart, 1967).

The research on that issue for the TMR is inconclusive, and many special educators believe it makes little difference which

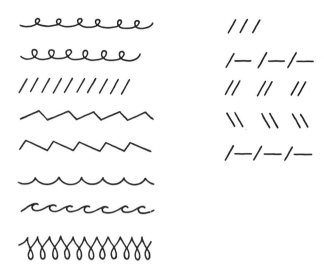

Fig. 8-8. Basic introductory handwriting movements. (From Reger, R., Schroeder, W., and Uschold, K.: Special education: children with learning problems. Copyright © 1968 by Oxford University Press, Inc. Reprinted by permission.)

is taught first. One recent report (Stasio, 1976), however, did find that the severely retarded made better progress with cursive than with printed writing. Deciding which to use still should depend on the individual. If the student has gross perceptual problems, cursive writing may be preferred. Otherwise, printing should be introduced first.

The professional literature is also in disagreement regarding whether lowercase or uppercase printed letters should be taught first or whether they should be taught simultaneously. One descriptive handwriting program for TMRs (Sharp, 1973) suggests only printed uppercase letters be taught because (1) this reduces by half the total number of letters to be learned, and (2) these printed uppercase letters are found on safety words or signs in the community (e.g., POISONS, MEN, STOP). This approach, called the Edwards Method, uses only six basic strokes: down, across, slant left, slant right, circle left, and circle right. Over a five-year period with 300 students, Sharp found that TMR children can and do learn to write using this method.

The question might not actually be lowercase vs. uppercase but which lowercase and which uppercase letters should be taught first. The decision should be based on the specific skills necessary for letter formation. The order of presentation then should be (1) uppercase straight line letters, (2) lowercase straight line letters, (3) uppercase curved and circular letters, and (4) lowercase curved and circular letters.

Following is a sequence for teaching printed letters (Bender et al., 1976).

1. Straight line uppercase and lowercase printed letters
   a. Uppercase: AEFHIKLMNTVWXYZ
   b. Lowercase: iklrtvwxyz
2. Curved and circular uppercase and lowercase printed letters
   a. Uppercase: BCDGJOPQRSU
   b. Lowercase: abcdefghjmnopqsu

It should also be noted that only six different pencil strokes are necessary for making lowercase printed letters (Spaulding and Spaulding, 1962). (See Fig. 8-9.)

The cursive letter sequence should also follow a certain pattern based on the movements necessary. The letter sequence suggested by Dubrow (1968) is i, u, w, t, r, s, n, m, v, x, e, l, b, h, k, f, c, a, g, d,

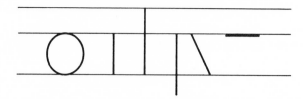

Fig. 8-9. Basic strokes necessary for making lowercase printed letters.

q, o, p, j, y, and z. For the few students who proceed to this advanced level, a check should be made for the most commonly made errors, five of which follow:

1. Failure to close letters (a, b, f, etc.)
2. Closing top loops (l like t, e like i)
3. Looping nonlooped strokes (i like e)
4. Using straight up and down strokes rather than rounded strokes (n like v, c like i)
5. Failure to bring end strokes up or down

Additionally, teachers can make errors in the teaching of handwriting. Hofmeister (1973) found that special education teachers are sometimes guilty of (1) massed practice without supervision, (2) no immediate feedback, (3) failure to provide a good model, and (4) no differentiation made between good and poor work. These are teacher-made errors and should be controlled for in teaching writing to the TMR.

The following general techniques are offered for consideration when teaching handwriting to the TMR:

1. Make sure the child possesses adequate readiness skills.
2. Check for writing posture (elbow on the desk, nonwriting hand holding the paper, fingers on the pencil correctly, feet on the floor, proper head tilt).
3. Follow a sequenced format for development of skills.
4. Avoid having the child commit unnecessary errors. Tasks presented must be within his capabilities.
5. For beginners, use large crayons or pencils.
6. Provide physical assistance initially.
7. Build in success on early tasks.
8. Use newsprint, since it is inexpensive and available in large sheets.
9. Tape the paper to the desk if necessary.
10. Provide pencil grips for cerebral palsy child if necessary.
11. Use paper with raised lines.*
12. Include all the senses (e.g., visual, auditory, tactile, kinesthetic).

There are many activities for teaching the specific skills; following are only a few:

1. Practice in holding pencil-shaped objects (e.g., chalk, crayons)
2. Tracing exercises using templates (letters, shapes, etc.)
3. Arranging pictures in a left-to-right progression
4. Dot-to-dot activities
5. Chalkboard activities (introductory movements)
6. Sandbox activities
7. String, bead, pegboard, and lacing activities

Table 8-4 contains possible handwriting programs and materials listed with the publisher. Publishers' addresses can be found in Appendix A.

Spelling

The spelling program may be initiated in conjunction with reading or writing and should only be a functional activity. For the TMR the spelling activities might include name, address, city, state, words of current interest (Christmas, circus, etc.),

---

*Right-Line Paper, Modern Educational Corporation, Tulsa, Okla.

Table 8-4. Handwriting programs and materials

Program or materials	Publisher
Alphabet Practice Cards (easy print paper, prespaced primary paper, and cursive alphabet developmental activities)	Ideal School Supply Co.
Better Handwriting for You (two printing workbooks, one transitional workbook, and six cursive workbooks)	Noble and Noble Publishers, Inc.
Color-cued control paper, dot-to-dot pattern sheets, chubbi stumps (large wax crayons), pencil grips, and alphabet templates	Developmental Learning Materials
Training Fun With Writing (six separate but related workbooks entitled *I Can Print, My Printing Book, Using My Printing, Learning to Write, Writing Words,* and, *Using Writing*)	Mafex Associates, Inc.

and words important to the student (other family members' names, pets, etc.). Several general principles for teaching spelling to the TMR follow:

1. Use only important functional words.
2. Be systematic in the approach.
3. Do not include spelling rules.
4. Integrate the words in other activities and curriculum areas.
5. Teach spelling *after*, not before, the student learns to write.

It should be realized that only a few older students will ever be able to spell even the basic words, so spelling as a skill is an insignificant aspect of the curriculum. One spelling program that deserves consideration is *Train-ing Fun With Spelling*, published by Mafex Associates. This program consists of six separate but related workbooks for spelling: *Learning Words, Using Words, Everyday Words, Words Around Us, Holiday Words,* and *My Family Words*.

ARITHMETIC

The world we live in is a "quantitative world." Society requires some limited mathematical knowledge even for semi-independent living. Even simple productive tasks such as counting in a closely supervised sheltered workshop require some quantitative skills. Some understanding of numbers is also demanded by everyday encounters with things such as the telephone, house numbers, and admission prices. The experiences students have with math will to some degree determine the efficiency with which they lead their daily lives. Math should be a part of the academic program, since research has demonstrated that most trainable children are capable of learning some mathematics (Bellamy and Cuttars, 1975; Bellamy et al., 1974; Coleman, 1971).

The arithmetic program for TMR students consists of prerequisite arithmetic skills plus the basic math skills and the application of their use in other areas. It also includes measurement, vocabulary, time, and money.

Development

The normal sequence of math skills are number readiness, basic math vocabulary, sets, whole numbers, basic math operation, fractions, and measurement (Primes, 1971). The TMR can make advances following the same developmental sequence with the exception of sets and fractions.

Assessment

Arithmetic assessment may simply consist of a check sheet using the skills listed on pp. 200 and 201. Either the child has these skills or he does not, and instruction can proceed from that point. Formal instruments are of little value with the TMR in math. For older, higher-level ability TMRs the subsections Addition, Subtraction, Money (recognizing money, counting, making change, etc.), Measurement (distance, heat, weight), and Time (clocks, holidays, seasons) of the *Key Math Diagnostic Arithmetic Test* (Connolly et al., 1971) may have some value.

Skills to be developed

The basic math skills to be developed in the TMR include readiness skills, number skills, vocabulary, monetary concepts, mea-

surement, basic math processes, and time
and calendar skills.

Readiness skills

Classification (grouping of objects by some
common characteristic, such as color, size,
shape).

One-to-one correspondence (matching numbers or objects).

Seriation or ordering (counting objects in
order).

Other readiness skills for higher level math:
flexibility (5 + 5 = 10, but 4 + 6 also =
10), reversibility (5 + 4 = 9, and 9 - 4 =
5), and conservation (given amount of
clay remains the same although in different shapes).

Number skills

Counts orally.

Counts objects.

Selects a certain number of objects from a
group.

Identifies and names numerals.

Counts by twos, fives, or tens.

Adds objects.

Subtracts objects.

Vocabulary

Addition words and sign—plus (+), more,
add, sum.

Subtraction words and sign—minus (-),
take away, subtract, less.

One more than, all, some, none, dozen, more-
less, next.

Ordinal words—first, second, third.

Time words—night, day, noon, morning,
afternoon, yesterday, today, tomorrow, minute, second, hour, half hour.

Money words—penny, nickel, dime, quarter,
half-dollar, dollar.

Seasonal words—fall, winter, spring, summer.

Measurement words—heavy, light, big, little,
inch, foot, yard.

Monetary concepts

Identifies and names basic coins.

Identifies and names basic currency.

Identifies and names the money symbols—
cent and dollar signs.

Can read price tags.

Fig. 8-10. Telling time is within the capabilities of many TMRs. (Courtesy Greenwich, Conn.,
Public Schools.)

Understands simple coin conversions.

Can count change.

Can make simple change.

Can independently purchase small-value items.

Measurement

Can discriminate by size (big-little, large-small, long-short, tall-short, thick-thin, wide-narrow, full-empty).

Can read a weight scale.

Can read a thermometer.

Can use a ruler to measure objects, distance, and height.

Can use measuring cups and spoons.

Basic math processes

Addition (one-digit numbers, no carrying and carrying; two-digit numbers, no carrying and carrying).

Subtraction (one-digit numbers, no borrowing; two-digit numbers, borrowing and no borrowing).

Time and calendar skills

Can name certain time of the day (morning, noon, afternoon, night).

Can name the days of the week.

Can name the months of the year.

States the number of days in week, months in a year, weeks in a year.

Can name the current day and date.

Can name the major holidays.

Can tell time by the hour, half hour, quarter hour, and minute.

As Sengstock and Wyatt (1976) point out, the concepts of measurement such as weight, linear and liquid measure, and temperature will soon have to be taught to the retarded using the metric system. This of course poses problems for the mentally retarded in trying to make the conversions; therefore it is recommended that instruction focus only on teaching the metric system. The following measurement concepts of the metric system should be taught:

Linear: meter, millimeter, centimeter, and kilometer

Liquid: liter, milliliter

Temperature (Celsius): freezing (0°), boiling (100°), body temperature (37°)

Weight: gram, milligram, kilogram

The following techniques are useful in teaching arithmetic to the TMR.

Fig. 8-11. Concrete counting materials such as the abacus should be used in developing number concepts in the TMR. (Courtesy Bossier Parish, La., Public Schools.)

1. Determine readiness level and abilities.
2. Do not teach addition and subtraction skills at the same time.
3. Use concrete materials as much as possible.
4. Always use real money.
5. Use other areas of curriculum to reinforce and teach math skills (e.g., physical education and music).
6. Frequently review previously learned material, since this is necessary for reinforcement.
7. Make frequent use of items such as an abacus, a cash register, number line games, flannel boards, dice, cards.

Programs and materials

Many programs and materials for teaching basic arithmetic skills exist, but only a few directly relate to the mentally retarded. Programs and materials for possible use are listed in Table 8-5. Addresses for publishers are provided in Appendix A.

SUMMARY

Functional academic skills for the TMR consist of reading, writing and spelling, and arithmetic. Each area was once thought to be beyond the capabilities of this group, but recent research indicates otherwise. The decision to include or exclude academics for TMRs should not be made on preconceived stereotyped ideas about their categorical level. Instead, the decision as to what skills students are taught must be based on teacher assessment of their readiness and capabilities.

Reading primarily consists of readiness skills, word attack skills, and reading com-

Table 8-5. Programs and materials for teaching basic arithmetic skills

Program or materials	Publisher	Program or materials	Publisher
Arithmetic Step by Step	Continental Press	Teachers handbook of games, ideas, and activities to teach arithmetic	Educational Service, Inc.
Calendars, counting frames, blocks, magnetic boards, flannel boards with counting shapes, measurement devices	R. H. Stone Products	Touch Beaded Alphabet Chart, Groovy Letters and Numerals	Ideal School Supply Co.
Concrete materials for teaching number concepts, calendars, clocks, pegboards	The Judy Co.	Training for Independence (teaching the counting of objects and identification of coins), sorting box and accessories, number hole templates, abacuses (large and small), ordinal/cardinal puzzles, Moving Up in Time, Today's Weather Box, clocks, Moving Up in Money, Shopping Lists (games)	Developmental Learning Materials
Cuisenaire Rods	Cuisenaire Co. of America, Inc.		
Design cubes, form boards, puzzles, wooden numbers	Creative Playthings		
DISTAR Arithmetic I	Science Research Associates		
Manipulative and concrete materials for teaching number concepts	A. Daigger & Co.	Training Fun With Numbers Kit (All About You, Counting Numbers, How the Numbers Grow, Working with Numbers, Numbers Around Us, Everyday Numbers), It's About Time, Time Teller, abacus/clock calendar	Mafex Associates, Inc.
Number Facts Mastery Program	Edmark Associates		
Number relationships, time concepts, games, manipulative materials	Teaching Resources Corp.		
Pacemaker Arthmetic Readiness, Time, Telling Time	Fearon Publishers, Inc.		
Parquetry Blocks Training Kit	Prentice-Hall, Inc.	Walk on Number Lines, Counting Time, Montessori Numbers Match Kit, Number Worm, Stepping Stones, indoor-outdoor thermometer	Childcraft
Ready Go Math and Records (math readiness vocabulary and concepts, math readiness addition and subtraction)	Educational Activities, Inc.		
Stern Structural Arithmetic	Houghton Mifflin Co.		

prehension. TMRs will spend most of their time in a reading program on developing readiness skills and sight vocabulary. Only occasionally will students achieve higher level word attack or comprehension skills. It should also be remembered that factors other than intelligence affect the ability to read. These include perceptual abilities, emotional and social adjustment, socioeconomic factors, physical factors, and language skills.

The major sight vocabulary word groups identified in this chapter were safety words, public signs, public building titles, months, days, family titles, public titles, basic colors, weather words, directional words, body parts, home and furniture words, clothing words, numbers, fruits and vegetables, and action words. For more advanced students three reading programs were recommended and discussed: (1) Peabody Rebus Reading Program, (2) DISTAR, and (3) Edmark Reading Program.

Writing and spelling are other academic skills that can, to a limited degree, be taught to TMRs. The prerequisite skills for writing (visual-motor integration and laterality) and their subskills were listed, and procedures, techniques, and materials for their development were offered. Also described was the sequence for teaching writing skills.

Mathematics is the last academic area discussed in this chapter. The major areas in which to develop math skills other than readiness skills are (1) number skills, (2) vocabulary, (3) monetary concepts, (4) measurement, (5) basic math processes (addition and subtraction), and (6) time and calendar skills. These appear to be within the capabilities of the TMR and also are necessary to function adequately in everyday school, community, and family life.

REFERENCES AND SUGGESTED READINGS

A catalog of instructional objectives for TMR students, Tallahassee, Fla., 1974, Florida State Department of Education.

Apffel, J. A.: Some TMRs can read, Educ. Train. Ment. Retard. 9(4):199-202, 1974.

Apffel, J. A., Kelleher, J., Lilly, M. S., and Richardson, R.: Developmental reading for moderately retarded children, Educ. Train. Ment. Retard. 10(4):229-236, 1975.

Ayllon, T., Kelly, K., Barnes, J., and Letson, J. W.: A nine-month token reinforcement program for the trainable retarded, Atlanta, 1972, Atlanta Public Schools.

Barrett, T. C., editor: The evaluation of children's reading achievement, Newark, Del., 1967, International Reading Association.

Bellamy, G. T., Greiner, C., and Buttars, K.: Arithmetic computation for trainable retarded students: continuing a sequential instructional program, Train. Sch. Bull. 70:230-240, 1974.

Bellamy, T., and Buttars, K. L.: Teaching trainable level retarded students to count money: toward personal independence through academic instruction, Educ. Train. Ment. Retard. 10(1):18-26, 1975.

Bender, M., Valletutti, R. J., and Bender, R.: Teaching the moderately and severely handicaped: curriculum, objectives, strategies, and activities, vol. III, Baltimore, 1976, University Park Press.

Bijou, S. W.: The Edmark Reading Program, 1972, Seattle, Edmark Associates.

Bijou, S. W., Birnbraver, J. S., Kidder, J., and Tague, C.: Programmed instruction as an approach to the teaching of reading, writing, and arithmetic to retarded children, Psychol. Rec. 16:505-522, 1966.

Brown, L., and Perlmutter, L.: Teaching functional reading to trainable level retarded students, Educ. Train. Ment. Retard. 6(2):74-84, 1971.

Coleman, R.: A pilot demonstration of the utility of reinforcement techniques in trainable programs, Edu. Train. Ment. Retard. 6:74-84, 1971.

Connolly, A. J., Nachtman, W., and Pritchett, E. M.: Key math diagnostic arithmetic test, Circle Pines, Minn., 1971, American Guidance Service, Inc.

Delchant, E. V.: Improving the teaching of reading, ed. 2, Englewood Cliffs, N.J., 1970, Prentice-Hall, Inc.

Dubrow, H. C.: Learning to write, Cambridge, Mass., 1968, Educators Publishing Service, Inc.

Ekwall, E. E., Diagnosis and remediation of the disabled reader, Boston, 1976, Allyn & Bacon, Inc.

Engelman, S.: Classroom techniques: teaching reading to children with low mental age, Educ. Train. Ment. Retard. 2(9):193-201, 1967.

Engelmann, S., and Bruner, E. C.: DISTAR reading: an instructional system, Chicago, 1969, Science Research Associates.

Feinberg, P.: Sight vocabulary for the TMR child and adult: rationale, development and application, Educ. Train. Ment. Retard. 10(4): 246-251, 1975.

Fredericks, H. D.: The teaching research curriculum for moderately and severely handicapped, Springfield, Ill., 1976, Charles C Thomas, Publisher.

Fuller, R.: Breaking down the IQ walls: severely retarded people can learn to read, Psychol. Today 8(5):96-100, 1974.

Gillespie, P. H., and Johnson, L. E.: Teaching reading to the mildly retarded child, Columbus, Ohio, 1974, Charles E. Merrill Publishing Co.

Hammill, D. D.: Problems in writing. In Hammill, D. D., and Bartel, N.: Teaching children with learning and behavior problems, Boston, 1975, Allyn & Bacon, Inc.

Hofmeister, A. M.: Five common instructional errors in teaching writing, Teach. Except. Child. 5(1):30-33, 1973.

Lerner, J. W.: Children with learning disabilities, ed. 2, Boston, 1976, Houghton Mifflin Co.

Lutz, J.: Expanding spelling skills: new words and ways for revised spelling activities, Dansville, N.Y., 1963, F. A. Owen Publishing Co.

Noble, J. K.: Better handwriting for you, New York, 1966, Noble & Noble Publishers, Inc.

Peterson, D. L.: Functional mathematics for the mentally retarded, Columbus, Ohio, 1973, Charles E. Merrill Publishing Co.

Pope, L.: Guidelines to teaching remedial reading to the disadvantaged, Brooklyn, N.Y., 1967, Book-Lab, Inc.

Primes: mathematics content authority list: K-6, Harrisburg, Pa., 1971, Pennsylvania State Department of Education.

Ramming, J.: Using the chalkboard to overcome handwriting difficulties, Academic Therapy 4: 49-51, 1968.

Reger, R., Schroeder, W., and Uschold, K.: Special education: Children with learning problems, New York, 1968, Oxford University Press.

Richardson, E., Oestereicher, M. H., Bialer, I., and Winsberg, B.: Teaching beginning reading skills to retarded children in community classrooms: a programmatic case study, Ment. Retard. 13(1):11-15, 1975.

Ruvin, H.: An evaluation of academics for the tainable mentally retarded, paper presented at the 40th Annual International Convention of the Council for Exceptional Children, Chicago, 1970.

Sengstock, W. L., and Wyatt, K. E.: Meters, liters, and grams: the metric system and its implications for curriculum for exceptional children, Teach. Except. Child. 8(2):59-65, 1976.

Sharp, R.: Teaching writing to trainable children: the Edwards Method, The Pointer 18(1):60-61, 1973.

Skinner, B. F., and Krakower, S.: Handwriting with writing and see, Chicago, 1968, Lyons & Carnahan.

Smith, R. M.: Clinical teaching: methods of instruction for the retarded, ed. 2, New York, 1974, McGraw-Hill Book Co.

Spalding, R. B., and Spalding, W. T.: The writing road to reading, New York, 1962, William Morrow & Co., Inc.

Stasio, J. T.: Cursive and manuscript writing, The Pointer 21(1):54-55, 1976.

Warren, S. A.: Academic achievement of trainable pupils with five or more years of schooling, Train. Sch. Bull. 60:75-88, 1963.

Woodcock, R., Clark, C. L., and Davies, C. O.: Peabody Rebus Reading Program, Circle Pines, Minn., 1969, American Guidance Service.

CHAPTER 9

DEVELOPING RECREATION AND LEISURE TIME SKILLS

Recreation and leisure time activities played an insignificant role in early education and habilitation programs for the mentally retarded. The few recreational provisions prior to the 1940s existed primarily as a means of preserving order, maintaining institutional morale, and preventing boredom (Witt, 1971). Following World War II, recreation became recognized as beneficial and practical for the mentally retarded, but development was slow until the late 1960s. Some of the major problems that have hindered expansion of recreation services are (1) few qualified recreation leaders trained in recreation and aware of the unique problems of the retarded, (2) not enough practical guidelines for program planning and implementation, (3) lack of public awareness, (4) inadequate transportation resources, and (5) insufficient financial support for modifying existing facilities and establishing new recreational areas, facilities, and programs (National Association for Retarded Citizens, 1973).

The magnitude of these problems has diminished as greater emphasis has been placed on the recreation and leisure time area of curriculum. Numerous organizations and groups (e.g., AAMD, CEC, AAHPER, NARC, American Camping Association, Boy Scouts of America, National Recreation and Parks Association) have expanded their operations to include recreational services for the retarded. Newer groups were formed (e.g., National Therapeutic Recreation Society), and increased federal funding was made available (Sengstock and Stein, 1967).

Equally important has been a demonstrated need for recreation and leisure time skills as a part of the curriculum. Research results indicate TMRs spend the majority of their leisure time watching television or listening to the radio, going to the movies, visiting friends and family, or doing nothing (Katz and Yekutiel, 1974). This also appears true whether the retardate is institutionalized, living at home, or employed. The statistics in Table 9-1 indicate the need for increased emphasis on teaching the retarded functional recreational and leisure time skills. Note that hobbies, a desired leisure time skill, rank near the bottom.

THERAPEUTIC RECREATION

In response to the growing importance of leisure time, a new professional specialty has emerged: therapeutic recreation ser-

Table 9-1. Leisure time activities
of the retarded*

Type of activity	Rank
Stays home (watches television, reads, listen to radio)	1
Goes to movies or theater	2
Visits friends and family	3
Stays home and does nothing	4
Attends social clubs of various types	5
Attends sport meetings	6
Pursues hobbies	7
Does volunteer work	8

*From Katz, S., and Yekutiel, E.: Leisure time problems of
mentally retarded graduates of training programs, Ment.
Retard. **12**(3):55, 1974.

vice (Nesbitt, 1970). The professional who
provides this service is called a therapeutic
recreation specialist. By definition, therapeutic recreation service is a professional
service that provides recreational and related activities especially designed to meet
the needs of individuals who possess some
significant degree of illness or disability
(Kraus, 1973). The foundation of therapeutic recreation service is the view that
the handicapped are also entitled to personal fulfillment in their leisure.

The goals of therapeutic recreation, as
it relates to the mentally retarded, consist
of the following (Kraus, 1973):

- Improvement in physical growth and development, motor skills, and physical fitness
- Prevention of social isolation
- Development of skills for the creative and
  constructive use of leisure time
- Achievement of community independence
- Improvement in general knowledge and environmental contacts
- Improvement in the morale and quality of
  family living by making the retardate less of
  a family burden

The need for more therapeutic recreation specialists is great and parallels the
views of professionals and families of the
retarded who desire for the TMR (1) a
greater use of community facilities and services, (2) an adherence to normalization
principles, and (3) independence and enjoyment of adult life beyond one vocational involvement. Opportunities, however,

for professional preparation in the field of
therapeutic recreation are increasing, with
over seventy-five universities offering degrees (Luckey and Shapiro, 1974).

There is also a need for therapeutic recreation services. Guidelines for developing
these public services for the retarded or
handicapped follow.*

1. Public understanding and support
   a. The public should accept the philosoph-
      ical view that every handicapped person
      is entitled to leisure, to opportunities for
      cultural and recreational participation, and
      to services which make participation pos-
      sible.
   b. The public should encourage the pro-
      vision of compensatory cultural, recrea-
      tional, and leisure service and activities
      as a means of correcting an imbalance in
      opportunities that exist for the handi-
      capped, such as the homebound, who
      need such services.
   c. The public should accept the fact that
      funds should be provided for cultural,
      recreational, and leisure services for handi-
      capped.
2. Goals of agencies
   a. The goals of agencies should include a
      sincere desire to achieve equality of op-
      portunity for handicapped persons to
      participate in recreational, cultural, and
      leisure activities.
   b. Agencies should actively seek to increase,
      expand, and improve programs for the
      handicapped. This should include the
      development and use of program and
      personnel standards.
   c. Agencies should organize and provide
      services and programs with the aim of
      enhancing the voluntary assimilation of
      activity of handicapped with nonhandi-
      capped.
   d. Within the existing framework of recrea-
      tion philosophy and program, agencies
      should strive to meet educational, voca-
      tional, social, and health needs of the
      handicapped.
   e. Agencies should seek the direct involve-
      ment of handicapped in policy-making,
      planning, development, implementation,

*From Nesbitt, J. A.: The therapeutic recreation
specialist as a change agent: guidelines for policy
and curriculum development. In Neal, L. L.,
editor, Recreation's role in the rehabilitation of
the mentally retarded, Eugene, Ore., 1970, University of Oregon, pp. 41-42.

and evaluation of programs that are provided.

f. Recreation personnel at all levels should strive to determine, understand, and serve the personal and individual needs of handicapped persons.

g. Agencies should conduct programs of public education designed to enhance public awareness and understanding of the handicapped and acceptance of handicapped in cultural, recreational, and leisure activities.

3. Special features of programs for handicapped

a. Special means should be employed in promoting and informing handicapped about leisure, cultural, and recreational opportunities, such as directories and telephone referral.

b. Associations and agencies at the national, state, and local levels should find means to surmount both real and imagined problems related to possible accidents and liability in providing service to handicapped persons.

c. Agencies should have written statements in relation to the handicapped which set forth their program goals, the role and function of units within their organization, relationships with other agencies, etc.

d. Leisure education and recreation counseling should be provided for handicapped clients with the aims of enhancing individual satisfaction in leisure through the acquisition of appropriate knowledge, skills, attitudes, and habits and, enhancing the ability of the handicapped to independently direct their own leisure.

e. Measures should be taken to provide for maximum utilization of existing and planned areas and facilities by the elimination of architectural barriers.

f. Measures should be taken to provide for maximum adaptation of existing equipment for use by handicapped.

g. Agencies should place major emphasis on providing a wide range of transportation services for handicapped.

4. Policy-making and administration

a. Personnel at all levels, from policy-making to volunteer, should be brought into direct contact with handicapped and made aware of the particular needs and problems of the handicapped.

b. Agencies should use existing knowledge and insight into the organization and provision of recreation services for handicapped.

c. Agencies should apply formal procedures and methods of identifying handicapped

clients and determining recreation and leisure needs.

d. Agencies should take action based on their existing awareness of the needs of the handicapped.

e. Agencies should prepare long-range plans that relate to the anticipated needs and problems of the handicapped.

f. Agencies should seek opportunities for cooperation, coordination, and liaison with and among other public and private agencies concerned with meeting the needs of the handicapped.

g. Agencies should establish or participate in formal representative councils and/or committees organized to coordinate efforts to meet the cultural, recreational, and leisure needs of handicapped.

5. Financing

a. Agencies should take appropriate steps to assure that adequate funds are provided for recreation services for handicapped.

b. New methods of financing recreation programs for handicapped should be found. Possible sources include the federal and state governments, foundations, public donations.

6. Personnel practices

a. Increased numbers of community-based recreation personnel should be provided to work with handicapped.

b. Agencies should recruit increased numbers of volunteers, including volunteers who are handicapped, to enhance the overall recreation for handicapped program capacity.

7. Formal education and training

a. Orientation and in-service training should be provided for all personnel associated with recreational, cultural, and leisure services, from policy-makers through aides, to increase awareness of the leisure, cultural, and recreational needs and potential of the handicapped.

b. Therapeutic recreation service training should be provided for all personnel working directly with the handicapped, either full-time or part-time.

c. Cooperative relationships should be developed among therapeutic recreation service sites, community recreation programs, and colleges and universities offering recreation education programs.

8. Research

a. Research should be conducted with the aim of evaluating the level and status of delivery of services in relation to needs, and evaluating methods and procedures being used.

b. Applied and demonstration research should

be undertaken with a view to effecting immediate improvement and expansion of recreation and leisure services for handicapped.

A sequentially based activity program is necessary for the retardate to receive maximum benefit. A suggested curriculum hierarchy for developing leisure time and play skills for the TMR follows (Wehman, 1975):

Level 1: Action on play materials—play behavior directed on or with different types of commercial toys and play material.

Level 2: Passive leisure—progressively more involved areas of passive recreation that are largely spectator in nature and require little of the individual (e.g., radio, television, playing records, looking at books, or attending sporting or entertainment events).

Level 3: Game activity—participation in popular low-organization individual and team games.

Level 4: Hobby activity—development of hobbies (e.g., art, caring for pets, music, scrapbooks, collections).

Level 5: Active socialization—activities (e.g., parties, scouting, clubs) that encourage development of new friends and acquaintances.

In the actual provision of specific activities for a recreation and leisure time curriculum for the retarded, the following guidelines are suggested:

1. When possible and feasible, allow some self-choice in the selection of activities rather than compelling participation.

2. Provide activities in which the child can be active away from school or after completing an educational program.

3. Place emphasis on activities that contribute to confidence, competence, and accomplishment.

4. When possible, involve those who are to be served in planning programs.

5. Integrate the TMR with other children when possible (Kraus, 1973).

RECREATION ACTIVITIES

Recreation and leisure time skills for the retarded are, in effect, one and the same, since what is recreational can also fill leisure time and vice versa. However, popular conceptualization of this curriculum area distinguishes between recreational activities and leisure time activities. This separation will be used in the presentation of specific curriculum activities for the TMR.

The list of possible recreational activities is endless; therefore only those major activities having relevance to TMRs will be presented. The decision to include an activity, of course, should depend on the group's ability to benefit from and enjoy the activity. The major activities include bicycling, bowling, camping, hiking, scouting, and swimming.

Bicycling

A functional and enjoyable national pastime of many children and adults is bicycling. This is a difficult skill for some TMRs to acquire, but it is within the capabilities of many older students. One technique to develop bicycling ability is to weld a bicycle to a barrel (filled with sand or concrete) in such a way that it moves forward and around the barrel. This lead-up activity can be performed on any size bicycle, boys' or girls', and gives the student a feel for riding. After this activity comes the attachment of training wheels to a regular bicycle. Training wheels keep the bike from tipping over but allow full participation in bicycling. When the student develops the necessary skills of pedaling, steering, balance, etc., the training wheels can be adjusted (raised) and eventually removed. If bicycling is beyond a child's capabilities, an alternative might be a large tricycle, the type often used by adults. Bicycling is a useful activity and encourages safety, family and social participation, care of a possession, exercise, and ecological concern.

Bowling

Another recreational activity that can be enjoyed by the student and his family is bowling. Prerequisite skills (depending on ability and age) necessary for the mentally retarded include (1) basic movement, (2) perceptual skills, and (3) physical skills. After these skills are minimally developed, practice and experience in low-organization activities should be provided. A number of simulated commercial bowling games are available and serve this purpose. If funds are limited, use any type of playground ball for a bowling ball and use milk cartons or coffee cans for pins.

At this "bowling" level the teacher has control over the size and weight of the ball, the number of pins to knock down, and the distance of each person from the pins. This is ideal, since these modifications allow *all* to bowl. Emphasis should also focus on the delivery of the ball. A one-step delivery should be taught first, leading up to the four-step delivery. The procedure for a one-step delivery includes (1) proper stance, (2) pendulum swing, and (3) underarm push-away motion. Emphasize the smoothness with which the ball should meet the ground.

The last step consists of actual bowling at a commercial lane. Adaptations for some students, such as rolling the ball with both hands or from a stationary position (for physically small children), or other rule changes may be necessary. Keeping score has been successfully taught to 14- to 21-year-old TMR students using a step-by-step approach (Landry and Garcia, 1972). Prerequisite skills found necessary were the ability to count to 100 and counting by tens, a basic understanding and possession of the skills of addition and subtraction, and the ability to read and write *strike, bowl, spare, pin,* and *frame.*

Bowling is a Special Olympics sport, and many communities sponsor special bowling leagues. Many bowling alley managers may also provide reduced rates for your class and/or an instructor to assist in this phase of your recreational program. Bowling is fun, provides many benefits, and should be included in a recreation and leisure time curriculum for TMRs.

Camping

The movement in recent years for camping as an activity for the mentally retarded and other handicapped populations has been remarkable. This movement follows the enthusiasm for camping felt by the general population. Camping of any type by anyone provides tremendous enjoyment, benefits, and great educational potential because it departs from traditional learning environments (i.e., schools or classrooms).

Camping can develop the physical, social, emotional, esthetic (arts, crafts, music), and cognitive selves in addition to providing related outdoor educational skills and knowledge. Shea (1977) sums it up best in the following statement:

> Nature's classroom provides opportunities to add true meaning and understanding to the thinking, reading, and computing skills presented in the classroom. Nature provides opportunities to apply the principles of science, math, physics, ecology, and conservation to the real world.

One camping program, Camp Confidence (a northern Minnesota therapeutic camp), even provides year-round camping (instead of summer only) and recreational experiences for mentally retarded citizens of Minnesota (Klappholz, 1976). This comprehensive camping program includes the following facilities:

1. Two year-round cabins with kitchen, toilet, and fireplace
2. A ski chalet with a nature crafts center, outdoor education library, winter sports equipment, and toilets
3. The foster grandparent cabin with a wood stove
4. A vocational training shop and classroom
5. A main waterfront with a sand beach, dock, and diving raft
6. A boat marina
7. A centrally heated bathhouse with toilets and showers
8. A 5-acre nature playground with tree houses, rope swings, ladders, and bridges
9. A 4-acre wildlife sanctuary with trained, tame, and wild animals
10. An outdoor skating rink with warming house
11. A ski hill with electrical rope tow

Fig. 9-1. Day camping offers the TMR new learning experiences as well as recreational opportunities. (From Shea, T. M.: Camping for special children, St. Louis, 1977, The C. V. Mosby Co.)

12. A ten-site tenting area with tents, fireplaces, and tables
13. Day camping areas with fireplaces and tables
14. Screened picnic shelters with fireplaces
15. Miles of nature trails and cross-country ski trails
16. Fifteen hundred feet of wheelchair sidewalks around the main camping area
17. Two fish houses with four holes, stove, and fishing tackle
18. Gardens
19. An archery range
20. A wilderness camping area
21. A pioneer camp with two log cabins
22. A maintenance building

The following major activities and sports are also found in the Camp Confidence program:

Camp living skills
  Bed making
  Camp safety
  Care of appliances
  Cooking (indoors)
  Food planning
  Housekeeping
  Personal hygiene
  Physical fitness
  Simple first aid
Nature crafts
  Bark crafts

Fig. 9-2. Overnight camping can aid the TMR in developing independent living skills. (From Shea, T. M.: Camping for special children, St. Louis, 1977, The C. V. Mosby Co.)

Bird feeder construction
Birdhouse construction
Clay molding
Indian lore
Insect collections
Kite construction
Leaf collections
Leather work
Natural dye work
Picture crafts
Plaster casts
Sand casting
Sculpture
Shells and nuts
Snowshoe construction
Totem pole construction
Weaving
Nature study
  Animal hibernation
  Animal tracking
  Conservation activities
  Native animal study
  Native fish study
  Native ivy identification
  Native plant study
  Native tree study
  Nature hike
  Nature photography

Nature sounds
Scavenger hunt
Sensory experiences
Simple astronomy
Weather station activities
Wildlife sanctuary
Outdoor living skills
  Axmanship
  Compass reading
  Dressing game and fish
  Estimating distances
  Game laws
  Knot tying
  Outdoor cooking
  Proper dress for the season
  Shelter building
  Tent camping
  Trapping and snaring
Seasonal sports
  Archery
  Boating
  Canoeing instruction
  Canoeing
  Cross-country skiing
  Downhill skiing
  Fishing
  Hayrides
  Ice safety

Ice skating
Life jacket safety training
Pontoon riding
Roller skating
Rowing instruction
Snowmobiling
Sleigh riding
Swimming
Swimming instruction
Tobogganing
Tubing

Although most camps are not as elaborate as this one, it does indicate what is possible if enough businesspeople, citizens, professionals, and parents become interested and involved.*

Types of camps for the retarded include the day camp, the residential camp, and the wilderness camp. The day camp holds the most advantages for the majority of TMRs; the residential camp has value for many; and a modified wilderness camp is the least feasible of the three types (Shea, 1977). For an in-depth discussion of the specifics of camping, management procedures, and correlated activities, the reader is encouraged to consult the following books.

Camping for Special Children by T. M. Shea.

This excellent text contains a section on camping with the mentally retarded and includes a comprehensive review of the day camp, the evening camp, the preschool day camp, the residential camp, and the wilderness camp. Each type of camp is discussed by purpose and objectives, administration, physical factors, necessary equipment and materials, the training of needed personnel, program descriptions, and advantages and limitations of each.

Day Camping for Developmentally Disabled and Exceptional Children: Guidelines for Establishing Day Camp Program by C. Arslaner, C. R. Curry, S. A. Keck, and G. Salzman.

Published in 1970 as *Day Camping for the Trainable and Severely Mentally Retarded*, this book contains useful instructions on administration of a day camp, physical, arts and crafts, and music activities, as well as a chapter on solving camp behavior problems. All activities are described in detail and relate to the camping experience.

*For detailed background on operation and financing, refer to "Year-Round Camping for the Mentally Retarded" in *The Physical Activities Report,* no. 413, 1976.

Student Council for Exceptional Children Summer Camps With the Handicapped by L. W. Jones, R. C. Jones, and P. Putman.

This last resource is a booklet showing how college CEC students at the University of Tennessee provided low-cost residential camping experiences for the mentally retarded. Sections of the publication include staffing, physical environment, financing, camp curriculum, equipment and supplies, transportation, and insurance considerations.

Additional resources include the following organizations:

American Camping Association
Bradford Woods
Martinsville, Ind. 46151
National Camping Association
353 West 56th St.
New York, N.Y. 10019
National Catholic Camping Association
1785 Massachusetts Ave., N.W.
Washington, D.C. 20036
National Park Service
U.S. Department of the Interior
Washington, D.C. 20402
National Recreation and Park Association
1601 N. Kent St.
Arlington, Va. 22209

Hiking

A hike is a trip on foot with a definite goal in mind. City hikes can include a walk to the corner store, a museum, a playground, a movie, a restaurant, or a friend's home. Country hikes can be a walk around a pond or lake or through a forest trail, a foothills climb, or a nature hike.

On any hike, especially a country hike, time should be taken to learn more about nature and the environment. The outdoors lends itself to developing the senses, our mechanisms for learning. Possible ways to exercise the senses on nature hikes are listed:

Vision: Do you see any animals? Any trees? Are there any clouds? What color are they? Do you see any plants?
Listening: Do you hear any sounds? What is making the sound? Is it a bird? What kind of bird? An airplane? Water?
Touching: What does the bark of a tree feel like? Different leaves? Dirt? Sand? Rocks? Is the water cold?
Smelling: Do you smell anything? What is it? Is it smoke? How do flowers smell? Pine trees?

Fig. 9-3. Hiking can be an enjoyable activity for the TMR. (From Shea, T. M.: Camping for special children, St. Louis, 1977, The C. V. Mosby Co.)

Other nature walk activities include (1) collecting insects, leaves, pine cones, etc. to study and discuss in class, (2) walking quietly and trying to see animals, (3) picking up trash, etc. left by others, (4) trying to name the different trees, (5) giving each student a picture of something to find, (6) taking photographs of interesting places during the nature hike, and (7) taking a picnic.

Scouting

The Boy Scouts of America (Cub Scouts, Boy Scouts, and Explorer Scouts) emphasize character development and citizenship, as well as physical and mental development through training and experience. These aims also apply to the retarded but on a different level of understanding. The scouting program, in a belief that scouting should be made available to *all* boys and girls, has recently designed a special advancement and recognition program for mentally retarded scouts (Boy Scouts of America, 1975). Scoutmasters of regular troops who wish to include the TMR or scoutmasters of special troops (TMRs only) should consult the following special program components.*

Scouting for the Mentally Retarded (no. 3058).
This is a 32-page handbook describing the total program from progress award requirements (e.g., tenderfoot award) to specific scout badge requirements. The TMR can earn merit badges in knot typing, hiking, twelve ideas, swimming, flag, symbols, camping, citizenship, first aid, and cooking.

My Scout Badge Record Book (no. 3051)
This is the student's record book for progress award requirements, scouting badge requirements, and skill awards. Skill awards are similar to merit badges and are given for camping, citizenship, communications, community living, conservation, cooking, environment, family living, first aid, hiking, physical fitness, and swimming. Components for the requirements are listed, and the scoutmaster writes in the date completed and his signature.

---

*These materials and additional information are available by writing Boy Scouts of America, North Brunswick, N.J. 08902.

Fig. 9-4. Scouting affords the TMR active social and community participation opportunities. (Courtesy Boy Scouts of America, North Brunswick, N.J.)

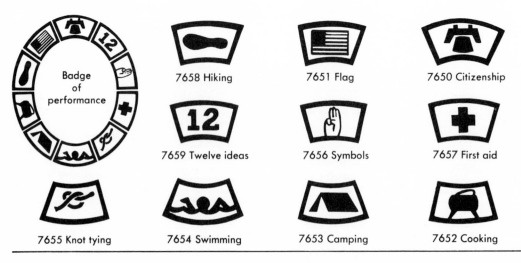

Badge of performance

7658 Hiking

7651 Flag

7650 Citizenship

7659 Twelve ideas

7656 Symbols

7657 First aid

7655 Knot tying

7654 Swimming

7653 Camping

7652 Cooking

Fig. 9-5. Emblem scout badges available in the special scouting program.

Embroidered Emblem Scout Badges

This is a series of ten special emblems that are sewn around the badge of performance (e.g., tenderfoot, second class) and worn on the left shirt pocket of the scout uniform. (See Fig. 9-5.)

Swimming

Swimming and aquatic activities provide the retarded with opportunities to improve motor development, physical fitness, body control, self-concept, and social skills, in addition to their therapeutic and recreational values. Swimming can assist the fearful child because he gains confidence at being able to exhibit control over water; it can also benefit the aggressive child, who can hit the water to his heart's content, and it can reduce tension in the hyperactive or nervous child because of the fatigue factor (Moran and Kalakian, 1974).

It is of critical importance to teach the child to feel secure in and around water before beginning serious attempts to teach him to swim. Introductory activities for the water should be made with confidence but with the firm understanding that the rules of the water must be obeyed. Several sequential activities that might help introduce the TMR child to the water follow (Joseph P. Kennedy, Jr. Foundation, 1974):

1. Take a shower together with bathing suits on.
2. Walk around the edge of the pool; point out shallow and deep ends.
3. Sit together on pool edge in the shallow end, splashing water with the feet.
4. Walk around together in the shallow end.
5. Wet a towel and put it on the child's face.
6. Splash water with the hands.
7. Put your face in the water and blow bubbles "like a motorboat."
8. Hold your breath out of the water and then in the water, face under only.
9. Drop a large object to the bottom of the shallow end of the pool and have a student retrieve it by reaching under water.

After the basic introductory activities, the child can work on higher-skill activities such as bobbing up and down in waist-deep water (completely submerged), jellyfish and turtle floats, and other floating activities, such as the prone float, prone glide, and prone kick glide. The next skills to develop include the back float, back glide, back kick glide, and changing from front to back and from back to front. The strokes can then be introduced (e.g., arm stroke front, finning, arm stroke back). After these strokes are mastered, more advanced students can progress to jumping and diving activities (level-off jumping, jump and tread water, sitting dive from side of pool, kneeling dive from side of pool, standing dive from side of pool) and water stunts (e.g., tuck, handstand, front and back somersaults). The accompanying evaluation checklist can be used for a swimming instructional program, either as an initial assessment or as a measure for charting progress.

The American National Red Cross (1974) recommends five basic survival, or safety swimming, skills for each student. These are (1) breath control, (2) prone float and recovery, (3) back float and recovery, (4) turning over, and (5) changing direction. These skills should be included in a swimming program for the retarded.

The instructor who teaches swimming to the TMR should keep the following points in mind:

1. Use tact and persuasion with some children, if necessary, for new experiences in swimming.
2. Work on a ratio of one instructor or volunteer for each student.
3. Pay particular attention to students who have a history of seizures.
4. Keep explanations and demonstrations brief.
5. For children susceptible to respiratory infections (e.g., Down's syndrome), make sure they dry thoroughly, especially the hair.
6. Give all students opportunities to experience some success during every lesson.

TMR SWIMMING EVALUATION CHECKLIST

Name _____   Class _____

Skills	Number of times, distance, or amount of time	Date	Comments
Taking shower			
Entering pool			
Walking in shallow end of pool			
Putting face in water			
Blowing bubbles			
Bobbing			
Jellyfish float			
Turtle float			
Prone float			
Prone glide			
Prone kick glide			
Back float			
Back glide			
Back kick glide			
Front-to-back maneuver			
Back-to-front maneuver			
Arm stroke front			
Finning			
Arm stroke back			
Level-off jumping			
Jumping in and treading water			
Sitting dive from side of pool			
Kneeling dive from side of pool			
Standing dive from side of pool			

Fig. 9-6. Physical assistance is often necessary in teaching some swimming skills to the TMR. (Courtesy Bossier Parish, La., Public Schools.)

7. You may allow flotation devices (e.g., water wings) to be used, but they are recommended only after the student has made physical and mental adjustments to the water.

8. Repetition can be boring, so vary the skills practice with some fun games.

9. Do not force a student to try a new skill that he fears.

10. Be responsible: be aware of safety factors.

This last point of safety in swimming instruction is extremely important. The usual pool hazards exist, of course, but when conducting a swimming program with students who might have visual, motor, or balance problems, safety becomes an intensified concern. Some of the *special* safety considerations follow:

1. Assist students with balance difficulties in walking on wet decks.

2. Watch carefully those TMR children with cerebral palsy.

3. Watch for signs of fatigue in TMR children subject to seizures.

4. Teach standard pool safety rules.

5. Have on file a physician's report of each child's health status and an emergency card. (See Appendix C for forms.)

LEISURE TIME ACTIVITIES

The major leisure time activities or skills to be discussed in this section include arts and crafts, music (rhythm, singing, dancing), and hobbies. As with recreational activities, the decision to include a leisure time activity should depend on the group's ability to benefit from and enjoy the pastime.

Arts and crafts

The arts and crafts component of curriculum for the TMR has historically consumed an extraordinarily large part of the instructional day. It may have been thought that art was an area where achievement was possible or that educators lacked an understanding of what constituted curriculums; therefore art was overemphasized. Whatever past reasons, it is now clear that

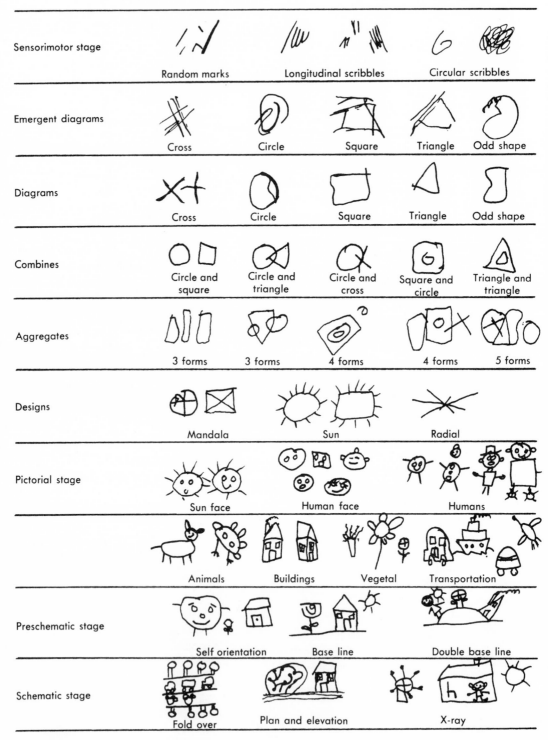

Fig. 9-7. Stages of art development. (From Marr, J., and Lubin, M.: Art for the mentally retarded as taught through a developmental sequence, unpublished paper, University of Kentucky, Lexington, Ky., 1976.)

Table 9-2. Basic art skill development*

Specific skills	Activity	Technique	Materials
1. To be able to draw with a crayon	a. Scribble with crayon freely b. Guide crayons purposefully in any direction, as over a cardboard shape c. Color within the outline of a picture d. Produce a representational drawing	Demonstrate and/or take child's hand with the crayon in it and help to hold and guide it around the page	Crayons Paper Cardboard shapes
2. To be able to trace around a shape with a pencil	a. Trace geometric shapes b. Trace around seasonal type stencils c. Trace around hand to make turkey	Help child to lean pencil against the model as he is moving the pencil	Pencil Paper Geometric shapes Seasonal shapes
3. To be able to paste	Paste (precut) construction paper shapes on a larger sheet	Assist child in applying a small amount of paste to the underside of the cutout, then turn it over and press it down on the page	Paste Cut out construction paper shapes 9 × 12-inch construction paper sheet
4. To be able to tear construction paper and then paste it	Tear construction paper into small strips or pieces, then paste them on a larger sheet	Assist child to tear paper and apply paste to one side of the paper and then turn it over and press it down on the larger sheet	Construction paper Paste 9 × 12-inch construction paper sheet
5. To be able to punch around shapes	Punch holes around animal, geometric, or seasonal shapes with a corn holder on a rug sample until the shape can be punched out with the fingers	Demonstrate and/or take child's hand with corn holder and assist him in punching holes around the shape; then punch it out; holes must be very close	Small rug sample Corn holder Various shapes drawn on construction paper
6. To be able to use a pair of scissors	a. Cut on lines on narrow strips of paper b. Cut out geometric or seasonal shapes c. Cut pop-up valentine card and fold along lines d. Cut butterfly wings from tissue paper; use two different colors of tissue paper; cut one about 1 inch smaller than the other	Assist child to hold scissors and cut along lines or around shapes Assist child to pinch wings in the middle and twist pipe cleaner for body and antennae	Scissors Narrow strips of lined paper Geometric or seasonal shapes Construction paper in butterfly shape
7. To be able to cut and then paste	Cut any desired shape from newspaper and paste it on black construction paper background	Assist child to cut newspaper and apply paste to one side; turn it over and press it down on the black construction paper	Newspaper Black construction paper Scissors Paste
8. To be able to cut, paste, and color	Make paper cup flower from muffin cups	Assist child to cut slits down into the center of a small, colored, paper muffin cup, leaving the bottom uncut, glue the bottom of cup to a large sheet of construction paper; color the center; draw leaves and stem	Scissors Paper cup Glue Crayons 9 × 12-inch construction paper

*From Craig, C.: Art for the TMR student, unpublished paper, University of New Orleans, New Orleans, La., 1976.

arts and crafts should be included as a subject area but not to the point of domination.

Alkema (1971) and Osdol (1972) have indicated some of the values of art for the TMR:

1. Development of fine motor skills (co-ordination and muscular control) through manipulation activities
2. Development of independence and self-expression by creative experiences
3. Development of general mental ability and readiness skills (e.g., color, shape, size, texture, following directions)
4. Development of social skills (e.g., sharing, working in groups)
5. Relief of nervous tension and promotion of emotional adjustment
6. Development of feelings of personal satisfaction, achievement, and success
7. Development of some objects that may be of use and have beauty

Research studies (Freasier, 1971; Gaitskell and Gaitskell, 1953; Winkelstein et al., 1973) and expert opinion (Eisner, 1972; Kramer, 1971; Lowenfeld and Brittain, 1970; Semmel, 1961; Thomkinson, 1973) surprisingly and generally conclude the following about art and the mentally retarded.

1. The retarded often do not profit from art activities. The primary reason offered was that teachers present too many new skills and materials too quickly. Attention should first be given to the acquisition of basic art skills.

2. Art creativity is often suppressed when a heavy reliance is made on predrawn figures and coloring book pictures. These figures and objects are often beyond the child's ability to reproduce, so that when the child does attempt to draw he becomes frustrated. He will often say, "My picture doesn't look right" or "My picture is no good."

3. The art curriculum often consists of too many short-term nonmeaningful activities, the results of which are often attractive but rarely involve art or education.

The child's need for continuity of purpose and direction in art is largely ignored.

4. Too often the art project is more "teacher made" than "student made."

5. The product rather than the experience has often been found to be the principle art education goal.

6. Many art projects taught are beyond the student's capabilities.

The art teacher of TMRs should keep in mind the group's or individual's developmental art level. The normal developmental art sequence with corresponding chronological age ranges is listed in Table 9-1. Illustrations of the first nine stages (the last two are rarely achieved by TMRs) are presented in Fig. 9-7.

Art for the TMR can be aimed at creative as well as at product goals (specific art projects). Whereas few or no art skills are needed to be creative, many basic art skills are necessary for specific projects. These basic skills, a sample activity or two, techniques for teaching, and necessary materials are listed in Table 9-2. Once a basic proficiency is developed, the students can progress to higher level of arts and crafts projects. The list of possible projects or activities might include finger painting, crayon-resist drawings, self-portraits, various types of printing (block, potato), papier mâché, dyed bean or rice pictures, making puppets and masks, collages, woodworking, weaving, clay molding, and watercolor painting. Many of these art projects and others can be made using scrap and inexpensive materials. A list of arts and crafts materials follows:

Acorns
Aluminum foil
Aluminum plates
Baking cups
Baking pans (foil)
Batting
Beads
Blocks of wood
Bottle caps
Braid
Burlap
Buttons
Cardboard rolls (toilet paper and paper towels)

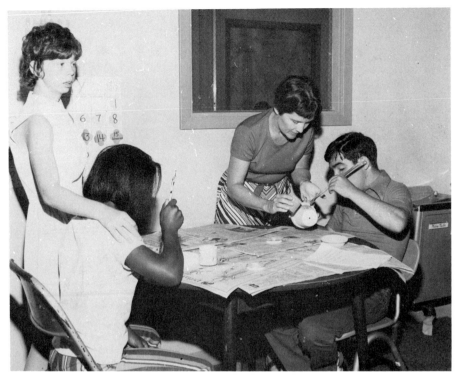

Fig. 9-8. Arts and crafts activities provide numerous benefits for the TMR of any age. (Courtesy Bossier Parish, La., Public Schools.)

Carpet samples
Cartons (all sizes)
Catalogues
Cereal boxes
Cheese boxes
Cigar boxes
Clay
Clothespins
Cloth pieces
Coat hooks
Coffee cans
Colored construction paper
Cork stoppers
Corrugated cardboard (all sizes)
Crayons
Crepe paper
Dried beans
Dried peas
Egg boxes
Eggshells
Feathers
Felt pieces
Floor tile
Glass jars
Glitter
Ice cream boxes
Lace

Light bulbs
Macaroni (all shapes)
Masking tape
Magazines
Marbles
Milk containers
Newspapers
Oatmeal boxes
Paint and sprays
Paper bags
Paper cups
Paper plates
Pinecones
Pipe cleaners
Plastic bottles
Ice cream sticks
Potato chip cans
Ribbon
Rice
Rope
Salt boxes
Sandpaper
Sawdust
Seashells
Shoe boxes
Shoelaces
Sponges

Spools (all sizes)
Stamps
Straws
String
Tin cans
Tongue depressors
Toothpicks
Twine
Varnish (clear)
Wallpaper samples
Wire coat hangers
Yarn

Two valuable teacher resources for the art teacher are *Art Projects for the Mentally Retarded Child* (Sussman, 1976) and *Art for the Exceptional* (Alkema, 1971). Both contain numerous specific activities, special occasion activities (e.g., for Thanksgiving, Halloween, Christmas), and illustrations.

Musical activities

Active involvement in music and related activities provides a number of benefits for the TMR, among them communication (listening and speaking), physical development (basic movements, perceptual-motor, fine motor), social development (group participation and peer interaction), cognitive development (following directions, attention span, academics), and emotional development (release of tension and self-satisfaction). Musical activities can also serve as major recreational or leisure time skills and include rhythms, singing, and dancing.

Rhythms. Rhythms are basic, natural flowing, balanced movements of part or all of the child's body and can be performed freely, with structure, or creatively. In rhythms and in all musically related activities, teachers and aides should participate, since students tend to follow or imitate the adult's attitude and movement. Popular tunes or favorite children's music can be used in the rhythms area. Areas of instruction and possible activities are listed:

A. Free movement
  1. Develop simple rhythm in time to the music
    a. Sway the body
    b. Shake the body
    c. Move the hands in a circle
    d. Move the hands up and down
    e. Jump up, forward, sideways, or backward
B. Rhythm coordination
  1. Clap hands to music
  2. Stamp feet to the music
C. Basic locomotor rhythms
  1. Even rhythm motions
    a. Walk to music
    b. Run to music
    c. Jump to music
    d. Hop to music
    e. Leap to music
    f. March to music
  2. Uneven rhythm motions
    a. Skip to music
    b. Slid to music
    c. Gallop to music
D. Nonlocomotor rhythms
  1. Head movements to music
  2. Torso movements to music
  3. Arm movements to music
  4. Leg movements to music
E. Imitative or creative movements
  1. Animal imitations
    a. Dog chasing a ball
    b. Cat stretching
  2. Plant imitations
    a. Plant growing
  3. Tree imitations
    a. Tall tree
    b. Wind blowing a tree
  4. Insect imitations
    a. Crawling insects (ants, bugs, etc.)
    b. Fly
    c. Butterfly
    d. Grasshopper
  5. Everyday objects
    a. Bus
    b. Car
    c. Train
    d. Boat
    e. Truck
F. Playing rhythm instruments
  1. Rhythm sticks
  2. Bells
  3. Drum
  4. Sand blocks
  5. Kazoo
  6. Harmonica
  7. Tambourine
  8. Maracas
  9. Bongos
  10. Xylopipes
  11. Triangle

Many instruments for the rhythms and other musical areas can be played and enjoyed by the TMR. These instruments can be bought or, in most cases, made. Making the instruments saves money and offers additional opportunities to develop related vocational skills (e.g., sanding, hammering, cutting). With only a little imagination and some materials the following rhythm instruments can be made: (1) rhythm sticks (from dowels or old drumsticks), (2) tambourines (from old drum heads), (3) drums (from cardboard boxes), (4) kazoos (from bamboo), (5) sand blocks (from old two-by-fours), (6) maracas (from tubes with rice, pop bottle caps tied together, dried gourds), (7) triangles (from bent metal rod, played with a nail), and (8) bongos (from large cylindrical boxes).

Singing. Singing is another expressive music experience that can be enjoyed by all students. It is relaxing, fun, and can be used to develop breath control for students who need it. Action songs and singing games are best to teach, since they involve the students in the activity. Some typical nonaction songs (e.g., "Twinkle Twinkle Little Star," "Row, Row, Row Your Boat," "Pop Goes the Weasel") can become action songs with the addition of body motions. The specific songs and depth of involvement should depend on the ages and abilities of the class. Here are a few suggested action songs that can be taught to the retarded child*:

Bluebird, Bluebird
Eensy Weensy Spider
Farmer in the Dell
Found a Peanut
Here We Go 'Round the Mulberry Bush
He's Got the Whole World in His Hands
Hokey Pokey
If You're Happy and You Know It
London Bridge is Falling Down
Looby Loo
Musical Chairs
Skip to My Lou
The Bus
This Old Man
Three Blind Mice
Where is Thumbkin

---

*Most songs listed can be found in *Music Activities for Retarded Children,* Gingland and Stiles, 1965.

Additional songs that can be sung and enjoyed by retarded students include the following:

Christmas
Away in a Manger
Jingle Bells
Jolly Old Saint Nicholas
Up on the Housetop
Deck the Halls
Frosty the Snowman
Rudolph the Red-Nosed Reindeer
We Wish You a Merry Christmas
American folk and western
Dogie Song
Home on the Range
I'm Singing in the Saddle
Going to Leave Ol' Texas
She'll be Coming 'Round the Mountain
Halloween
Five Little Pumpkins
Pumpkin Man
There Was an Old Witch
Halloween is Coming
Jack O'Lantern
Mother Goose and nursery rhymes
Baa Baa Black Sheep
Twinkle, Twinkle Little Star
Rock-a-Bye Baby
Mary Had a Little Lamb
Pease Porridge Hot
Patriotic
America
This Land is Your Land
America the Beautiful
God Bless America
Star Spangled Banner
Valentine
Valentines
When You Send a Valentine
Easter
It's Easter
Easter Parade
Peter Cottontail
Fairest Lord Jesus

The singing teacher should be enthusiastic, love to sing, put the singers at ease, thoroughly know all the songs, and acquire a large repertoire of songs (Pomeroy, 1964). For introducing new songs, the teacher or song leader should select one that is simple, short, and has a catchy tune and slowly repeat the words many times.

Dance. Closely related to rhythmic activities are dance activities. Dancing can be performed merely as a social activity for enjoyment, fun, or relaxation. Dance, as do other musical activities, has therapeutic value. It provides opportunities for group feelings, expression, belonging, and releasing tension.

There are enough dances and modifications of dance activities for retarded persons of all ages and functioning abilities to make it enjoyable, challenging, and satisfying. Dancing can include basic dance steps, positions, and waltzes for all students; for older, more capable students, folk and square dancing can be taught.

Square dancing requires that the participants listen, understand, and know left, right, forward, and back, plus other commands as needed (e.g., clockwise). Standard square dances include "The Virginia Reel," "Turkey in the Straw," "She'll be Coming 'Round the Mountain," and "Oh, Suzanna." Square dancing is an especially suited social and recreational activity for adolescent and adult TMRs.

All musically related activities can be expanded to include pageants, celebrations, drama, talent shows, and specials. Rhythms, singing, and dancing truly offer the TMR endless opportunities for learning positive fun and enjoyment during leisure time.

Listed in Table 9-3 are some music materials and resources with publishers.

Hobbies and other recreation-leisure time activities

A hobby can include any specialized interest that occupies a person's time. It is usually an individually based activity but could possibly be a group activity. Any of the recreational and leisure time activities discussed in this chapter could be a hobby. Others include collections (coins, stamps, rocks, seashells, match covers, etc.), gardening, scrapbooks, pet care, horseback riding, skating (roller and/or ice), playing cards (e.g., Old Maid, Go Fish), and quiet games (e.g., Bingo, checkers, puzzles). A useful reference guide for these and other recreational–leisure time activities is *Manual for Constructive Leisure Time Activities* (Blackwell and Frederick, 1972).* This book contains specific information on introducing, teaching, equipment, facilities, and learning skills necessary for fifty-seven activities.

SUMMARY

Early recreation and leisure time development efforts were designed primarily to preserve order, maintain morale, and prevent boredom. It was not until the 1960s that the true value and need of purposeful recreation became known. The movement was so strong that a new discipline, therapeutic recreation, was born. Therapeutic recreation was founded on the premise that the handicapped individual is also entitled to personal and social fulfillment of leisure time.

The importance of recreation is easily recognized: it provides opportunities for development in all areas of behavior, in-

Table 9-3. Music materials and resources

Materials or resources	Publisher
Books: *Games and Music Red Book* and *Singing School Series*	C. C. Birchard & Co.
Rhythm instruments: koko drum, Hohner tub drum, and Makuhi-bamboo sticks	Childcraft
Rhythm instruments: rhythm sticks, bells, tambourines, drums, tom blocks, xylopipes, maracas, and bongo drums	Dick Blick
Records: "Honor Your Pardner," marches, rope-skipping rhythms, "Rhymes and Routines," and "Music for Movement Expression"	Educational Actitivies
Books: *Singing Our Way, Book 1, The Kindergarten Book,* and *The First Grade Book*	Ginn & Co.
Records: "Singing Fun," "More Singing Fun I and II," and song books	Mafex Associates
Books: *Music for Early Childhood* and *New Music Horizon Series*	Silver Burdett Co.
Book: *Music Time*	The Viking Press
Books: *Songs for the Nursery School* and *Musical Experiences of Little Children*	The Willis Music Co.

---

*Mafex Associates, Inc., 90 Cherry St., Johnstown, Pa. 15902.

cluding the physical, social, and personal areas. The retarded certainly need these experiences, since research results indicate that most spend their leisure time at home watching television or listening to the radio. If realistic integration into the mainstream of society is to be achieved, then recreation and leisure time activities must be included in the curriculum.

The major recreational activities in which most TMRs can actively participate include bicycling, bowling, camping (day and residential), hiking, scouting, and swimming. The major leisure time activities discussed include arts and crafts, music (rhythm, singing, dancing), and hobbies and other recreational–leisure time possibilities. Additional resources for each area were also provided.

REFERENCES AND SUGGESTED READINGS

A curriculum guide in arts and crafts for the educable mentally retarded, Augusta, Me., 1975, Maine State Department of Educational and Cultural Services.

Alkema, C. J.: Art for the exceptional, Boulder, Colo., 1971, Pruett Publishing Co.

Amary, I. B.: Creative recreation for the mentally retarded, Springfield, Ill., 1975, Charles C Thomas, Publisher.

Arslaner, C., Curry, C. R., Keck, S. A., and Salzman, G.: Day camping for the developmentally disabled and exceptional children: guidelines for establishing day camp programs, Springfield, Ill., 1970, Illinois Department of Mental Health.

Avedon, E. M.: Therapeutic recreation service, Englewood Cliffs, N.J., 1974, Prentice-Hall, Inc.

Blackwell, R., and Frederick, B.: Manual for constructive leisure times activities, Johnstown, Pa., 1975, Mafex Associates.

Cameron, R.: The uses of music to enhance the education of the mentally retarded, Ment. Retard. 8:32-34, 1970.

Carlson, B. W., and Gingland, D. R.: Play activities for the retarded child, Nashville, Tenn., 1961, Abingdon Press.

Craig, C.: Art for the TMR student, unpublished paper, University of New Orleans, New Orleans, La., 1975.

Deaver, M. J.: Sound and silence: developmental learning for children through music, Pikeville, Ky., 1975, Curriculum Development and Research, Inc.

Endres, R.: Northern Minnesota therapeutic camp, J. Health Phys. Ed. Rec. 75:75-76, May, 1971.

Families play to grow, Washington, D.C., 1974, Joseph P. Kennedy, Jr. Foundation.

Freasier, A.: Print art: sequential task programming for the trainable mentally retarded, Educ. Train. Ment. Retard. 5:98-107, 1971.

Frye, V., and Peters, M.: Therapeutic recreation, Harrisburg, Pa., 1972, Stackpole Books.

Fun with movement, rhythm, and dance, Washington, D.C., 1974, Joseph P. Kennedy, Jr. Foundation.

Fun in the water, Washington, D.C., 1974, Joseph P. Kennedy, Jr. Foundation.

Gingland, D. R., and Stiles, W. E.: Music activities for retarded children: a handbook for teachers and parents, Nashville, Tenn., 1965, Abingdon Press.

Gober, B.: Swimming for trainable mentally retarded, Challenge 3(5):1-3, 1968.

Improving teaching skills for working with the mentally retarded, Hartford, Conn., 1972, The Greater Hartford Association for Retarded Children and Connecticut State Department of Health.

Jones, L. W., Jones, R. C., and Putnam, P.: SCEC summer camps with the handicapped, paper presented at the 54th International Council for exceptional Children Convention, Chicago, Ill., 1976.

Katz, S., and Yekutiel, E.: Leisure time problems of mentally retarded graduates of training programs, Ment. Retard. 12(3):54-57, 1974.

Kelley, J. D., editor: Expanding horizons in therapeutic recreation, II, Urbana-Champaign, Ill., 1974, University of Illinois.

Kellogg, R.: Analyzing children's art, Palo Alto, Calif., 1970, National Press Books.

Kerr, J., and Savage, S.: Incremental art curriculum model for the mentally retarded, Except. Child. 39:193-199, 1972.

Klappholz, L., editor: Year-round camping for the mentally retarded, The Physical Activities Report no. 413, 1976.

Kraus, R.: Therapeutic recreation services: principles and practices, Philadelphia, 1973, W. B. Saunders Co.

Landry, N., and Garcia, R.: Bowling scorekeeping for the trainable, The Pointer, 17(1):60-63, 1972.

Linford, A. G., and Jeanrenaud, C. V.: Systematic instruction for retarded children: the Illinois program, Part IV: Motor performance and recreation instruction, 1972, Danville, Ill., The Interstate Printers & Publishers, Inc.

Luckey, R. B., and Shapiro, I. G.: Recreation: an essential aspect of habilitative programming, Ment. Retard. 12(5):33-35, 1974.

Marr, J., and Lubin, M.: Art for the mentally retarded as taught through a developmental sequence, unpublished paper, University of Kentucky, Lexington, Ky., 1975.

McCowan, L. L.: Horseback riding for the handicapped, Augusta, Me., 1972, The Olivet College Press.

Moran, J. M., and Kalakian, L. H.: Movement experiences for the mentally retarded or emotionally disturbed child, Minneapolis, Minn., 1974, Burgers Publishing Co.

Nesbitt, J. A.: The therapeutic recreation specialist as a change agent: guidelines for policies and curriculum development. In Neal, L. L., editor: Recreation's role in the rehabilitation of the mentally retarded, Monograph no. 4, Eugene, Ore., 1970, The University of Oregon.

Nesbitt, J. A., Brown, P. D., and Murphy, J. F.: Recreation and leisure service for the disadvantaged, Philadelphia, 1970, Lea & Febiger.

O'Morrow, G. S.: Therapeutic recreation: a helping profession, Englewood Cliffs, N.J., 1976, Prentice-Hall, Inc.

Osdol, B.: Art education for the mentally retarded, Ment. Retard. 10(2):51-53, 1972.

Peters, M. L.: Music and the exceptional child, Therap. Rec. 2(3):3-8, 1968.

Pomeroy, J.: Recreation for the physically handicapped, New York, 1964, Macmillan Publishing Co.

Reynolds, G: Swimming: a vehicle for rehabilitation or habilitation of the mentally retarded. In Neal, L. L., editor: Recreation's role in the rehabilitation of the mentally retarded, Eugene, Ore., 1970, The University of Oregon.

Robins, F., and Robins, J.: Educational rhythmics for mentally and physically handicapped children, New York, 1968, Association Press.

Scouting for the mentally retarded, North Brunswick, N.J., 1975, Boy Scouts of America.

Sengstock, W. L., and Stein, J. V.: Recreation for the mentally retarded: a summary of major activities, Except. Child. 33:491-497, 1967.

Semmel, M.: Art education for the mentally retarded, School Arts 60:17-22, 1961.

Shea, T. M.: Camping for special children, St. Louis, 1977, The C. V. Mosby Co.

Shivers, J. S., and Fait, H. F.: Therapeutic and adapted recreational services, Philadelphia, 1975, Lea & Febiger.

Steinhauser, M.: Art for the mentally retarded child, School Arts 69:30-31, 1970.

Sussman, E. J.: Art projects for the mentally retarded child, Springfield, Ill., 1976, Charles C Thomas, Publisher.

Swimming for the handicapped, Washington, D.C., 1974, American National Red Cross.

Tomkinson, E.: School art—creative or gimmicky, Instructor 83:21-22, 1973.

Uhlin, D.: Art for exceptional children, Dubuque, Iowa, 1972, William C. Brown, Co., Publishers.

Wehman, P.: A leisure time activities curriculum for the developmentally disabled, Madison, Wis., 1975, University of Wisconsin.

Winkelstein, E., Shapiro, B., and Shapiro, P.: Art curricula and mentally retarded preschoolers, Ment. Retard. 11(3):6-9, 1973.

Witt, P. A.: A historical sketch of recreation for the mentally retarded, Ment. Retard. 9(1):50-53, 1971.

CHAPTER 10

DEVELOPING ECONOMIC USEFULNESS AND VOCATIONAL SKILLS

In past years the mentally retarded, especially the trainable, were not given serious consideration for inclusion in vocational training programs leading to employment. This population went unemployed, were provided with mundane, unskilled, and menial tasks, or were given purposeless activities in an unstructured sheltered workshop. Reasons for this vocational potential stereotyping include (1) low ability in many individuals, (2) unavailability of higher-level jobs and tasks, and (3) minimal expectation by professionals providing training and evaluation. Low-level tasks and skills may be the maximum level of attainment for many vocational age and adult TMRs but should not be standard practice or terminal goals for the total population. Recent research (Bellamy et al., 1975; Bellamy and Synder, 1976; Brown et al., 1971; Gold, 1972; Gold, 1973; Levy, 1975) indicates the following factors pertinent to vocational skills and the TMR:

1. TMRs can participate effectively in far more vocational opportunities than are usually provided.

2. TMRs are capable of producing qualitatively and quantitatively above what is presently found.

3. TMRs can earn significant wages performing economically useful work.

Opportunities for vocational training and experiences have increased significantly in the last ten years and probably account, in part, for greater vocational attainment in the TMR. Institutions for the retarded are indicative of this opportunity change. Goldberg (1957) found that vocational training experiences for institutional residents were exclusively within institutional work stations, and only 31% of the workers received payment. Richardson, replicating the study in 1975, found that of those residents receiving vocational training, only 64% were trained in a work area of the institution and 90% received payment of some type. Alternative training environments indicated were sheltered workshops (institution and community based), community jobs, or other opportunities (prevocational evaluation programs, halfway houses, part-time day work).

The TMR should be granted the opportunity for full participation in society based on ability, and this includes vocational participation. This chapter will focus on factors affecting vocational performance, skills to be developed, assessment, vocational evaluation, materials for the vocational school program, and basic information on the roles of the sheltered workshop and vocational rehabilitation.

FACTORS AFFECTING VOCATIONAL PERFORMANCE

Successful vocational performance for any population is complex and dependent on many factors, some relating directly to the job tasks and some only indirectly related. Factors also develop over a long period of time and do not suddenly become important at the vocational level (CA of 16+). Many of the necessary skills are developed throughout the entire educational program.

Brolin (1976) has reached the following conclusions regarding the retarded and his relationship to and development of vocational skills:

1. Work personality (one's unique set of abilities and needs) develops but at a slower pace than in the nonretarded.

2. Work personality is determined by the interaction and influence of genetic and environmental factors.

3. Early childhood experiences and relationships are important.

4. Parents significantly affect work personality development.

5. The work personality of the retarded is less complex than that of the average individual.

6. Positive success experiences and reinforcers are important in attainment of vocational abilities.

Some of the general aspects of development that influence later success in the vocational area can be and usually are taught elsewhere in the curriculum. They include physical, cognitive, social, and vocational factors and are listed (Albin, 1973; Fiester and Giambra, 1972; Stabler, 1974).

Physical aspects
  Eye-hand coordination
  Finger dexterity
  Manipulative ability
  Manual dexterity
  Motor coordination
Cognitive-related aspects
  Decision making

  Mental capacity
  Psycholinguistic abilities
  Spatial judgment
Social aspects
  Ability to accept criticism
  Ability to meet crisis situations
  Conformity
  Respect for others
  Self-evaluation
  Tolerance
Vocational aspects
  Adjustment to repetitive work
  Economy of time
  Interest in job or tasks
  Performance on the job
  Perseverance
  Safety awareness and practice
  Work habits
  Work responsibility

These general aspects are factors relating to any job, but especially to the types of jobs performed by the retarded. TMR adults are employed primarily in service and manufacturing jobs (Peterson and Jones, 1964; Stabler, 1974). The technical and specific vocational concerns (e.g., evaluation, workshop operation) relating to the retarded must include the vocational rehabilitation specialist. These concerns will be discussed later in the chapter.

SKILLS TO BE DEVELOPED

Considerable time in the prevocational and vocational level instruction day (one fourth to one half) should be spent on developing related vocational skills. These skills may be taught as a subject, through other curriculum areas (art, physical education, etc.), or both.

The skills to be taught include economically useful skills and vocationally related skills. All TMR students should have opportunities to develop their skills, but it must be remembered that not all will attain a high proficiency level. These skills are important for the student who, after an educational program, enters a sheltered workshop, community group home, or other living-employment situation.

I. Economically and domestically useful skills
  A. Use of common household items
    1. Can opener

2. Dryer
3. Iron
4. Phonograph
5. Radio-television
6. Stove
7. Toaster
8. Washer
9. Vacuum cleaner
B. Contributions to the family
   1. Cleans floors, rugs, sink, etc.
   2. Clears dishes from table
   3. Folds clothes
   4. Hangs up own clothes
   5. Makes own bed
   6. Prepares simple foods
   7. Serves food
   8. Sets table (dishes and utensils)
   9. Sews
   10. Takes out trash or garbage
   11. Washes and dries dishes (hand or machine)
   12. Washes car
   13. Washes clothes
C. Gardening and yard work
   1. Picks up and carries away leaves
   2. Rakes leaves
   3. Trims shrubs or bushes

4. Uses common garden or yard tools (rake, hoe, etc.)
5. Waters lawn or garden
II. Vocational skills
   A. Use of vocationally-related tools
      1. Broom
      2. Hand saw
      3. Hammer
      4. Map
      5. Paintbrush
      6. Pencil sharpener
      7. Sandpaper
      8. Screwdriver
   B. Work habits and attitudes (work personality)
      1. Adjustment skills
         a. Can work with adults
         b. Can work with co-workers
         c. Can adjust to new assignments
         d. Can adjust to work environment
      2. Directional skills
         a. Can and will follow verbally administered directions
         b. Has self-directed work behavior (i.e., keeps working or reads work task)
         c. Can accept correction

Fig. 10-1. Gardening and yard work are economically useful skills within the capabilities of most TMRs. (Courtesy Greenwich, Conn., Public Schools.)

Fig. 10-2. Home-living area at the vocational level can provide opportunities for developing economically and domestically useful vocational skills. (Courtesy Greenwich, Conn., Public Schools.)

3. Interpersonal skills
   a. Has acceptable personality
   b. Has acceptable social behavior
   c. Is socially responsible
   d. Shows adequate self-concept
4. Motivation
   a. Desires to work
   b. Has positive attitude toward work
   c. Is willing to work routinely
5. Personal appearance
   a. Dresses appropriately for work
   b. Has necessary personal hygiene habits
6. Punctuality
   a. Starts work on time
   b. Attends work regularly
C. Necessary or relevant functional academic skills
   1. Reading
      a. Knows functional words (safety word signs, community words, etc.)
      b. Knows specific job-related words
   2. Writing
      a. Knows name, address, and telephone numbers
   3. Math
      a. Recognizes and uses numbers

   b. Recognizes and uses common measurements
   c. Tells time
   d. Has knowledge of money
D. Specific vocational tasks
   1. Assembling (e.g., nuts, bolts, washers)
   2. Colates (e.g., pages for booklets)
   3. Folds letters
   4. Packages
   5. Sorts (by color, texture, design, shape)
   6. Types
   7. Weaves
   8. Wraps
E. Other necessary independent skills
   1. Uses a time clock
   2. Uses public transportation
   3. Uses the telephone (personal and public)

ASSESSMENT

It has been recommended that standardized, vocationally-related instruments be used with the retarded because informal measures (i.e., subjective opinion) and intelligence quotient scores possess little vocational predictability powers (Albin,

Table 10-1. Nonverbal interest tests for the TMR

Name of test	Areas of interest	Publisher and date
AAMD-Becker Reading Free Vocational Interest Inventory	Males (automation, building trade, clerical, animal care, food service, patient care, horticulture, janitorial, personal service, laundry service, materials handling)	AAMD, 1975
	Females (laundry, light industrial, clerical, food service, patient care, horticulture, housekeeping)	
Picture Interest Inventory	Interpersonal, natural, mechanical, business, esthetic, scientific	California Test Bureau/McGraw-Hill, 1958
Wide Range Interest-Opinion Test	Art, drama, sales, management, social service, mechanics, and outdoor	Guidance Associates of Delaware, 1972
Vocational Interest and Sophistication Assessment	Males (construction, maintenance, farmgrounds, food service, garage, industrial, laundry)	Edward R. Johnstone Training and Research Center, 1963
	Females (business, clerical, food service, housekeeping, industrial, laundry)	

Table 10-2. Vocational aptitude assessment instruments

Name of test	Major skill(s) assessed	Publisher and date
Bennet Hand Tool Dexterity Test	Motor control and use of tools	Psychological Corporation, 1965
Crawford Small Parts Dexterity Test	Fine eye-hand coordination (uses tweezers and screwdriver)	Psychological Corporation, 1956
MacQuarie Test for Mechanical Ability	Eye-hand coordination and finger dexterity	California Test Bureau, 1943
Minnesota Rate of Manipulation Test	Gross arm-hand manipulatory movement	American Guidance Service, 1969
Nonreading Aptitude Test Battery	General learning ability, verbal aptitude, numerical ability, spatial aptitude, form perception, motor coordination, finger dexterity, manual dexterity	United States Employment Service, 1973
O'Conner Finger Dexterity and O'Conner Tweezer Dexterity Tests	Insertion of pins into pegboard holes by hand and use of tweezers	Western Psychological Services, no date
Purdue Pegboard	Hand, finger, and arm dexterity and fingertip coordination	Science Research Associates, 1948
Stromberg Dexterity Test	Speed and accuracy of arm and hand movements	Psychological Corporation, 1951

1973; Song and Song, 1969). Although intelligence may certainly be important, Brolin (1976) has suggested that its significance to vocational success is obscured by the interaction of the large number of other variables.

The two types of vocational assessment instruments for the vocational level and adult TMR are those relating to interest and aptitude. Evaluation of vocational or work skills will be discussed later.

Vocational interest testing

Follow-up studies of vocational failures in retarded populations indicated that most individuals had a lack of interest in their jobs. This lack of interest caused secondary difficulties such as little motivation and poor work habits (e.g., late, slow), all of which led to unsuccessful job performance. Interest in one's job is as important for the retarded worker as it is for the nonretarded worker.

Vocational interest testing has only recently become important for the educable level vocational program. Education and rehabilitation specialists have never given serious consideration to interest testing for TMRs for the following reasons:

1. The TMR is not considered a competent, productive employee.

2. The TMR has limited exposure to the

vocational world and therefore cannot select a valid job.

3. Most interest inventories either do not contain realistic job choices for the TMR or depend too heavily on verbal abilities and wide experiences.

Even though it is not known if TMRs (vocational level or adults) can accurately determine their vocational interests, this possibility deserves consideration at the vocational level. Presently there are at least four nonverbal interest assessment measures that merit use. These are listed and described in Table 10-1.

Vocational aptitude

Vocational aptitude tests for the mentally retarded have primarily been used to assess manual ability. Table 10-2 lists several standardized vocational aptitude instruments that can be used with higher skilled TMRs. Little research has attempted to relate these scores to vocational performances of the TMR. Also, the published norms for the test are probably not valid for the retarded. A retarded individual, for example, may score low on a dexterity test, compared with the test norms, but still may possess enough dexterity skills to handle many vocational tasks.

VOCATIONAL EVALUATION

Many public school systems have extended the age range for TMRs to 21 or above and employ teachers as the only professionals. At this level, however, another discipline besides education is needed: vocational rehabilitation. To repeat, education and training for the TMR is not restricted to the domain of any single profession or discipline. The vocational rehabilitation specialists becomes a valuable member of the team at this level in the curriculum and should be used extensively for vocational evaluations.

The two primary means by which work ability can be ascertained are work sample performance tests and rating scales. More comprehensive work sample evaluation systems might also be applicable for some of the more capable TMRs.

Work sample performance tests

Work samples are simulations of tasks or work activity found in certain jobs. As a technique for vocational evaluation, work samples have met with acceptance because of their numerous advantages. Some of the major advantages follow (Pruitt, 1970; Sinick, 1962):

1. Typically administered psychological tests are ineffective for many students (especially minority students).

2. They approximate real jobs.

3. The simplest skill can be evaluated.

4. Personal characteristics can also be determined.

5. Work samples can be devised for the multihandicapped (e.g., retarded and cerebral palsy).

6. Actual work behavior can be observed.

7. The student or client prefers a work task of this type rather than a test.

Disadvantages or limitations also exist and are listed:

1. There is no definite predictability of vocational success.

2. Evaluation, for the most part, is subjective.

3. Work attitude and motivational problems escape detection.

4. There do not exist enough work samples from the major occupational families.

5. Work samples can be expensive and time-consuming to develop.

The ideal work sample involves (1) conducting a community job survey, (2) analyzing the job, (3) constructing the work sample, (4) establishing norms, (5) writing a manual, and (6) administering and evaluating the work sample (Brolin, 1976). One of the keys to developing the work sample is the job analysis. One job analysis form that can be used not only for establishing the basis for the job samples but also for determining the job market of your community is provided in Appendix C.

Possible work sample evaluation systems for TMRs are scarce. One, *The Wide Range Employment Sample Test* (WREST), also called the *Jastak-King*

Work Samples, has unique applicability and potential for TMRs. The WREST also contains workshop norms.

The battery of ten work samples includes tasks that many TMRs perform as adult workers. The work samples of the WREST follow:

1. Single and double folding, posting, labeling, and stuffing
2. Stapling
3. Bottle packaging
4. Rice measuring
5. Screw assembly
6. Tag stringing
7. Swatch pasting
8. Collating
9. Color and shade matching
10. Pattern making

The battery takes approximately 90 minutes administration time and requires no academic skills on the part of the client. Directions for administration are explicit, and no training for the evaluator is required. Occasionally, an adult TMR might be able to complete selected portions of more advanced work sample systems. Although most samples of the systems are inappropriate or too difficult, they are also listed:

TOWER (*Testing, Orientation, and Work Evaluation in Rehabilitation*). 110 work samples; related to *Dictionary of Occupational Titles.*
JEVS (*Jewish and Employment Vocational Services of Philadelphia*). 28 work samples; related to *Dictionary of Occupational Titles.*
SVES (*Singer Vocational Evaluation System*). 17 occupational clusters; related to *Dictionary of Occupational Titles.*
COATS (*Comprehensive Occupational Assessment and Training System*). Job matching, employability attitude, 10 work samples, living skills.

Rating scales

The most frequently used evaluation of vocational performance is the *rating scale.* In this procedure, a rater is asked to record information on a client relative to overall job performance.

Dunn (1973) states that behavior rating scales make two assumptions, which pose

Table 10-3. Vocational rating scales

Name of scale	Areas of assessment	Publisher and date
A Scale of Employability for Handicapped Persons (Workshop Scale Revision by Bolton, 1970)	Attitudinal conformity to work role, maintenance of quality, acceptance of work demands, interpersonal security, speed of production	Jewish Vocational Service, 1963
San Francisco Vocational Competency Scale	Vocational competence—motor skills, cognition, responsibility, social-emotional behavior	Psychological Corporation, 1968
Vocational Adjustment Rating for the Mentally Retarded	Large number of specific traits considered to be either directly or indirectly related to work success; may be used as two separate tests	In Daniels, L. K.: An experimental edition of a rating scale of vocational adjustment for the mentally retarded, Train. Sch. Bull. pp 92-98, 1972
Vocational Adjustment Rating Scale for the Retarded	Work ability, work habits, withdrawn behavior, aggressive behavior, bizarre behaviors	In Song, R. H., and Song, A. Y.: Development of a vocational adjustment rating scale for the retarded, J. Counsel. Psychol. **18**(2):173-176, 1971
Work Adjustment Rating Form	Amount of supervision required, realism of job goals, teamwork, acceptance of rules/authority, work tolerance, perseverance in work, extent of assistance sought, importance attached to job training	In Bitter, J. A., and Bolanovich, D. J.: WARF: a scale for measuring job readiness behaviors, Am. J. Ment. Defic. **74:**616-620, 1970.
Work Habits Rating Scale	Learning, comprehension, performance, attitude toward work, interpersonal relationships	Missouri State Department of Education, 1970
Work Habits Scale (Part of Vocational Capacity Scale)	Learning and comprehension, attitude toward work, performance, interpersonal relationships	MacDonald Training Center Foundation, Inc., 1972

limitations for accurate assessment: (1) the measured behaviors can be rated on a continuous scale, and (2) rating scales can obscure situation-specific responses. In spite of these criticisms, Timmerman and Doctor (1974), after reviewing numerous scales, state that rating scales in theory have considerable merit and are good tools to use for the evaluation of progress by comparing the client's current performance with past performances. Vocational rating scales, areas of assessment, and publishers and dates are provided in Table 10-3.

VOCATIONAL PREPARATION MATERIALS

The teacher of the vocational level TMR class has the task of providing appropriate vocationally-related activities. Many items suited for skill development in this curriculum area are common materials often used at lower instructional levels or different curriculum areas. The materials needed for specific vocationally-related tasks are listed (Missouri State Department of Education, 1970):

Sorting
   Colored beads and laces
   Colored pegs and boards
   Blocks
   Lotto games
   Sorting box by U.S. Toy
   Form board by Playskool
   Coordination board by Hoover Brothers
   Playskool work bench
   Flannel board and aids
   Inset cylinders from Creative Playthings
   Dominoes
   Parquetry blocks
   Construction paper
   At least 4 sizes of nails
   Containers
Packaging
   Buttons, plastic disks, pop bottle tops, etc.
   Sacks
   Stapler
   Pencils
   Marking pens
Tying
   Shoes and laces
   Gaskets with holes in center
Assembling
   Puzzles in varying degrees of difficulty
   Nuts, bolts, and washers

Collating
   Paper materials
Letter folding
   Envelopes
   Paper
Weaving
   Looper looms
   Nylon loopers
   Rug looms
   Rags
   Rug filler
Sewing
   Craft articles such as comb cases
   Pyrolace lacing
   Sewing cards
   Cloth yard goods
   Needles
   Thread
   Buttons
   Sewing machine
Wrapping
   Newspaper
   Sturdy wrapping paper
   Gift wrapping paper
   String
   Ribbon
   Cellophane tape
Maintenance work
   Sponges
   Buckets
   Cleaning cloths
   Wastebaskets
   Cleanser
   Broom
   Dustpan
   Dishpan
   Tea towels
   Drainer
   Detergents
   Plate scrapers
   Trays
   Garbage pails
   Scrubbers
   Waxers
   Vacuum sweeper
   Mops
Use of tools
   Nuts and bolts
   Hammer
   Pliers
   Screwdriver
   Finishing nails
   Wood for project
   Sanding blocks
   Sandpaper
   Linseed oil
   Paint
   Paintbrushes
   Turpentine

Patterns
Phillips screwdriver
Common wrenches
Hand saws
Electric saw
Masking tape

ROLES OF THE SHELTERED WORKSHOP AND VOCATIONAL REHABILITATION

To be a vital part of society means, in part, to contribute to the work force. The feeling of contributing is important regardless of the type of job one performs. Being a dishwasher, busboy, kitchen helper, janitor, or bottle filler—each is important and can be performed with dignity. Not all individuals have the ability to perform highly skilled, technical or, professional jobs, but they nevertheless make their contributions. The retarded often need extensive preparation for even the simplest jobs. This preparation can be provided in the vocational area of curriculum (e.g., skill classes and activity centers), sheltered workshops, and, in some instances, by the services of vocational rehabilitation. The latter two will be examined in terms of their general relation to the TMR, since both play an active role in developing vocational competence in mentally retarded or other handicapped individuals.

Sheltered workshop

Many larger school districts have their own sheltered workshop and activities center for the vocational level TMR, whereas smaller districts send their students to a community-based workshop. A sheltered workshop, by definition, is a facility that utilizes work experience and related services to assist the handicapped individual toward productive vocational status. The sheltered workshop is not to be confused with the rehabilitation workshop, a facility that heavily emphasizes evaluative aspects of competitive employment. It is also more transitional (six weeks to six months), as opposed to the longer-term employment that sheltered workshops often provide.

Sheltered workshops have been in operation for many years, sponsored by volun-tary agencies such as Volunteers of America, Salvation Army, United Cerebral Palsy, National Association for Retarded Citizens, Easter Seal Society, and Goodwill Industries of America. Others are administered and controlled by churches, hospitals, school districts, and institutions. There are an estimated 2,000 rehabilitation workshops financed by one of three sources: (1) fees from agencies that refer clients, (2) subcontract work and money received from services, and (3) contributions.

A comprehensive workshop for the retarded includes the following phases: (1) screening and admissions, (2) evaluation, (3) personal adjustment training, (4) general vocational training; and (5) selective training (for outside or workshop jobs). The workshop can serve as interim employment for some and terminal employment for others.

Most facilities have a staff composed of a director, evaluators, work supervisors, counselors, a subcontract procurement specialist, and other specialists, depending on the size. The workshops are usually governed by a board of directors, who oversee the total operation. The modern workshop has developed into a business enterprise while still providing the necessary services. Barton (1971) suggests that, as a business enterprise, the workshop shares certain demands and realities with other small businesses. As a business, the workshop must:

1. Be competitive for subcontract work and customers.
2. Meet delivery schedules.
3. Provide a quality product.
4. Exercise cost control and other production efficiencies.
5. Respond to market trends, demands, and needs.

The operation of sheltered workshops and other rehabilitation services has been the subject of concern in the last few years (Olshansky, 1973; Williams, 1973). Two of the concerns or criticisms are that workshops do not provide realistic work environments and do not adhere to normalization principles. To provide a more realistic work environment, Barton (1971) and Brown, Johnson, Gadberry, and Fenrick (1971) suggest the following:

1. The clients' efforts should have economic value.

2. Clients' wages should be related to their productivity.

3. Clients should be treated as other nonworkshop workers (i.e., regular work, time for lunch and breaks, follow rules and regulations, etc.).

4. The foreman should remember that he is a boss and not a buddy.

5. Vocational training environments should be more challenging.

Power and Marinelli (1974), writing on the concept of normalization in the sheltered workshop, suggest that (1) pay should be increased; (2) clients should be treated with more normal expectations; (3) there should exist a wide variety of work tasks; (4) the workshop should be in a regular business location; and (5) there should be a change in attitude and behavior of the staff. When these changes are made, a person is then working in a "normal" atmosphere, and attitudes toward self and job will be more like those of the general population.

The physical areas of the sheltered workshop are also important to normalization and overall operation. Space is needed for production, evaluation, storage, and offices. Locker space, restrooms, and snack areas are also needed. The actual space depends on the number and type of clients, the number of staff workers, and the extent of the services. The building should be accessible to public transportation and located on the ground floor. The community workshop in Boston and the Shaffer Rehabilitation Center in Greely, Colorado, are examples of buildings and facilities that serve normalization goals.

The many specific jobs and contracts performed by the retarded in a sheltered workshop include tasks such as assembling, sorting, packaging, performing mailing operations, general repairs, and providing home arts services. Very few studies exist

that indicate what IQs are necessary to perform certain jobs, but Delp (1957) reported the following figures[*]:

Jobs	IQ
Farm	
Cleaning chickens	30
Wheeling grain	30
Husking corn, washing vegetables	38
Picking apples	38
Thinning plants	38
Cleaning automatic water fountains	42
Feeding mash and grain	42
Setting onions	44
Cutting trees	44
Tractor plowing, etc.	51
Tractor seeding	52
Machine-setting plants	52
Pruning fruit trees	52
Hand spraying	55
Greenhouse	
Cleaning greenhouse	42
Grounds	
Raking leaves	31
Hand mowing	31
Using sickle	34
Repairing roads	40
Trimming lawn edges	40
Cleaning grass from flagstones	40
Laundry	
Pulling washers	26
Delivering to cottages	26
Operating extractor	37
Operating washer	37
Operating mangle	37
Sorting laundry by cottage	47
Ironing shirts	51
Dietary	
Cleaning root vegetables	36
Drawing and cleaning poultry	37
Cleaning stoves	44
Mopping floors, washing tables	44
Dishing food at stove	45
Operating potato peeler	45
Assisting at stove, cooking	53
Pantry	
Placing food on tables	30
Wet-mopping floors	32
Washing dishes	47
Setting tables	47

---

[*]Delp, H. A.: Criteria for vocational training of the mentally retarded, a revised concept of the necessary mental level, Train. Sch. Bull., pp. 14-20, 1957. The author notes that even these figures should not be considered rock bottom. They are merely reflective of the lowest IQ that has been successfully used on the job.

Housekeeping

Sweeping, dry scrubbing	32
Cleaning tub and toilet	34
Washing windows	40
Waxing floors and linoleum	42
Sorting and counting laundry	47
Assisting in clothes room	54

Carpentry

Rough sanding, cleaning	53

Miscellaneous

Pressing by hand, sewing room	40

On overall vocational training of TMRs, research indicates the following conclusions (Brown et al., 1971; Crosson, 1969; Huddle, 1967):

1. Behavior modification principles are effective for developing complex workshop tasks.

2. Initial performance is low, but they make progress.

3. They work best in small groups.

4. Supervisor (social) praise and encouragement is sufficient for a reasonable production level.

5. If properly motivated, only minimal supervision is needed.

Basic standards for sheltered workshops prepared by the federal government (Rehabilitation Services Administration, Social and Rehabilitation Services, U.S. Department of Health, Education, and Welfare) can be found in *Standards for Rehabilitation Facilities and Sheltered Workshops* (1969). The seven basic standards for sheltered workshops are listed.* Consult the book for the specific criteria for each standard.

1. *Organization and administration.* The organizational and administrative structure of the facility shall contribute effectively to the achievement of its goals.

2. *Services.* The program of services shall be planned and operated in relation to present and future needs of its clients. These services shall be of such a quality and so applied that they constitute an effective program which achieves the objectives of rehabilitation for the individual client.

3. *Staff.* The staff of the facility shall be competent, professionally ethical, and qualified for positions held.

4. *Clients.* The facility shall observe client personnel policies and practices that protect the interest of the client.

5. *Records and reports.* The facility shall maintain accurate and complete records and prepare and distribute reports as necessary to the achievement of its goals.

6. *Community relations.* The facility shall develop broad community and professional acceptance in order to implement effectively its program goals.

7. *Safety.* The physical plant of the facility and its environment shall be such that the safety and health of the staff and clients are protected.

The following questions offered by Brolin (1973) can also be used to determine whether a sheltered workshop is providing necessary service and meeting its intended goals. A facility that can answer these questions affirmatively will be more likely to meet client needs.

- Does the rehabilitation facility have a well-qualified staff?
- Is the facility housed in a building conducive to rehabilitation operation?
- Does the facility have meaningful evaluative, work adjustment, counseling, social, and vocational training programs?
- Does the staff give the clients enough supervision?
- Does the facility work closely with the family?
- Does the facility issue meaningful and appropriate evaluation, training, and placement reports?
- Does the facility provide a dynamic placement, follow-up, and research program?
- Does the facility have frequent and meaningful preservice and in-service training programs?

Vocational rehabilitation

At its inception, vocational rehabilitation was considered to be a service of retraining for employment rather than for correcting or reducing the disability through medical or therapeutic treatment. The Barden–La Follette Act (Public Law 113) of 1943 instituted provisions for corrective surgery, therapeutic treatment, hospitalization, transportation, occupational licenses, occupational tools and equipment, maintenance during training, placement or

*From Standards for rehabilitation facilities and sheltered workshops, Washington, D.C., 1969, U.S. Department of Health, Education, and Welfare.

retention in employment, prostheses, medical examinations, and guidance counseling. Special provisions for the mentally retarded and blind were also contained in the act. Several amendments have been made since then, but the most significant for the TMR has to be the Rehabilitation Act of 1973. One of the aims was to improve services to the mentally retarded by mandating that state rehabilitation agencies adhere to the following provisions:

1. Give priority emphasis for services to individuals with the most severe handicaps.

2. Focus research, demonstration, and training activities on rehabilitating the severly handicapped.

3. Make the agency's resources more accessible.

4. Assure client involvement and approval in the determination and delivery of vocational rehabilitation services.

5. Stimulate new programs and services for the disabled.

Eligibility for rehabilitation services is based on (1) the presence of a physical or mental disability; (2) the existence of a substantial handicap to employment, and (3) reasonable expectation that vocational rehabilitation services may render the individual capable of gainful occupation (competitive, sheltered, homebound). Services (not including diagnosis, evaluation, counseling, planning, vocational training, training supplies, and placement—which are normally provided) are dependent on the ability to pay and can include the following divisions:

1. *Medical diagnosis*—to find out about any physical conditions that might limit the kinds of work an individual can do.

2. *Counseling and testing*—to help the client aim for the right kind of job, in keeping with his interest, aptitudes, capacities, and limitations.

3. *Medical and hospital care*—if needed, to attend to physical problems that may stand in the way of preparation for work.

4. *Prosthetic appliances*—if needed for a physical disability.

5. *Training for a job*—whatever kind is suitable: personal adjustment training, prevocational training, vocational training, occupational training center, sheltered workshop, on-the-job training, any other necessary instruction. The training must lead toward a definite job goal.

6. *Maintenance and transportation*—provided during rehabilitation, if needed.

7. *Tools and equipment for the job*—again, if needed.

8. *Job placement*—a position most suitable for the person's aptitudes, abilities, and training.

9. *Job follow-up*—to make certain that the person and the employer are both satisfied; to furnish whatever further adjustments are needed; to provide services necessary to ensure that the client gets off to a proper start.

Vocational rehabilitation services for the TMR are sometimes direct but in many states are indirectly provided. A state's rehabilitation agency, for example, might purchase services from workshops operated by private nonprofit organizations.

SUMMARY

The trainable mentally retarded can develop many economically useful and vocational skills. The opportunities to develop these skills should be provided in the curriculum. Although many specific job skills or tasks can be taught at the vocational level (CA 16+), the general factors of development (physical, cognitive, social, vocational) that relate to later success in vocational endeavors can be learned from earlier instructional levels.

The specific skills to be developed were listed and focused on economically and domestically useful skills (use of common household items, contributions to the family, gardening and yard work) and vocational skills (use of vocationally-related tools, work habits and attitudes, necessary or relevant functional academic skills, specific vocational tasks, other necessary independent skills).

Assessment for this area of curriculum was discussed and appropriate tests presented. Vocational interest tests and vocational aptitude tests were the two assessment measures examined. Work samples and vocational rating scales are the two frequently used vocational evaluation measures. Those samples and rating scales best designed for the TMR were presented.

The chapter concluded by examining the roles of the sheltered workshop and vocational rehabilitation. Their general functioning, applicability, and value to the TMR were noted.

REFERENCES AND SUGGESTED READINGS

A curriculum for the intellectually disabled trainable, Tallahassee, Fla., 1970, Florida State Department of Education.

Albin, T. J.: Relationships of I.Q. and previous work experience to success in sheltered employment, Ment. Retard. 11(3):26, 1973.

Barton, E. H.: The rehabilitation workshop and the foreman's role, San Francisco, 1971, University of San Francisco.

Bellamy, G. T., and Snyder, S.: The trainee performance sample: toward the prediction of habilitation costs for severely handicapped adults, AAHPER Rev. 1(4):17-36, 1976.

Bellamy, T., Peterson, L., and Close, D.: Habilitation of the severely and profoundly retarded: illustrations of competence, Educ. Train. Ment. Retard. 10:174-186, 1975.

Brolin, D.: Vocational evaluation: special education's responsibility, Educ. Train. Ment. Retard. 39:619-624, 1973.

Brolin, D. E.: Vocational preparation of retarded citizens, Columbus, Ohio, 1976, The Charles E. Merrill Publishing Co.

Brown, L., Johnson, S., Gadberry, E., and Fenrick, N.: Increasing individual and assembly line production rates of retarded students, Train. Sch. Bull. 67:206-212, 1971.

Curriculum guide for teachers of trainable mentally retarded children, Jefferson City, Mo.; 1970, Missouri State Department of Education.

Daniels, L. K., editor: Vocational rehabilitation of the mentally retarded, Springfield, Ill., 1974, Charles C Thomas, Publisher.

Daniels, L. K., and Stewart, J. A.: A vocational adjustment rating scale for the mentally retarded, Train. Sch. Bull. 68:10-14, 1969.

Delp, H. A.: Criteria for vocational training of the mentally retarded, a revised concept of the necessary mental level, Train. Sch. Bull. 54: 14-20, 1957.

Dunn, D. J.: Situational assessment: models for the future, Menomonie, Wis., 1973, University of Wisconsin-Stout, Research and Training Center.

Elkin, L.: Predicting productivity of trainable retardates on experimental workshop tasks, Am. J. Ment. Defic. 71:576-580, 1967.

Elkin, L.: Predicting performance of the mentally retarded on sheltered workshop and non-institutional jobs, Am. J. Ment. Defic. 72:533-539, 1968.

Fiester, A. R., and Giambra, L. M.: Language indices of vocational success in mentally retarded adults, Am. J. Ment. Defic. 77:332-337, 1972.

Fraenkel, W. A.: Preparing for work, Washington, D.C., The President's Committee on Employment of the handicapped.

Fudell, S., and Peck, J.: How to hold your job, New York, 1967, The John Day Co.

Gellman, W.: The principles of vocational evaluation Rehabil. Lit. 29:98-102, 1968.

Gold, M.: Stimulus factors in skill training on a complex assembly task: acquisition, transfer and retention, Am. J. Ment. Defic. 76:517-526, 1972.

Gold, M. W.: Factors affecting producing by the retarded: base rate, Ment. Retard. 11(6):41-45, 1973.

Goldberg, I. I.: A survey of the present status of vocational rehabilitation of the mentally retarded residents in state supported institutions, Am. J. Ment. Defic. 61(6):698-705, 1957.

Huddle, D.: Work performance of trainable adults as influenced by competition, cooperation, and monetary reward, Am. J. Ment. Defic. 72:198-211, 1967.

Jastak, J. F., and King, D. E.: Wide-range employment sample test, supplement to manual, Wilmington, Del., 1972, Guidance Associates of Delaware, Inc.

Katz, K.: Job role playing in the classroom, J. Spec. Educ. Ment. Retard. 8:152, 1972.

Lane, P. A., Soares, L. M., and Silverstone, L. S.: Objective: vocational rehabilitation within public education, Bridgeport, Conn., Bridgeport Public Schools.

Leff, R. B.: Teaching the TMR to dial the telephone, Ment. Retard. 12(2):12-13, 1974.

Levy, S. M.: The development of work skill training procedures for the assembly of printed circuit boards by the severely handicapped, Review 1(1):1-10, 1975.

Neff, W. S.: Work and human behavior, New York, 1968, Atherton Press.

Nelson, N.: Workshops for the handicapped in

the United States, Springfield, Ill., 1971, Charles C Thomas, Publisher.

Nitzberg, J.: Functions of sheltered workshop supervisors (shop teachers), J. Spec. Educ. Ment. Retard. 7(2):86-89, 1971.

Olshansky, S.: Evaluating workshop evaluations, Rehabil. Record 14(5):24-25, 1973.

Olshansky, S., and Beach, D.: A five-year follow-up of mentally retarded clients, Rehabil. Lit. 35 (2):48-49, 1974.

Peterson, R. O., and Jones, E. M.: Guides to jobs for the mentally retarded, revised edition, Pittsburgh, 1964, American Institutes for Research.

Power, P. W., and Marinelli, R. P.: Normalization and the sheltered workshop, Rehabil. Lit. 35(3):66-72, 1974.

Pruitt, W.: Basic assumptions underlying work sample theory, J. Rehabil. 36(1):24-26, 1970.

Richardson, J. B.: A survey of the present status of vocational training, Ment. Retard. 13(1):16-20, 1975.

Sinick, O.: Client evaluation: work task approach, Rehabil. Record 3(2):6-8, 1962.

Song, A., and Song, R.: Prediction of job efficiency of institutionalized retardates in the community, Am. J. Ment. Defic. 73:567-571, 1969.

Stabler, E. M.: Follow-up study of retarded clients from a training workshop, Ment. Retard. 12(3):7-9, 1974.

Standards for rehabilitation facilities and sheltered workshops, Washington, D.C., 1969, United States Department of Health, Education, and Welfare.

Timmerman, W. J., and Doctor, A. C.: Special applications of work evaluation techniques for prediction of employability of the trainable mentally retarded, Stryker, Ohio, 1974, Quadco Rehabilitation Center, Inc.

Tobias, J., and Gorelick, J.: Work characteristics of retarded adults at trainable levels, Ment. Retard. 1:338-344, 1963.

Wagner, E. E., and Hawver, D. A.: Correlation between psychological tests and sheltered workshop performance for severely retarded adults, Am. J. Ment. Defic. 70(4):685-691, 1965.

Williams, H. A.: Toward a federal partnership with exceptional children, presented at National Topical Conference on Career Education of Exceptional Children and Youth, New Orleans, La., February, 1973.

APPENDIX A

Publishers of tests, materials, and equipment for TMR programs

This alphabetical list of publishers is provided so that the teacher or administrator can request more specific information relating to tests or materials mentioned in the text.

Adams County School District
Commerce City, Colo. 80022

Alla Associates, Inc.
7600 Red Rd., Suite 104
South Miami, Fla. 33143

Allied Educational Council
P.O. Box 78
Galien, Mich. 49113

Amateur Athletic Union
3400 W. 86th St.
Indianapolis, Ind. 46208

American Alliance for Health, Physical Education, and Recreation
1201 16th St., N.W.
Washington, D.C. 20036

American Association on Mental Deficiency
5201 Connecticut Ave., N.W.
Washington, D.C. 20015

American Guidance Service, Inc.
Publishers' Building
Circle Pines, Minn. 55014

Bio-Dyne Corporation
154 E. Erie
Chicago, Ill. 60611

BKR Educational Projects, Inc.
1970 S.W. 43rd Way
Fort Lauderdale, Fla. 33317

Dick Blick Co.
P.O. Box 1267
Galesburg, Ill. 61401

Borg-Warner Educational Systems
7450 N. Natchez Ave.
Nile, Ill. 60648

California Test Bureau/McGraw-Hill
Del Monte Research Park
Monterey, Calif. 93940

The Center for Applied Research in Education, Inc.
521 5th Ave.
New York, N.Y. 10017

Childcraft Educational Corporation
20 Kilmer Rd.
Edison, N.J. 08817

Communication Research Associates, Inc.
Box 11012
Salt Lake City, Utah 84111

Consulting Psychologists Press, Inc.
577 College Ave.
Palo Alto, Calif. 94306

Continental Press, Inc.
Elizabethtown, Pa. 17022

Cooperative Educational Service Agency #12
412 E. Slifer
Portage, Wis. 53901

Coronet Films
65 E. South Water St.
Chicago, Ill. 60601

Creative Playthings, Inc.
P.O. Box 330
Princeton, N.J. 08540

Cuisenaire Company of America, Inc.
9 Elm Ave.
Mount Vernon, N.Y. 10550

Decca Records % N.C.A. Records
100 Universal City Plaza
Universal City, Calif. 91618

Developmental Learning Materials
3305 N. Ashland Ave.
Chicago, Ill. 60657

Walt Disney Educational Media Co.
800 Sonora Ave.
Glendale, Calif. 91201

Edmark Associates
13241 Northup Way
Bellevue, Wash. 98005

Educational Activities, Inc.
Box 392
Freeport, N.Y. 11520

Educational Performance Associates
563 Westview Ave.
Ridgefield, N.J. 07657

Educational Service, Inc.
P.O. Box 219
Stevensville, Mich. 49127

Educational Teaching Aids
159 W. Kinzie St.
Chicago, Ill. 60610

Educators Publishing Service, Inc.
301 Vassar St.
Cambridge, Mass. 02138

Encyclopedia Britannica Educational Corp.
425 N. Michigan Ave.
Chicago, Ill. 60611

ESU #14
Box 414
Sidney, Neb. 69162

Fearon Publishers
6 Don's Dr.
Belmont, Calif. 94002

Field Educational Publications, Inc.
2400 Hanover St.
Palo Alto, Calif. 94002

George Peabody College for Teachers
Institute of School Learning and Individual
   Differences
Nashville, Tenn. 37203

GEM
P.O. Box 2339, Station A
Champaign, Ill. 61820

**Georgia Division of Early Childhood and
   Special Education**
Department of Education
Atlanta, Ga. 30334

Ginn & Co.
988 Monroe Dr.
Dallas, Texas 75229

Guidance Associates of Delaware
1526 Gilpin Ave.
Wilmington, Del. 19806

H & H Enterprises, Inc.
Box 3342
Lawrence, Kan. 66044

Hallmark Films and Recordings, Inc.
1511 E. North Ave.
Baltimore, Md. 21213

Harcourt Brace Jovanovich, Inc.
757 Third Ave.
New York, N.Y. 10017

Harris County Center for the Retarded, Inc.
3550 W. Dallas
Houston, Texas 77019

Houghton Mifflin Co.
53 W. 43rd St.
New York, N.Y. 10036

Houston Test Co.
P.O. Box 35152
Houston, Texas 77035

Hubbard Scientific Co.
P.O. Box 104
Northbrook, Ill. 60062

Ideal School Supply Co.
8316 S. Birkhoff
Chicago, Ill. 60620

Instructional Media, Inc.
8141 E. 44th St.
Tulsa, Okla. 74145

The Interstate Printers and Publishers
19-27 N. Jackson St.
Danville, Ill. 61832

Jefferson Parish School Board
519 Huey P. Long Ave.
Gretna, La. 70053

The Judy Co.
310 N. Second St.
Minneapolis, Minn. 55401

Learning Arts
P.O. Box 917
Wichita, Kan. 67201

The Learning Business
30961 Agoura Rd., Suite 325
Westlake Village, Calif. 91361

J. B. Lippincott Co.
E. Washington Square
Philadelphia, Pa. 19105

Louisiana State Division of Mental Retardation
P.O. Box 44215
Baton Rouge, La. 70804

Mafex Associates, Inc.
90 Cherry St.
Johnstown, Pa. 15902

Macdonald Training Center Foundation, Inc.
4424 Tampa Bay Blvd.
Tampa, Fla. 33624

McGraw-Hill Book Co.
330 W. 42nd St.
New York, N.Y. 10036

Melton Book Co.
111 Leslie St.
Dallas, Texas 75207

Charles E. Merrill Publishing Co.
1300 Alum Creek Dr.
Columbus, Ohio 43216

Metropolitan Toronto Association for
Retarded Children
186 Beverly St.
Toronto 2B
Ontario, Canada

Millikin Publishing Co.
1100 Research Blvd.
St. Louis, Mo. 63132

Milton Bradley Co.
Springfield, Mass. 01101

Modern Educational Corporation
P.O. Box 721
Tulsa, Okla. 74101

Ohio State University Press
Publications Sales Division
2070 Neil Ave.
Columbus, Ohio 43210

Peterson Co.
555 Lancaster Ave.
Reynoldsburg, Ohio 43068

Phonovisual Products, Inc.
12216 Parklawn Dr.
Rockville, Mass. 20852

Prentice-Hall, Inc.
Educational Books Division
Englewood Cliffs, N.J. 07632

PREP Inc.
1575 Parkway Ave.
Trenton, N.J. 08628

Project ACTIVE
Township of Ocean School District
Oakhurst, N.J. 07755

Project ADAPT
Tri-counties Regional Center
22 W. Michetorena
Santa Barbara, Calif. 93101

The Psychological Corporation
757 3rd Ave.
New York, N.Y. 10017

Random House, Inc.
201 E. 50th St.
New York, N.Y. 10022

Reporting Service for Children
563 Westview Ave.
Ridgefield, N.J. 07657

Research Press Co.
2612 N. Mattis Ave.
Champaign, Ill. 61820

Rocky Mountain Special Education Instructional
Materials Center
University of Northern Colorado
Greeley, Colo. 80631

Science Research Associates, Inc.
259 E. Erie
Chicago, Ill. 60611

Silver Burdett Co.
Park Ave. and Columbia Rd.
Morristown, N.J. 07960

Society for Visual Education, Inc.
1345 Diversey Parkway
Chicago, Ill. 60614

Stanwix House, Inc.
3020 Chartiers St.
Pittsburgh, Pa. 15204

State Schools for the Severely Handicapped
P.O. Box 480
Jefferson City, Mo. 65101

C. H. Stoelting Co.
424 North Homan Ave.
Chicago, Ill. 60624

R. H. Stone Products
13735 Puritan
Detroit, Mich. 48227

Suburban Publications
Box 3444
Champaign, Ill. 61820

Teaching Resources Corporation
100 Boylston St.
Boston, Mass. 02116

Texas Education Agency
Department of Special Education
201 E. 11th St.
Austin, Texas 78712

Fern Tripp
2035 E. Sierra Way
Dinuba, Calif. 93618

University of Connecticut
School of Physical Education
Storrs, Conn. 06268

University of Illinois Press
Urbana, Ill. 61801

University of Iowa
Bureau of Educational Research and Service
Iowa City, Iowa 52240

University of Kansas
Lawrence, Kan. 66044

University of Michigan Press
Ann Arbor, Mich. 48103

University of Washington
Child Development and Mental Retardation
   Center
Seattle, Wash. 98195

The Viking Press, Inc.
625 Madison Ave.
New York, N.Y. 10022

Webster Publishing Co.
Manchester Rd.
Manchester, Mo. 63011

Western Psychological Services
12031 Wilshire Blvd.
Los Angeles, Calif. 90025

The Willis Music Co.
Florence, Ky. 41042

Winter Haven Lions Research Foundations
P.O. Box 111
Winter Haven, Fla. 33880

Word Making Productions
P.O. Box 1858
Salt Lake City, Utah 84110

APPENDIX B

Directory of agencies, professional organizations, and publications that contribute to the education of TMRs

---

This appendix affords the inexperienced, as well as the knowledgeable experienced, professional easy access to the names and addresses of various agencies (public, private, and nonprofit), professional organizations, and professional journals that in some way contribute to the education of the TMR. More specific information on their services, publications, membership requirements, etc. is available on request.

AGENCIES

Bureau of Education for the Handicapped
U.S. Office of Education
7th and D St., S.W.
Washington, D.C. 20202

Center for Law and Social Policy
1600 20th St., N.W.
Washington, D.C. 20009

International League of Societies for the Mentally Handicapped
12 Rue Forestiere
Brussels 5, Belgium

Joseph P. Kennedy, Jr. Foundation
1701 K St., N.W.
Washington, D.C. 20006

National Center for Law and the Handicapped, Inc.
1235 N. Eddy St.
South Bend, Ind. 46617

National Council on the Rights of the Mentally Impaired
1600 20th St., N.W.
Washington, D.C. 20009

Office of Mental Retardation Coordination
HEW North Building, Room 3744
330 Independence, S.W.
Washington, D.C. 20201

President's Committee on Mental Retardation
Washington, D.C. 20201

State-Federal Information Clearing House for Exceptional Children
Council for Exceptional Children
1920 Association Dr.
Reston, Va. 22091

PROFESSIONAL ORGANIZATIONS

American Association for the Education of the Severely/Profoundly Handicapped
P.O. Box 15287
Seattle, Wash. 98115

American Association for Health, Physical Education, and Recreation
1201 16th St., N.W.
Washington, D.C. 20036

American Association on Mental Deficiency
5201 Connecticut Ave., N.W.
Washington, D.C. 20015

American Association of Special Educators
P.O. Box 168
Fryeburg, Me. 04037

The Canadian Association for the
  Mentally Retarded
Kinsmen Building
York University Campus
4700 Keele St.
Downsview (Toronto)
Ontario, Canada

The Council for Exceptional Children
Division on Mental Retardation
1920 Association Dr.
Reston, Va. 22091

National Rehabilitation Association
1522 K St., N.W.
Washington, D.C. 20005

PUBLICATIONS

American Journal of Mental Deficiency
  (research-oriented journal, published by
  AAMD; published bimonthly)
American Association on Mental Deficiency
5201 Connecticut Ave., N.W.
Washington, D.C. 20015

Challenge (newsletter dealing with physical
  education and recreation for the mentally
  retarded; published bimonthly)
American Association for Health, Physical
  Education, and Recreation
1201 16th St., N.W.
Washington, D.C. 20036

The Closer Look Report (periodic report intended
  to disseminate information to parents and
  others on current happenings and events in
  the world of the handicapped)
Closer Look, Inc.
P.O. Box 1492
Washington, D.C. 20013

Deficience Mentale (Mental Retardation)
  (journal published by the Canadian Association
  for Mental Retardation, which is primarily
  a parent's organization; published quarterly)
The Canadian Association for Mental Retardation
Kinsmen Building
York University Campus
4700 Keele St.
Downsview (Toronto)
Ontario, Canada

Education and Training of the Mentally
  Retarded (journal of the Division on Mental
  Retardation, The Council for Exceptional
  Children; published quarterly)
The Council for Exception Children
1920 Association Dr.
Reston, Va. 22091

The Exceptional Parent (publication geared
  toward the interests of parents of the mentally
  retarded child; published bimonthly)
Magazine
264 Beacon St.
Boston, Mass. 02116

The Journal of Rehabilitation (emphasis on
  rehabilitation programs for physically and
  mentally handicapped persons; published
  bimonthly)
National Rehabilitation Association
1522 K St., N.W.
Washington, D.C. 20005

Mental Retardation (official publication of AAMD
  dealing with articles on all aspects of mental
  retardation; published bimonthly)
American Association on Mental Deficiency
5201 Connecticut Ave., N.W.
Washington, D.C. 20015

Mental Retardation News (newspaper covering
  the news in the field of mental retardation,
  primarily for parents and advocates of mental
  retardation)
National Association for Retarded Citizens
2709 Avenue E East
Arlington, Texas 76010

NRA Newsletter (apprises professionals and laypersons of current issues and developments
  in the area of rehabilitation; published
  bimonthly)
National Rehabilitation Association
1522 K St., N.W.
Washington, D.C. 20005

Outlook (newsletter giving information on
  physical education and recreation for the
  mentally retarded; published five times during
  the school year)
American Association of Health, Physical
  Education, and Recreation
1201 16th St., N.W.
Washington, D.C. 20036

PCMR Message (newsletter issued to inform the
  public of current interests and activities of
  the PCMR; published bimonthly)
President's Committee on Mental Retardation
Washington, D.C. 20201

The Pointer (journal designed for teachers of
  the mentally retarded; published three times a
  year in fall, winter, and spring)
Heldref Publications
4000 Albemarie St., N.W.
Washington, D.C. 20016

Programs for the Handicapped (booklet
describing new programs for the handicapped;
published monthly)
National Easter Seal Society for Crippled
Children and Adults
2023 W. Ogden Ave.
Chicago, Ill. 60612

Rehabilitation World (journal about human
restoration from throughout the world;
published quarterly)
Rehabilitation International, U.S.A.
20 W. 40th St.
New York, N.Y. 10018

Research and the Retarded (journal for the
exchange of ideas and information among
institutions and individuals involved with the
mentally retarded; published quarterly)
P.O. Box 247
Goldsboro, N.C. 27530

The Retarded Adult (journal for professionals
and laypersons concerned with mentally
retarded adults in various settings and
activities, including community, residence,
family, school, employment, treatment
facilities, and workshops)
American Association of Special Educators
107-20 125th St.
Richmond Hill, N.Y. 11419

Sharing Our Caring (newsletter for parents of
Down's syndrome children)
P.O. Box 196
Milton, Wash. 98354

Special Children (journal for parents and
professionals concerned with the handicapped;
published three times a year)
P.O. Box 168
Fryeburg, Me. 04037

APPENDIX C

Forms for teachers and administrators of programs for TMRs

The commonly needed forms in the operation of an educational program for TMRs are (1) an emergency information card, (2) parental or guardian consent forms for field trips, release of information, and photographs, (3) a medical examination form (for participation in physical education, summer camps, etc.), (4) a job analysis form for vocational or adult programs, and (5) a checklist for program quality.

EMERGENCY INFORMATION CARD

Name _____ Date of birth _____

Home address _____ Telephone _____

Mother's first name _____ Father's first name _____

Mother's place of employment _____ Telephone _____

Father's place of employment _____ Telephone _____

Neighbor or relative to contact in absence of parents _____

Name _____ Address _____ Telephone _____

Name of family or child's physician _____ Telephone _____

Hospital to be used in case of emergency _____

FIELD TRIP

I hereby give my permission for _____
                                    (Child's name)
to attend a field trip to _____ on _____
                           (Name of place)   (Date)
I also release all school employees and volunteers from any liability or accidents resulting from or associated with this field trip.

Signed _____

Date _____

RELEASE OF INFORMATION

This is to authorize _____ ,
                        (Name of school or school district)
_____ to release information
              (Address)
concerning _____
              (e.g., evaluation, school performance)
to _____
     (Name and address where information is to be released)

Signed _____

Date _____

PERMISSION FOR PHOTOGRAPHS

I hereby (give my consent, do not give my consent) to have my child _____
                                                                      (Name of student)
_____ photographed, both still and motion picture, in any activities associated with school.

Signed _____

Date _____

MEDICAL EXAMINATION FORM

Name_____

Age_____ Date of birth_____

Height_____ Weight_____

Pulse_____Urine analysis_____Blood pressure_____

Glasses: Yes____No____   Hernia: Yes____No____

	Normal
Eyes	_____
Ears	_____
Nose	_____
Throat	_____
Heart	_____
Lungs	_____
Abdomen	_____

Noted abnormalities_____

_____

_____

_____

General impression_____

_____

_____

	Yes	No	Type	Medication
Seizures	____	____	_____	_____
Allergies	____	____	_____	_____

Reaction to penicillin or other drugs: Yes____No____

   If so, what_____

                                                                 Date

Immunization: Oral Polio_____   _____

                 Measles_____   _____

                 Tetanus toxoid_____   _____

                 Smallpox_____   _____

                 Whooping cough_____   _____

                 Diphtheria_____   _____

Any recent illnesses, surgery, etc._____

_____

_____

Medications now being used_____

   Name_____Dosage_____

   Name_____Dosage_____

This student may participate in physical education or other activities requiring gross motor

movement: Yes____No____

Other limitations or restrictions (if any)_____

_____

_____

Date of examination_____

Signed_____, M.D.

JOB ANALYSIS FORM*

Job area _____ Job title _____ Sk SSk Unsk

Name of firm _____ Address _____

Nature of business _____ Number employed _____

Person interviewed _____ Position _____

NOTE: *It is most important* that the spaces allocated for *Comment* be used freely. The validity and completeness of your report will depend on the extent to which descriptive comments are included. *No job analysis is valid without detailed explanatory comment.*

Interviewer _____ Position _____

A. Qualifications

1. **Age:** Minimum _____ Maximum _____ Comment _____

2. **Sex:** Male _____ Female _____ Both _____ Preference _____

3. **Legal requirements:** License: Yes _____ No _____ Kind of license _____

   Bond: Yes _____ No _____ Cost _____ Who pays cost _____

4. **Union membership:** Open _____ Closed _____ Required _____

   Not required _____ Name of union _____ Name of local _____

   Address of local _____ Initial fee _____ Dues _____

5. **Experience:** None required _____ Some required _____ Degree _____

6. **Test:** Given _____ Not given _____ Kind _____

7. **Application blanks:** Needed _____ Not needed _____ Comment _____

   Assistance in filling out blanks: Yes _____ No _____ Comment _____

   Personal interview: Yes _____ No _____ Comment _____

8. **Health requirements:** _____

   Reasons: _____

   Medical examination: Yes _____ No _____ Comment _____

9. **Physical requirements:** _____

   Reasons: _____

   Hearing: Exceptional _____ Average _____ Not important _____

   Eyesight: Exceptional _____ Average _____ Not important _____

   Speech: Exceptional _____ Average _____ Not important _____

   Disqualifying physical factors: _____

10. **Educational requirements:** Grade _____ Comment _____

    Language skill: Grade _____ Comment _____

    Reading skill: Grade _____ Comment _____

    Writing skill: Grade _____ Comment _____

    Arithmetic skill: Grade _____ Comment _____

11. **Personality requirements:** Manners: Outstanding _____ Average _____

    Comment _____

*From University of Northern Colorado, Greeley, Colo.

Continued.

JOB ANALYSIS FORM—cont'd

Emotional stability: Very stable_____Average stability_____

Comment_____

Appearance: Important_____Unimportant_____Comment_____

Disposition: Important_____Unimportant_____Comment_____

Additional information:_____

12. **Essential skills (nonmanual):** Special information_____

_____

Travel knowledge: Local_____City_____None_____Comment_____

Telephone knowledge: Much_____Little_____None_____Comment _____

Directory knowledge: Much_____Little_____None_____Comment_____

Job time forms: Much_____Little_____None_____Comment_____

Job completion forms: Much_____Little_____None_____Comment_____

Cash register: Much_____Little_____None_____Comment_____

Time clock: Used_____Not used_____Comment_____

Customer relations: Much_____Little_____None_____Comment_____

Employer relations: Much_____Little_____None_____Comment_____

Employee relations: Much_____Little_____None_____Comment_____

13. **Essential skills (manual):** Unusual skills_____

_____

Tool knowledge: Much_____Little_____None_____Comment_____

Tools used:_____

_____

Machine knowledge: Much_____Little_____None_____Comment_____

Machines used:_____

_____

Manual dexterity: Outstanding_____Average_____None_____

Comment_____

Motor coordination: Outstanding_____Average_____None_____

Comment_____

Finger dexterity: Outstanding_____Average_____None_____

Comment_____

Speed: Outstanding_____Average_____None_____Comment_____

Precision: Outstanding_____Average_____None_____Comment_____

Accuracy: Outstanding_____Average_____None_____Comment_____

B. **Working conditions**

1. **Wages:** Weekly_____Bimonthly_____Monthly_____Piecework_____

Amount: Weekly_____Bimonthly_____Monthly_____Piecework_____

Overtime: Much_____Some_____None_____

Increases: Possible_____Impossible_____Comment_____

2. **Hours:** More than 40 _____ 40 hours _____ 35 hours _____ Unusual hours _____

   6-day week _____ 5½ _____ 5 _____ Comment _____

3. **Tenure:** Year-round _____ Seasonal _____ Comment _____

   Permanent _____ Uncertain _____ Comment _____

4. **Benefits:** Illness: Paid _____ Not paid _____ Comment _____

   Vacation: 2 weeks _____ 1 week _____ Less _____ With pay _____

   Without pay _____

   Hospital & medical services: Provided _____ Not provided _____

   Comment _____

   Pensions: Provided _____ Not provided _____ Comment _____

   Workmen's compensation: Provided _____ Not provided _____

   Comment _____

5. **Hazards:** Moral: Much _____ Some _____ None _____ Description _____

   Physical: Much _____ Some _____ None _____ Description _____

   Emotional: Much _____ Some _____ None _____ Description _____

   Health: Much _____ Some _____ None _____ Description _____

6. **Surroundings:** Very pleasant _____ Pleasant _____ Unpleasant _____

   Indoor _____ Outdoor _____ Both

   Noisy _____ Quiet _____ Average _____

   Hot _____ Cold _____ Average _____

   Wet _____ Dry _____ Average _____

   Description

7. **Works with:** Many _____ Some _____ Alone _____ Comment _____

8. **Supervision:** Much _____ Some _____ Little _____ Comment _____

   Employer _____ Employee _____ Foreman _____ Fellow worker _____

   Comment _____

   Sympathetic _____ Unsympathetic _____ Impersonal _____

9. **Training possibilities:** Many _____ Some _____ None _____ Comment _____

10. **Induction training:** Employer _____ Foreman _____ Fellow worker _____

    None _____

11. **Physical activities:** Description _____

CHECKLIST FOR PROGRAM QUALITY*

A. The school undertakes the pursuit of behavioral and instructional objectives that grow out of the need of each family unit to find ways and means of establishing and maintaining the normalization of its life cycle. These objectives are achieved by:
1. The school and the home working as an educational team
2. Enabling the child to function in ways considered to be within the norms of his society
3. Giving each individual the opportunity to undergo the normal developmental experiences of his life cycle
4. Taking into consideration and respecting the choices, wishes, and desires of each child
5. Helping shape the attitudes and values of society to be more accepting and tolerant of differentness in appearance, demeanor, intelligence, speech and language, nationality, education, race, color, and ethnic background

B. The school develops procedures for early identification and referrals which include:
1. Work with community agencies (e.g., clinics)
2. Criteria for screening children (finding placement for every child)
3. Selection (exclusion practices should be eliminated)
4. Development of evaluation and dissemination practices

C. The school makes provision for physical facilities with:
1. Sufficient indoor space for movement
2. Sufficient outdoor space for movement
3. Adequate lighting
4. Sufficient wall space
5. Adequate toilet facilities adjoining rooms for young children
6. Adequate toilet facilities nearby for older children
7. Adequate storage space for wraps
8. Adequate storage space for supplies and equipment
9. Open shelves for books and blocks
10. Sink with hot and cold running water in each room
11. Homemaking equipment for older children

D. The school provides adequate transportation for:
1. Children for whom transportation is feasible
2. Children within a reasonable distance from the school

E. The school employs a certified special education teacher who:
1. Understands child growth and development
2. Has realistic expectations at all levels of functioning and recognizes that all children have some ability to learn
3. Meets the needs of children within a particular age range
4. Uses physical movement in activities (structured and unstructured)
5. Makes good use of music and other arts
6. Makes skillful use of time
7. Observes and records behavior of children and uses written reports effectively
8. Likes children and does not show that he may not like all children equally
9. Is prepared to distribute affection freely without infantilizing the child or intruding on him
10. Gives the child guidelines to behavior that are appropriate to his ability level
11. Maintains a balance between leaving the child free to find his own structure and giving him one to use
12. Enjoys seeing children in action
13. Does not readily become involved emotionally with individual children
14. Communicates on the child's level of understanding

15. Has physical stamina
16. Is human—may be frustrated on some occasions and maintain a sense of humor on others
17. Has the ability to suppress his own fears and maintain his composure in dealing with unexpected difficulties, objectionable behavior, or upsetting circumstances
18. Is realistic in seeing a child in relation to others
19. Subordinates himself in a child-centered approach
20. Provides sufficient opportunities for parent-teacher interaction
21. Establishes good relationships with co-workers
22. Views his own feelings toward a child realistically
23. Plans and carries out a consistent program that has continuity
24. Does not do for the child those things the child is able to do for himself

F. The school includes the class as an integral part of the school system by:
1. Integrating the class with children of normal intelligence as far as possible, rather than segregating it
2. Giving the teacher the same responsibility and privileges as other members of the faculty
3. Providing the teacher with support and direction from the principal
4. Providing supervision with reinforcement and assistance

G. The school develops cumulative records that include:
1. Results of psychological evaluations
2. Anecdotal records
3. Complete health records
4. Referrals to and from community agencies
5. Family background data
6. Written reports from teachers to parents
7. Written reports from parents to teachers
8. Records of parent-teacher conferences

H. The school arranges joint meetings of administrators, teachers, psychologists, and social workers to evaluate:
1. The child's social and emotional status
2. Problems regarding progress
3. Pressures and demands of school, home, and community
4. Plans for experiences in classroom, school, home, and community that will aid in development
5. Plans for moving children into other programs

I. The school facilitates evaluation of children by:
1. Encouraging teachers to make daily anecdotal records
2. Keeping cumulative records up-to-date
3. Checking cumulative records periodically to see what clues they contain
4. Interpreting effects of socioeconomic levels
5. Learning about emotional climate of the home
6. Encouraging written reports to parents
7. Encouraging written reports to teachers from parents
8. Encouraging teachers to visit homes
9. Inviting parents to visit the school
10. Showing willingness to learn from parents

J. The school arranges periodic conferences (weekly, in beginning stages) with parents of children to:
1. Review their progress
2. Consider their needs in home, school, and community
3. Encourage parental cooperation in school activities that affect their welfare
4. Explore possibilities for sharing with and learning from parents

Continued.

CHECKLIST FOR PROGRAM QUALITY—cont'd

5. Build a 24-hour-a-day schedule between each home and the school that contains experiences geared to the normalization of the life cycle of the family

K. Provision is made for meeting the special needs of children by:
1. Teachers
2. Administrators and supervisors
3. Psychologists
4. Physicians
5. Nurses
6. Social workers
7. Physical therapists
8. Parents

L. Provision is made for use of community resources in developing programs by:
1. Surveys of community resources
2. Supervised excursions
3. Help from parents and community agencies

M. Provision is made to participate in activities with other children:
1. In the classroom
2. In physical education classes
3. On the playground
4. In the cafeteria
5. In assemblies

N. The school provides in-service training by:
1. Meetings of special education teachers with each other
2. Meetings of special education teachers with teachers of other children
3. Workshops and study groups
4. Participation in conferences and conventions
5. Use of outside consultants
6. Flexible approach to identification procedures and their interpretation
7. Visits of teachers to other classes and schools
8. Study of methods of observation, recording, and reporting
9. Study of methods of charting the progress of each child
10. Openness to new ideas in instructional materials and classroom procedure
11. Openness to new ideas in administrative arrangements
12. Assistance in curriculum construction

O. The school interprets the program to:
1. Faculty members
2. The general public
3. Other educators
4. Related professions
5. Community agencies

P. The school includes programs in parent education by:
1. Involving parents as integral parts of the planning and execution of programs
2. Providing the assistance of administrators, teachers, a psychologist, therapists, and a social worker in meetings and conferences
3. Including parents in the regular P.T.A.

Q. The school explores possibilities for the child as he leaves the elementary school in:
1. The secondary school
2. A sheltered environment outside the home, if needed

R. The school follows up children who leave school to go to:
1. Homes
2. Residential schools
3. Other environments

APPENDIX D

Litton-TMR behavioral assessment checklist

The *Litton-TMR Behavioral Assessment Checklist* is intended to serve as a guide to indicate behavioral ability of school-age TMRs (CA 3 to 21) in the seven curriculum areas: (1) self-care, (2) basic communication, (3) social, (4) perceptual-motor/physical education, (5) functional academics, (6) recreation and leisure time, and (7) economic usefulness and vocational skills. Numbers (1 = low to 5 = high) and descriptors (never, seldom, occasionally, usually, always) are used to indicate the quality (degree) or quantity (frequency) of performance, depending on the specific skill or desired behavior. A student scoring a 1 or 2 never or seldom performs the behavior (e.g., flushes toilet after use). For another behavior, it might mean the quality of performance is low (e.g., polishes shoes). A 4 or 5 indicates the quality or quantity of the performance is sufficient. Those behaviors which only pertain to members of one sex (e.g., taking off or putting on a slip) should be marked through if the assessment is for a person of the opposite sex.

This checklist can be used as (1) a general assessment of behavioral functioning of students, (2) a measure to determine behavioral growth, and (3) an informal diagnostic tool to pinpoint deficiencies. The checklist can be completed by the teacher (after working with the child for a sufficient period of time), by the teacher interviewing the parent, or both. The behaviors scored low and needing attention should be task analyzed and sequenced before instruction is begun.

LITTON-TMR BEHAVIORAL ASSESSMENT CHECKLIST

Student's name _____ Date _____

Chronological age _____ Intelligence quotient _____

	Never	Seldom	Occa-sionally	Usually	Always
	1	2	3	4	5
I. SELF-CARE					
A. Feeding					
1. Eats soft and solid finger foods					
2. Can drink					
a. From a cup					
b. From a glass					
c. Through a straw					
d. From a water fountain					
3. Can eat with a					
a. Spoon					
b. Fork					
c. Knife					
B. Toileting					
1. Properly manipulates clothes before and after toileting					
2. Has bladder control					
a. During the day					
b. At night					
3. Has bowel control					
a. During the day					
b. At night					
4. Properly uses toilet tissue					
5. Flushes toilet after use					
6. Washes and dries hands					
C. Clothing					
1. Can undress and dress					
a. Socks (off/on)					
b. Shoes (off/on)					
c. T-shirt (off/on)					
d. Underwear (off/on)					
e. Pull-on pants (off/on)					
f. Slip-on dress (off/on)					
g. Coat (off/on)					
h. Cap or hat (off/on)					

	Never	Seldom	Occa-sionally	Usually	Always
	1	2	3	4	5
i. Mittens (off/on)					
j. Gloves (off/on)					
k. Slip (off/on)					
l. Scarf (off/on)					
m. Pajamas (off/on)					
n. Bra (off/on)					
2. Can unfasten and fasten clothes parts					
a. Unzips, zips					
b. Unsnaps, snaps					
c. Unbuttons, buttons					
d. Unbuckles, buckles					
e. Unlaces, laces					
f. Unhooks, hooks					
g. Unties, ties					
3. Appropriateness, care, and use of clothing					
a. Appropriateness					
(1) Identifies appropriate clothing for weather					
(2) Identifies appropriate clothing for different sexes					
(3) Identifies own clothing					
(4) Identifies dress clothing					
(5) Identifies work clothing					
(6) Identifies appropriate sizes					
(7) Identifies coordinated clothes					
b. Care and use					
(1) Select clean clothing					
(2) Adjust clothes on body for neatness					
(3) Uses a clothes brush					
(4) Folds clothes					
(5) Hangs clothes on hook or hanger					
(6) Properly disposes of dirty clothes					

Continued.

LITTON-TMR BEHAVIORAL ASSESSMENT CHECKLIST—cont'd

	Never	Seldom	Occa-sionally	Usually	Always
	1	2	3	4	5
b. Care and use—cont'd					
(7) Wipe shoes on mat when dirty					
(8) Polish shoes					
(9) Use an umbrella					
D. Personal grooming and health					
1. Hands					
a. Washes own hands when needed					
b. Dries own hands after washing					
c. Uses soap or soap dispenser					
d. Cleans own nails					
e. Uses an emery board					
f. Uses fingernail clippers					
g. Applies and removes nail polish					
2. Nose					
a. Blows and wipes his nose with handkerchief or tissue					
3. Teeth					
a. Brushes his teeth					
b. Uses dental floss					
4. Hair					
a. Combs his hair					
b. Brushes his hair					
c. Uses a hair dryer					
d. Puts hair in rollers					
e. Shampoos hair					
5. Face					
a. Washes and dries face					
b. Applies makeup					
6. Skin					
a. Applies skin moisturizer					
b. Uses an electric shaver					
7. Body					
a. Uses deodorant					

	Never	Seldom	Occa-sionally	Usually	Always
	1	2	3	4	5
b. Bathes or showers independently					
c. Uses mouthwash					
d. Takes care of self during menstruation					
E. Safety and first aid					
1. Home and sheltered employment					
a. Recognizes containers of poisonous substances					
b. Uses electrical devices safely					
c. Can identify potential fire hazards					
d. Identifies harmful or dangerous objects					
e. Uses bathtub or shower safely					
f. Properly disposes of plastic bag					
g. Recognizes stairways that are dangerous					
h. Uses tools safely					
2. School and recreation					
a. Enters, exits, and rides school bus in safe manner					
b. Uses safe practices around playground equipment					
c. Looks before crossing street					
d. Knows when to cross at intersections with traffic signal					
e. Practices rules of safety in recreational activities (e.g., swimming)					
3. Care of simple injuries					
a. Can apply antiseptic and creams					
b. Can apply adhesive or gauze bandages					
c. Can report or self-treat minor burns, animal and insect bites, small cuts, and nosebleed					

Continued.

LITTON-TMR BEHAVIORAL ASSESSMENT CHECKLIST—cont'd

	Never	Seldom	Occa-sionally	Usually	Always
	1	2	3	4	5
II. BASIC COMMUNICATION SKILLS					
A. Listening or receptive ability					
1. Can imitate motor movements					
2. Auditory perceptual skills—Student has adequate					
a. Auditory awareness					
b. Auditory focusing					
c. Auditory figure-ground					
d. Auditory discrimination					
e. Auditory memory					
f. Auditory sequencing					
g. Auditory blending					
h. Auditory association					
3. Knows environmental sounds					
4. Can recognize sounds in isolation					
5. Can listen for information					
6. Can follow directions					
7. Can listen for enjoyment					
B. Speaking or expressive skills					
1. Can gesture to communicate					
2. Can imitate sounds					
3. Knows vowel sounds					
4. Knows consonant sounds					
5. Can repeat words					
6. Can independently produce functional words					
7. Can identify pictures of commonly spoken words					
8. Can comprehend the meaning of commonly spoken words					
9. Can repeat functional phrases and sentences					
10. Can independently produce functional phrases and sentences					

	Never	Seldom	Occa-sionally	Usually	Always
	1	2	3	4	5

III. SOCIAL SKILLS

A. Self-control behaviors

1. Is emotionally stable in most everyday situations
2. Can control temper (not prone to verbal or physical outbursts)
3. Accepts changes in routine
4. Can accept losing in game situations
5. Can wait turn
6. Responds positively to authority
7. Respects criticism
8. Feels secure

B. Social amenities

1. Uses appropriate polite greeting and parting words (e.g., hello, goodbye)
2. Can perform proper physical social amenities (e.g., hand-shake, wave)
3. Can make simple introductions
4. Displays proper eating and table manners
5. Socially appropriate for specific environments

C. Group participation

1. Participates appropriately in team games
2. Interacts and enjoys group play
3. Behaves appropriately while attending assemblies, plays, etc.
4. Behaves appropriately on various modes of transportation
5. Behaves appropriately on field trips
6. Participates as a member of the family, class, group home, or residential unit

D. Personality

1. Has positive self-concept
2. Is enthusiastic and has fun in most work and social activities

Continued.

LITTON-TMR BEHAVIORAL ASSESSMENT CHECKLIST—cont'd

	Never	Seldom	Occa-sionally	Usually	Always
	1	2	3	4	5
D. Personality—cont'd					
3. Shows and accepts criticism					
4. Participates and displays some leadership in play and work					
5. Takes care of and distinguishes between personal property and property of others					
6. Complies with rules and regulations of school and home					
7. Is truthful and honest					
8. Is dependable					
E. Sex education					
1. Can recognize body parts and is aware of their function					
2. Is able to recognize and understand physical changes during puberty and adolescence					
3. Is knowledgeable and exhibits some understanding of the sexual self					
4. Understands peer relationships					
5. Is a responsible sexual being					
IV. PERCEPTUAL-MOTOR AND PHYSICAL SKILLS					
A. Basic movement					
1. Nonlocomotor skills					
a. Bends					
b. Kneels					
c. Rotates					
d. Sits					
e. Squats					
f. Stands					
g. Stops					
h. Stretches					
i. Swings					
j. Turns					
k. Twists					
2. Locomotor skills					
a. Crawls					

	Never	Seldom	Occa-sionally	Usually	Always
	1	2	3	4	5
b. Creeps					
c. Dodges					
d. Gallops					
e. Hops					
f. Jumps					
g. Leaps					
h. Marches					
i. Rolls					
j. Runs					
k. Skips					
l. Slides					
m. Starts					
3. Manipulative skills					
a. Bounces					
b. Carries					
c. Catches					
d. Climbs					
e. Falls					
f. Hangs					
g. Hits					
h. Jumps					
i. Kicks					
j. Lands					
k. Lifts					
l. Pulls					
m. Throws					
B. Perceptual-motor skills					
1. Has an adequate body image					
2. Has laterality (right from left)					
3. Has directionality					
a. Up/down					
b. Forward/backward					
4. Can coordinate eye-hand movements					
5. Has tactile and kinesthetic perception					

Continued.

LITTON-TMR BEHAVIORAL ASSESSMENT CHECKLIST—cont'd

	Never	Seldom	Occa-sionally	Usually	Always
	1	2	3	4	5
C. Physical fitness					
1. Organic performance					
a. Has adequate strength					
b. Is flexible					
c. Has adequate endurance					
2. Motor performance					
a. Balance					
(1) Static					
(2) Dynamic					
b. Has adequate agility					
c. Can run fast (speed)					
d. Has general coordination					
e. Can react quickly					
V. FUNCTIONAL ACADEMIC SKILLS					
A. Reading					
1. Visual skills					
a. Can discriminate					
(1) Color					
(2) Shape					
(3) Size					
b. Can match					
(1) Color					
(2) Shape					
(3) Size					
c. Has visual sequential memory					
2. Listening skills					
a. Auditory discrimination					
b. Auditory figure-ground					
c. Auditory association					
d. Auditory sequential memory					
3. Produces left-right sequences					
4. Identifies and names letters of alphabet					
a. Uppercase letters					
b. Lowercase letters					

	Never	Seldom	Occa-sionally	Usually	Always
	1	2	3	4	5
5. Identifies basic sight vocabulary words					
a. Safety words					
b. Public sign words					
c. Public building title words					
d. Months of the year					
e. Days of the week					
f. Family titles					
g. Public titles					
h. Basic color words					
i. Weather words					
j. Directional words					
k. Body part words					
l. Home and furniture words					
m. Clothing words					
n. Number words					
o. Fruit and vegetable words					
p. Action words					
B. Writing					
1. Prewriting skills					
a. Can hold pencil					
b. Can draw basic strokes					
(1) Down					
(2) Across					
(3) Slant right/left					
(4) Circle					
2. Tracing skills					
a. Can trace horizontal lines					
b. Can trace vertical lines					
c. Can trace shapes					
(1) Cross					
(2) Square					
(3) Circle					
(4) Triangle					
d. Can trace letters					
(1) Uppercase straight line letters					

Continued.

LITTON-TMR BEHAVIORAL ASSESSMENT CHECKLIST—cont'd

	Never	Seldom	Occa-sionally	Usually	Always
	1	2	3	4	5
d. Can trace letters—cont'd					
(2) Lowercase straight line letters					
(3) Uppercase curved and circular letters					
(4) Lowercase curved and circular letters					
e. Can trace numbers (0 to 10)					
f. Can trace age					
g. Can trace telephone number					
h. Can trace name					
3. Copying skills					
a. Can copy horizontal lines					
b. Can copy vertical lines					
c. Can copy shapes					
(1) Cross					
(2) Square					
(3) Circle					
(4) Triangle					
d. Can copy letters					
(1) Uppercase straight line letters					
(2) Lowercase straight line letters					
(3) Uppercase curved and circular letters					
(4) Lowercase curved and circular letters					
e. Can copy numbers (0 to 10)					
f. Can copy age					
g. Can copy telephone number					
h. Can copy name					
4. Can write independently					
a. Age					
b. Name					
c. Telephone number					
d. Address					

	Never	Seldom	Occa-sionally	Usually	Always
	1	2	3	4	5
e. Important words					
f. Important names					
C. Spelling					
1. Name					
2. Address					
3. City					
4. State					
5. Words of current interest (e.g., Christmas)					
6. Important words to student (e.g., names of family members)					
D. Math skills					
1. Readiness					
a. Can classify objects					
b. Understands one-to-one correspondence					
c. Understands seriation or ordering					
2. Number skills					
a. Can count orally					
b. Can count objects					
c. Can select certain number of objects from group					
d. Can identify and name numerals					
e. Can count by twos, fives, and tens					
f. Can add objects					
g. Can subtract objects					
3. Vocabulary					
a. Recognizes addition words and signs (e.g., plus [+], more, and sum)					
b. Recognizes subtraction words and signs (e.g., minus [-], take away, subtract, less)					
c. Knows other math vocabulary words (e.g., all, some, none, next)					

Continued.

LITTON-TMR BEHAVIORAL ASSESSMENT CHECKLIST—cont'd

	Never	Seldom	Occasionally	Usually	Always
	1	2	3	4	5
3. Vocabulary—cont'd					
d. Knows ordinal words (e.g., first, second)					
e. Knows time words (night, day, noon, minute, second, hour, half hour, etc.)					
f. Knows money words (e.g., penny, nickel, dime)					
g. Knows seasonal words (e.g., fall, winter, spring, summer)					
h. Knows measurement words (big, little, inch, foot, yard)					
4. Monetary concepts					
a. Can identify and name basic coins					
b. Can identify and name basic currency					
c. Can identify and name money symbols (i.e., ¢ and $)					
d. Can read price tags					
e. Understands simple coin conversions					
f. Can count change					
g. Can make simple change					
h. Can independently purchase small-value items					
5. Measurement					
a. Can discriminate by size					
b. Can read weight scale					
c. Can read thermometer					
d. Can use ruler to measure objects					
e. Can use measuring cups and spoons					
6. Basic math processes					
a. Addition					
(1) One-digit numbers (2) Two-digit numbers b. Subtraction					

	Never	Seldom	Occa-sionally	Usually	Always
	1	2	3	4	5
(1) One-digit numbers					
(2) Two-digit numbers					
7. Time and calendar skills					
a. Can name certain time of day					
b. Can name days of week					
c. Can name months of year					
d. Can state number of days in week, months in year, and weeks in year					
e. Can name current day and date					
f. Can name major holidays					
g. Can tell time by hour, half hour, quarter hour, and minute					
VI. RECREATION AND LEISURE TIME					
A. Recreational activities					
1. Participates in bicycling					
2. Participates in bowling					
3. Participates in camping					
4. Participates in hiking					
5. Participates in scouting					
6. Participates in swimming					
7. Participates in other recreational activities					
B. Leisure time activities					
1. Arts and crafts					
a. Can tear construction paper					
b. Can work with clay					
c. Can color with crayon					
d. Can trace shapes					
e. Can paint					
f. Can paste					
g. Can use scissors					
2. Musical activities					
a. Participates in free movement rhythms					
b. Participates in coordinated rhythms (e.g., claps hands)					

Continued.

LITTON-TMR BEHAVIORAL ASSESSMENT CHECKLIST—cont'd

	Never	Seldom	Occasionally	Usually	Always
	1	2	3	4	5
2. Musical activities—cont'd					
c. Participates in basic locomotor rhythms (e.g., walk, run, hop to music)					
d. Participates in nonlocomotor rhythms (i.e., movements of body)					
e. Participates in imitative or creative movements					
f. Can play rhythm instruments					
g. Participates in singing activities					
h. Participates in dancing activities					
VII. ECONOMIC USEFULNESS AND VOCATIONAL SKILLS **A.** Economically and domestically useful skills					
1. Uses common household items					
2. Contributes to his family (e.g., cleans, takes care of clothes)					
3. Contributes in gardening or yard work					
B. Vocational skills					
1. Uses vocationally-related tools (e.g., brush, hammer, screwdriver)					
2. Has acceptable work personality					
a. Is flexible and can work with others					
b. Can follow directions					
c. Has necessary interpersonal skills					
d. Has motivation to work					
e. Has acceptable dress and necessary personal hygiene skills					
f. Is punctual and completes assigned tasks					
3. Has relevant functional academic skills					

	Never	Seldom	Occa-sionally	Usually	Always
	1	2	3	4	5
a. Can read safety and community words					
b. Can write name, address, etc.					
c. Can use numbers					
d. Can tell time					
e. Knows money value					
f. Can use common measurements					
4. Can perform specific vocational tasks					
a. Can assemble					
b. Can collate					
c. Can fold letters					
d. Can package					
e. Can sort					
f. Can type					
g. Can weave					
h. Can wrap					
5. Can perform work-related independent skills					
a. Can use time clock					
b. Can use public transportation					
c. Can use telephone					

AUTHOR INDEX

SUBJECT INDEX